tactics

**Volume 3
by Sakura Kinoshita and
Kazuko Higashiyama**

HAMBURG // LONDON // LOS ANGELES // TOKYO

tactics Volume 3
ART & STORY BY: Sakura Kinoshita × Kazuko Higashiyama

Translation - Christine Schilling
English Adaptation - Lianne Sentar
Retouch and Lettering - Star Print Brokers
Production Artist - Mike Estacio
Graphic Designer - James Lee

Editor - Lillian Diaz-Przybyl
Digital Imaging Manager - Chris Buford
Pre-Production Supervisor - Erika Terriquez
Production Manager - Elisabeth Brizzi
Managing Editor - Vy Nguyen
Creative Director - Anne Marie Horne
Editor-in-Chief - Rob Tokar
Publisher - Mike Kiley
President and C.O.O. - John Parker
C.E.O. and Chief Creative Officer - Stuart Levy

A  Manga

TOKYOPOP and  are trademarks or registered trademarks of TOKYOPOP Inc.

TOKYOPOP Inc.
5900 Wilshire Blvd. Suite 2000
Los Angeles, CA 90036

E-mail: info@TOKYOPOP.com
Come visit us online at www.TOKYOPOP.com

ISBN: 978-1-59816-962-1
First TOKYOPOP printing: December 2007
10 9 8 7 6 5 4 3 2 1
Printed in the USA

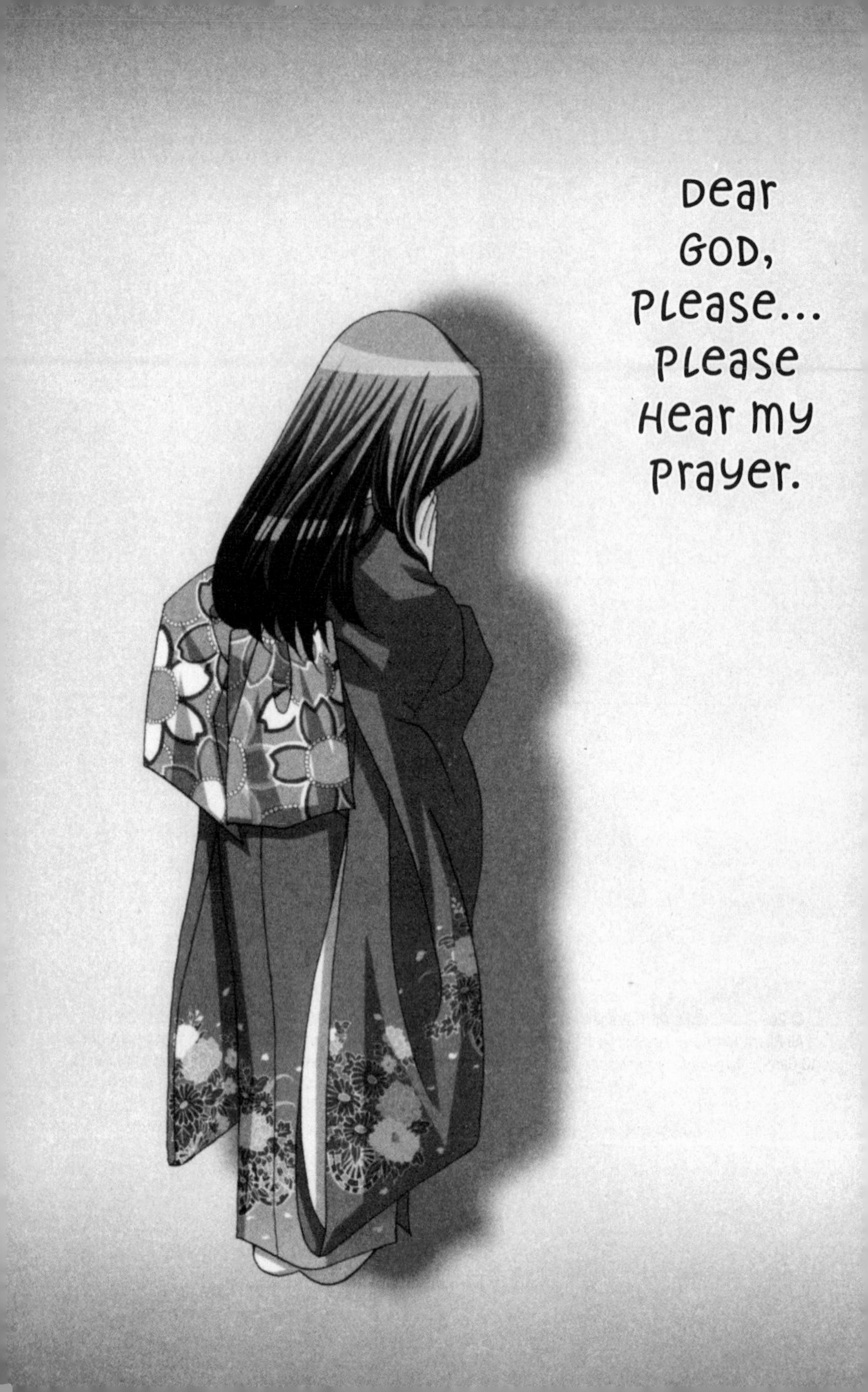
Dear GOD, please... please hear my prayer.

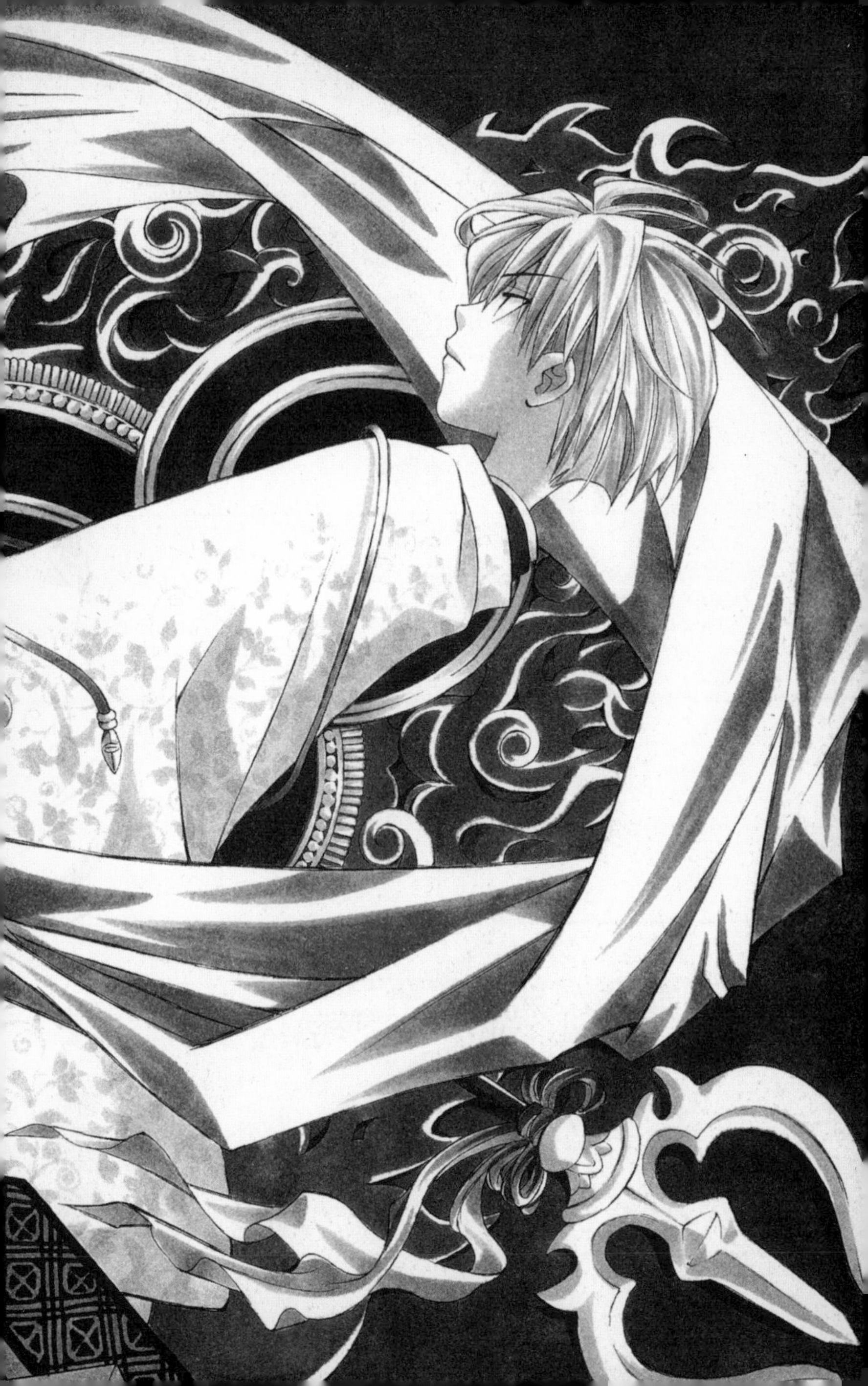

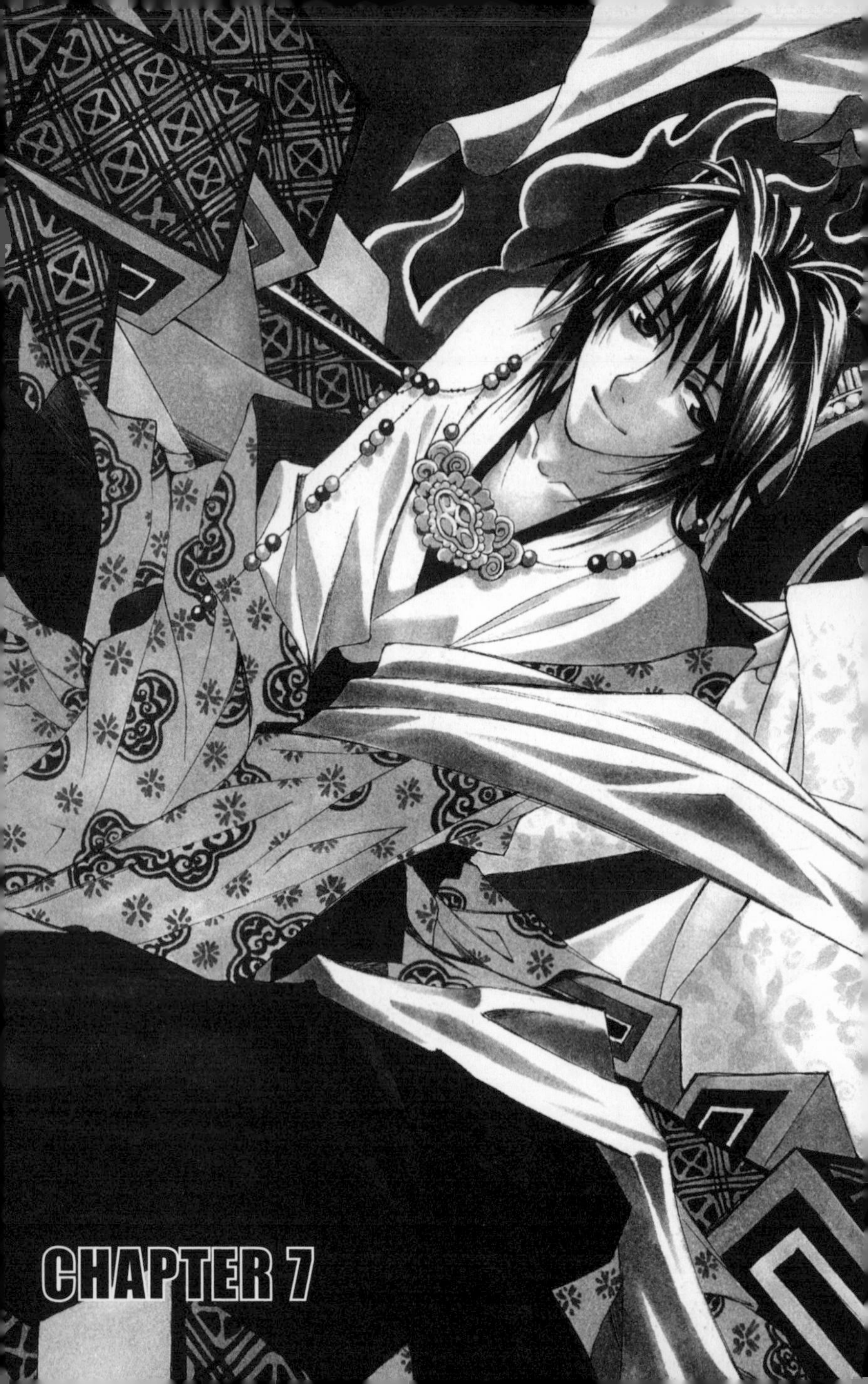
CHAPTER 7

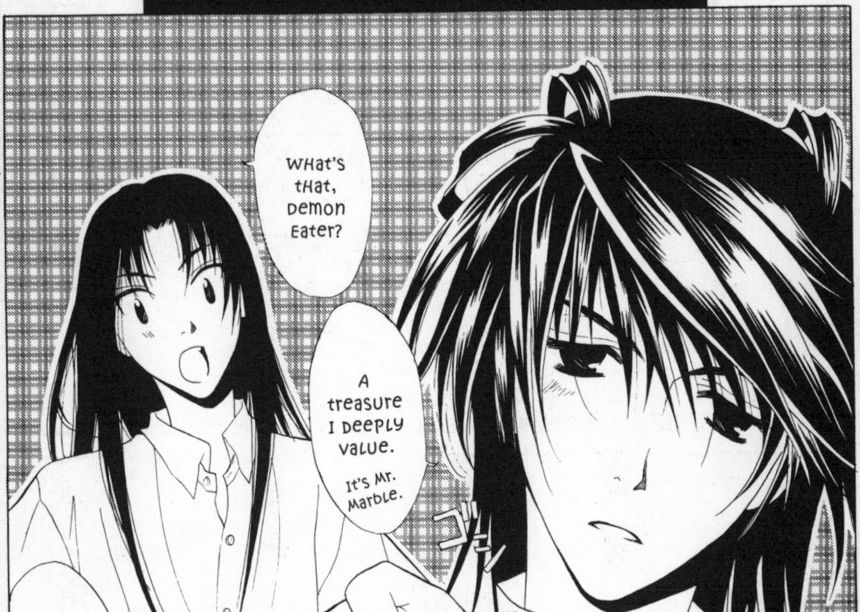
WHAT'S tHAT, DEMON EATER?
A treasure I DEEPLY VALUE.
It's Mr. MarbLe.
OOOOH, LEMME SEE!

tactics 3

CONTINUED ON PAGE 104.

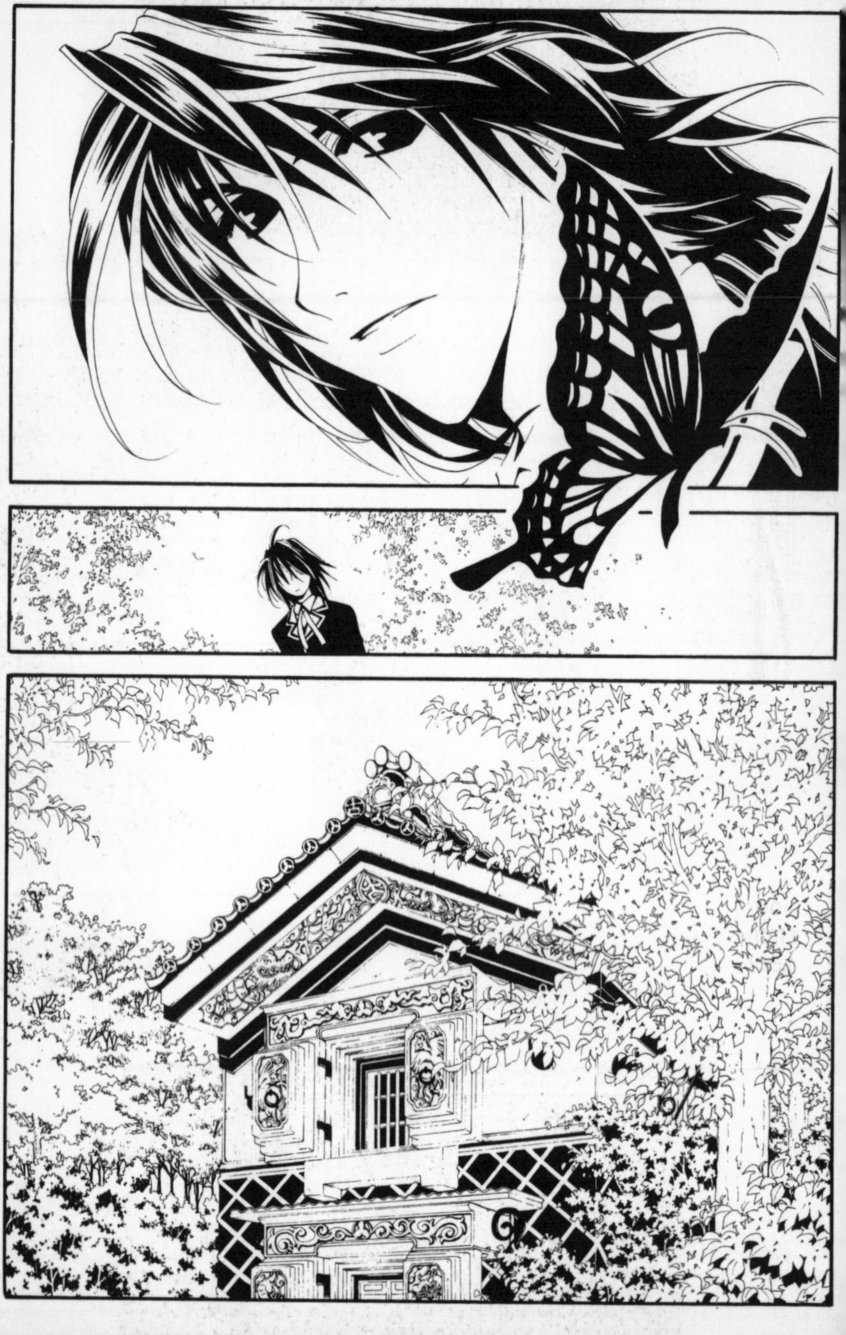

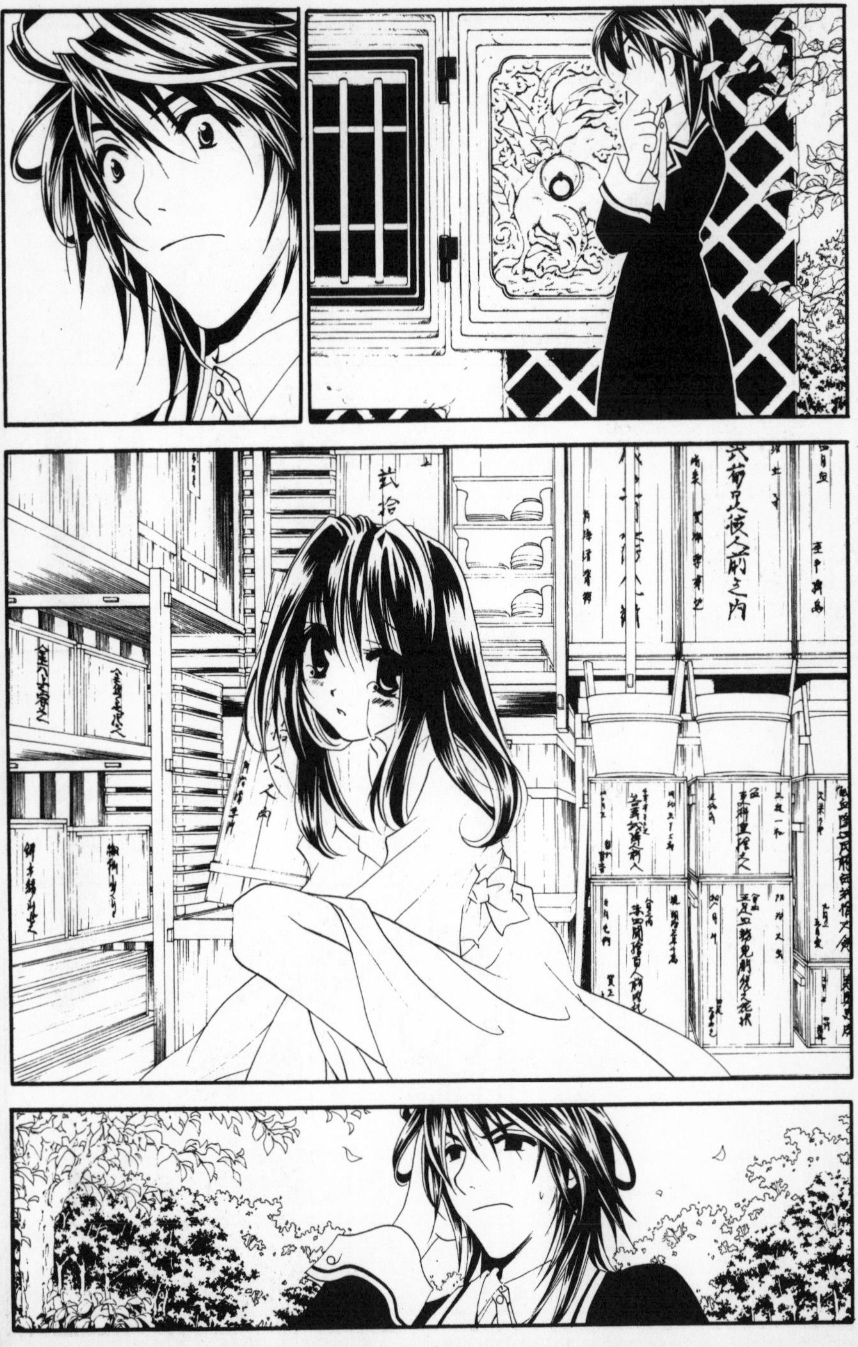

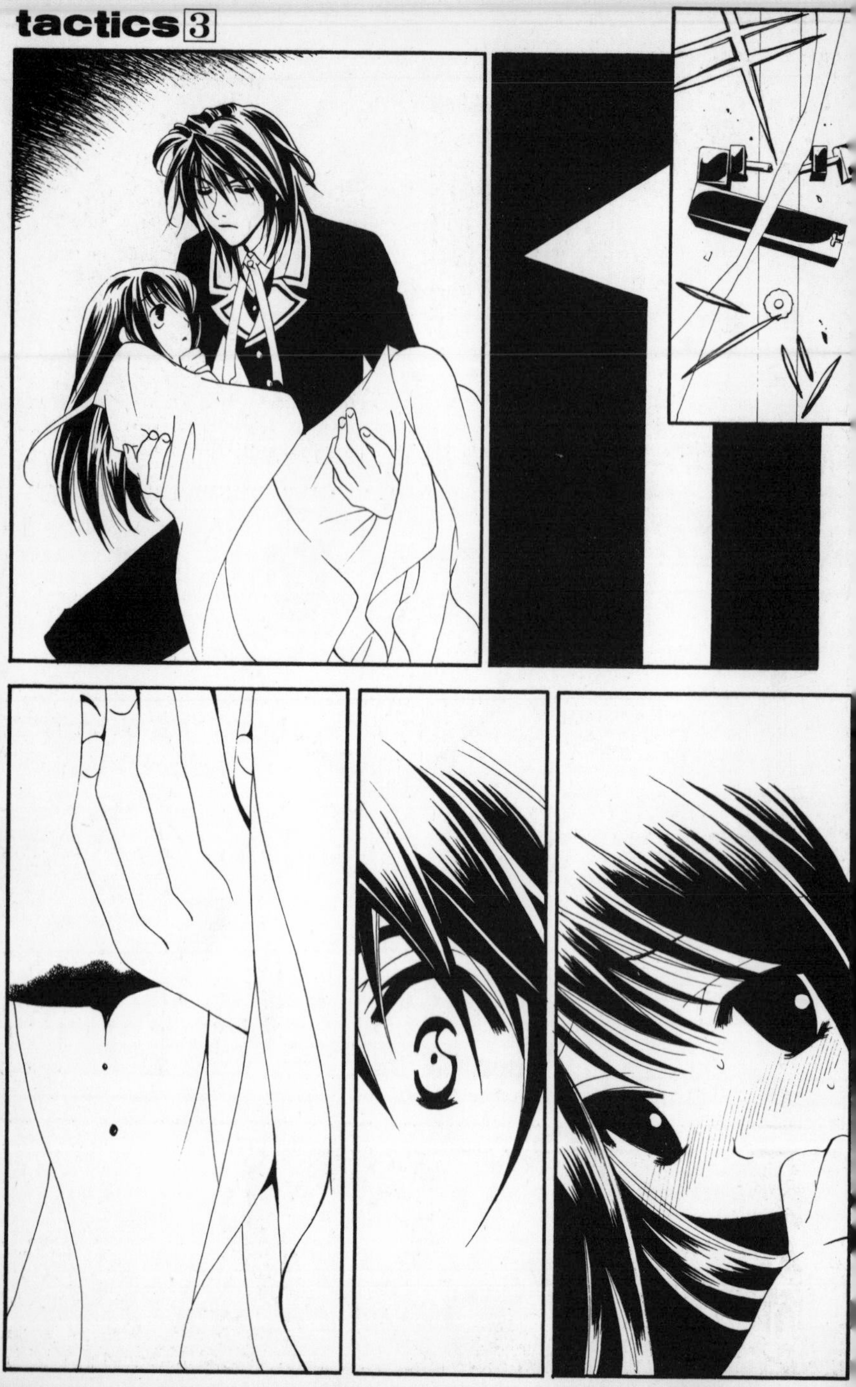

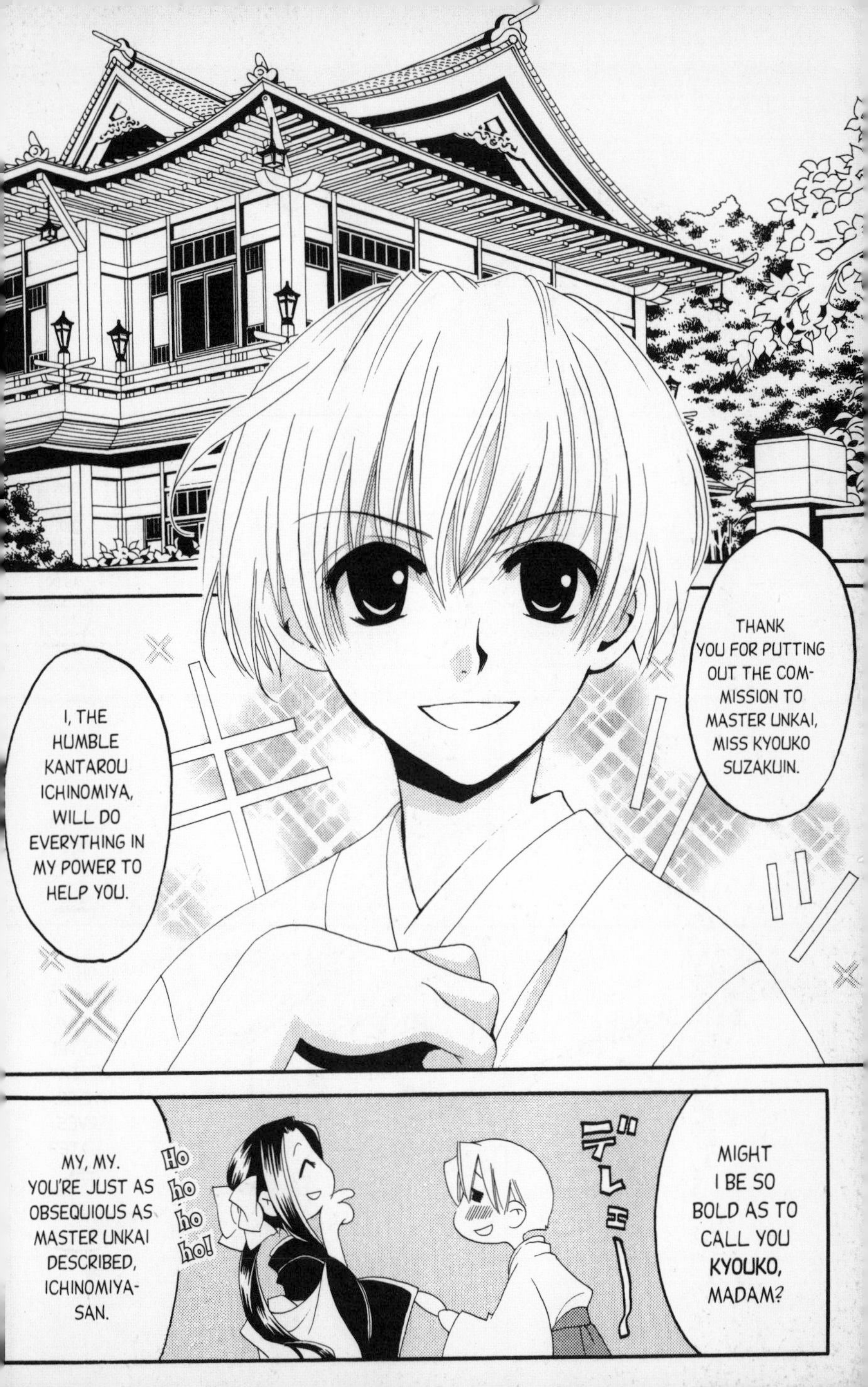
THANK YOU FOR PUTTING OUT THE COM-MISSION TO MASTER UNKAI, MISS KYOUKO SUZAKUIN.
I, THE HUMBLE KANTAROU ICHINOMIYA, WILL DO EVERYTHING IN MY POWER TO HELP YOU.
MIGHT I BE SO BOLD AS TO CALL YOU **KYOUKO,** MADAM?
デレ〜ー
Ho ho ho ho!
MY, MY. YOU'RE JUST AS OBSEQUIOUS AS MASTER UNKAI DESCRIBED, ICHINOMIYA-SAN.

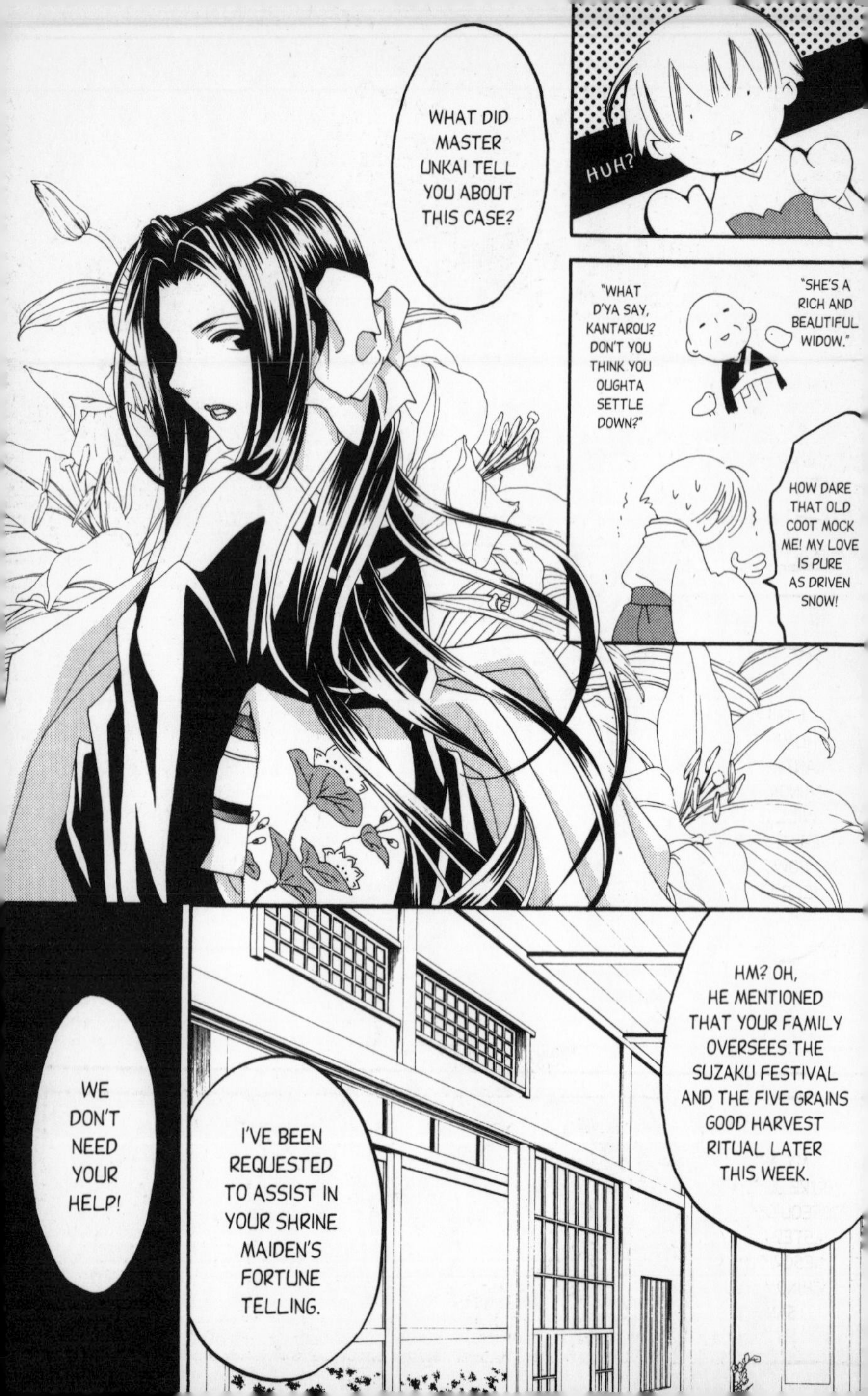
HUH?
"SHE'S A RICH AND BEAUTIFUL WIDOW."
"WHAT D'YA SAY, KANTAROU? DON'T YOU THINK YOU OUGHTA SETTLE DOWN?"
HOW DARE THAT OLD COOT MOCK ME! MY LOVE IS PURE AS DRIVEN SNOW!
WHAT DID MASTER UNKAI TELL YOU ABOUT THIS CASE?
HM? OH, HE MENTIONED THAT YOUR FAMILY OVERSEES THE SUZAKU FESTIVAL AND THE FIVE GRAINS GOOD HARVEST RITUAL LATER THIS WEEK.
I'VE BEEN REQUESTED TO ASSIST IN YOUR SHRINE MAIDEN'S FORTUNE TELLING.
WE DON'T NEED YOUR HELP!

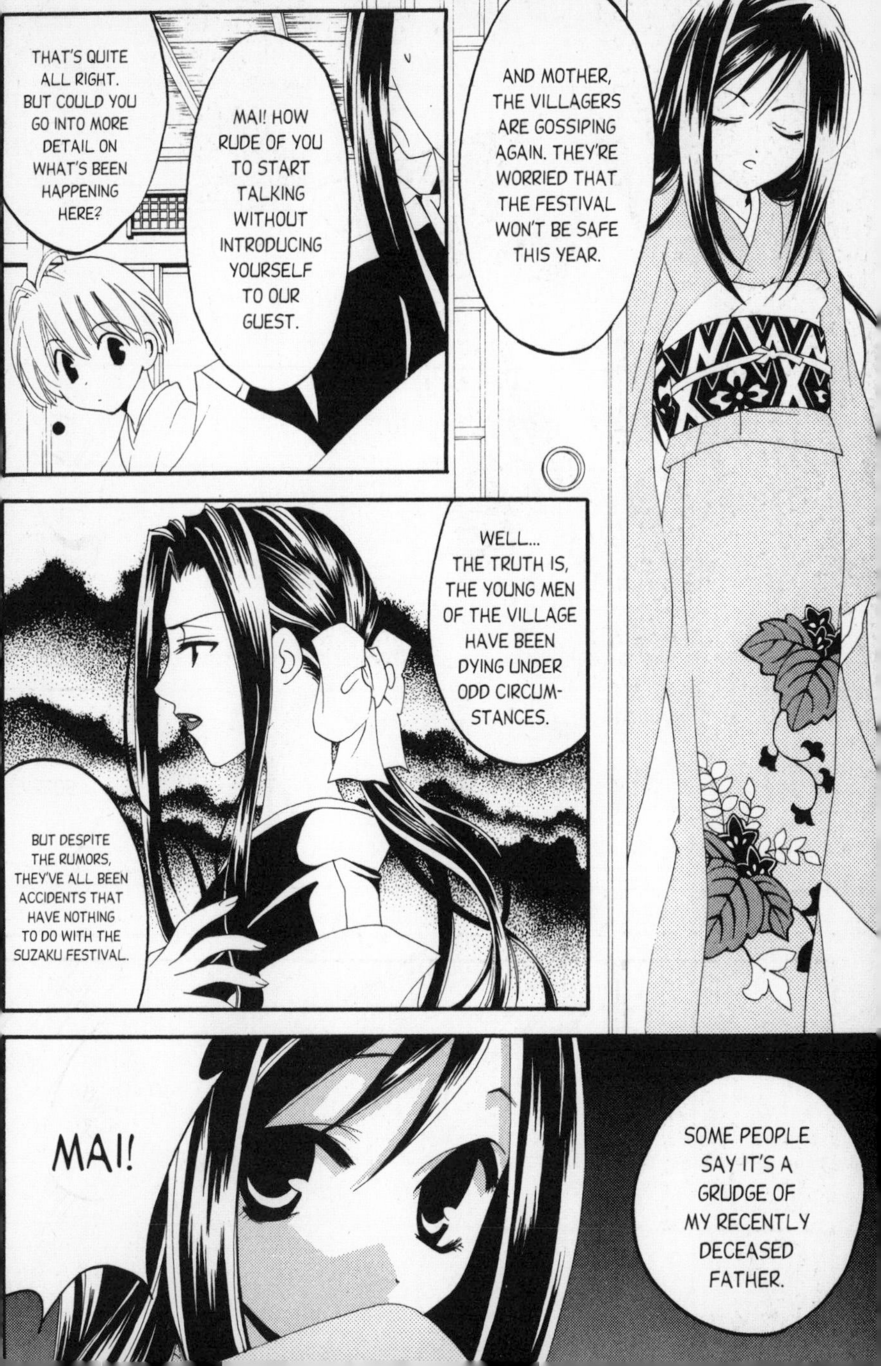
AND MOTHER, THE VILLAGERS ARE GOSSIPING AGAIN. THEY'RE WORRIED THAT THE FESTIVAL WON'T BE SAFE THIS YEAR.
MAI! HOW RUDE OF YOU TO START TALKING WITHOUT INTRODUCING YOURSELF TO OUR GUEST.
THAT'S QUITE ALL RIGHT. BUT COULD YOU GO INTO MORE DETAIL ON WHAT'S BEEN HAPPENING HERE?
WELL... THE TRUTH IS, THE YOUNG MEN OF THE VILLAGE HAVE BEEN DYING UNDER ODD CIRCUM-STANCES.
BUT DESPITE THE RUMORS, THEY'VE ALL BEEN ACCIDENTS THAT HAVE NOTHING TO DO WITH THE SUZAKU FESTIVAL.
SOME PEOPLE SAY IT'S A GRUDGE OF MY RECENTLY DECEASED FATHER.
MAI!

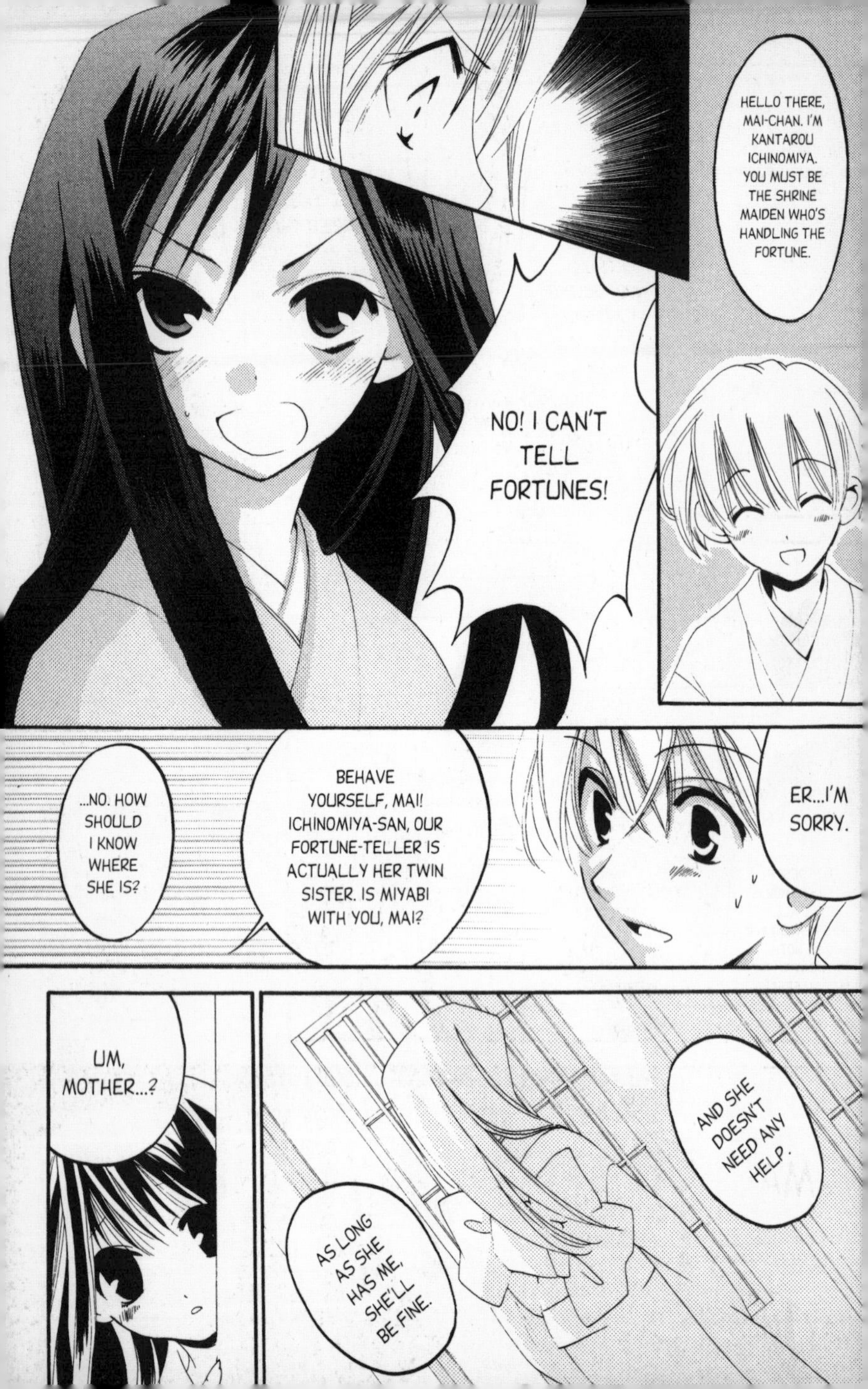

HELLO THERE, MAI-CHAN. I'M KANTAROU ICHINOMIYA. YOU MUST BE THE SHRINE MAIDEN WHO'S HANDLING THE FORTUNE.
NO! I CAN'T TELL FORTUNES!
ER...I'M SORRY.
BEHAVE YOURSELF, MAI! ICHINOMIYA-SAN, OUR FORTUNE-TELLER IS ACTUALLY HER TWIN SISTER. IS MIYABI WITH YOU, MAI?
...NO. HOW SHOULD I KNOW WHERE SHE IS?
AND SHE DOESN'T NEED ANY HELP.
AS LONG AS SHE HAS ME, SHE'LL BE FINE.
UM, MOTHER...?

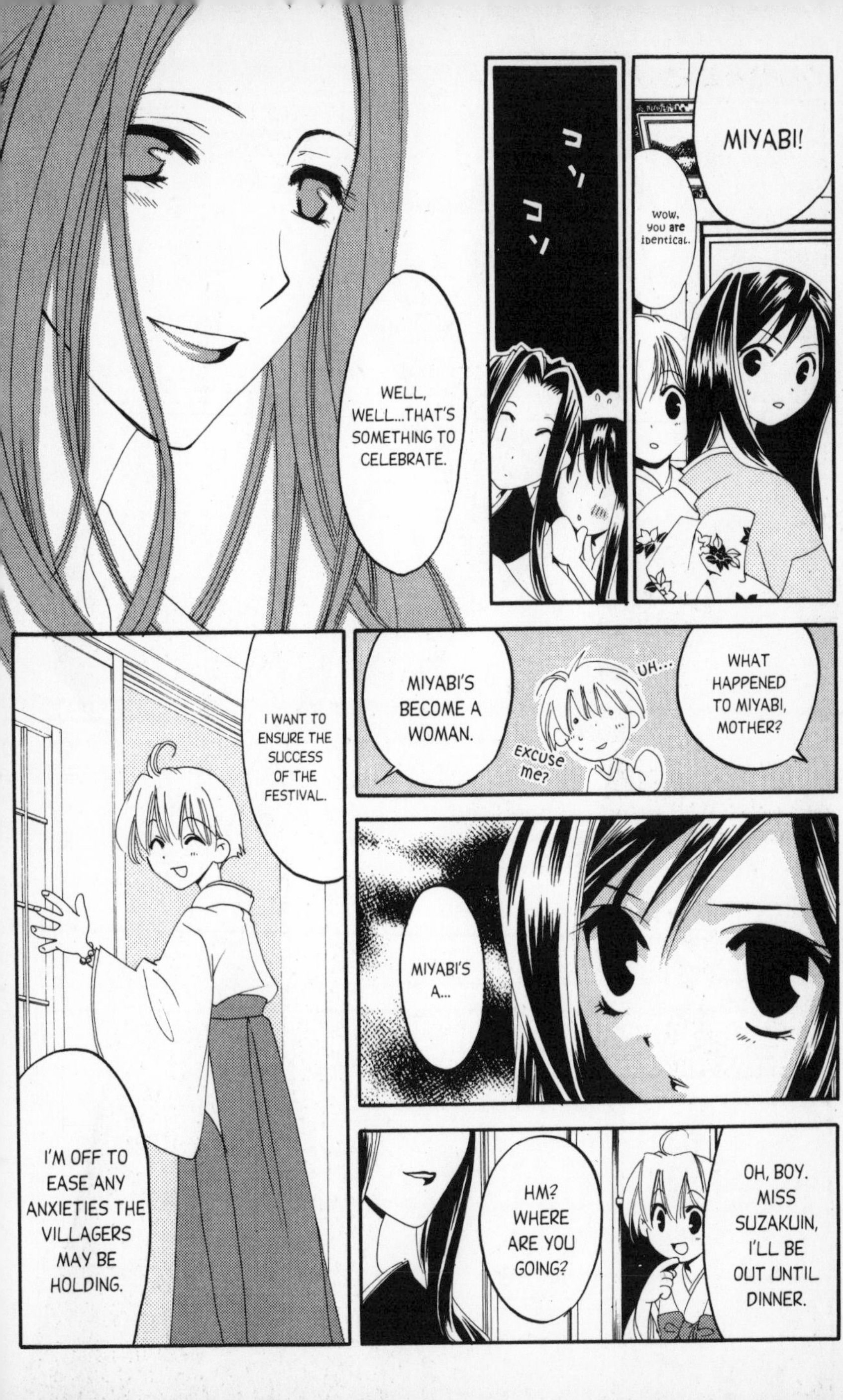
MIYABI!
wow, you are identical.
コソ コソ
WELL, WELL...THAT'S SOMETHING TO CELEBRATE.
WHAT HAPPENED TO MIYABI, MOTHER?
UH...
EXCUSE me?
MIYABI'S BECOME A WOMAN.
MIYABI'S A...
OH, BOY. MISS SUZAKUIN, I'LL BE OUT UNTIL DINNER.
HM? WHERE ARE YOU GOING?
I WANT TO ENSURE THE SUCCESS OF THE FESTIVAL.
I'M OFF TO EASE ANY ANXIETIES THE VILLAGERS MAY BE HOLDING.

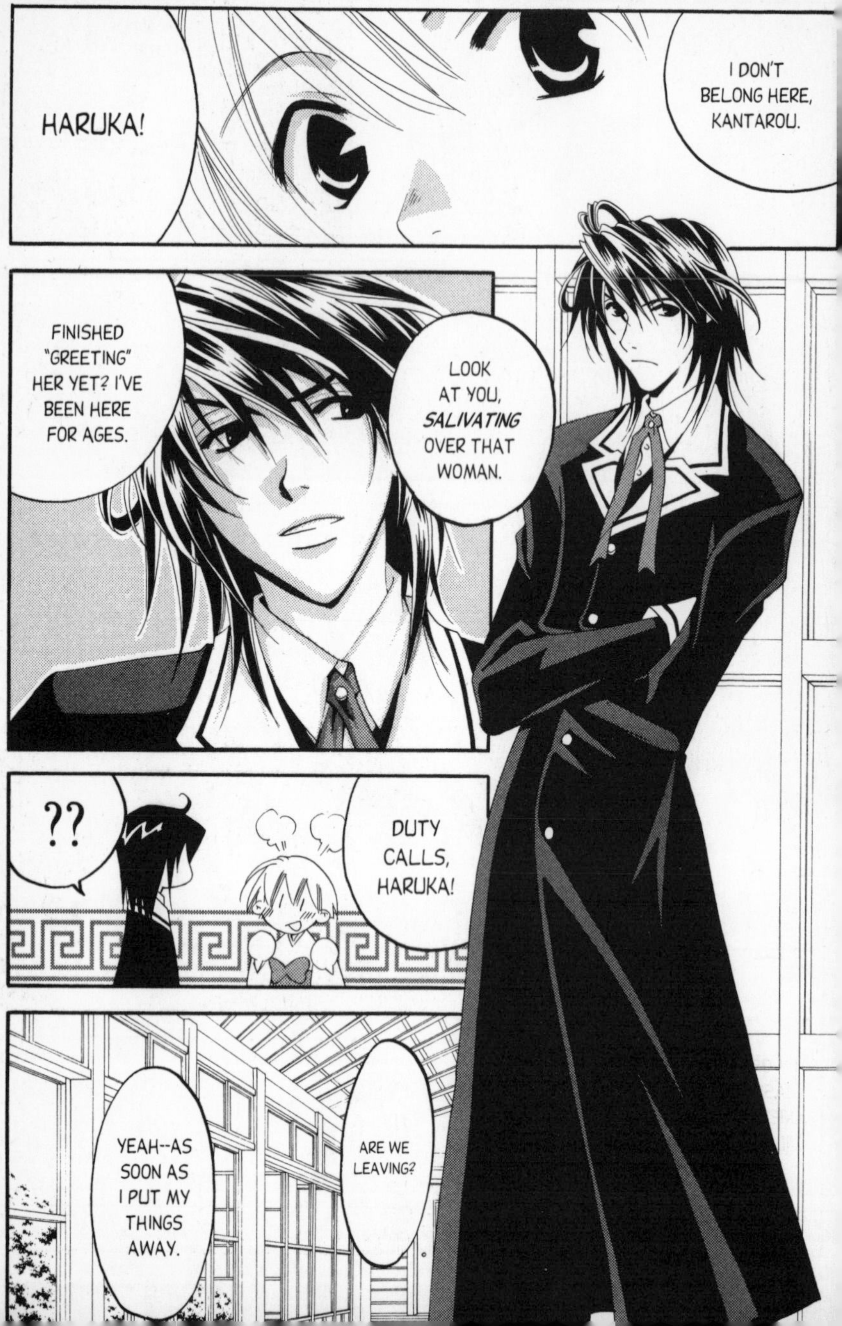
I DON'T BELONG HERE, KANTAROU.
HARUKA!
LOOK AT YOU, *SALIVATING* OVER THAT WOMAN.
FINISHED "GREETING" HER YET? I'VE BEEN HERE FOR AGES.
DUTY CALLS, HARUKA!
??
ARE WE LEAVING?
YEAH--AS SOON AS I PUT MY THINGS AWAY.

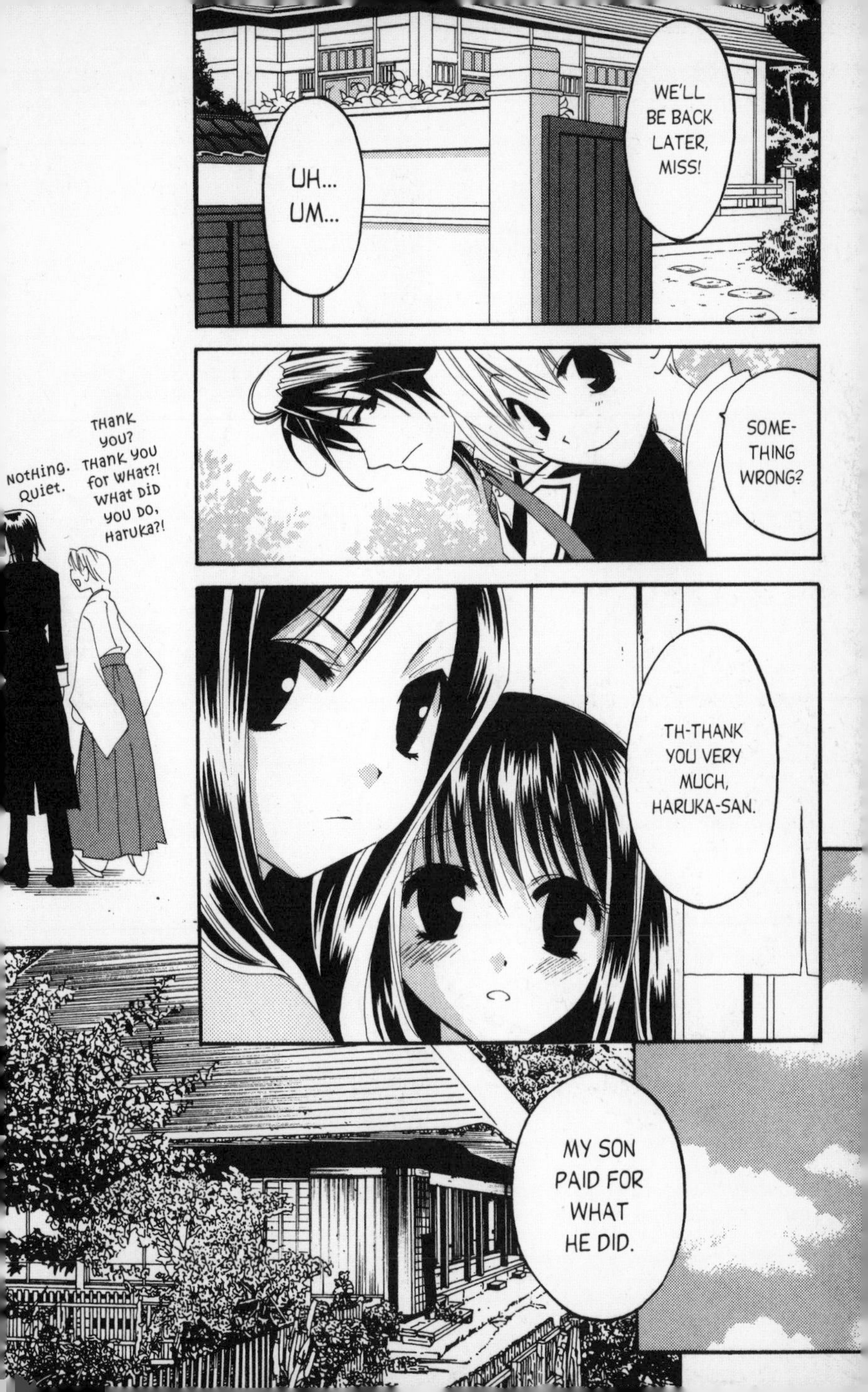
WE'LL BE BACK LATER, MISS!
UH... UM...
SOME-THING WRONG?
TH-THANK YOU VERY MUCH, HARUKA-SAN.
THANK YOU? THANK YOU FOR WHAT?! WHAT DID YOU DO, HARUKA?!
NOTHING. QUIET.
MY SON PAID FOR WHAT HE DID.

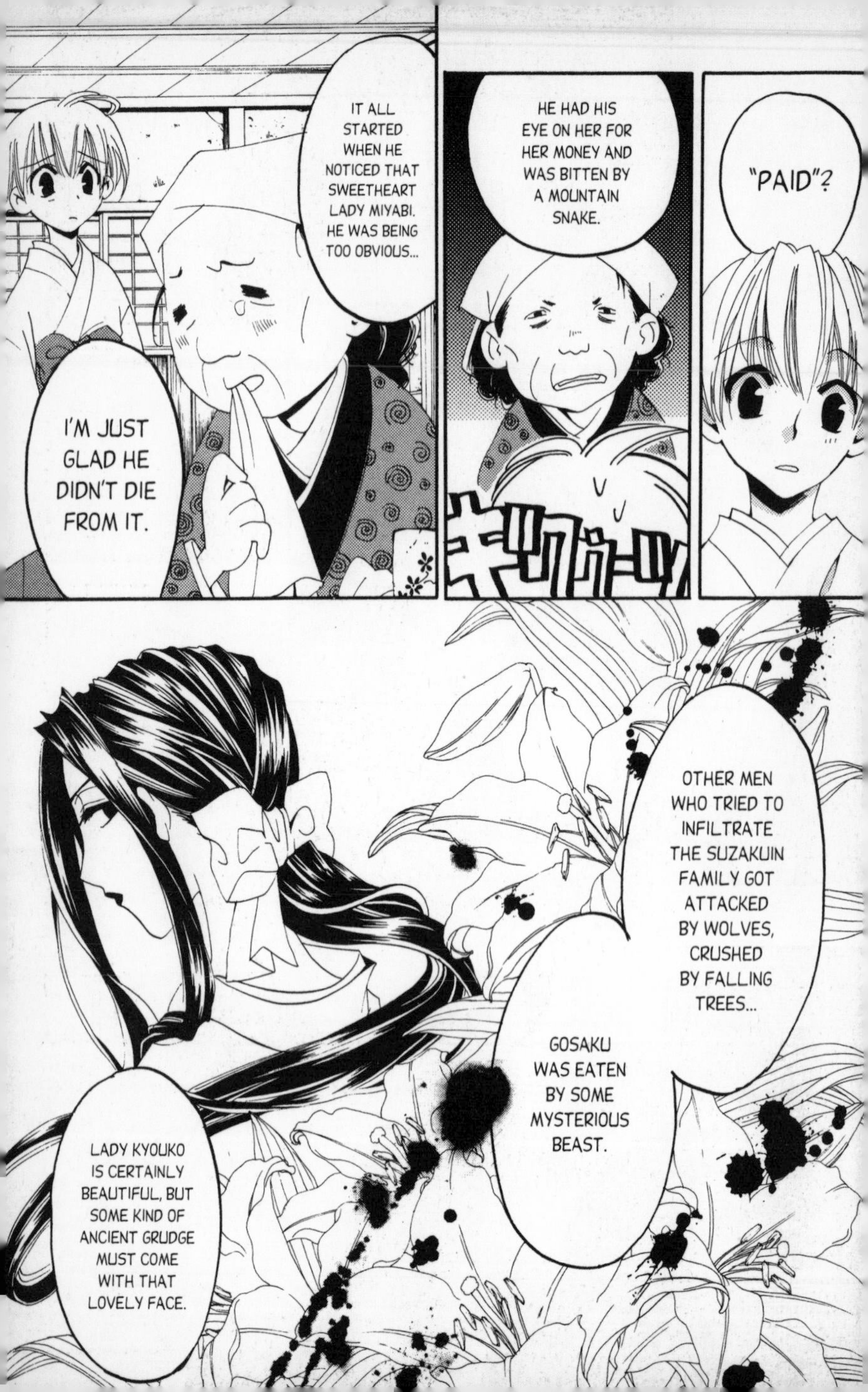
"PAID"?
HE HAD HIS EYE ON HER FOR HER MONEY AND WAS BITTEN BY A MOUNTAIN SNAKE.
IT ALL STARTED WHEN HE NOTICED THAT SWEETHEART LADY MIYABI. HE WAS BEING TOO OBVIOUS...
I'M JUST GLAD HE DIDN'T DIE FROM IT.
OTHER MEN WHO TRIED TO INFILTRATE THE SUZAKUIN FAMILY GOT ATTACKED BY WOLVES, CRUSHED BY FALLING TREES...
GOSAKU WAS EATEN BY SOME MYSTERIOUS BEAST.
LADY KYOUKO IS CERTAINLY BEAUTIFUL, BUT SOME KIND OF ANCIENT GRUDGE MUST COME WITH THAT LOVELY FACE.

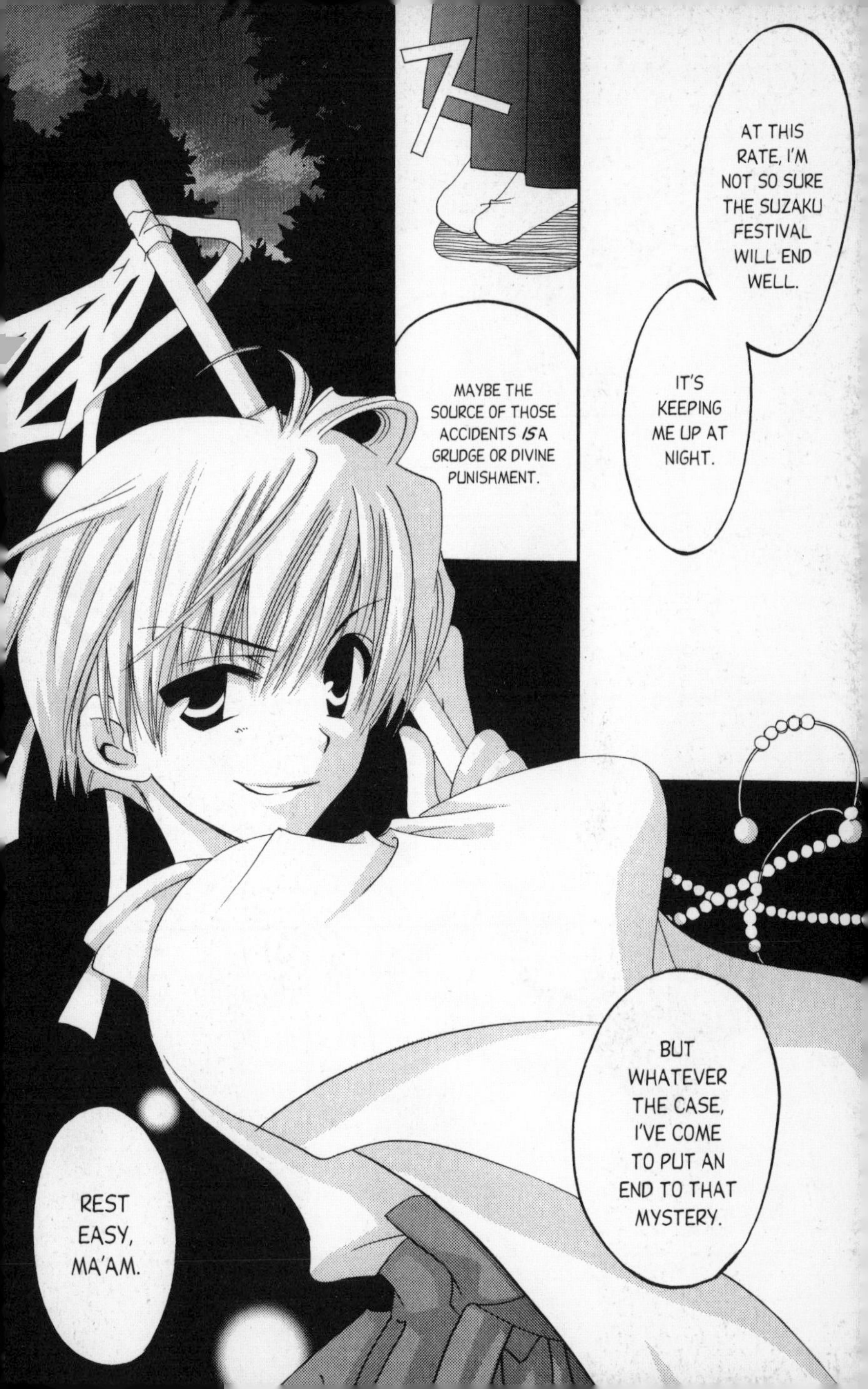
AT THIS RATE, I'M NOT SO SURE THE SUZAKU FESTIVAL WILL END WELL.
IT'S KEEPING ME UP AT NIGHT.
MAYBE THE SOURCE OF THOSE ACCIDENTS *IS* A GRUDGE OR DIVINE PUNISHMENT.
BUT WHATEVER THE CASE, I'VE COME TO PUT AN END TO THAT MYSTERY.
REST EASY, MA'AM.

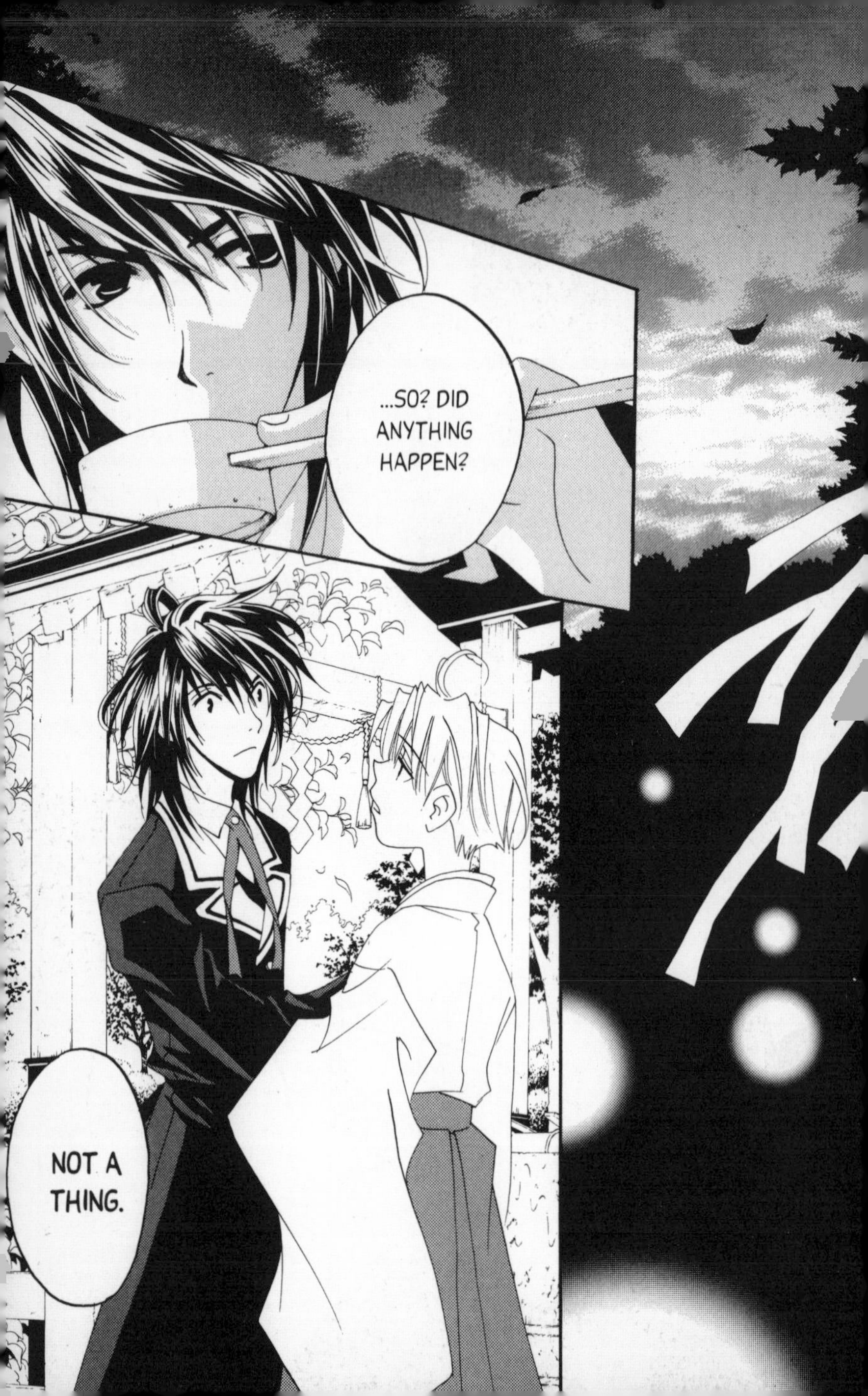
...SO? DID ANYTHING HAPPEN?
NOT A THING.

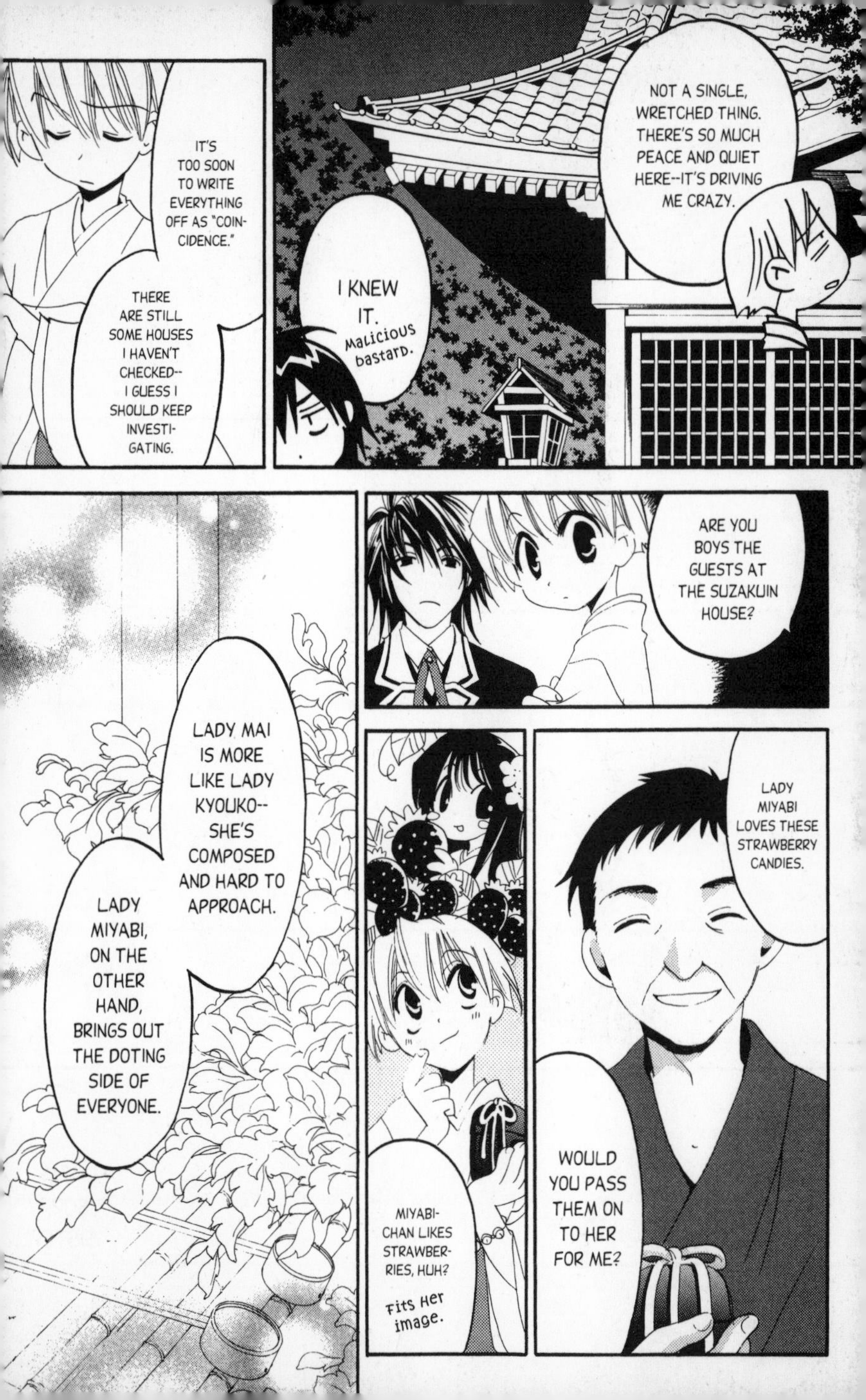
NOT A SINGLE, WRETCHED THING. THERE'S SO MUCH PEACE AND QUIET HERE--IT'S DRIVING ME CRAZY.
I KNEW IT.
Malicious bastard.
IT'S TOO SOON TO WRITE EVERYTHING OFF AS "COINCIDENCE."
THERE ARE STILL SOME HOUSES I HAVEN'T CHECKED-- I GUESS I SHOULD KEEP INVESTIGATING.
ARE YOU BOYS THE GUESTS AT THE SUZAKUIN HOUSE?
LADY MIYABI LOVES THESE STRAWBERRY CANDIES.
WOULD YOU PASS THEM ON TO HER FOR ME?
MIYABI-CHAN LIKES STRAWBERRIES, HUH?
Fits her image.
LADY MAI IS MORE LIKE LADY KYOUKO-- SHE'S COMPOSED AND HARD TO APPROACH.
LADY MIYABI, ON THE OTHER HAND, BRINGS OUT THE DOTING SIDE OF EVERYONE.

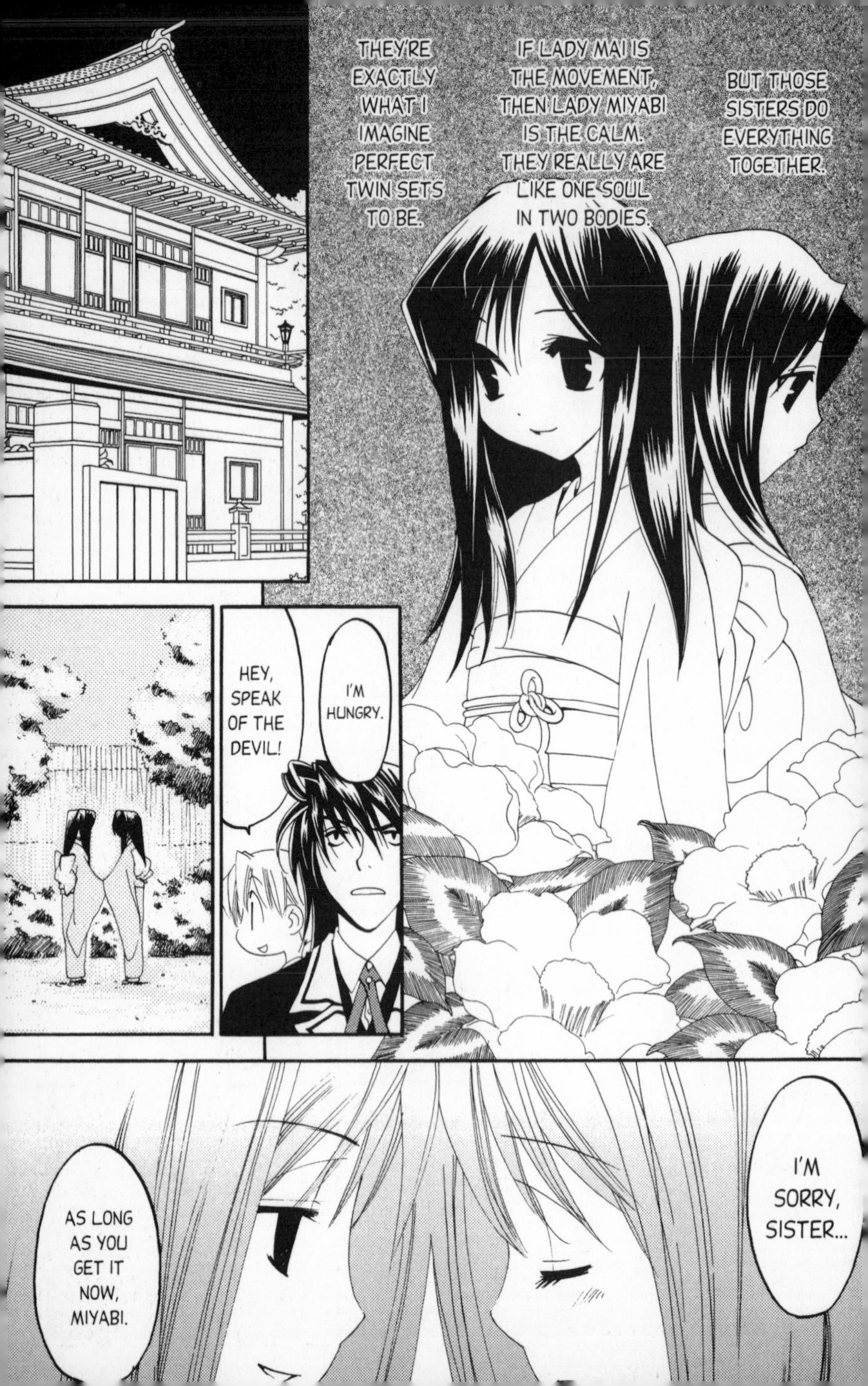
BUT THOSE SISTERS DO EVERYTHING TOGETHER.
IF LADY MAI IS THE MOVEMENT, THEN LADY MIYABI IS THE CALM. THEY REALLY ARE LIKE ONE SOUL IN TWO BODIES.
THEY'RE EXACTLY WHAT I IMAGINE PERFECT TWIN SETS TO BE.
I'M HUNGRY.
HEY, SPEAK OF THE DEVIL!
I'M SORRY, SISTER...
AS LONG AS YOU GET IT NOW, MIYABI.

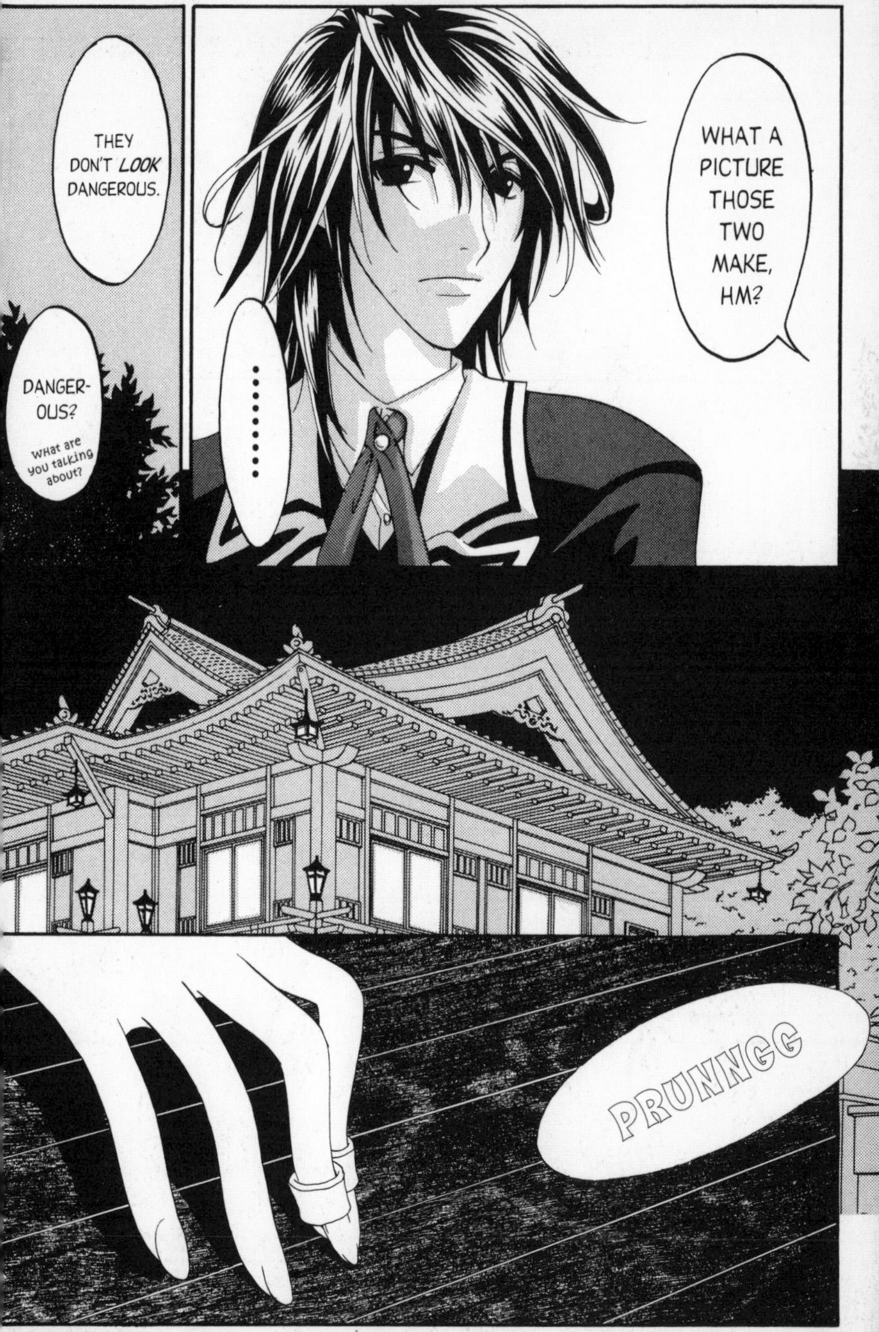
WHAT A PICTURE THOSE TWO MAKE, HM?
......
THEY DON'T *LOOK* DANGEROUS.
DANGER-OUS?
What are you talking about?
PRUNNGG

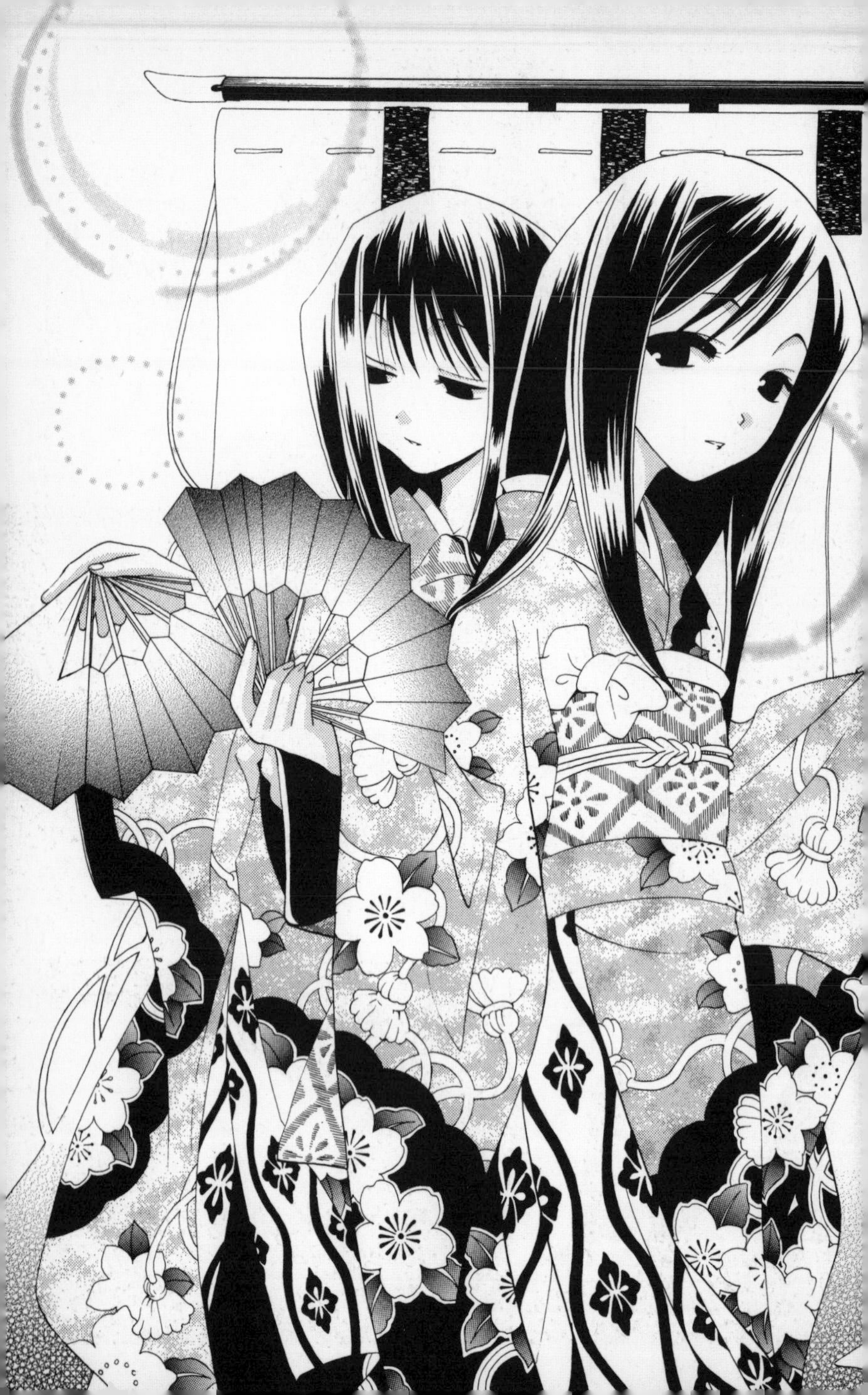

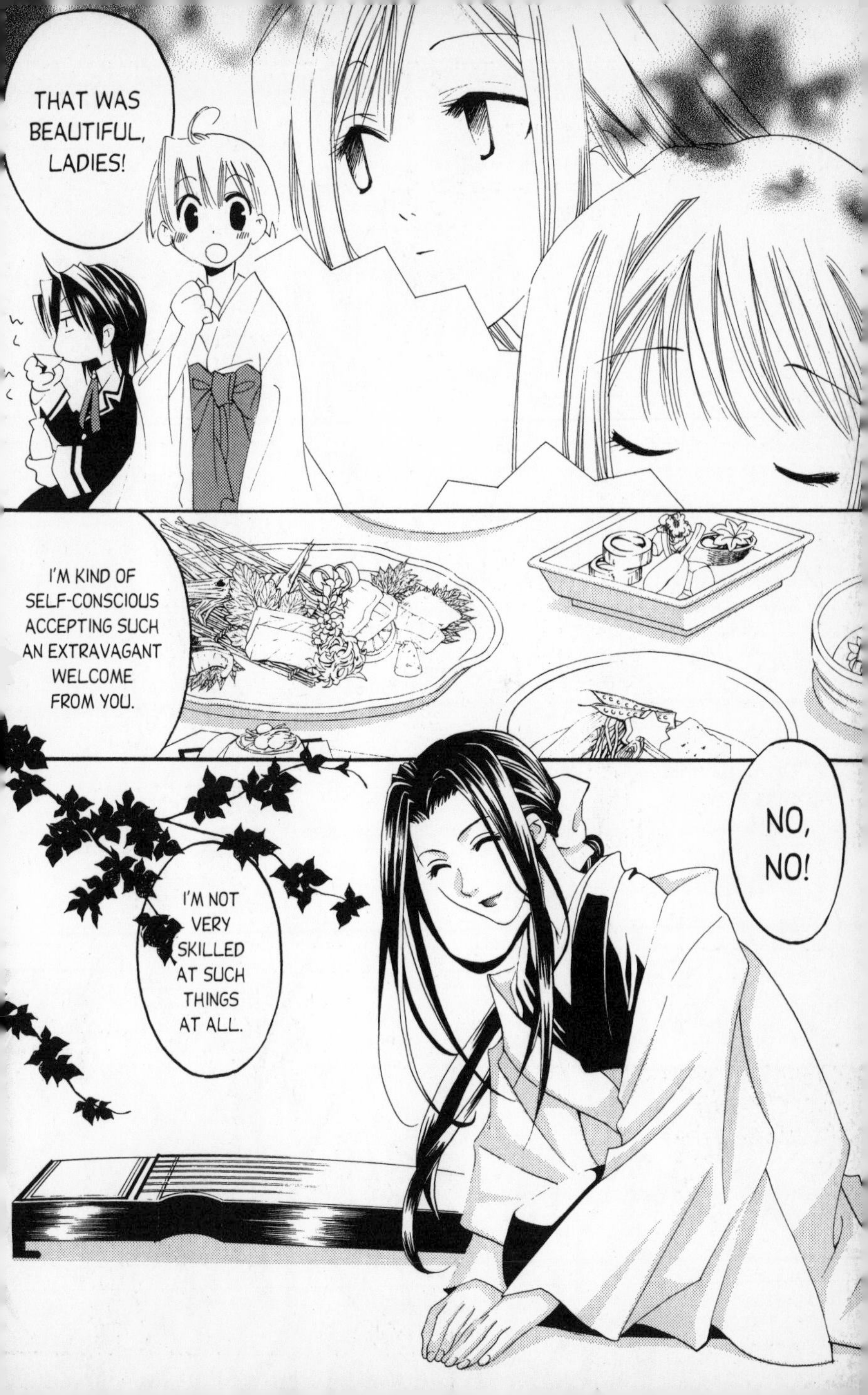
THAT WAS BEAUTIFUL, LADIES!
I'M KIND OF SELF-CONSCIOUS ACCEPTING SUCH AN EXTRAVAGANT WELCOME FROM YOU.
NO, NO!
I'M NOT VERY SKILLED AT SUCH THINGS AT ALL.

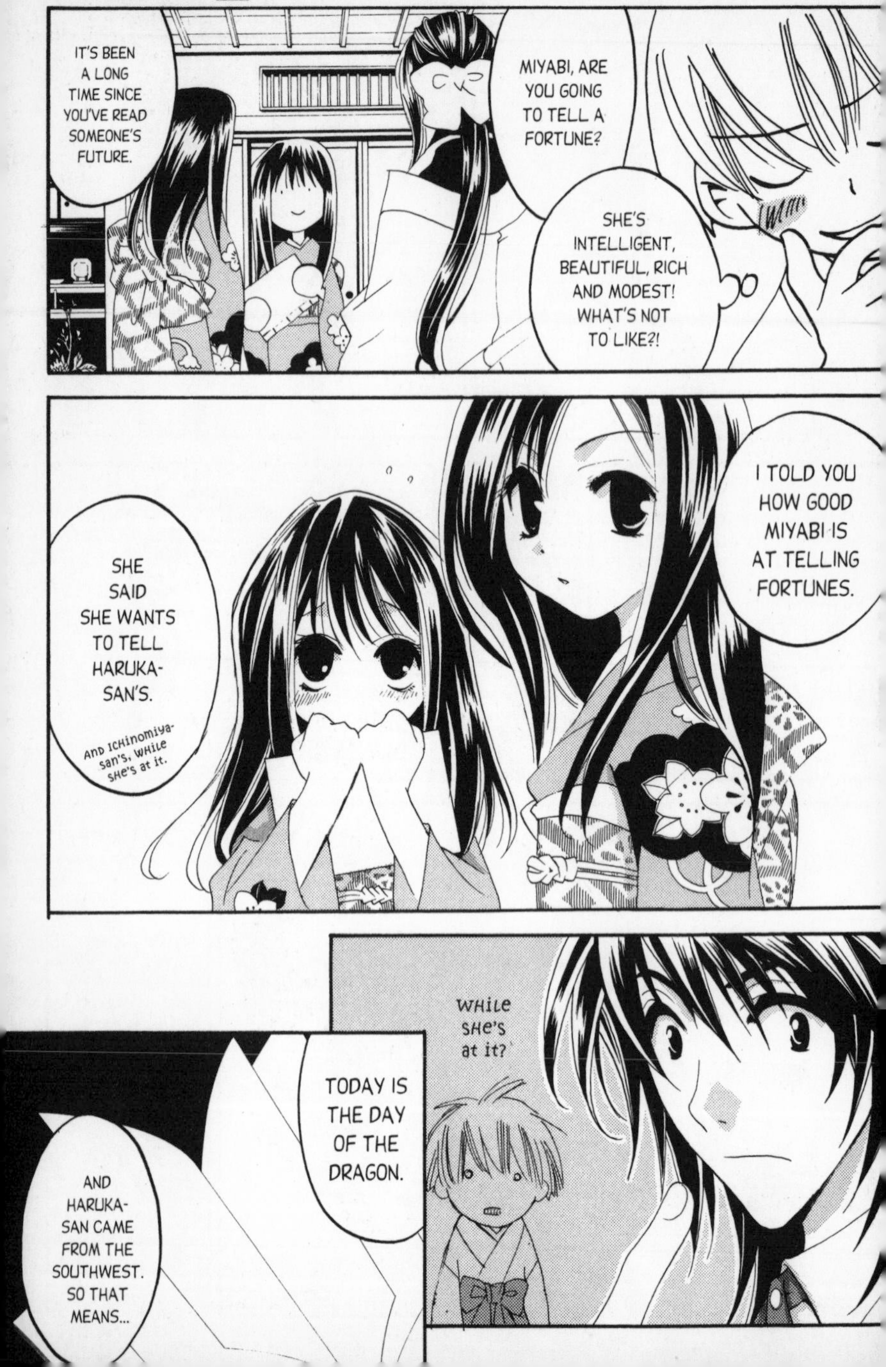
MIYABI, ARE YOU GOING TO TELL A FORTUNE?
IT'S BEEN A LONG TIME SINCE YOU'VE READ SOMEONE'S FUTURE.
SHE'S INTELLIGENT, BEAUTIFUL, RICH AND MODEST! WHAT'S NOT TO LIKE?!
I TOLD YOU HOW GOOD MIYABI IS AT TELLING FORTUNES.
SHE SAID SHE WANTS TO TELL HARUKA-SAN'S.
And Ichinomiya-san's, while she's at it.
While she's at it?
TODAY IS THE DAY OF THE DRAGON.
AND HARUKA-SAN CAME FROM THE SOUTHWEST. SO THAT MEANS...

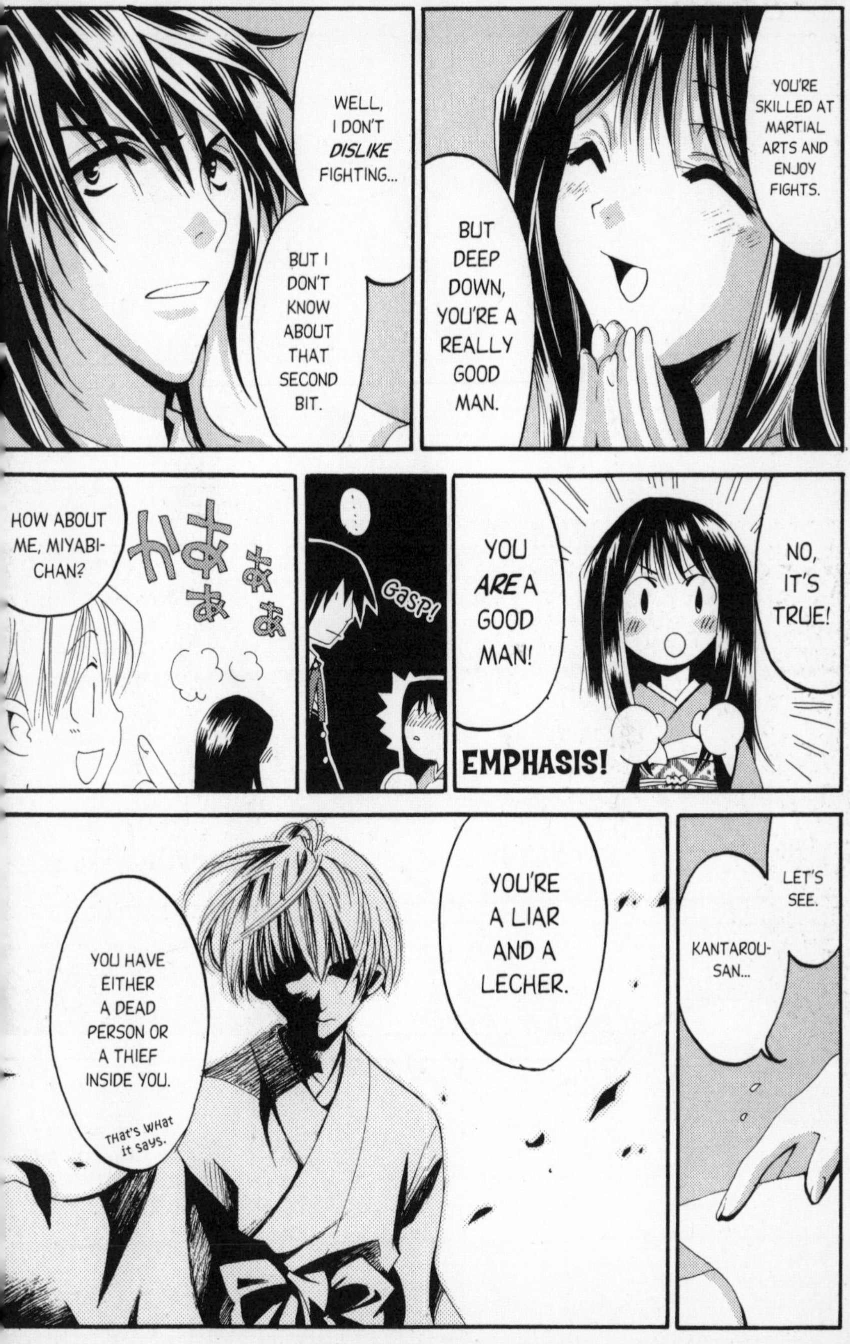
YOU'RE SKILLED AT MARTIAL ARTS AND ENJOY FIGHTS.
BUT DEEP DOWN, YOU'RE A REALLY GOOD MAN.
WELL, I DON'T *DISLIKE* FIGHTING...
BUT I DON'T KNOW ABOUT THAT SECOND BIT.
NO, IT'S TRUE!
YOU *ARE* A GOOD MAN!
EMPHASIS!
...!
GASP!
HOW ABOUT ME, MIYABI-CHAN?
かあぁぁぁ
LET'S SEE.
KANTAROU-SAN...
YOU'RE A LIAR AND A LECHER.
YOU HAVE EITHER A DEAD PERSON OR A THIEF INSIDE YOU.
THAT'S WHAT IT SAYS.

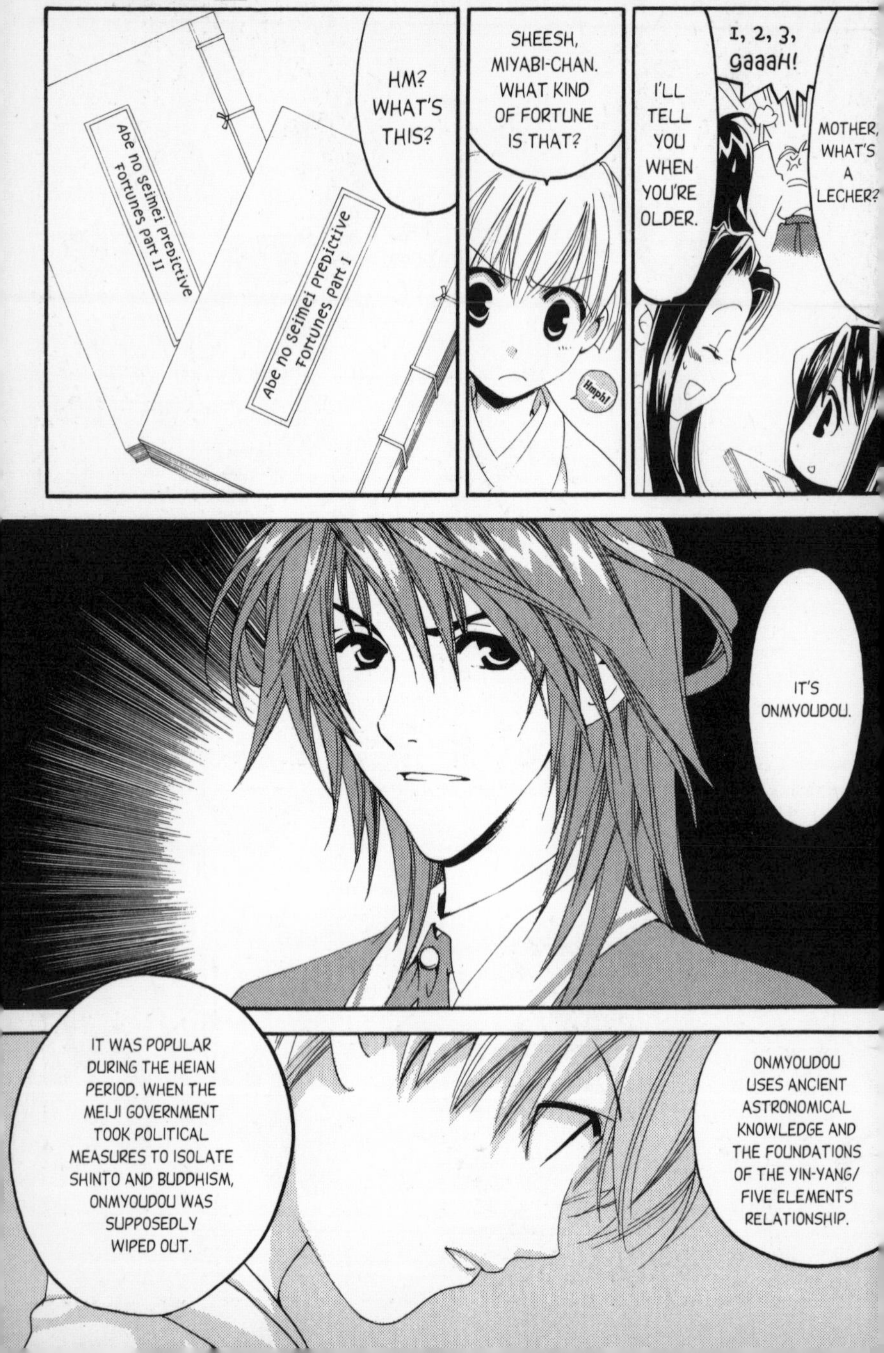
MOTHER, WHAT'S A LECHER?
1, 2, 3, gaaaH!
I'LL TELL YOU WHEN YOU'RE OLDER.
SHEESH, MIYABI-CHAN. WHAT KIND OF FORTUNE IS THAT?
Hmph!
HM? WHAT'S THIS?
Abe no Seimei predictive Fortunes part II
Abe no Seimei predictive Fortunes part I
IT'S ONMYOUDOU.
ONMYOUDOU USES ANCIENT ASTRONOMICAL KNOWLEDGE AND THE FOUNDATIONS OF THE YIN-YANG/ FIVE ELEMENTS RELATIONSHIP.
IT WAS POPULAR DURING THE HEIAN PERIOD. WHEN THE MEIJI GOVERNMENT TOOK POLITICAL MEASURES TO ISOLATE SHINTO AND BUDDHISM, ONMYOUDOU WAS SUPPOSEDLY WIPED OUT.

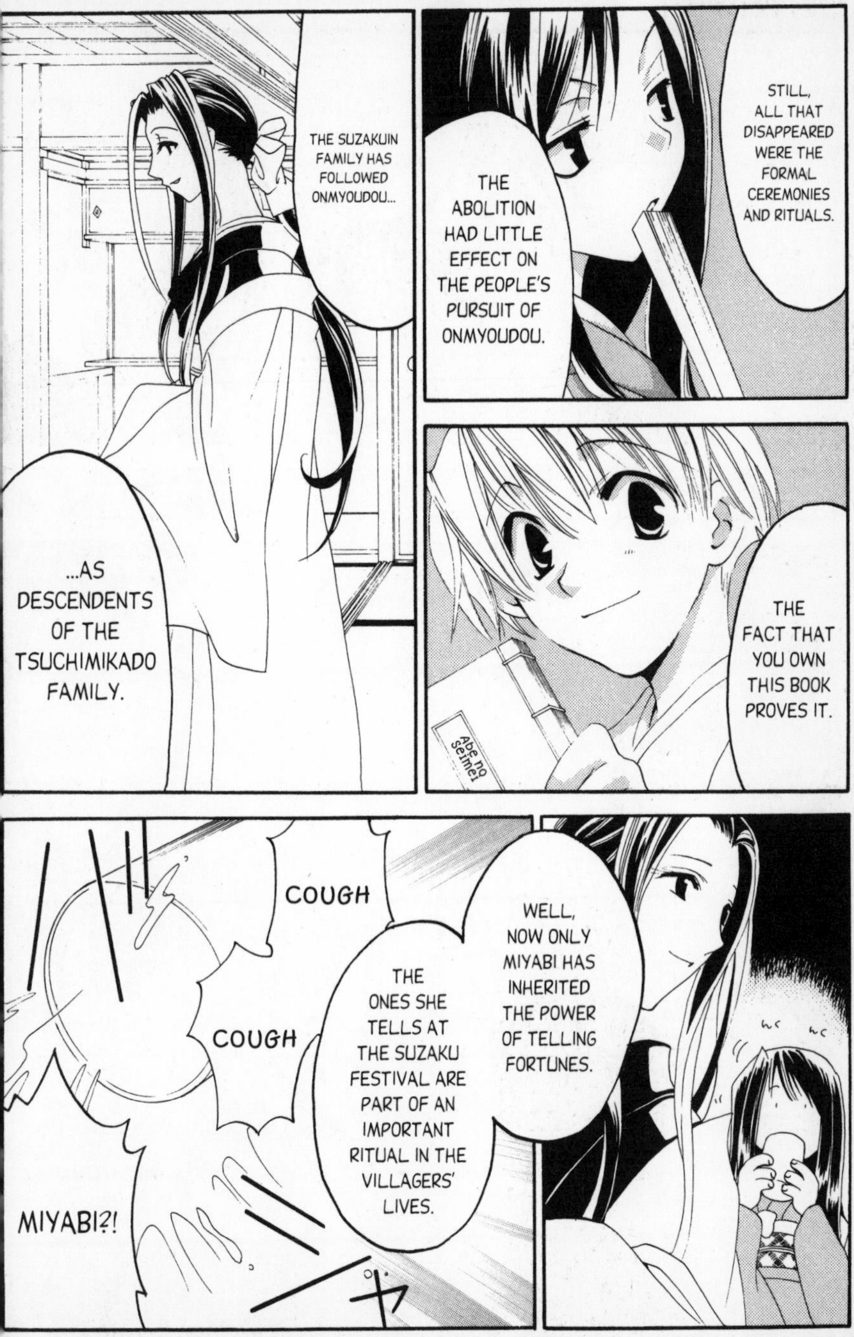
STILL, ALL THAT DISAPPEARED WERE THE FORMAL CEREMONIES AND RITUALS.
THE ABOLITION HAD LITTLE EFFECT ON THE PEOPLE'S PURSUIT OF ONMYOUDOU.
THE FACT THAT YOU OWN THIS BOOK PROVES IT.
Abe no Seimei
THE SUZAKUIN FAMILY HAS FOLLOWED ONMYOUDOU...
...AS DESCENDENTS OF THE TSUCHIMIKADO FAMILY.
WELL, NOW ONLY MIYABI HAS INHERITED THE POWER OF TELLING FORTUNES.
THE ONES SHE TELLS AT THE SUZAKU FESTIVAL ARE PART OF AN IMPORTANT RITUAL IN THE VILLAGERS' LIVES.
COUGH
COUGH
MIYABI?!

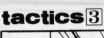

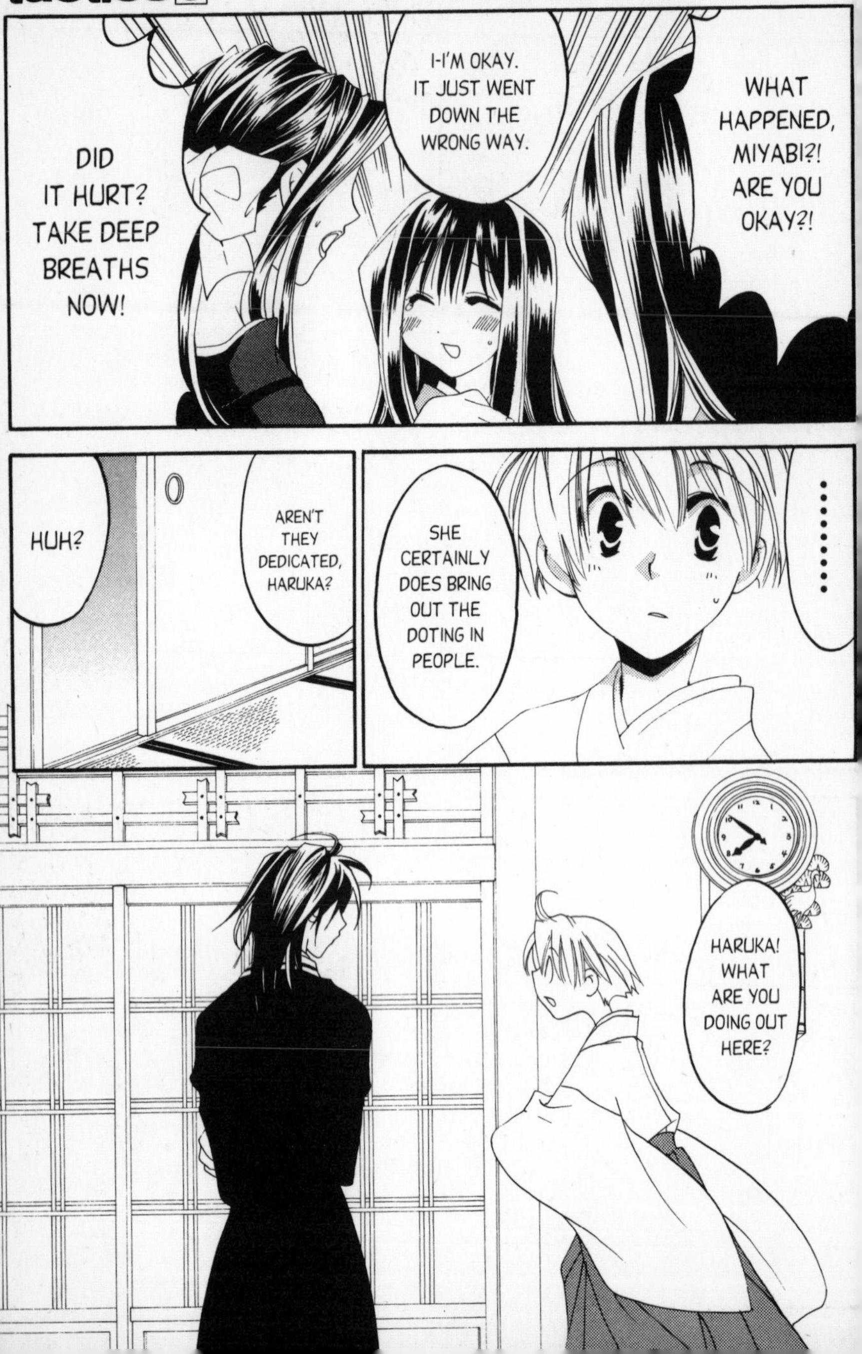
WHAT HAPPENED, MIYABI?! ARE YOU OKAY?!
I-I'M OKAY. IT JUST WENT DOWN THE WRONG WAY.
DID IT HURT? TAKE DEEP BREATHS NOW!
......
SHE CERTAINLY DOES BRING OUT THE DOTING IN PEOPLE.
AREN'T THEY DEDICATED, HARUKA?
HUH?
HARUKA! WHAT ARE YOU DOING OUT HERE?

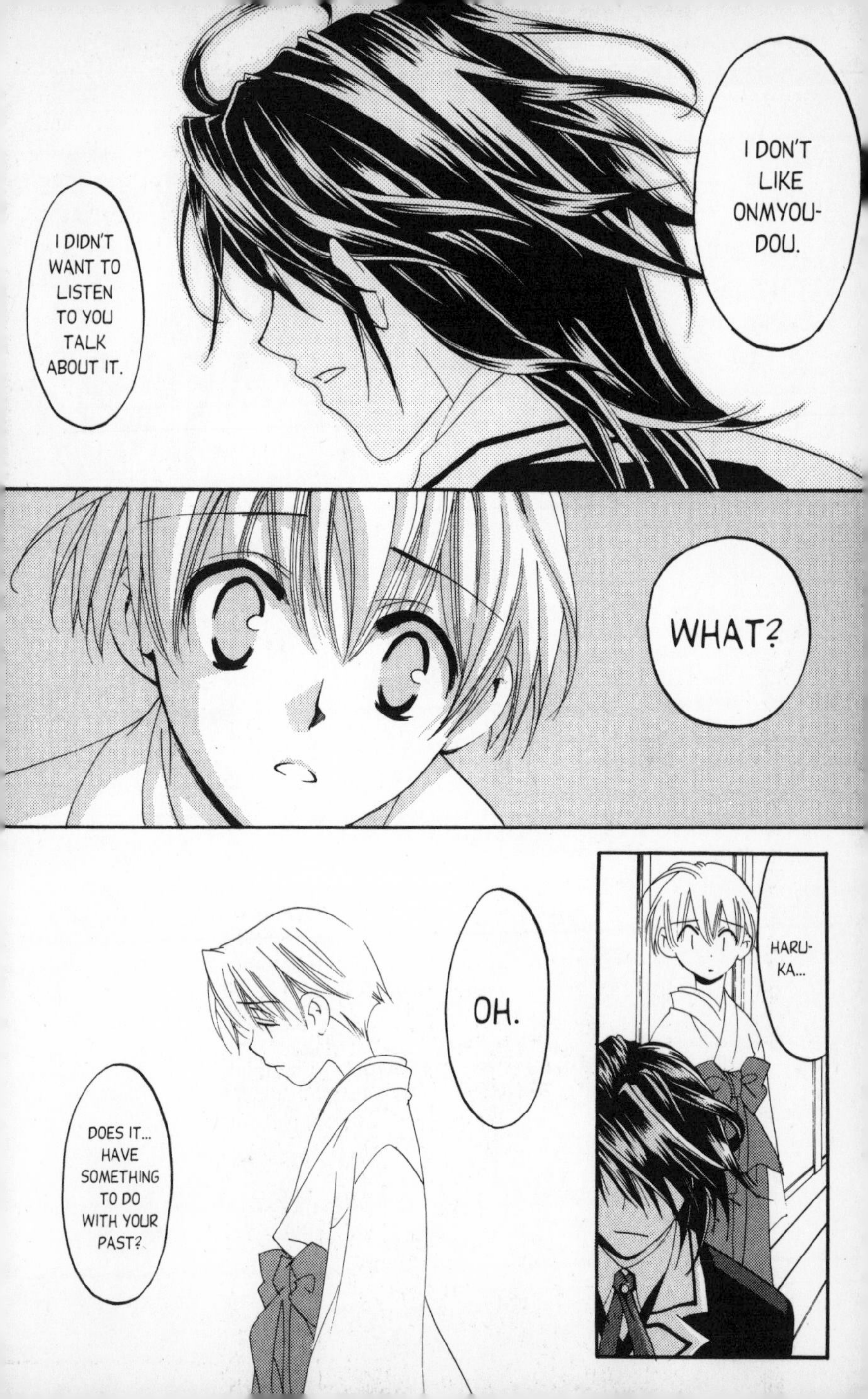
I DON'T LIKE ONMYOU-DOU.
I DIDN'T WANT TO LISTEN TO YOU TALK ABOUT IT.
WHAT?
HARU-KA...
OH.
DOES IT... HAVE SOMETHING TO DO WITH YOUR PAST?

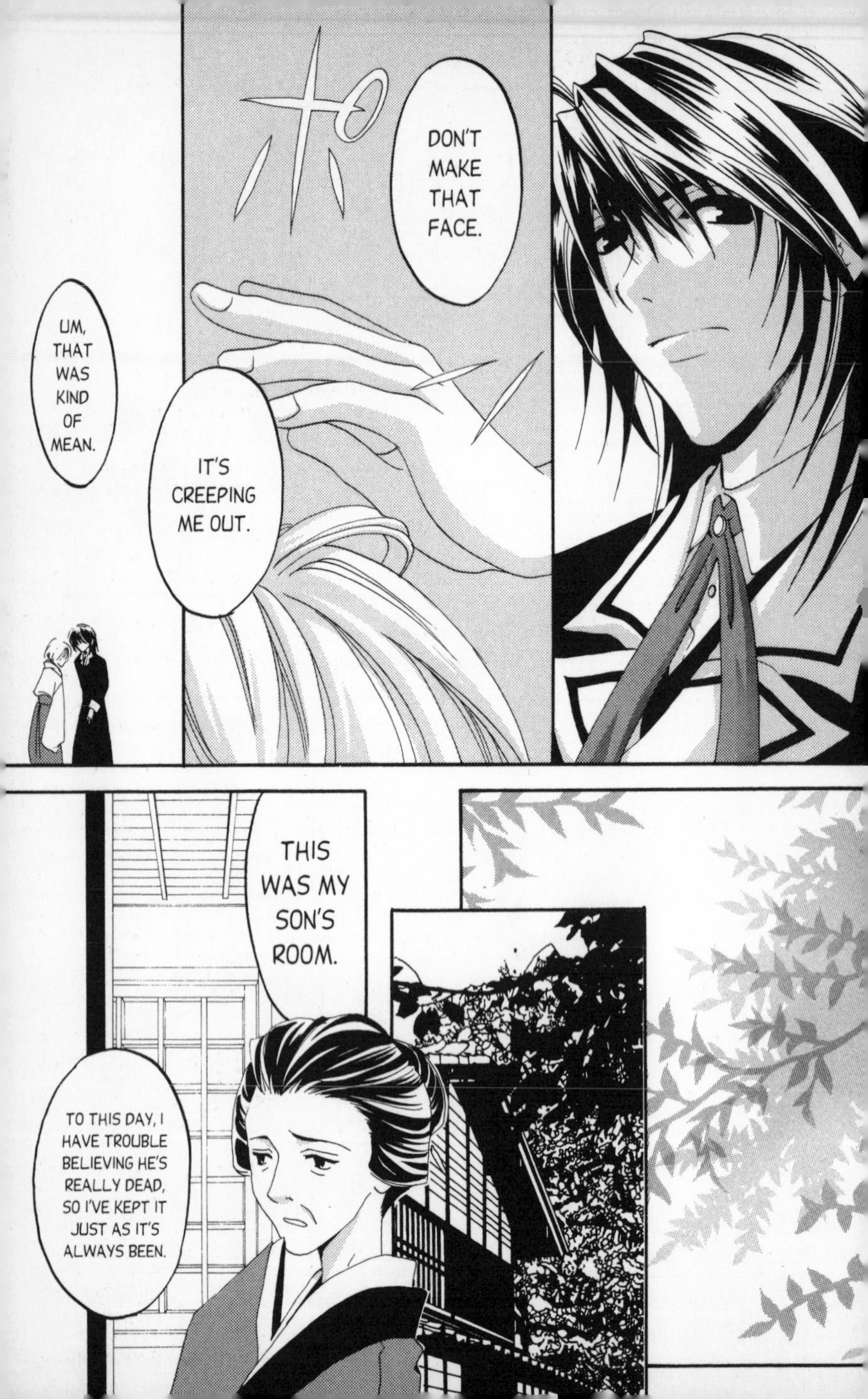

DON'T MAKE THAT FACE.
ポ
IT'S CREEPING ME OUT.
UM, THAT WAS KIND OF MEAN.
THIS WAS MY SON'S ROOM.
TO THIS DAY, I HAVE TROUBLE BELIEVING HE'S REALLY DEAD, SO I'VE KEPT IT JUST AS IT'S ALWAYS BEEN.

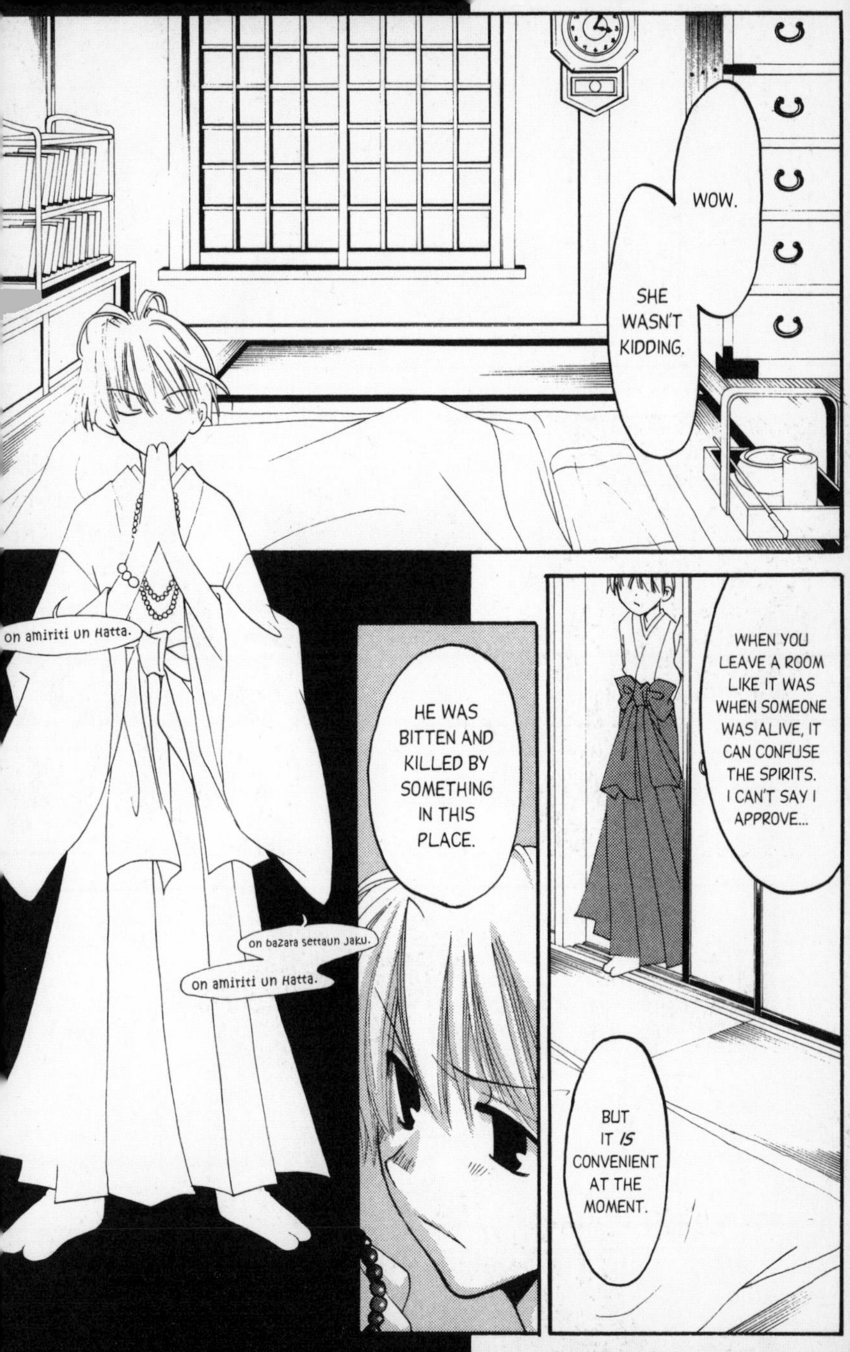
WOW.
SHE WASN'T KIDDING.
WHEN YOU LEAVE A ROOM LIKE IT WAS WHEN SOMEONE WAS ALIVE, IT CAN CONFUSE THE SPIRITS. I CAN'T SAY I APPROVE...
BUT IT *IS* CONVENIENT AT THE MOMENT.
HE WAS BITTEN AND KILLED BY SOMETHING IN THIS PLACE.
On amiriti un Hatta.
On bazara settaun jaku.
On amiriti un Hatta.

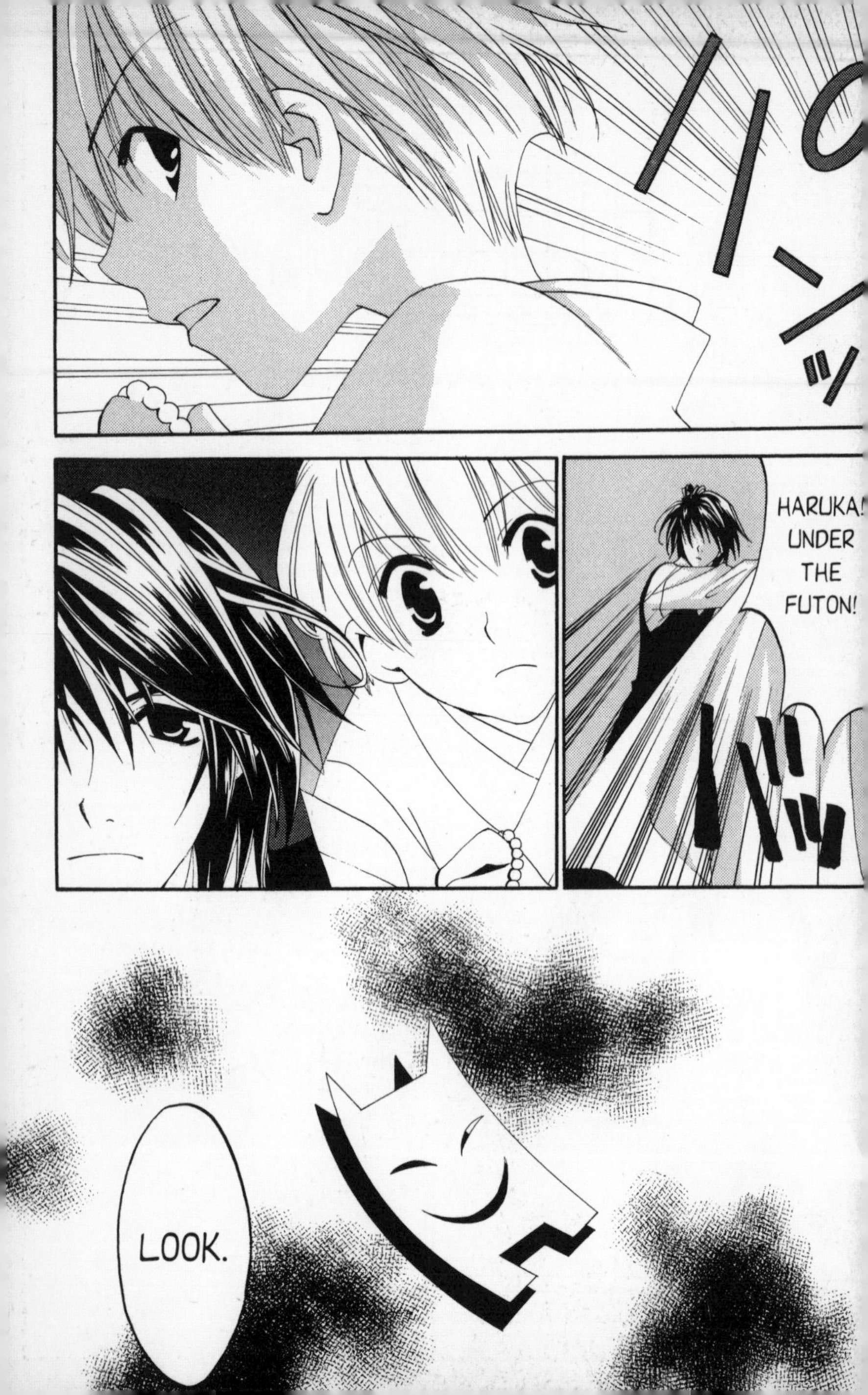
HARUKA! UNDER THE FUTON!
LOOK.

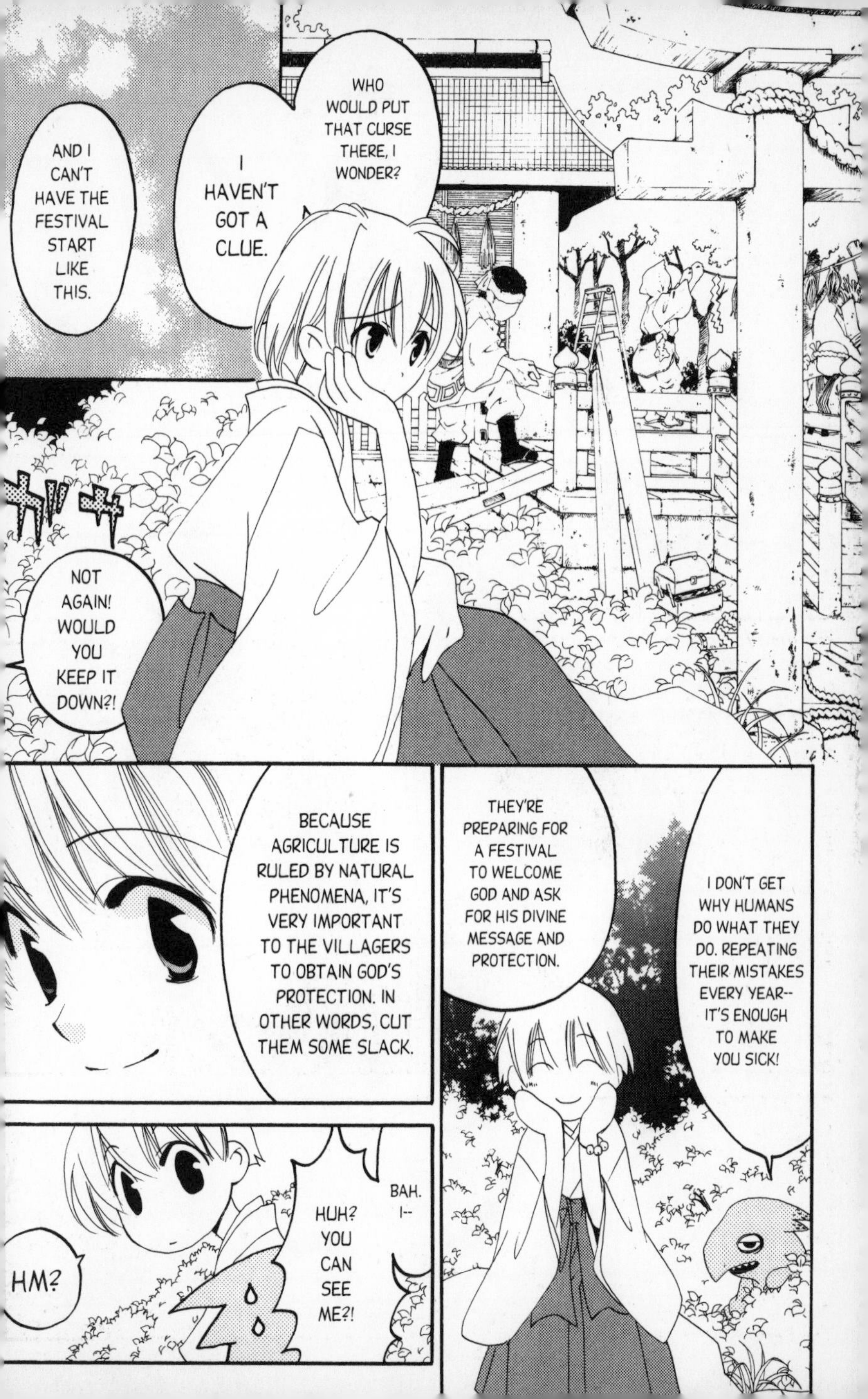
WHO WOULD PUT THAT CURSE THERE, I WONDER?
I HAVEN'T GOT A CLUE.
AND I CAN'T HAVE THE FESTIVAL START LIKE THIS.
NOT AGAIN! WOULD YOU KEEP IT DOWN?!
I DON'T GET WHY HUMANS DO WHAT THEY DO. REPEATING THEIR MISTAKES EVERY YEAR-- IT'S ENOUGH TO MAKE YOU SICK!
THEY'RE PREPARING FOR A FESTIVAL TO WELCOME GOD AND ASK FOR HIS DIVINE MESSAGE AND PROTECTION.
BECAUSE AGRICULTURE IS RULED BY NATURAL PHENOMENA, IT'S VERY IMPORTANT TO THE VILLAGERS TO OBTAIN GOD'S PROTECTION. IN OTHER WORDS, CUT THEM SOME SLACK.
BAH. I--
HUH? YOU CAN SEE ME?!
HM?

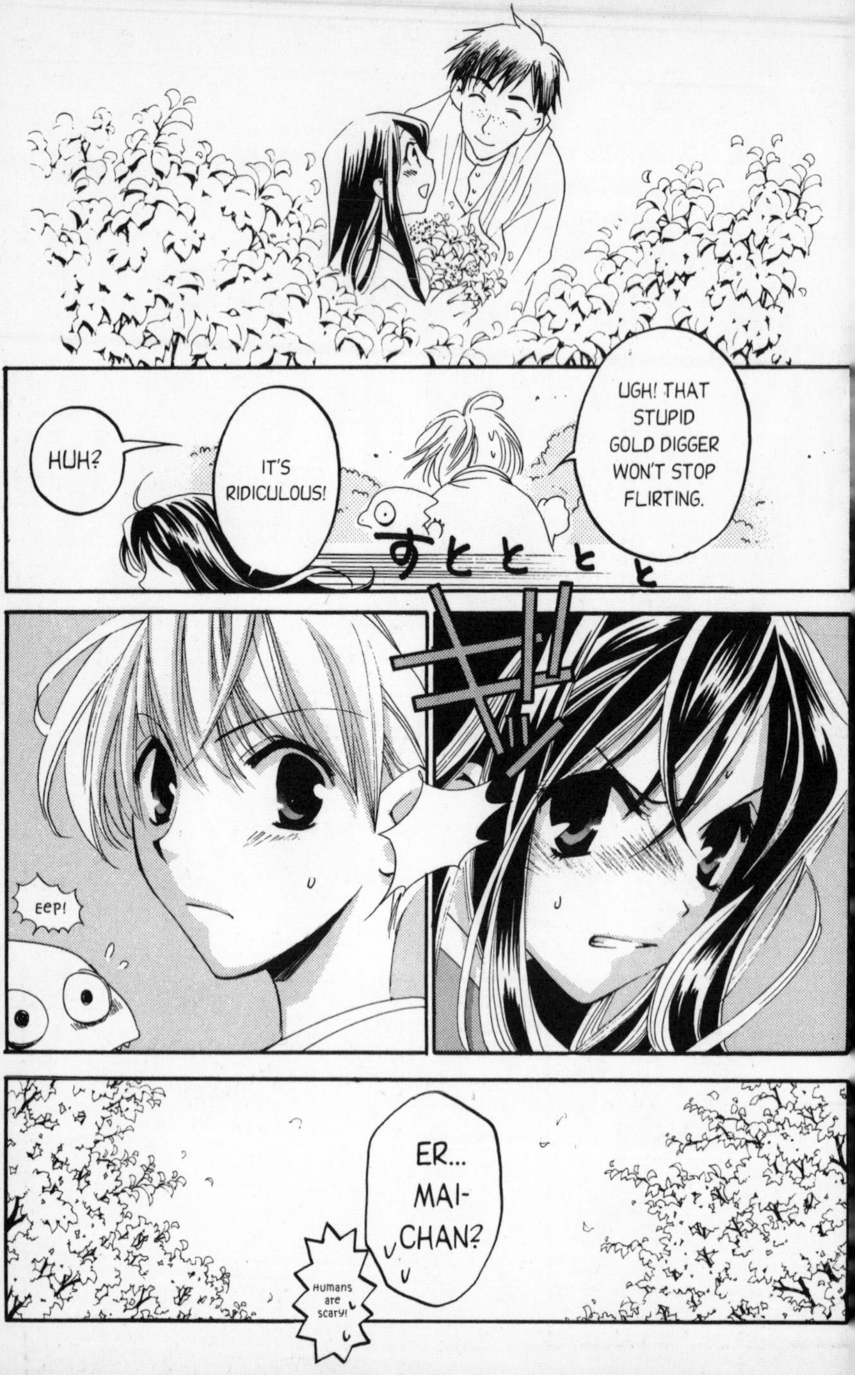
UGH! THAT STUPID GOLD DIGGER WON'T STOP FLIRTING.
IT'S RIDICULOUS!
HUH?
すととととと
EEP!
ER... MAI-CHAN?
Humans are scary!

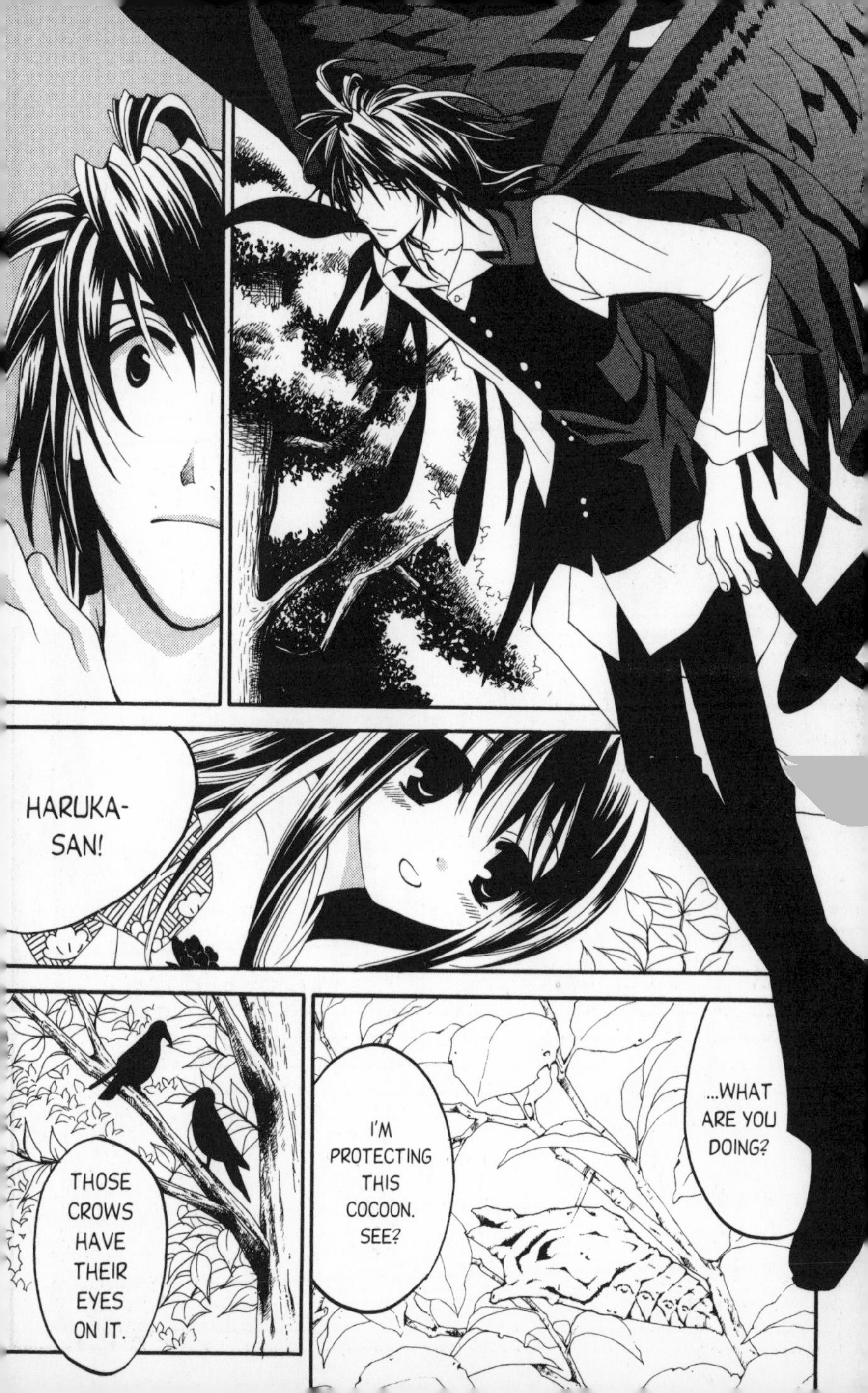
HARUKA-SAN!
...WHAT ARE YOU DOING?
I'M PROTECTING THIS COCOON. SEE?
THOSE CROWS HAVE THEIR EYES ON IT.

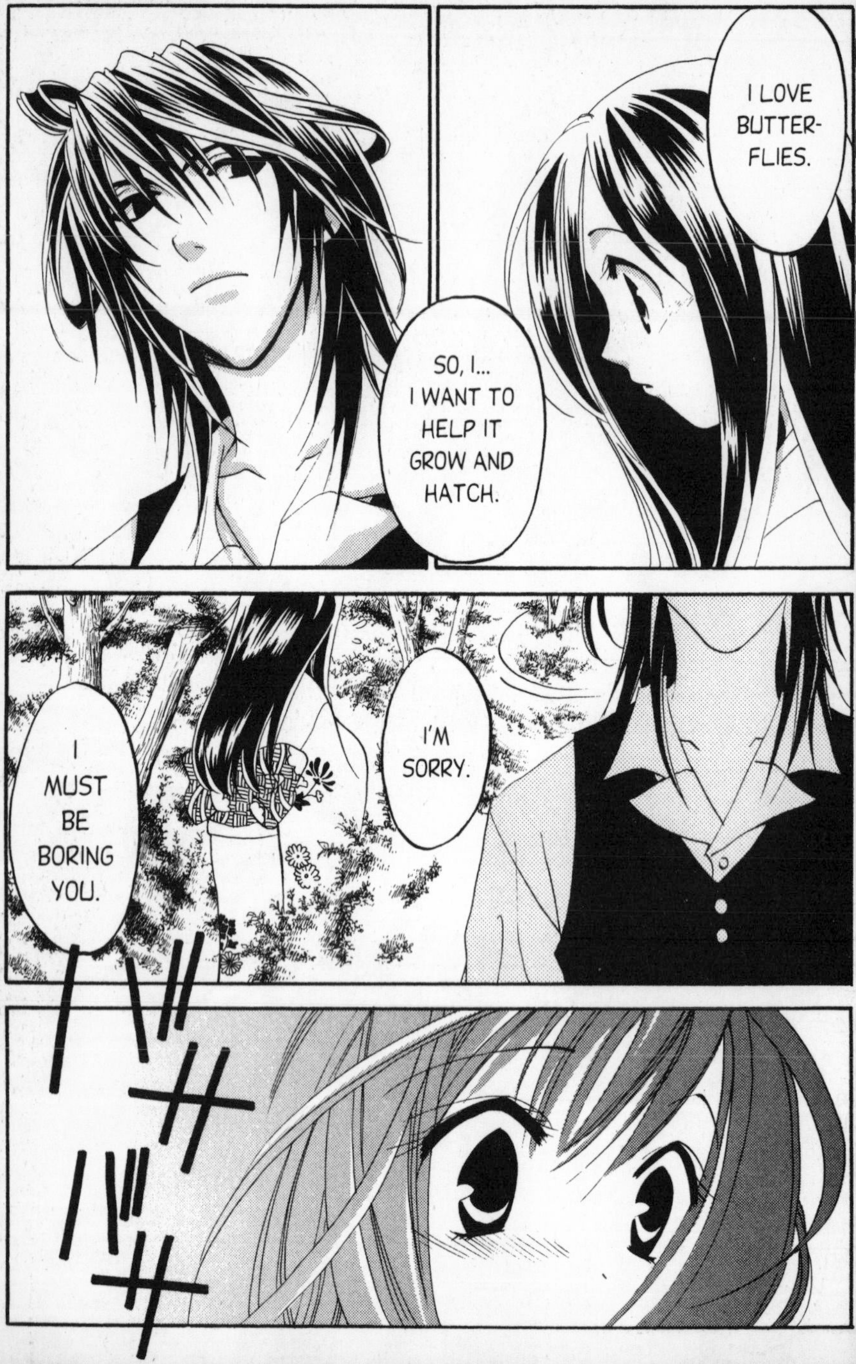
I LOVE BUTTER-FLIES.
SO, I... I WANT TO HELP IT GROW AND HATCH.
I'M SORRY.
I MUST BE BORING YOU.

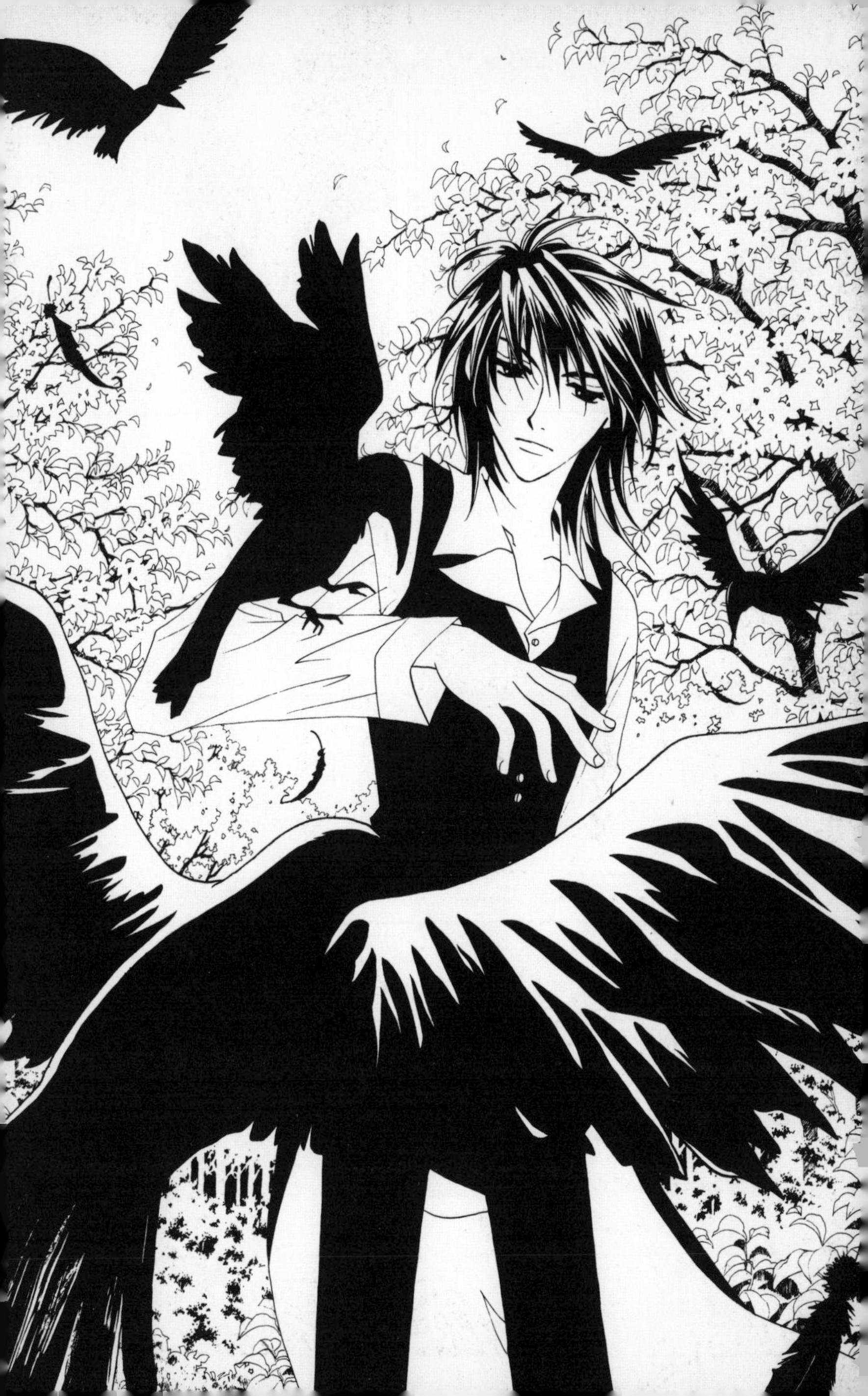

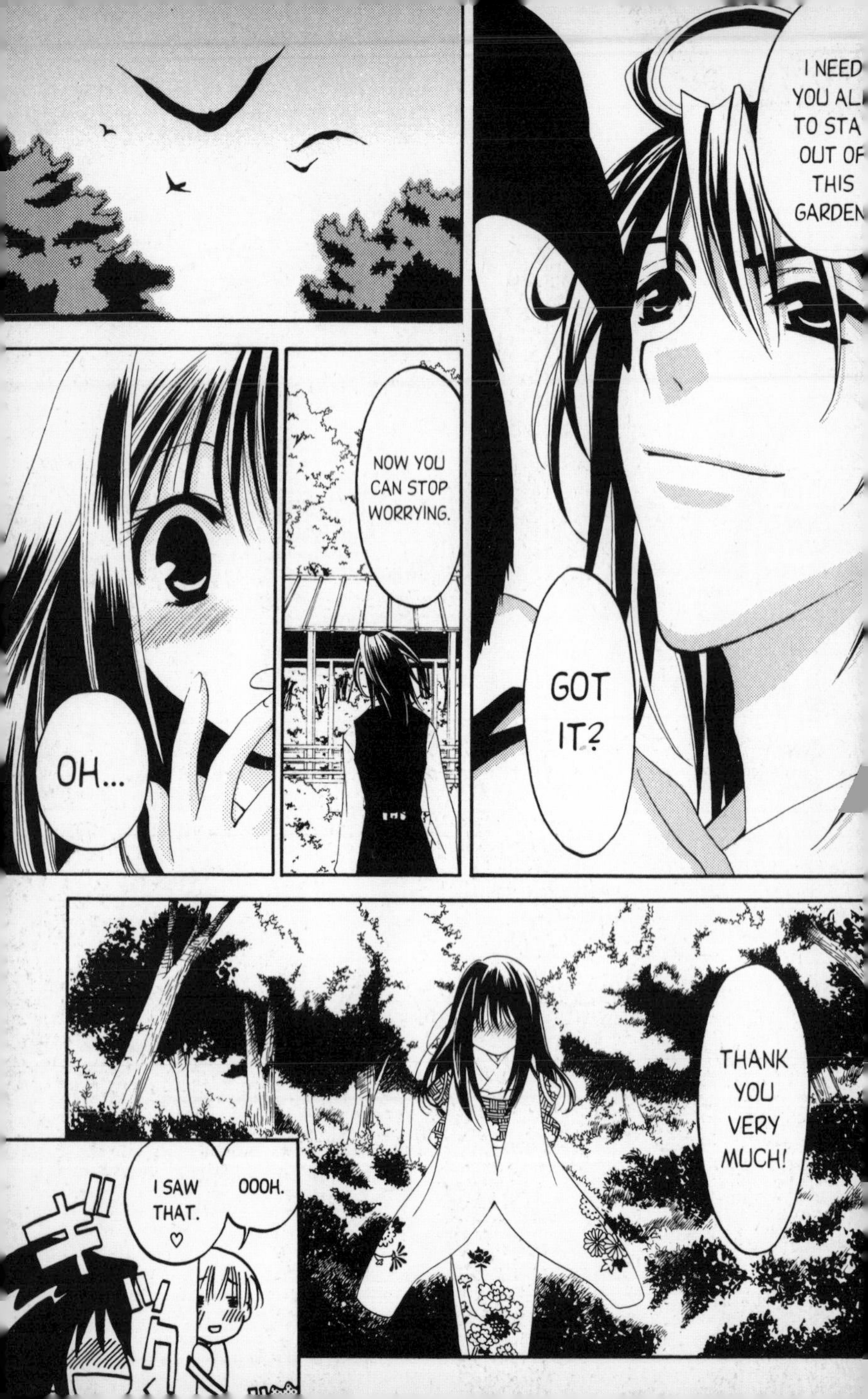

I NEED YOU AL TO STA OUT OF THIS GARDEN
GOT IT?
NOW YOU CAN STOP WORRYING.
OH...
THANK YOU VERY MUCH!
OOOH.
I SAW THAT. ♡

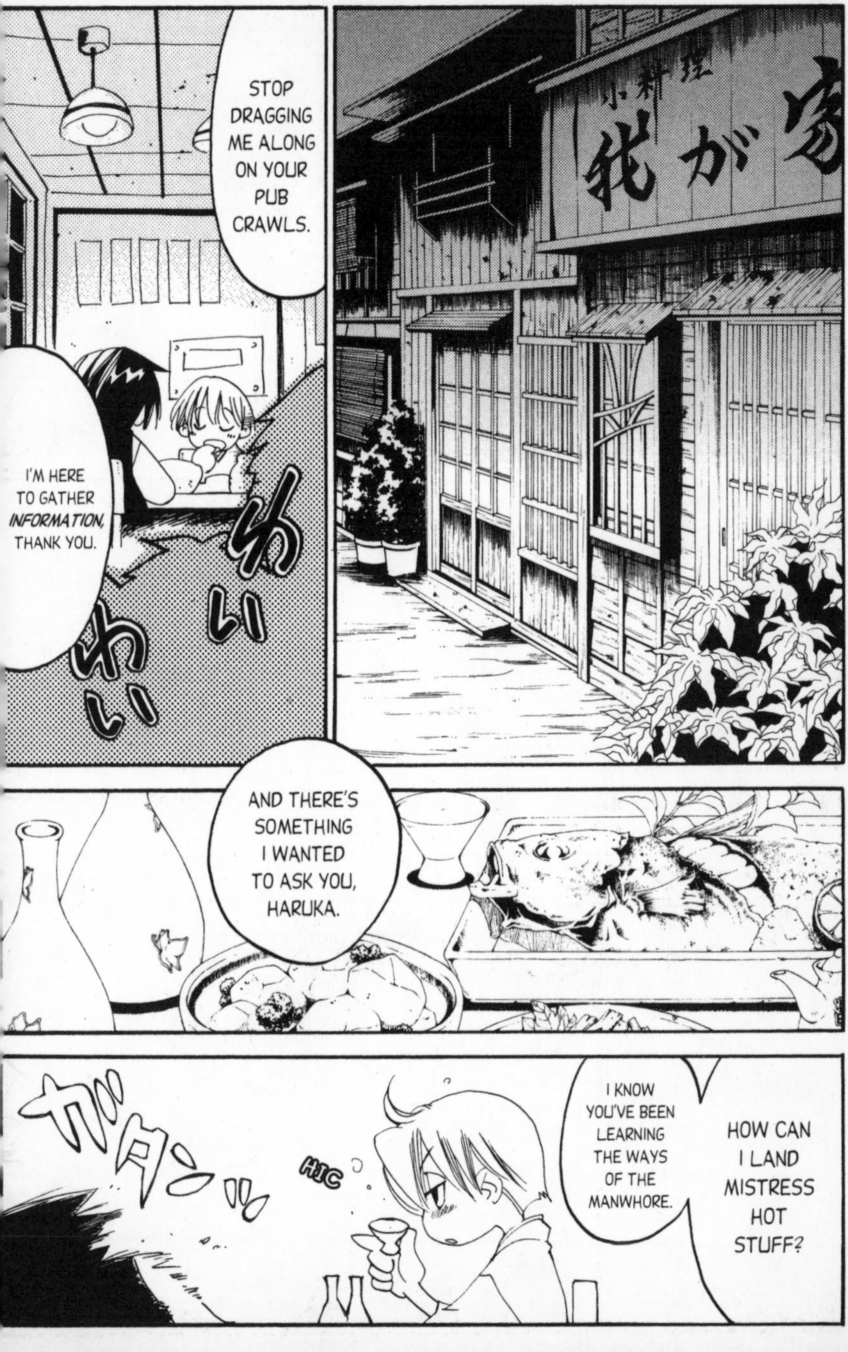

小料理
我が家
STOP DRAGGING ME ALONG ON YOUR PUB CRAWLS.
I'M HERE TO GATHER *INFORMATION,* THANK YOU.
わい
わい
AND THERE'S SOMETHING I WANTED TO ASK YOU, HARUKA.
I KNOW YOU'VE BEEN LEARNING THE WAYS OF THE MANWHORE.
HOW CAN I LAND MISTRESS HOT STUFF?
HIC
ガタン

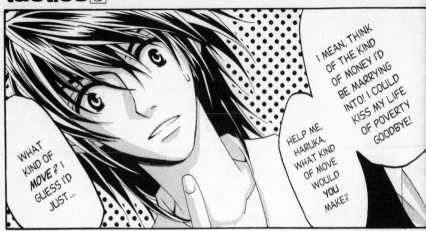

I MEAN, THINK OF THE KIND OF MONEY I'D BE MARRYING INTO! I COULD KISS MY LIFE OF POVERTY GOODBYE!
HELP ME, HARUKA. WHAT KIND OF MOVE WOULD YOU MAKE?
WHAT KIND OF MOVE? I GUESS I'D JUST...
YEAH, RIGHT. WHY WOULD I TELL YOU SOMETHING LIKE THAT?!
DON'T BE SELFISH, YOU LITTLE GIGOLO!
I WONDER IF THE FESTIVAL WILL WORK OUT THIS YEAR.
ALL WE CAN DO IS FOLLOW LADY MIYABI'S PREDICTIONS.
BUT AFTER EVERYTHING THAT'S HAPPENED AROUND THE SUZAKUIN FAMILY, I WOULDN'T BE SURPRISED TO SEE ANOTHER DISASTER.
HM... THAT'S THE FLIRT WHO GAVE FLOWERS TO MIYABI-CHAN EARLIER.

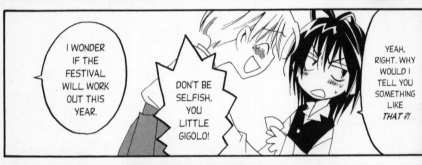

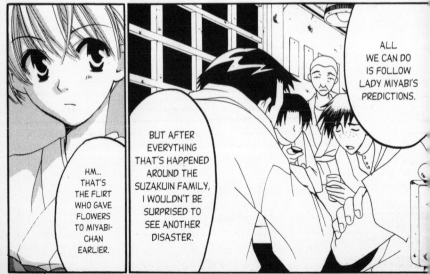

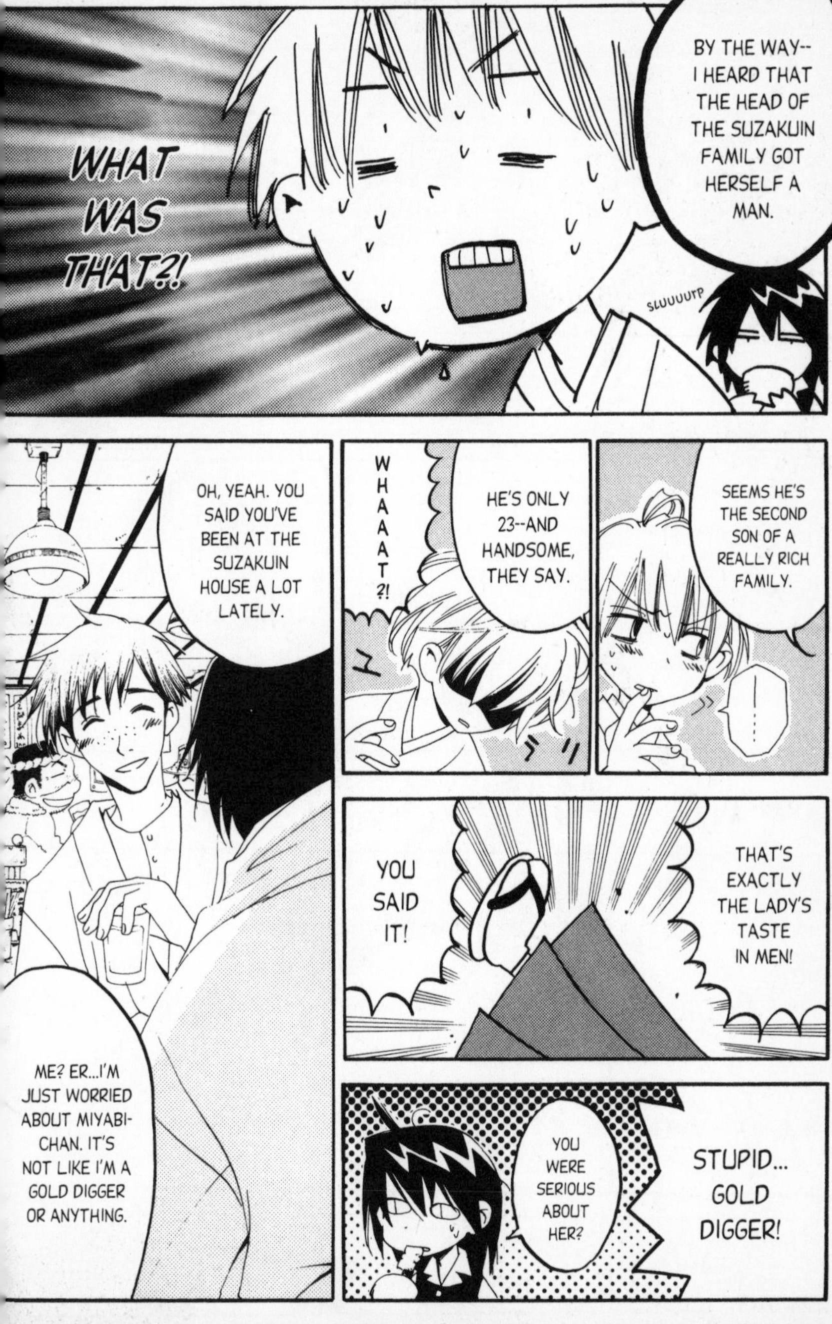

BY THE WAY-- I HEARD THAT THE HEAD OF THE SUZAKUIN FAMILY GOT HERSELF A MAN.
SLUUUURP
WHAT WAS THAT?!
SEEMS HE'S THE SECOND SON OF A REALLY RICH FAMILY.
HE'S ONLY 23--AND HANDSOME, THEY SAY.
WHAAAAT?!
THAT'S EXACTLY THE LADY'S TASTE IN MEN!
YOU SAID IT!
STUPID... GOLD DIGGER!
YOU WERE SERIOUS ABOUT HER?
OH, YEAH. YOU SAID YOU'VE BEEN AT THE SUZAKUIN HOUSE A LOT LATELY.
ME? ER...I'M JUST WORRIED ABOUT MIYABI-CHAN. IT'S NOT LIKE I'M A GOLD DIGGER OR ANYTHING.

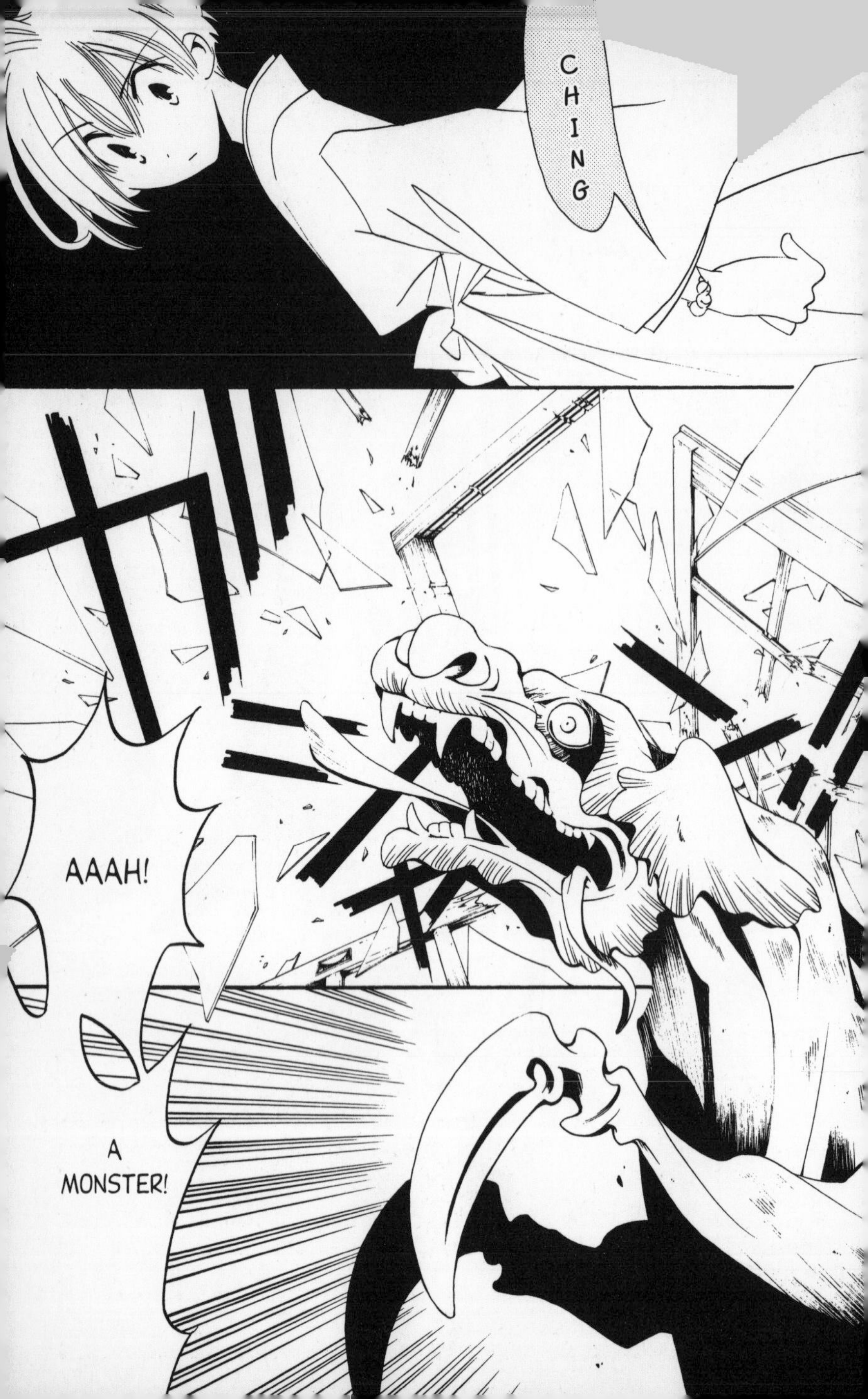
CHING
AAAH!
A MONSTER!

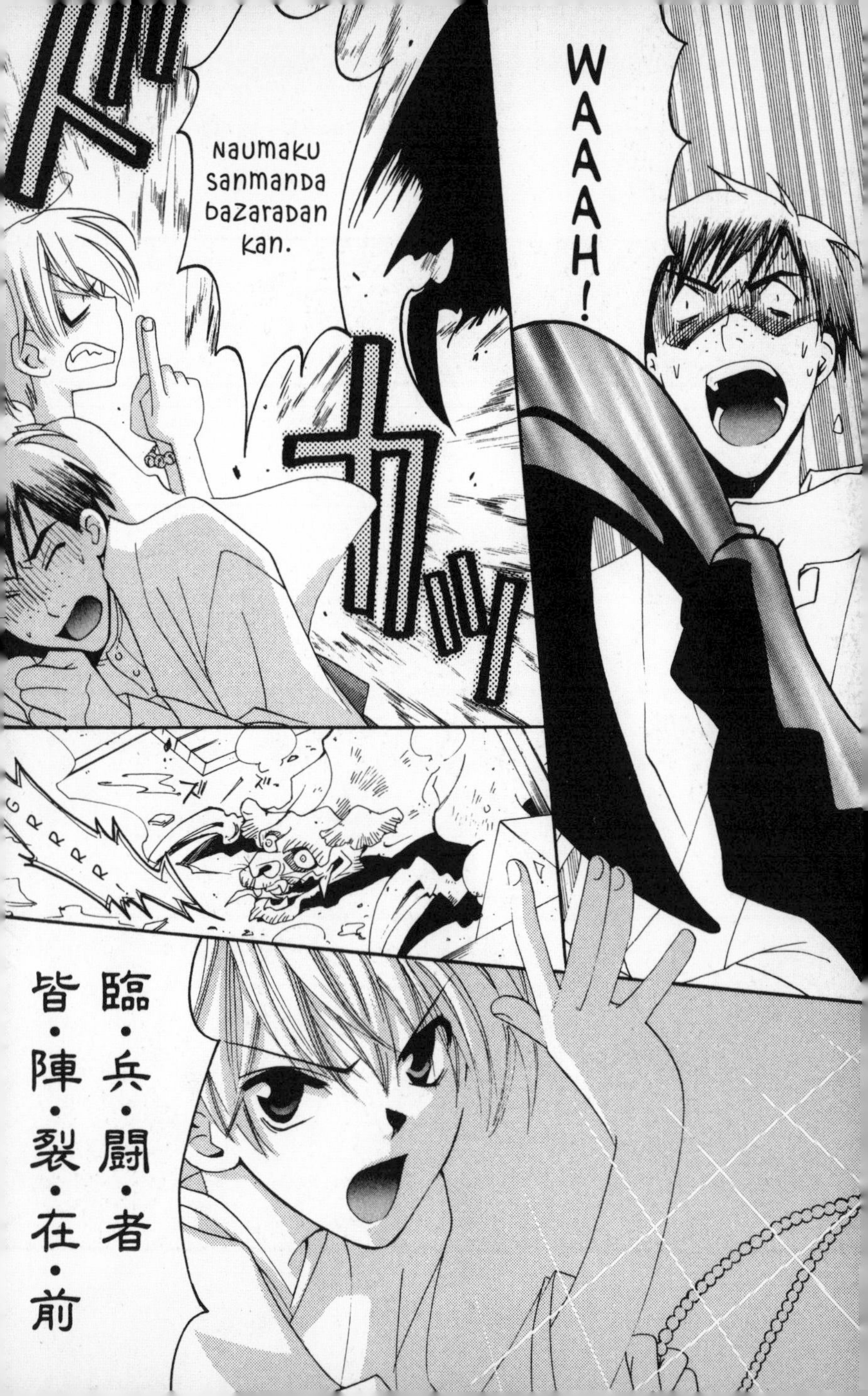

WAAAH!
ド
Naumaku sanmanda bazaradan kan.
カッ
GRRRR
臨・兵・闘・者
皆・陣・裂・在・前

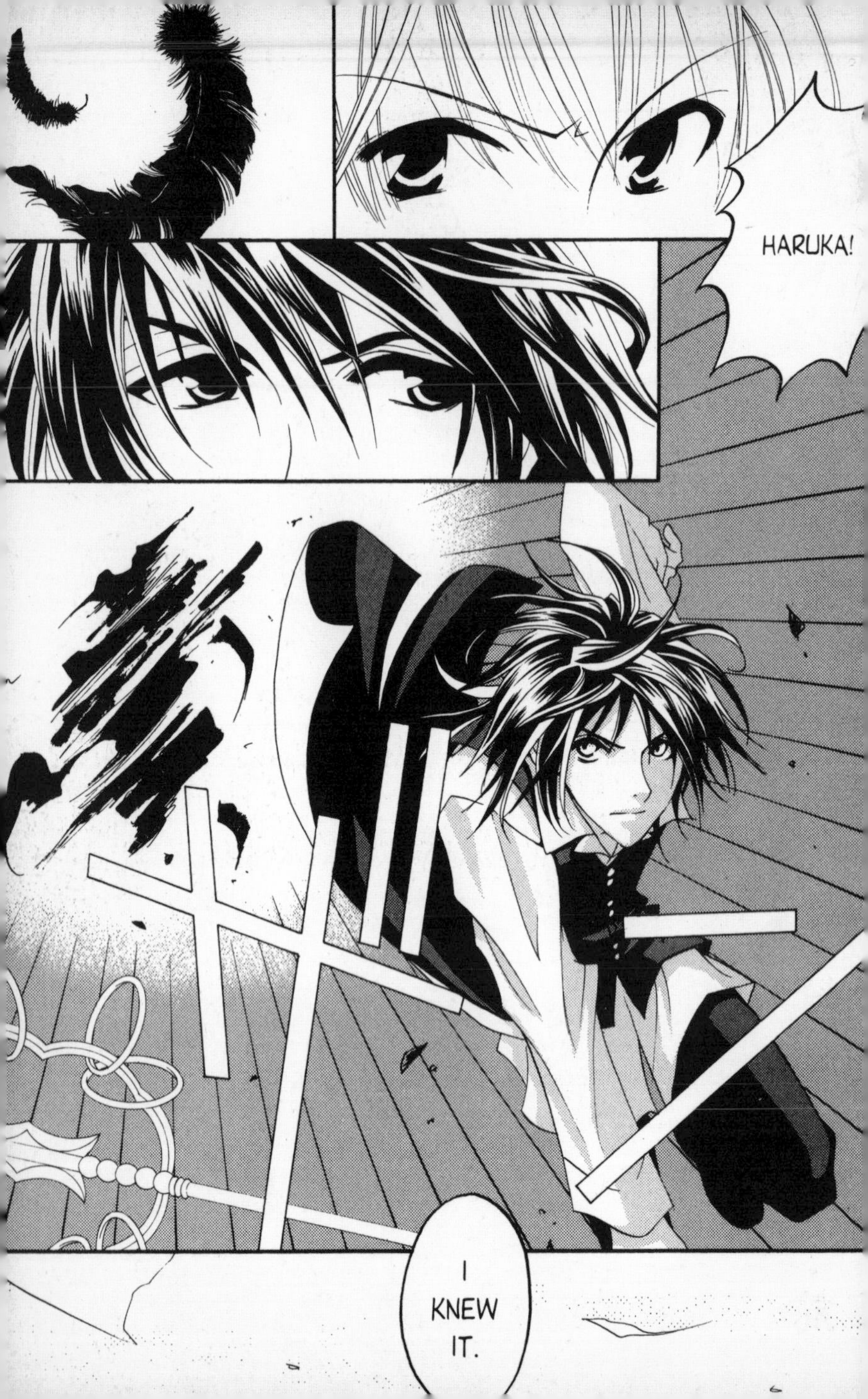
HARUKA!
I KNEW IT.

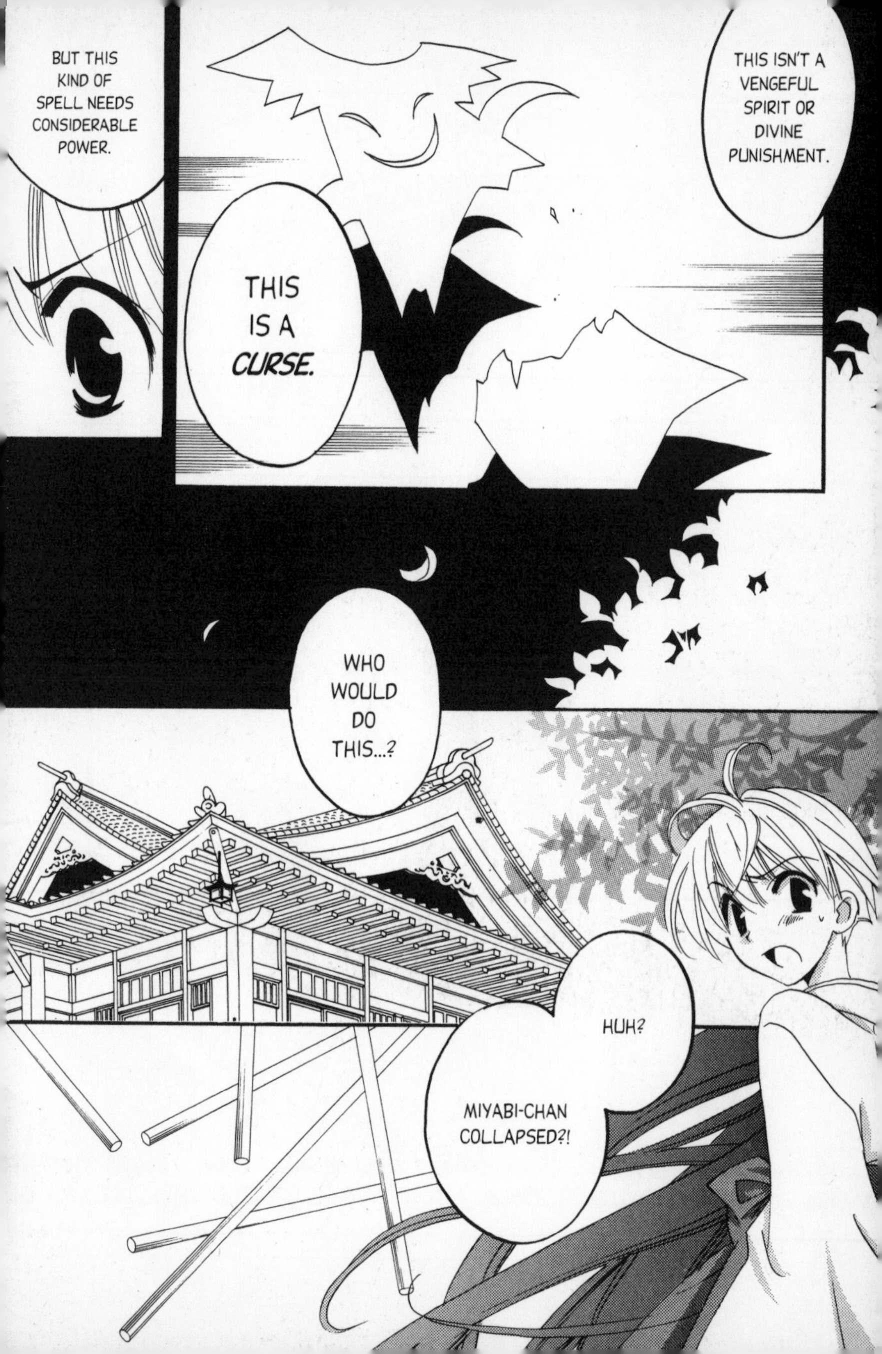
THIS ISN'T A VENGEFUL SPIRIT OR DIVINE PUNISHMENT.
THIS IS A *CURSE.*
BUT THIS KIND OF SPELL NEEDS CONSIDERABLE POWER.
WHO WOULD DO THIS...?
HUH?
MIYABI-CHAN COLLAPSED?!

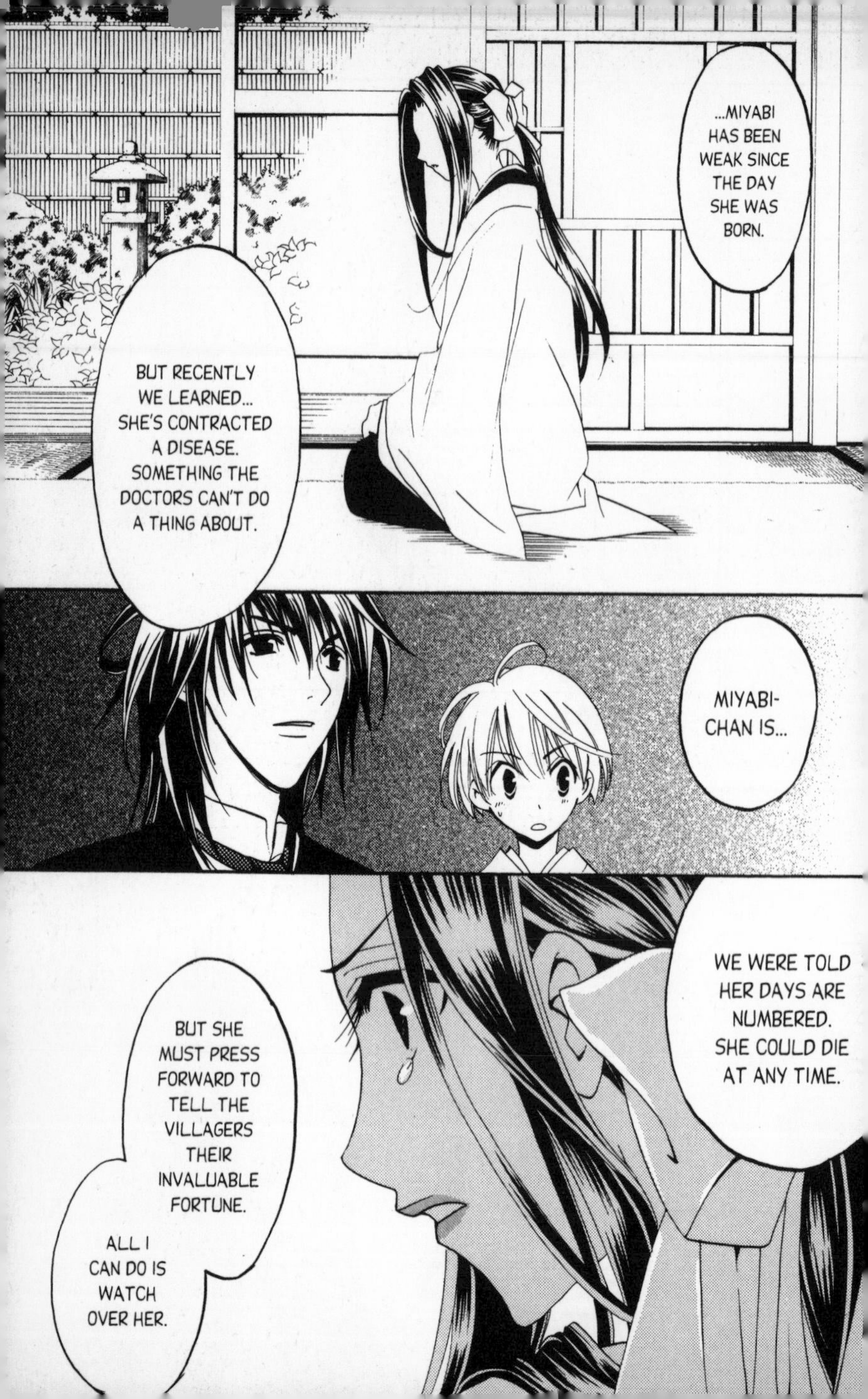
...MIYABI HAS BEEN WEAK SINCE THE DAY SHE WAS BORN.
BUT RECENTLY WE LEARNED... SHE'S CONTRACTED A DISEASE. SOMETHING THE DOCTORS CAN'T DO A THING ABOUT.
MIYABI-CHAN IS...
WE WERE TOLD HER DAYS ARE NUMBERED. SHE COULD DIE AT ANY TIME.
BUT SHE MUST PRESS FORWARD TO TELL THE VILLAGERS THEIR INVALUABLE FORTUNE.
ALL I CAN DO IS WATCH OVER HER.

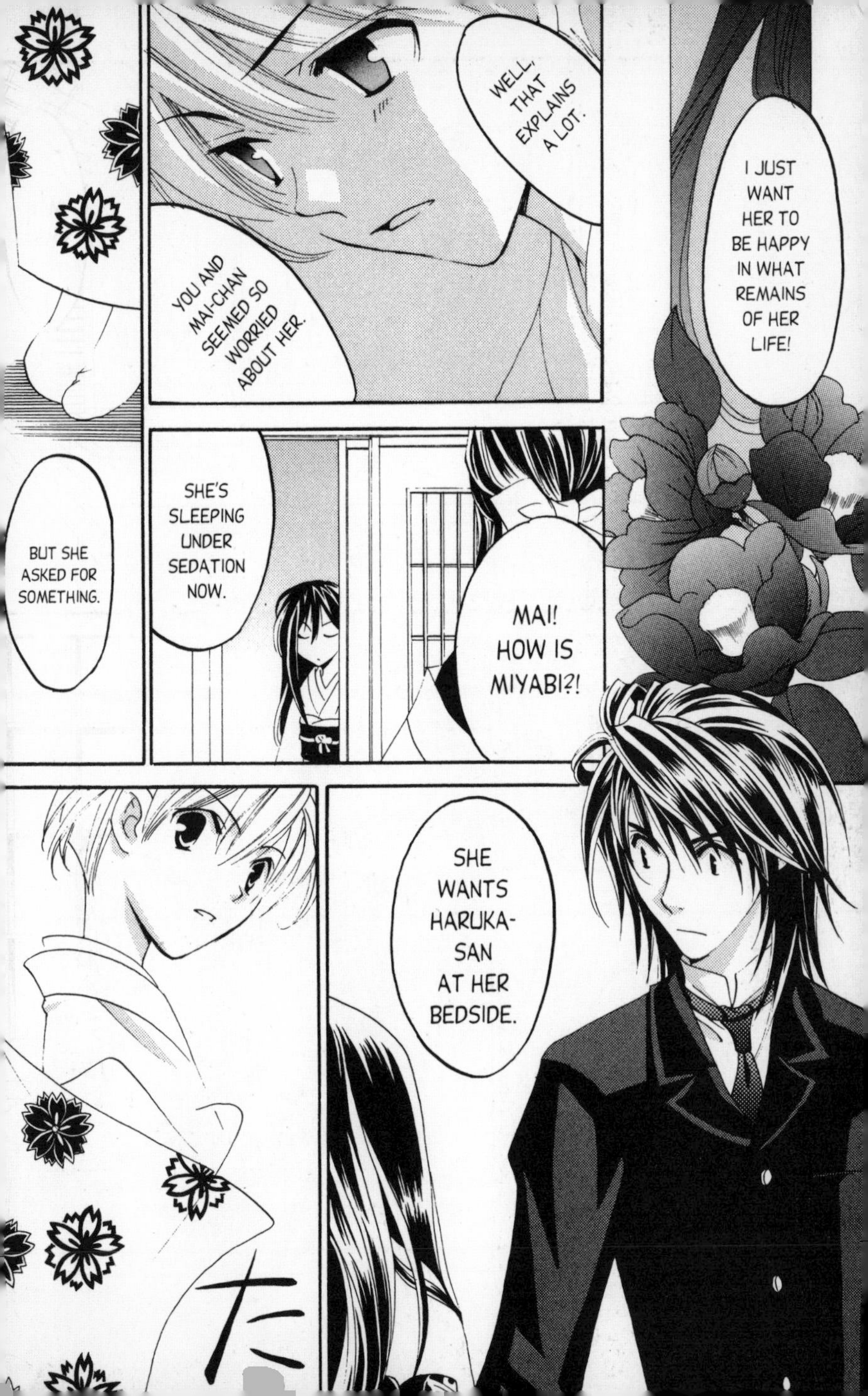
I JUST WANT HER TO BE HAPPY IN WHAT REMAINS OF HER LIFE!
WELL, THAT EXPLAINS A LOT.
YOU AND MAI-CHAN SEEMED SO WORRIED ABOUT HER.
MAI! HOW IS MIYABI?!
SHE'S SLEEPING UNDER SEDATION NOW.
BUT SHE ASKED FOR SOMETHING.
SHE WANTS HARUKA-SAN AT HER BEDSIDE.

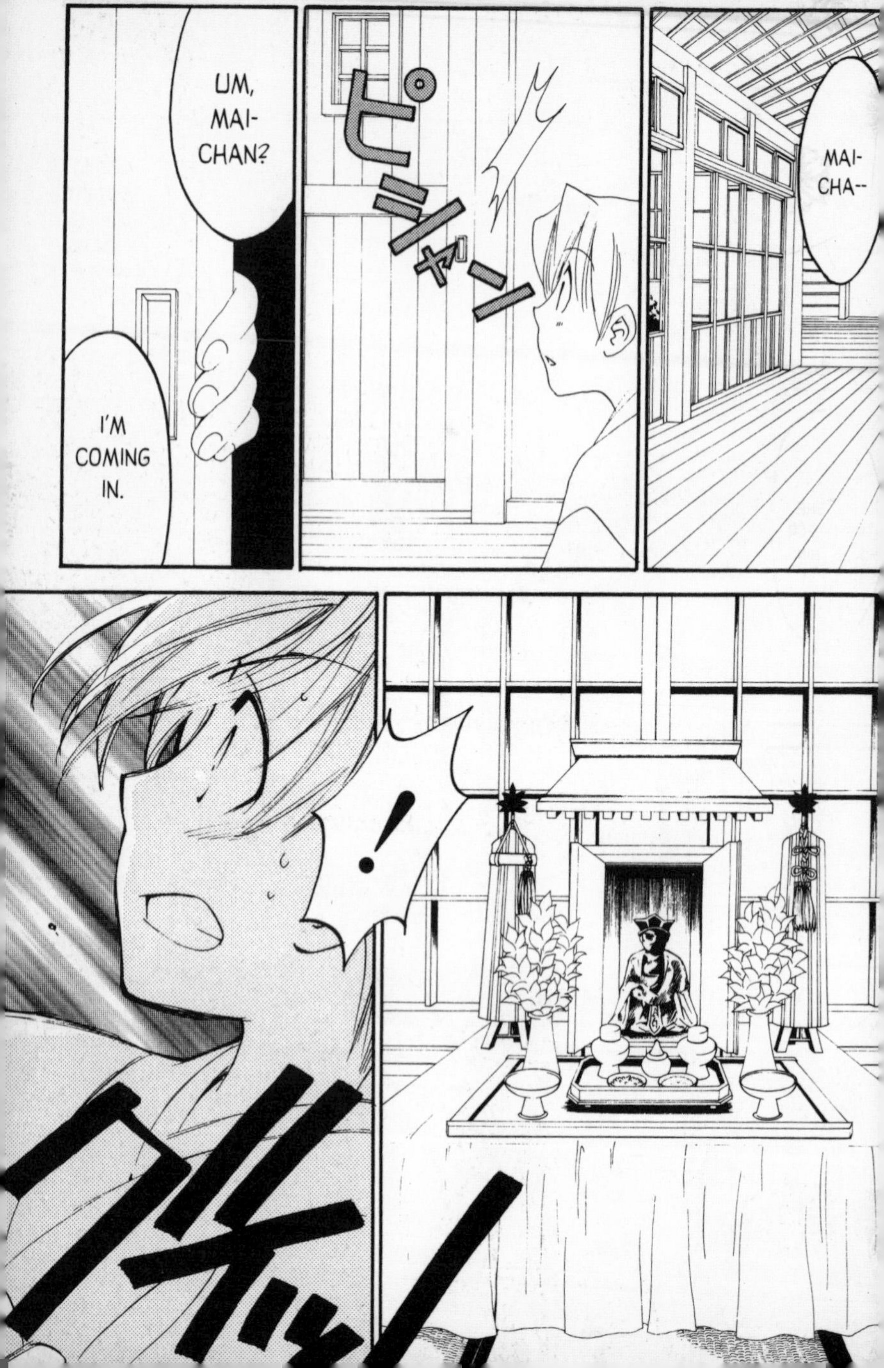
MAI-CHA--
ピシャーン
UM, MAI-CHAN?
I'M COMING IN.
!

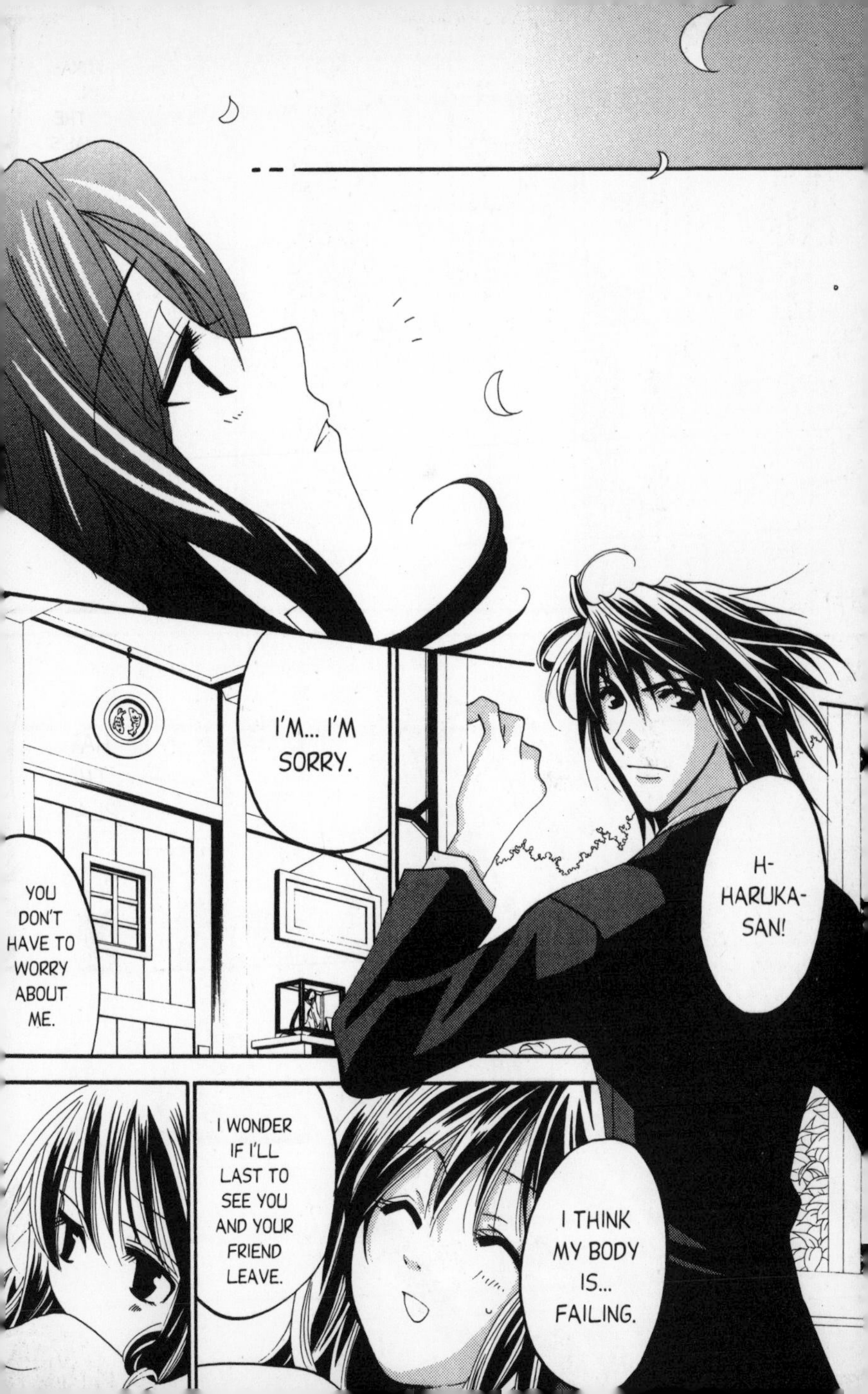

H- HARUKA-SAN!
I'M... I'M SORRY.
YOU DON'T HAVE TO WORRY ABOUT ME.
I THINK MY BODY IS... FAILING.
I WONDER IF I'LL LAST TO SEE YOU AND YOUR FRIEND LEAVE.

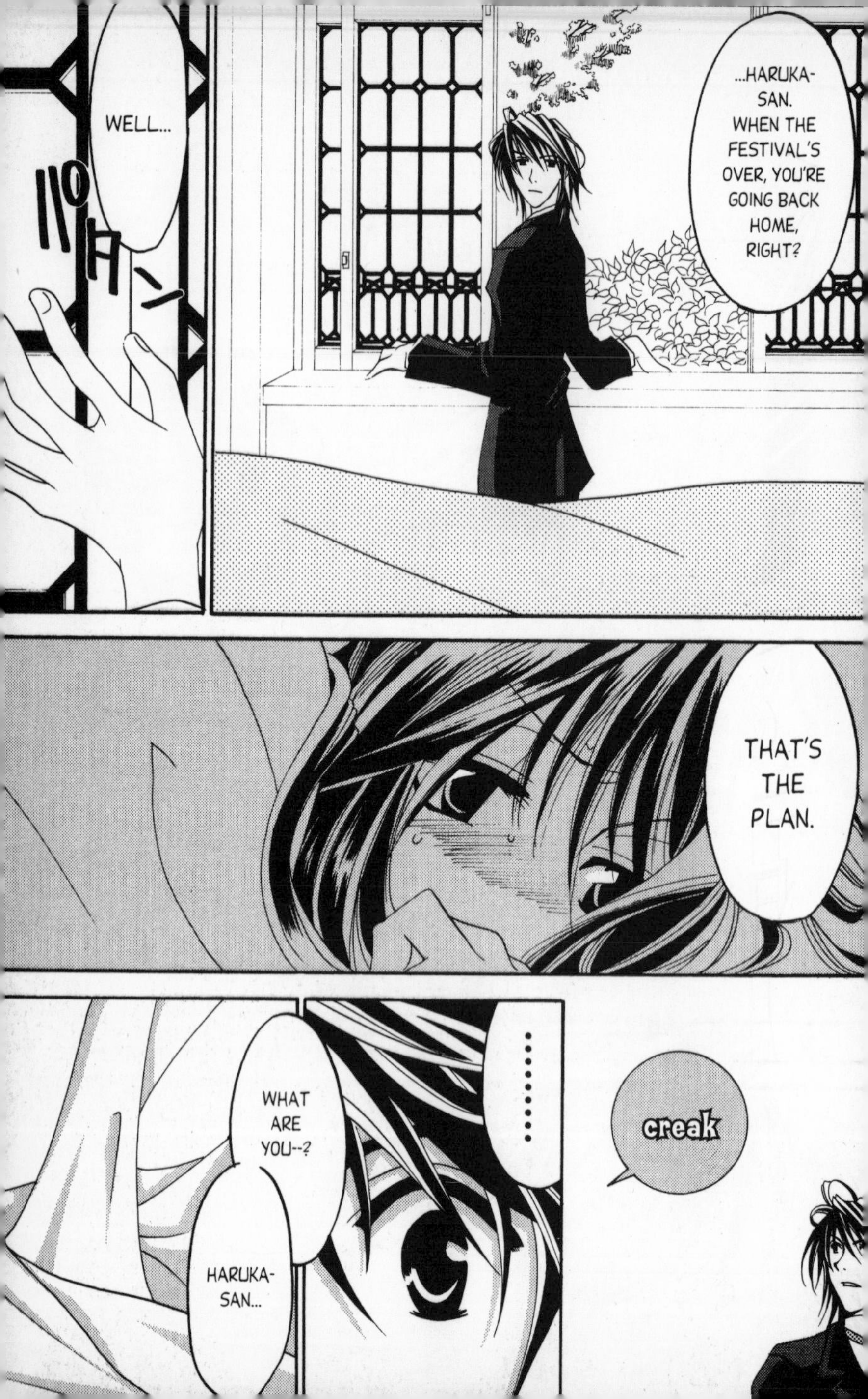
...HARUKA-SAN. WHEN THE FESTIVAL'S OVER, YOU'RE GOING BACK HOME, RIGHT?
WELL...
THAT'S THE PLAN.
creak
......
WHAT ARE YOU--?
HARUKA-SAN...

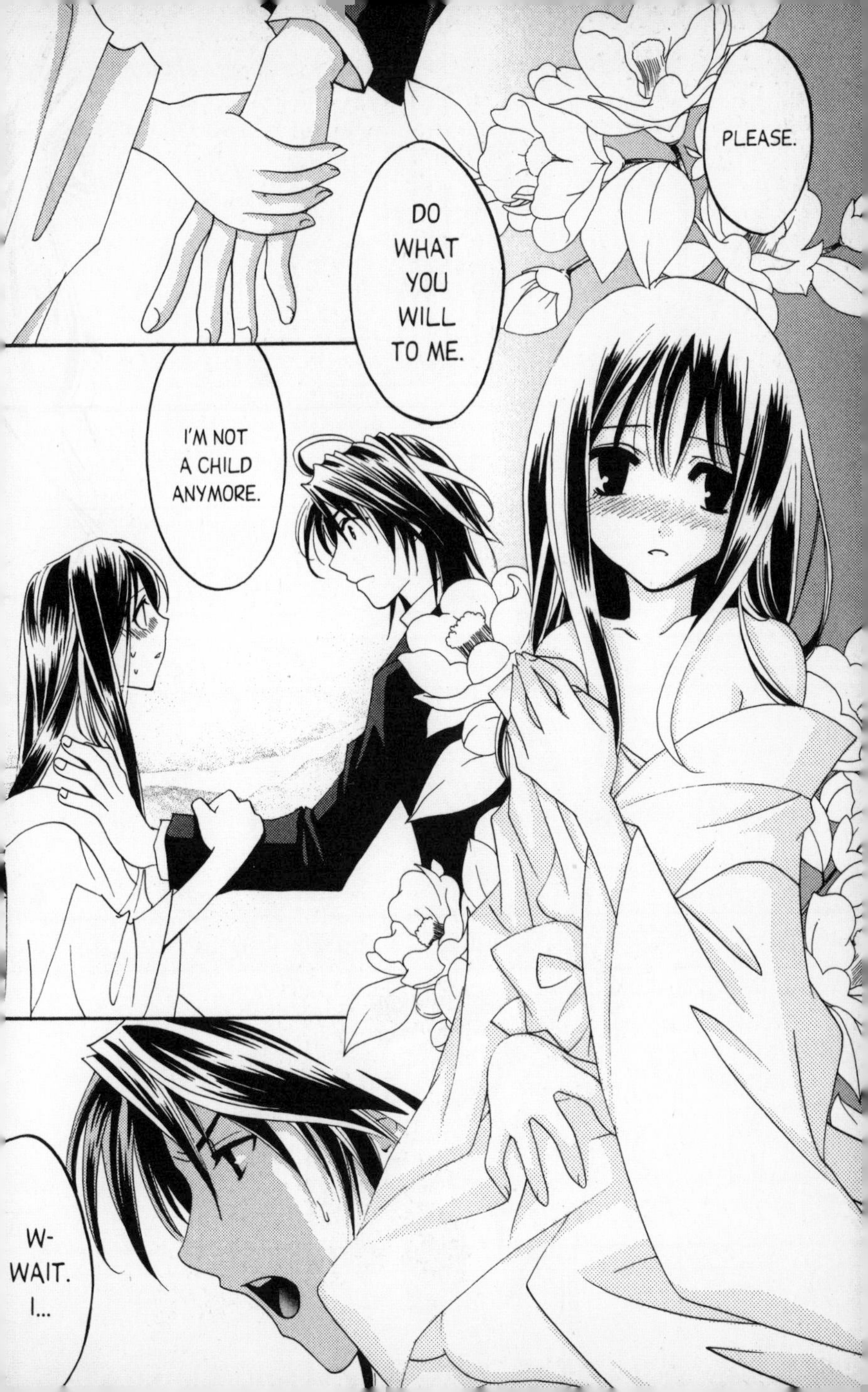
PLEASE.
DO WHAT YOU WILL TO ME.
I'M NOT A CHILD ANYMORE.
W-WAIT. I...

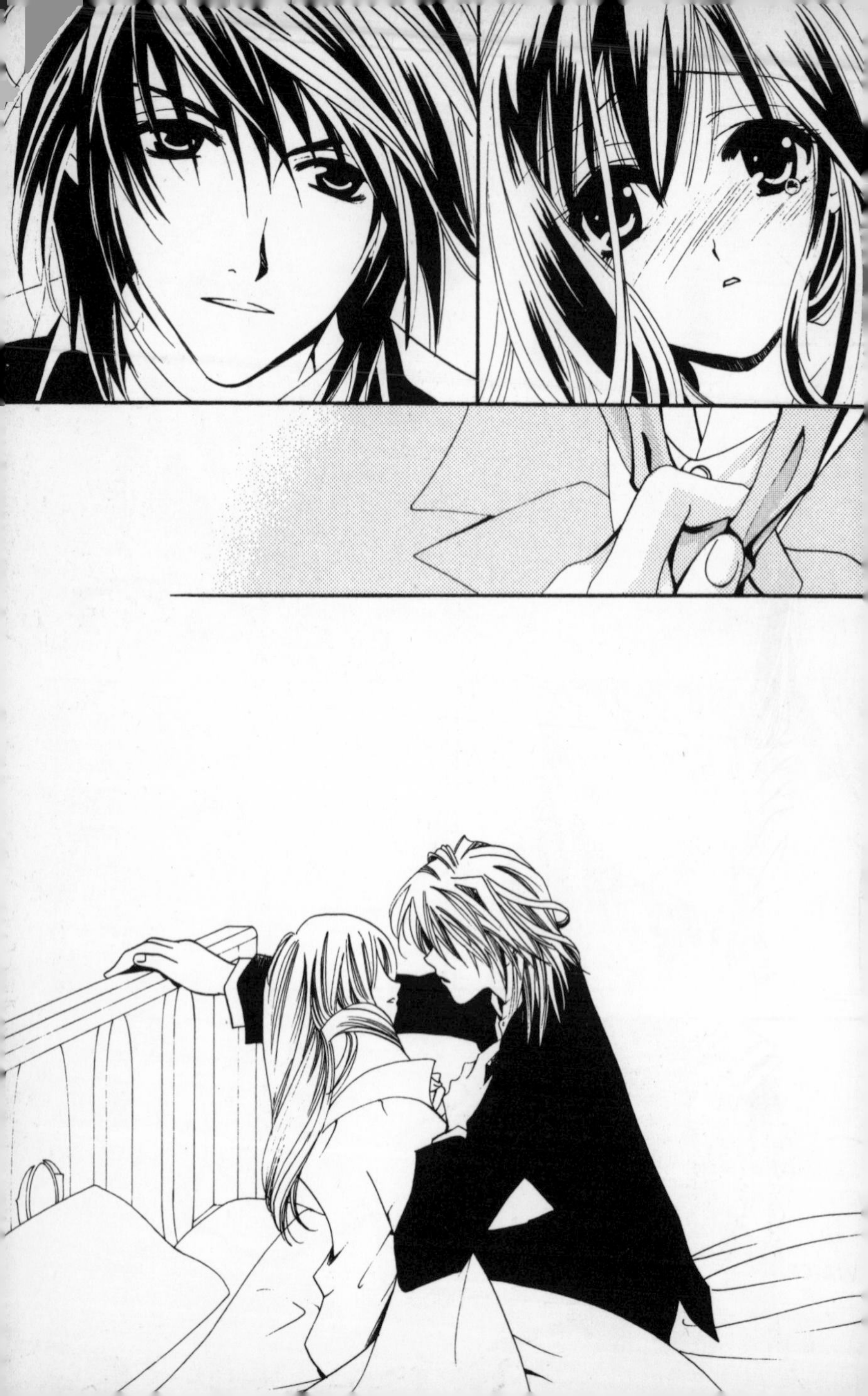

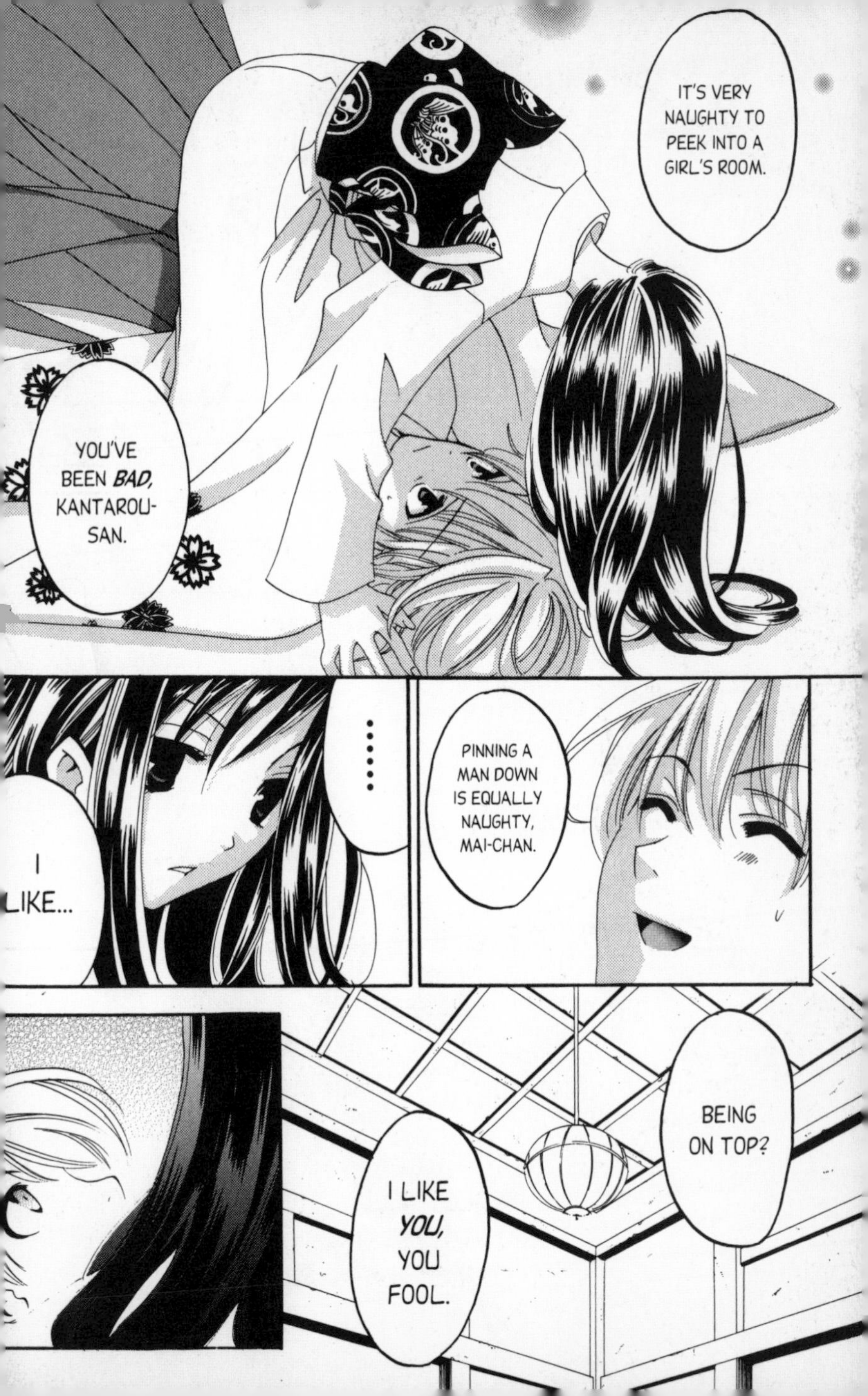
IT'S VERY NAUGHTY TO PEEK INTO A GIRL'S ROOM.
YOU'VE BEEN *BAD,* KANTAROU-SAN.
PINNING A MAN DOWN IS EQUALLY NAUGHTY, MAI-CHAN.
......
I LIKE...
BEING ON TOP?
I LIKE *YOU,* YOU FOOL.

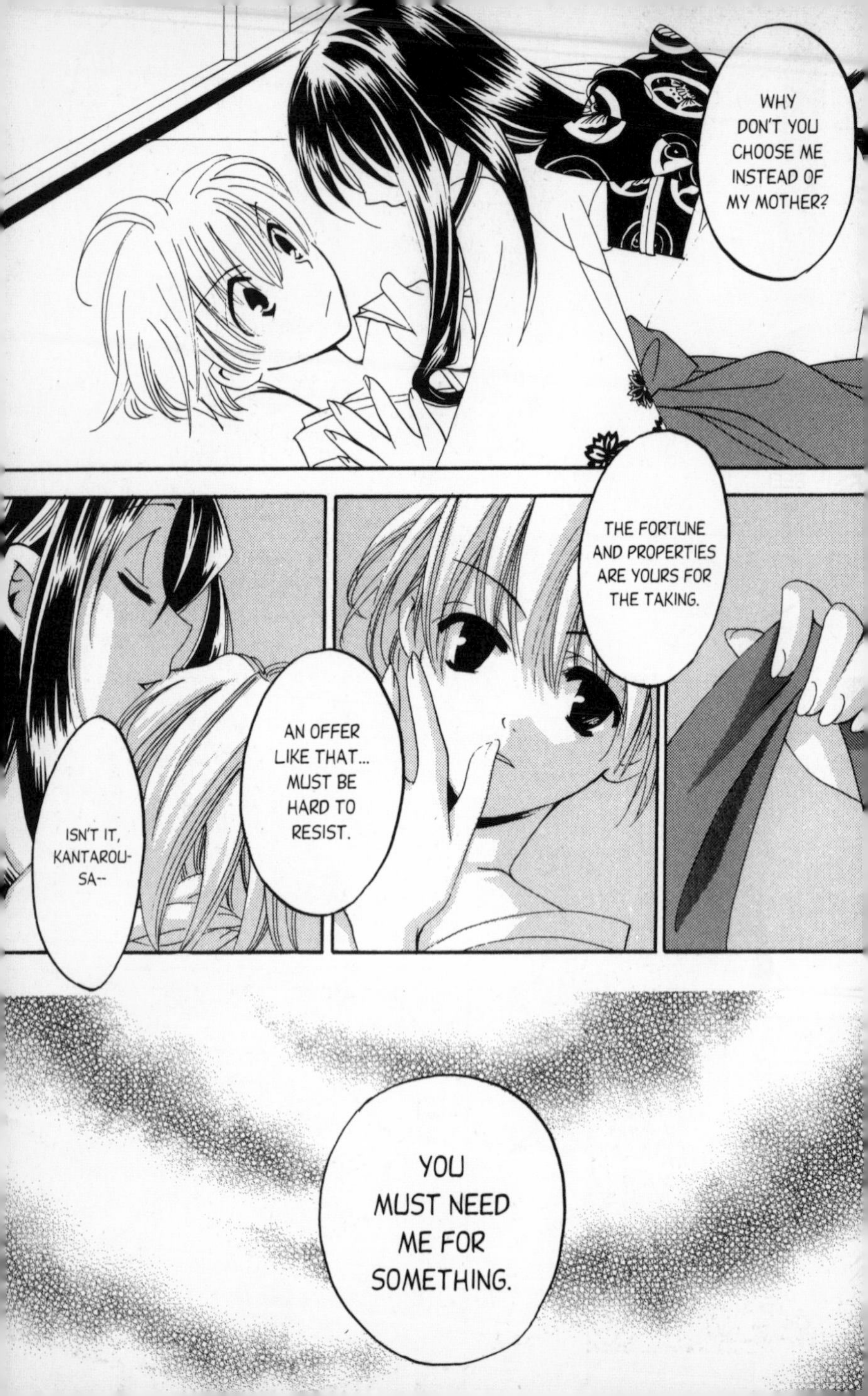
WHY DON'T YOU CHOOSE ME INSTEAD OF MY MOTHER?
THE FORTUNE AND PROPERTIES ARE YOURS FOR THE TAKING.
AN OFFER LIKE THAT... MUST BE HARD TO RESIST.
ISN'T IT, KANTAROU-SA--
YOU MUST NEED ME FOR SOMETHING.

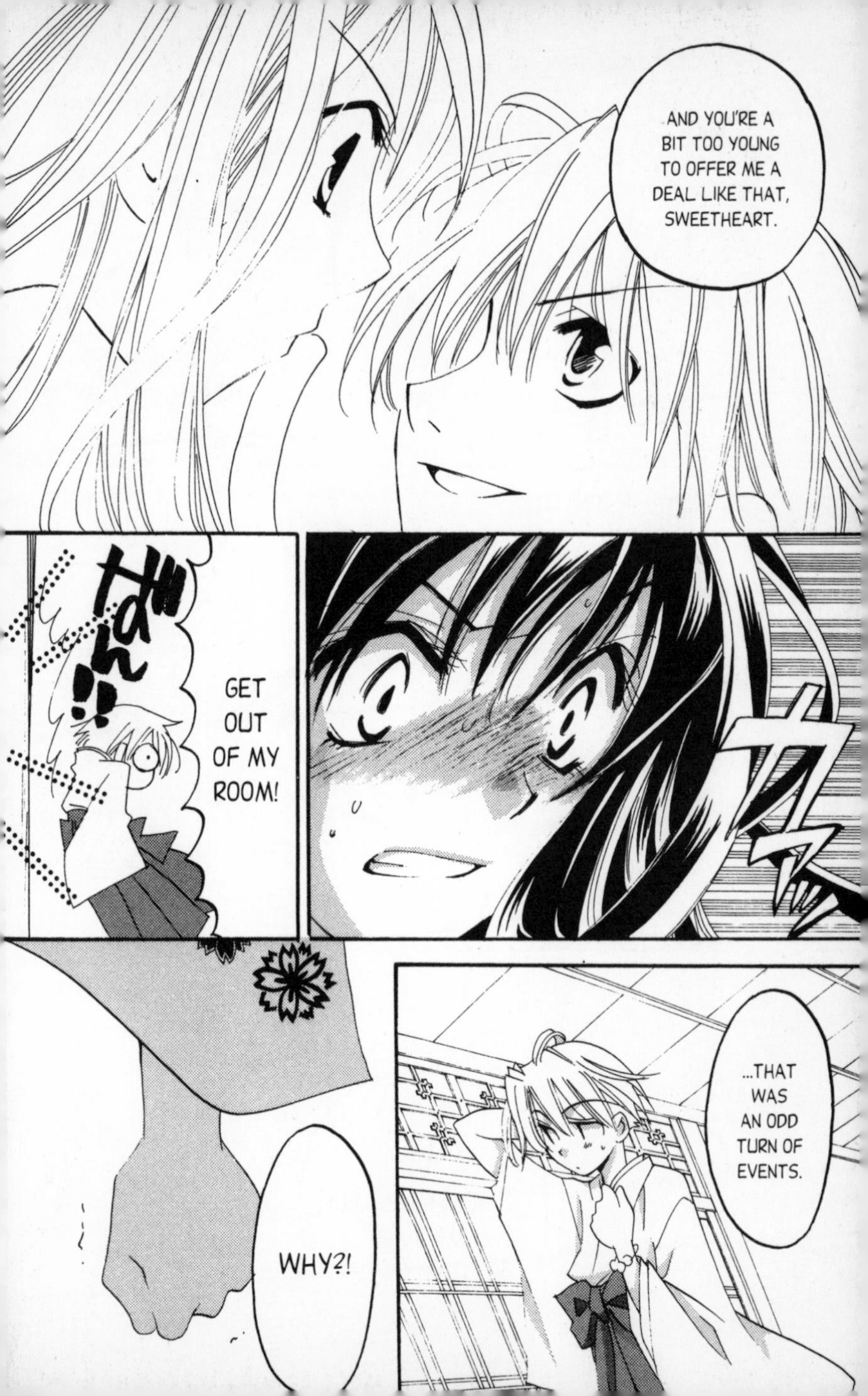
AND YOU'RE A BIT TOO YOUNG TO OFFER ME A DEAL LIKE THAT, SWEETHEART.
GET OUT OF MY ROOM!
...THAT WAS AN ODD TURN OF EVENTS.
WHY?!

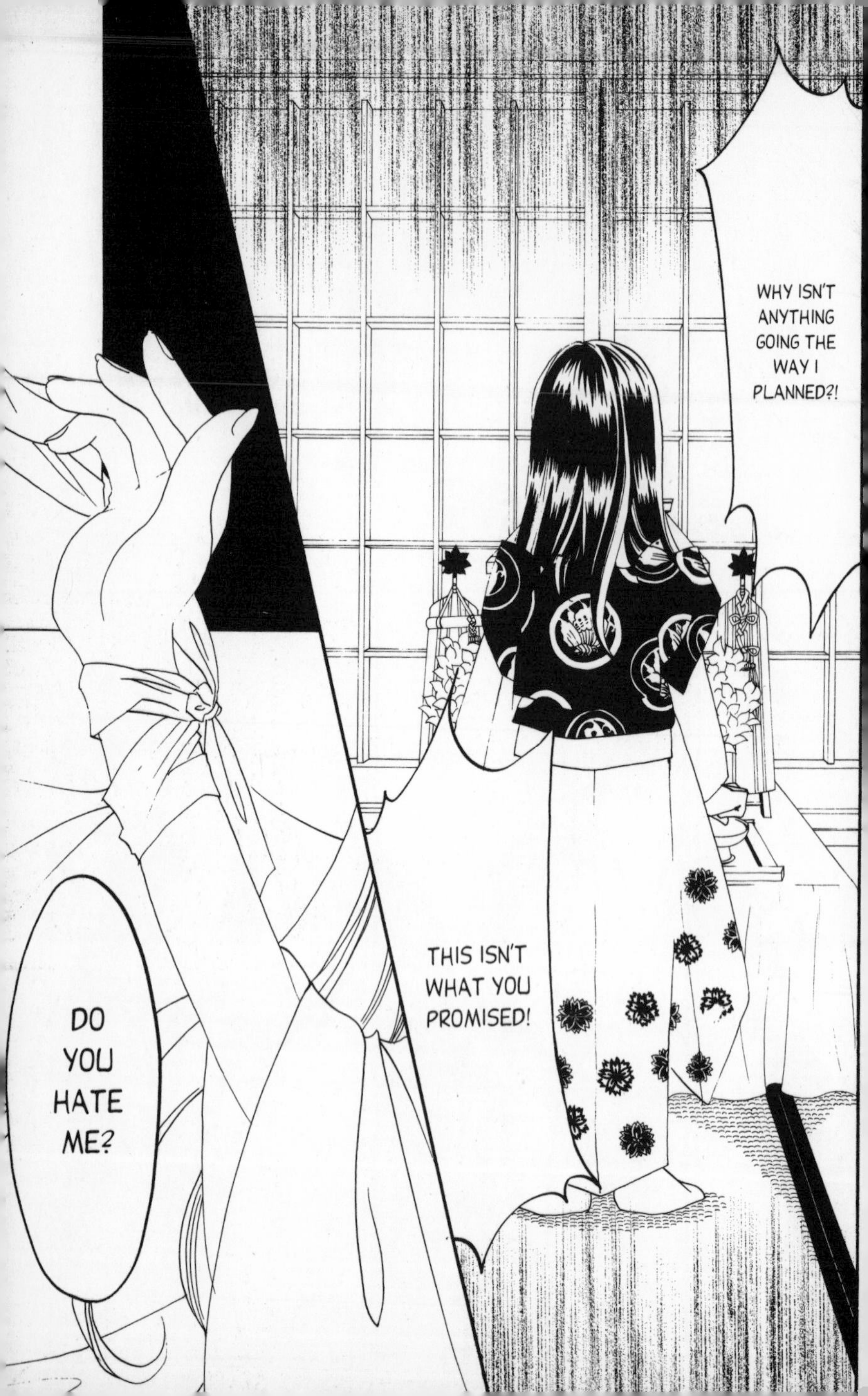
WHY ISN'T ANYTHING GOING THE WAY I PLANNED?!
THIS ISN'T WHAT YOU PROMISED!
DO YOU HATE ME?

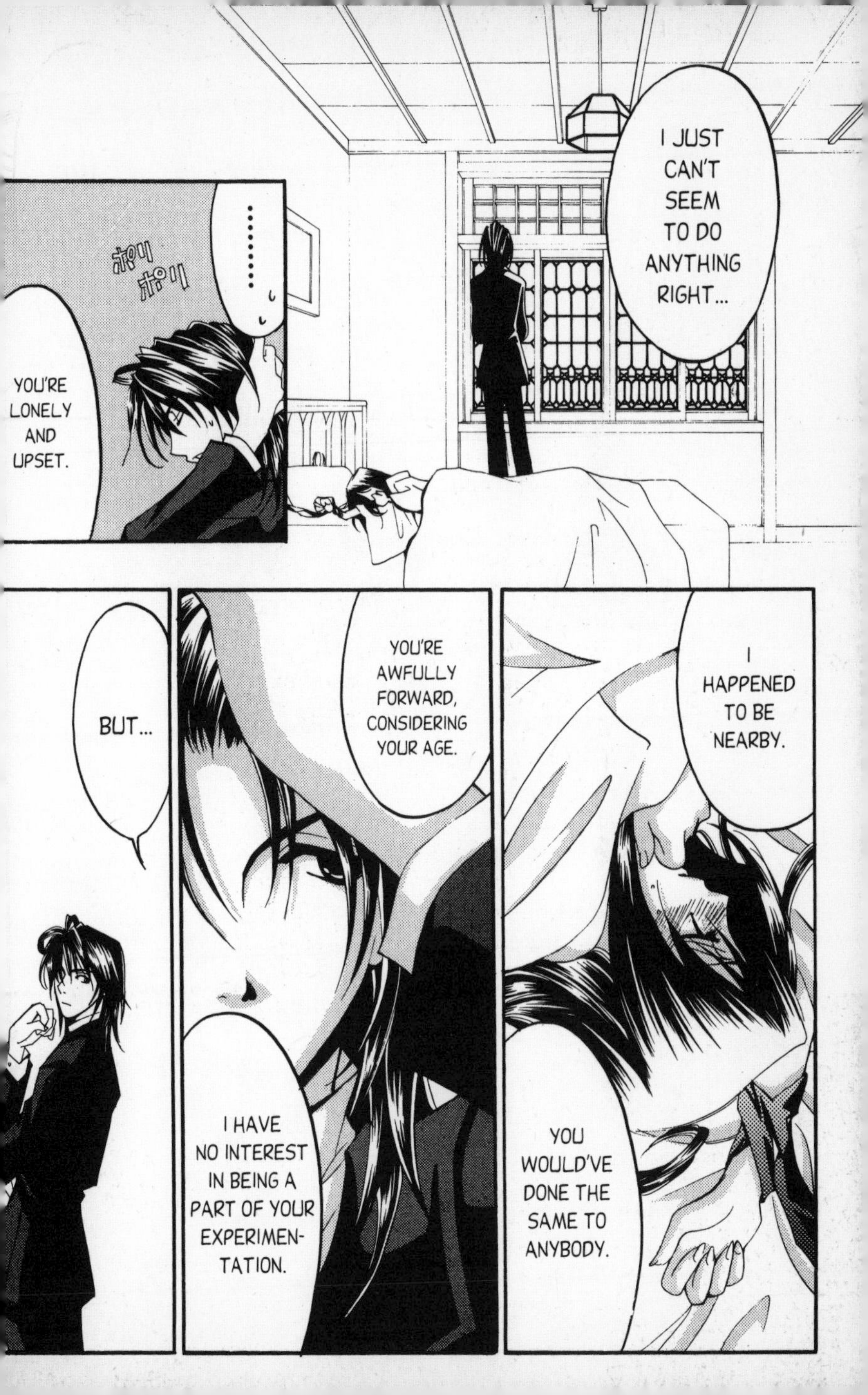

I JUST CAN'T SEEM TO DO ANYTHING RIGHT...
......
ポリ ポリ
YOU'RE LONELY AND UPSET.
I HAPPENED TO BE NEARBY.
YOU WOULD'VE DONE THE SAME TO ANYBODY.
YOU'RE AWFULLY FORWARD, CONSIDERING YOUR AGE.
I HAVE NO INTEREST IN BEING A PART OF YOUR EXPERIMENTATION.
BUT...

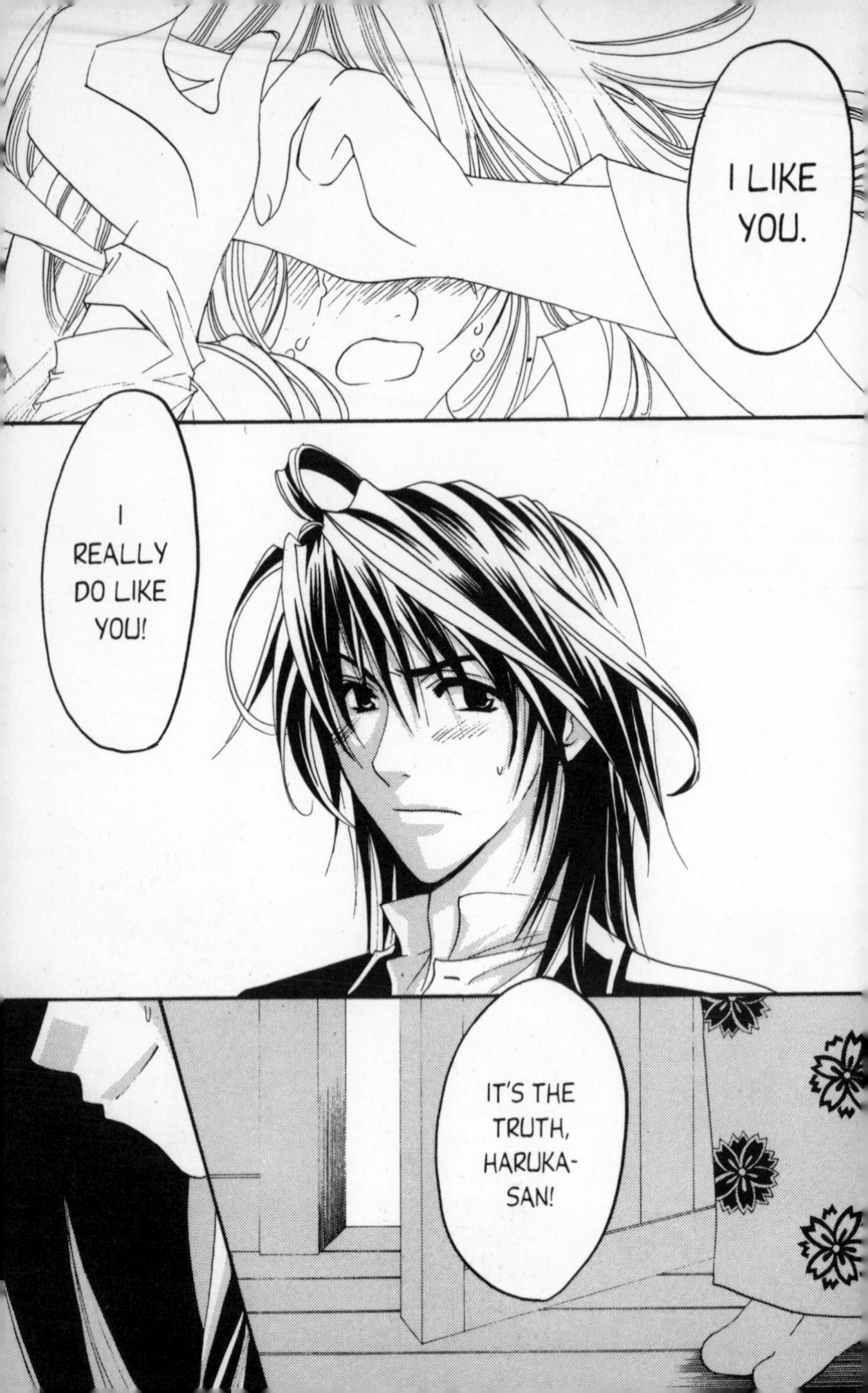
I LIKE YOU.
I REALLY DO LIKE YOU!
IT'S THE TRUTH, HARUKA-SAN!

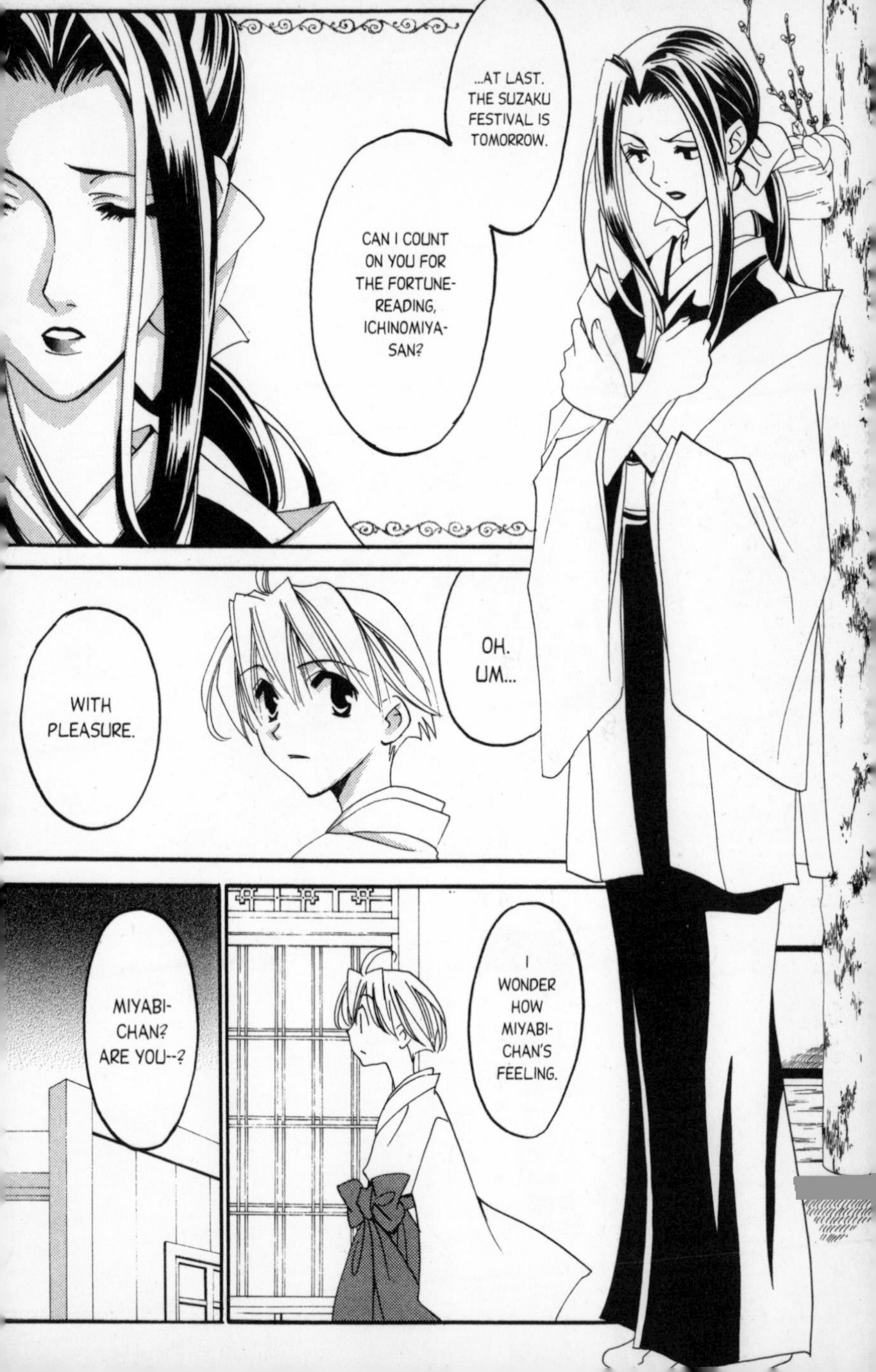
...AT LAST. THE SUZAKU FESTIVAL IS TOMORROW.
CAN I COUNT ON YOU FOR THE FORTUNE-READING, ICHINOMIYA-SAN?
WITH PLEASURE.
OH. UM...
I WONDER HOW MIYABI-CHAN'S FEELING.
MIYABI-CHAN? ARE YOU--?

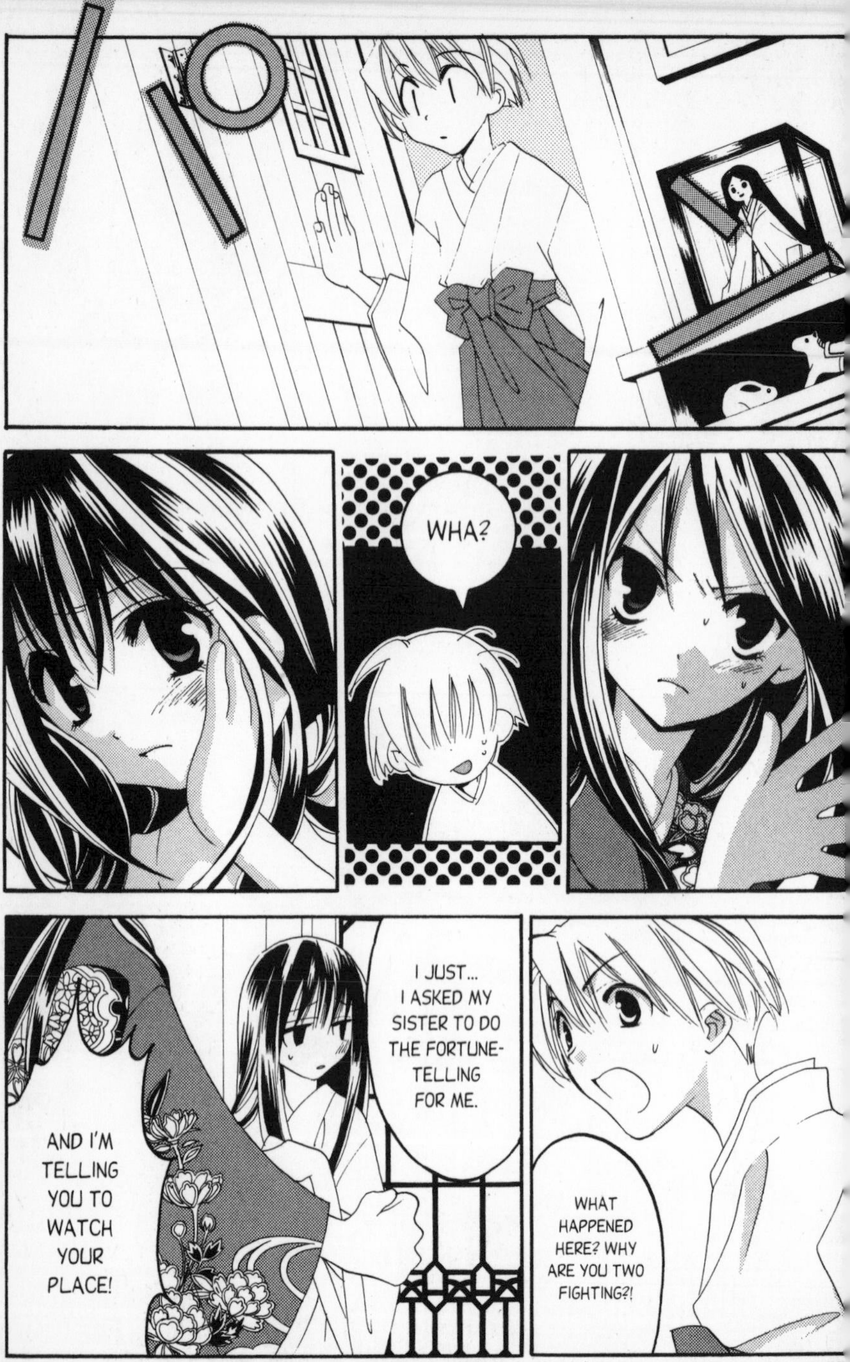
WHA?
WHAT HAPPENED HERE? WHY ARE YOU TWO FIGHTING?!
I JUST... I ASKED MY SISTER TO DO THE FORTUNE-TELLING FOR ME.
AND I'M TELLING YOU TO WATCH YOUR PLACE!

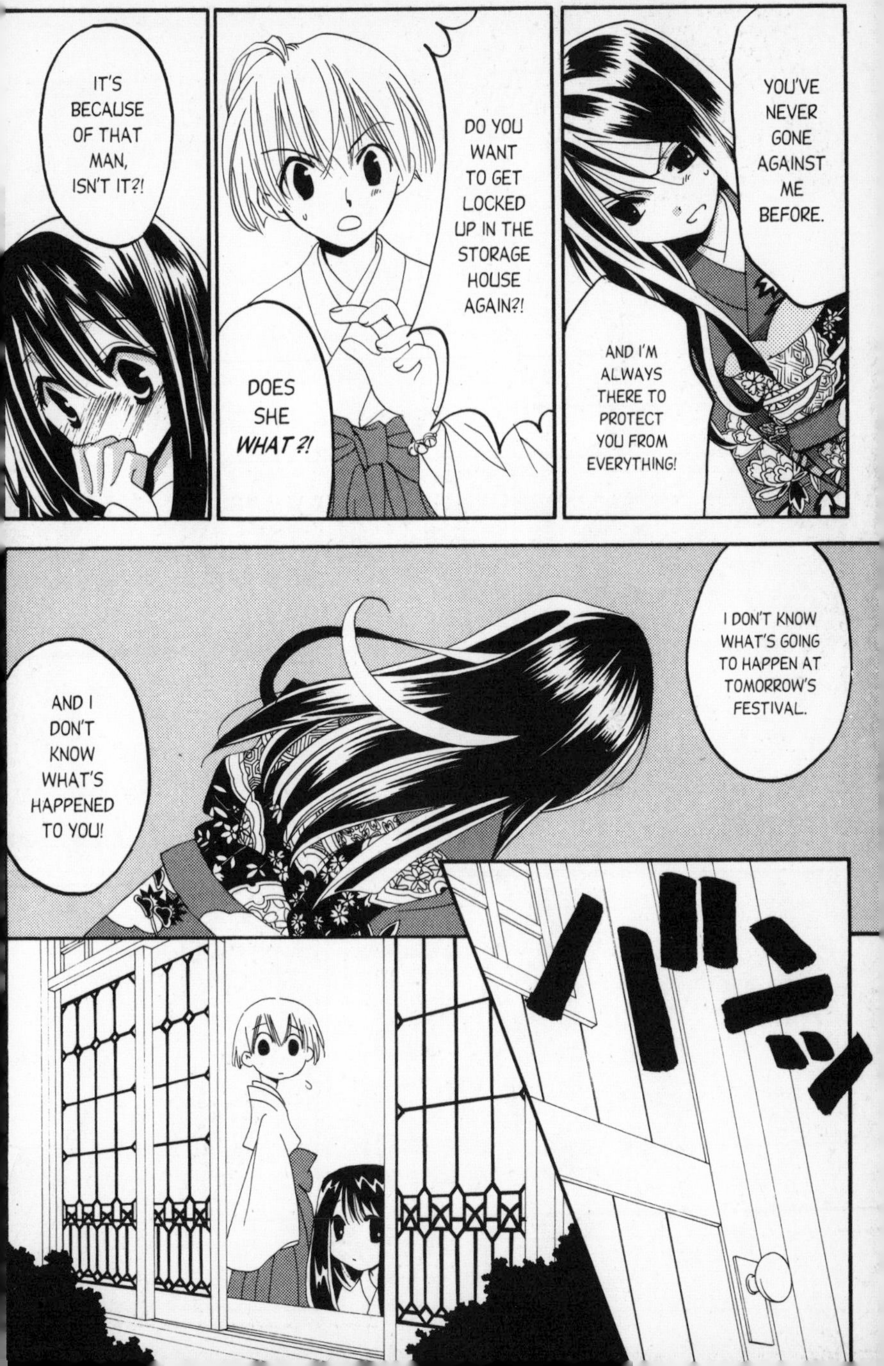
YOU'VE NEVER GONE AGAINST ME BEFORE.
AND I'M ALWAYS THERE TO PROTECT YOU FROM EVERYTHING!
DO YOU WANT TO GET LOCKED UP IN THE STORAGE HOUSE AGAIN?!
DOES SHE *WHAT*?!
IT'S BECAUSE OF THAT MAN, ISN'T IT?!
I DON'T KNOW WHAT'S GOING TO HAPPEN AT TOMORROW'S FESTIVAL.
AND I DON'T KNOW WHAT'S HAPPENED TO YOU!
バンッ

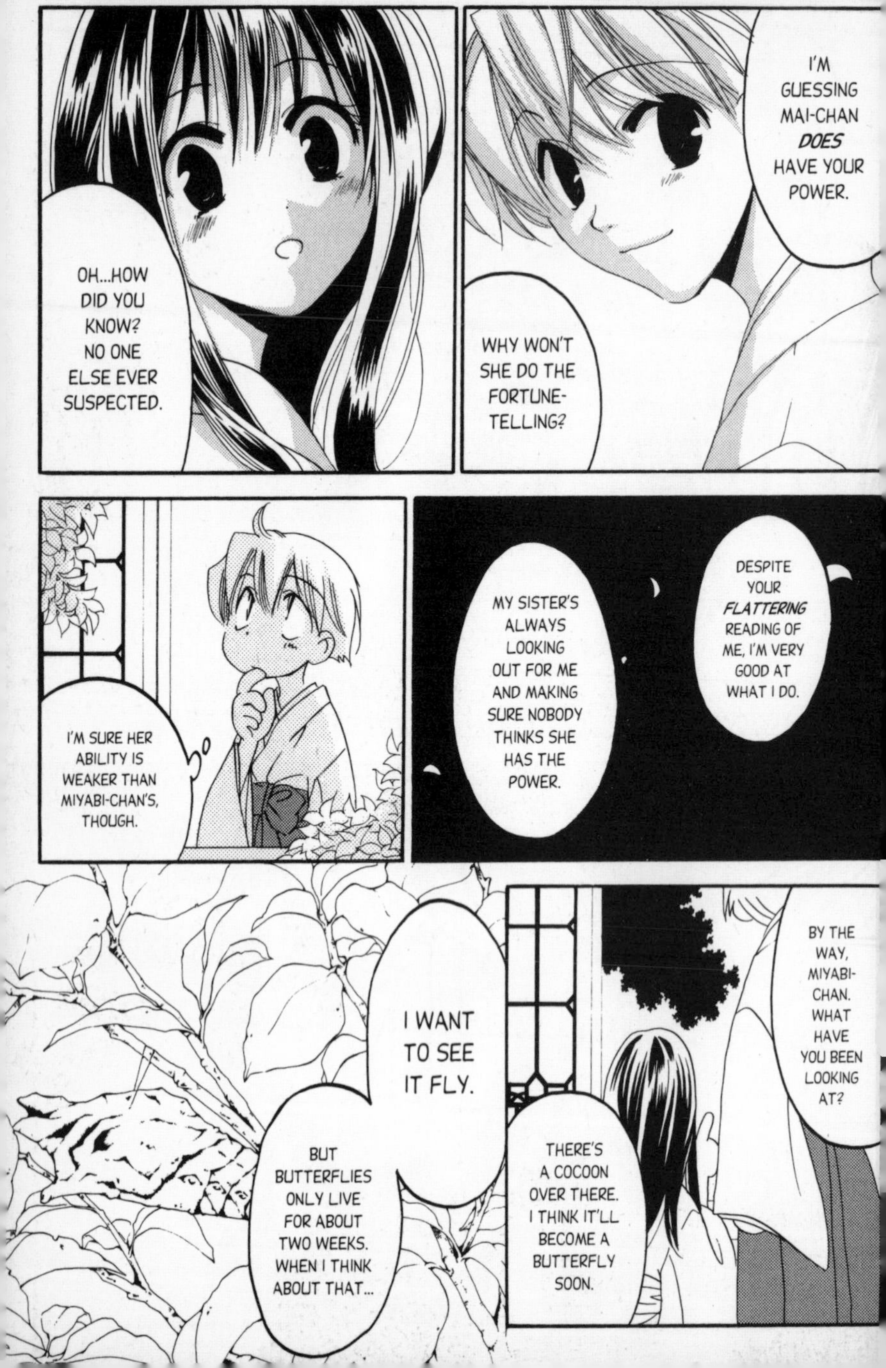
I'M GUESSING MAI-CHAN *DOES* HAVE YOUR POWER.
WHY WON'T SHE DO THE FORTUNE-TELLING?
OH...HOW DID YOU KNOW? NO ONE ELSE EVER SUSPECTED.
DESPITE YOUR *FLATTERING* READING OF ME, I'M VERY GOOD AT WHAT I DO.
MY SISTER'S ALWAYS LOOKING OUT FOR ME AND MAKING SURE NOBODY THINKS SHE HAS THE POWER.
I'M SURE HER ABILITY IS WEAKER THAN MIYABI-CHAN'S, THOUGH.
BY THE WAY, MIYABI-CHAN. WHAT HAVE YOU BEEN LOOKING AT?
THERE'S A COCOON OVER THERE. I THINK IT'LL BECOME A BUTTERFLY SOON.
I WANT TO SEE IT FLY.
BUT BUTTERFLIES ONLY LIVE FOR ABOUT TWO WEEKS. WHEN I THINK ABOUT THAT...

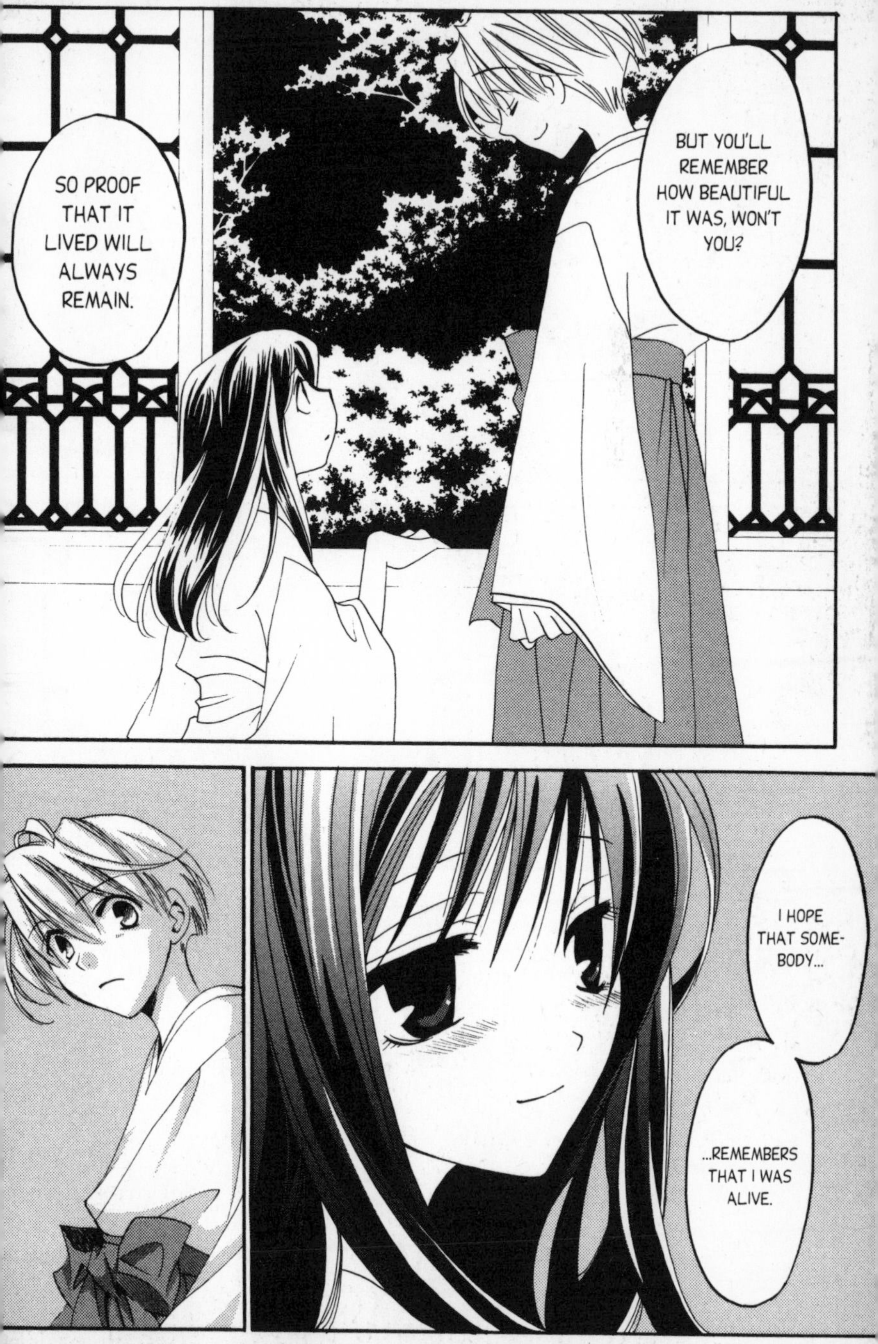
BUT YOU'LL REMEMBER HOW BEAUTIFUL IT WAS, WON'T YOU?
SO PROOF THAT IT LIVED WILL ALWAYS REMAIN.
I HOPE THAT SOME-BODY...
...REMEMBERS THAT I WAS ALIVE.

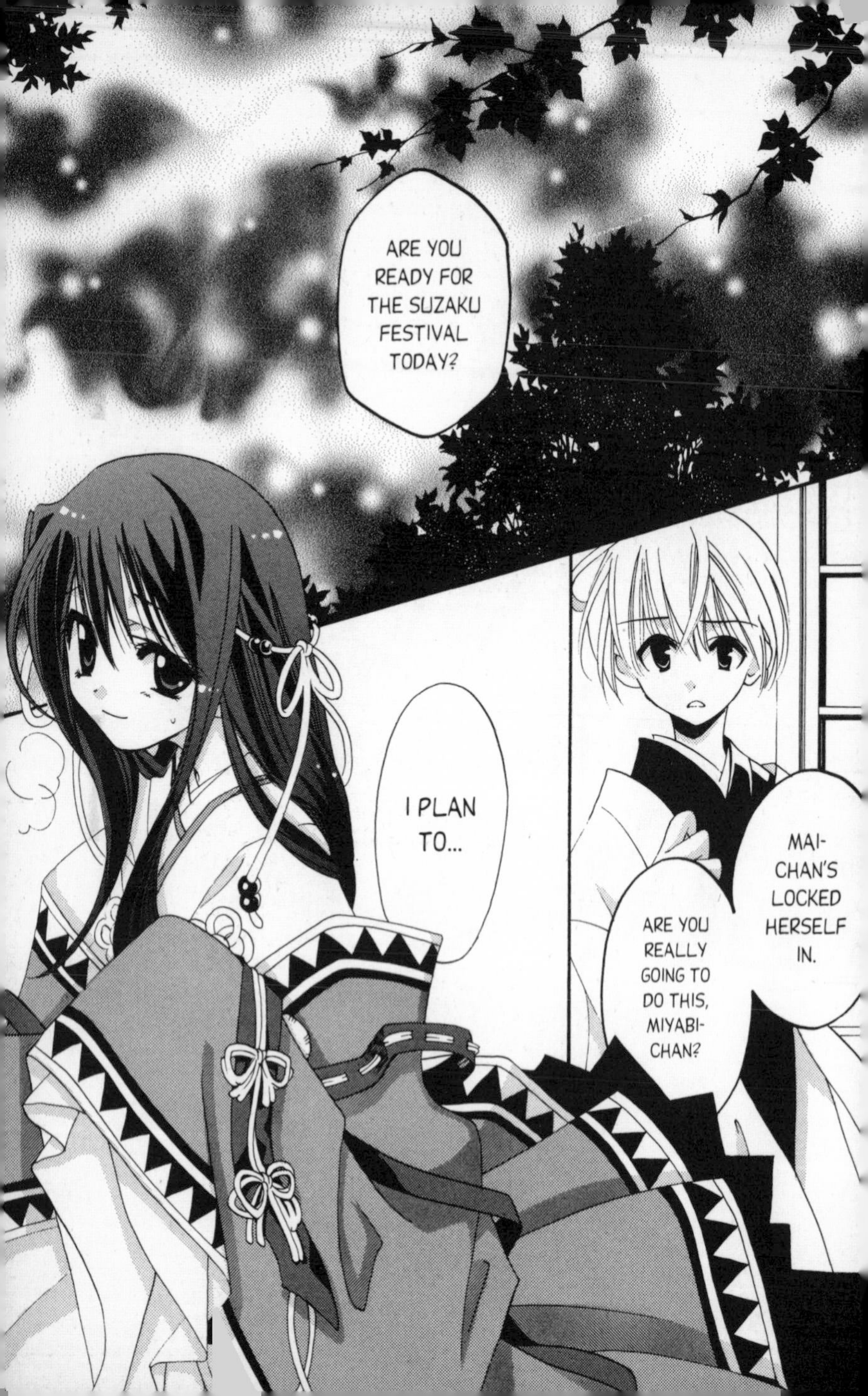
ARE YOU READY FOR THE SUZAKU FESTIVAL TODAY?
MAI-CHAN'S LOCKED HERSELF IN.
ARE YOU REALLY GOING TO DO THIS, MIYABI-CHAN?
I PLAN TO...

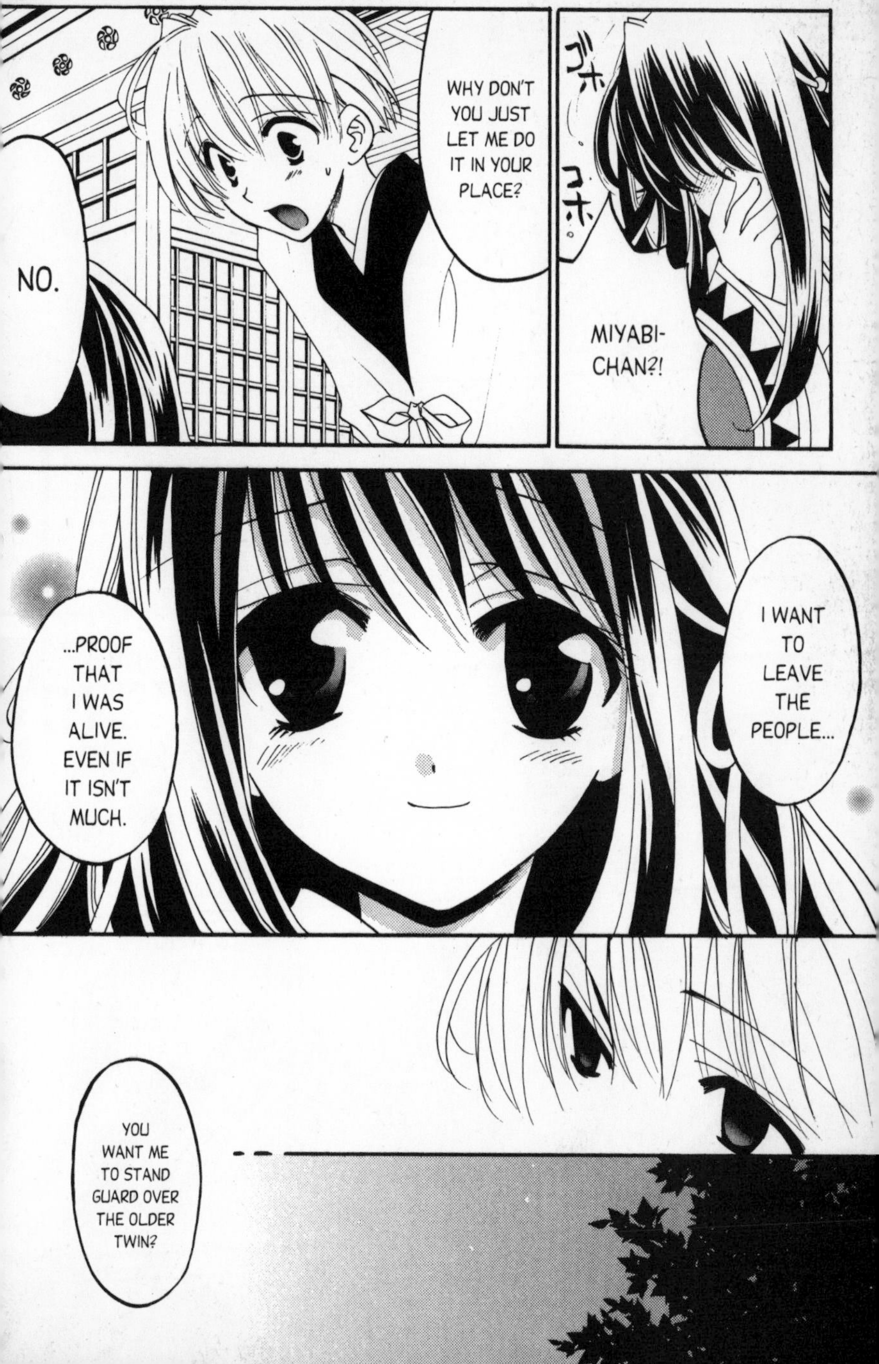
ゴホ
コホ
MIYABI-CHAN?!
WHY DON'T YOU JUST LET ME DO IT IN YOUR PLACE?
NO.
I WANT TO LEAVE THE PEOPLE...
...PROOF THAT I WAS ALIVE. EVEN IF IT ISN'T MUCH.
YOU WANT ME TO STAND GUARD OVER THE OLDER TWIN?

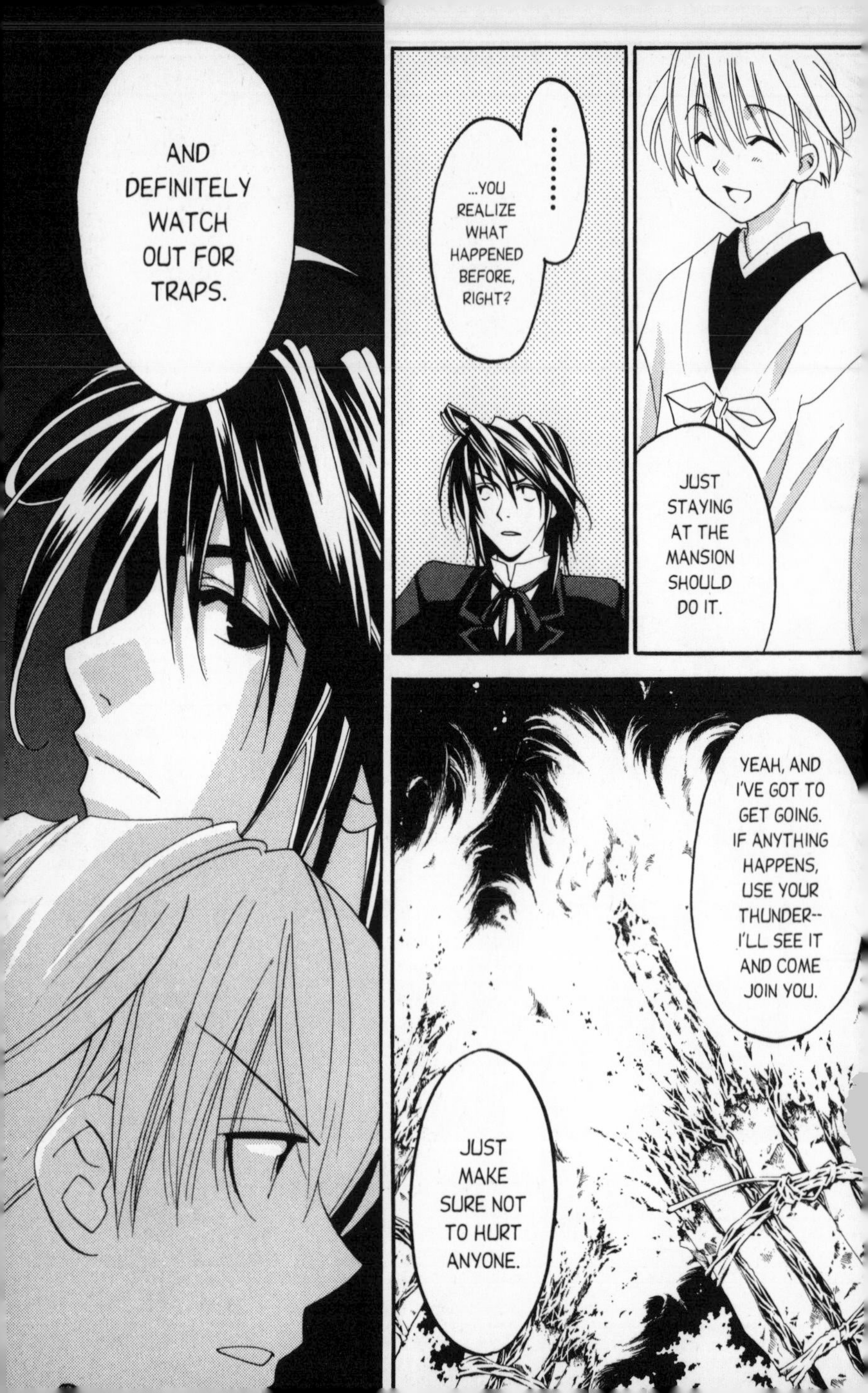
JUST STAYING AT THE MANSION SHOULD DO IT.
......
...YOU REALIZE WHAT HAPPENED BEFORE, RIGHT?
YEAH, AND I'VE GOT TO GET GOING. IF ANYTHING HAPPENS, USE YOUR THUNDER-- I'LL SEE IT AND COME JOIN YOU.
JUST MAKE SURE NOT TO HURT ANYONE.
AND DEFINITELY WATCH OUT FOR TRAPS.

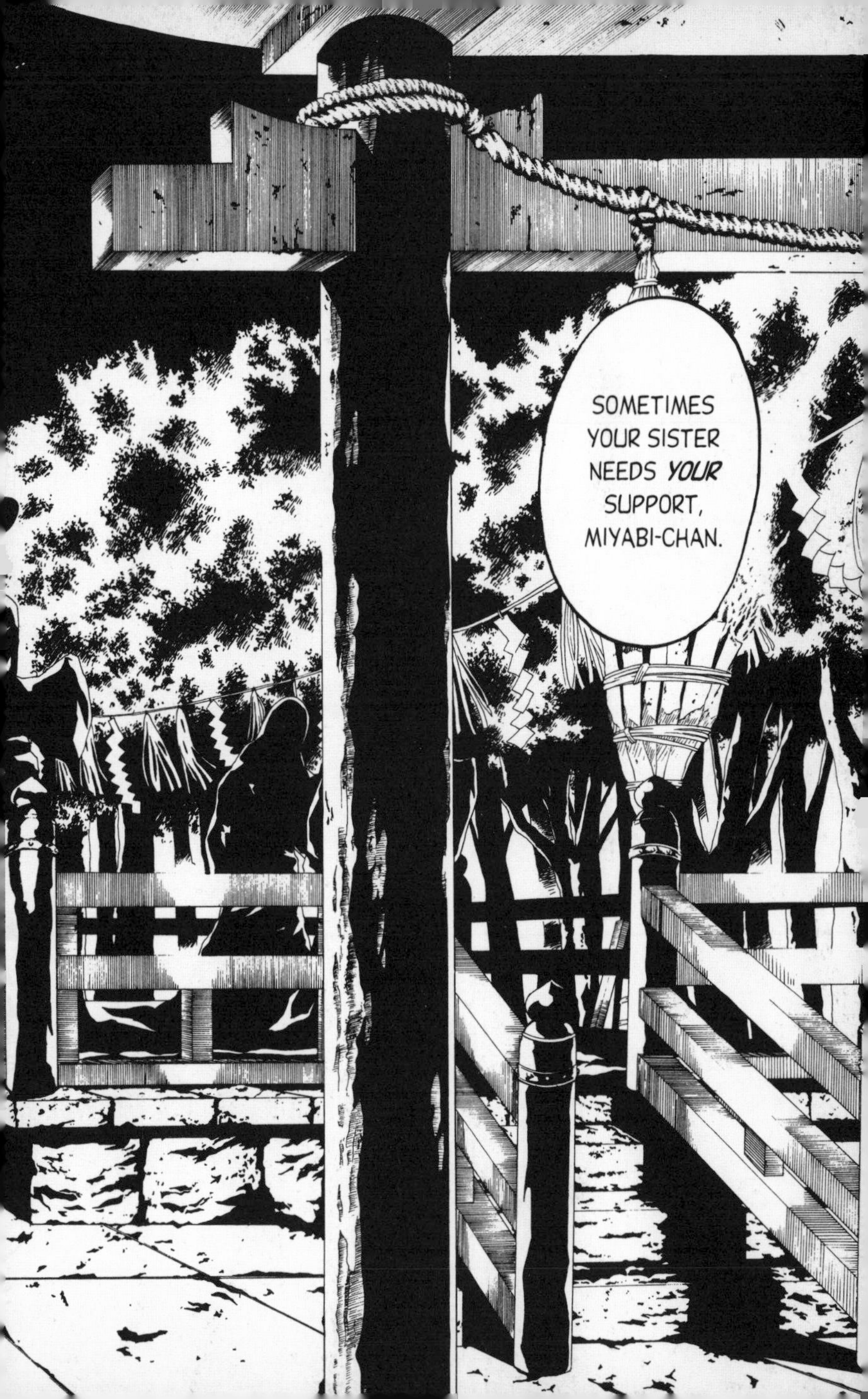
SOMETIMES YOUR SISTER NEEDS *YOUR* SUPPORT, MIYABI-CHAN.

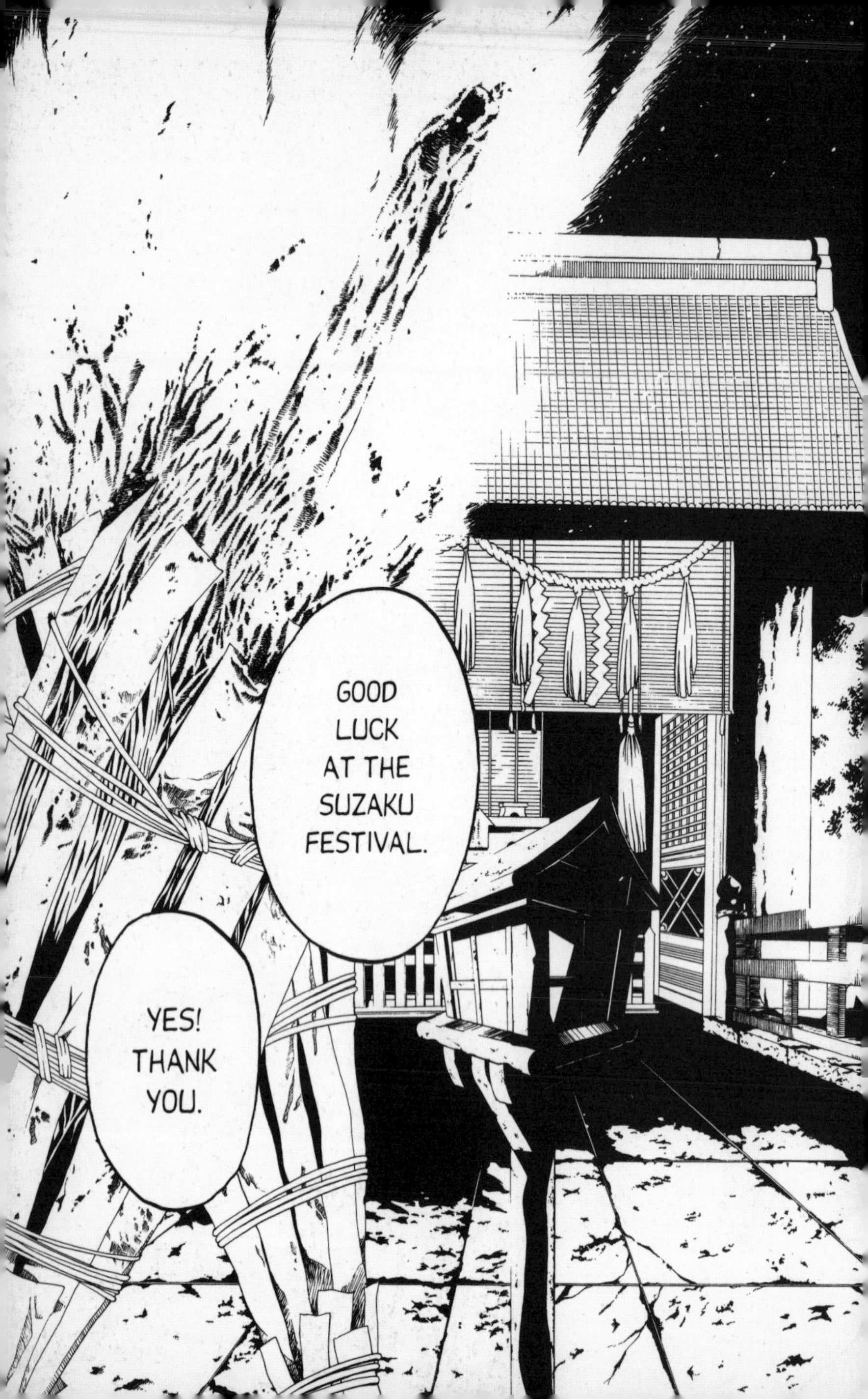
GOOD LUCK AT THE SUZAKU FESTIVAL.
YES! THANK YOU.

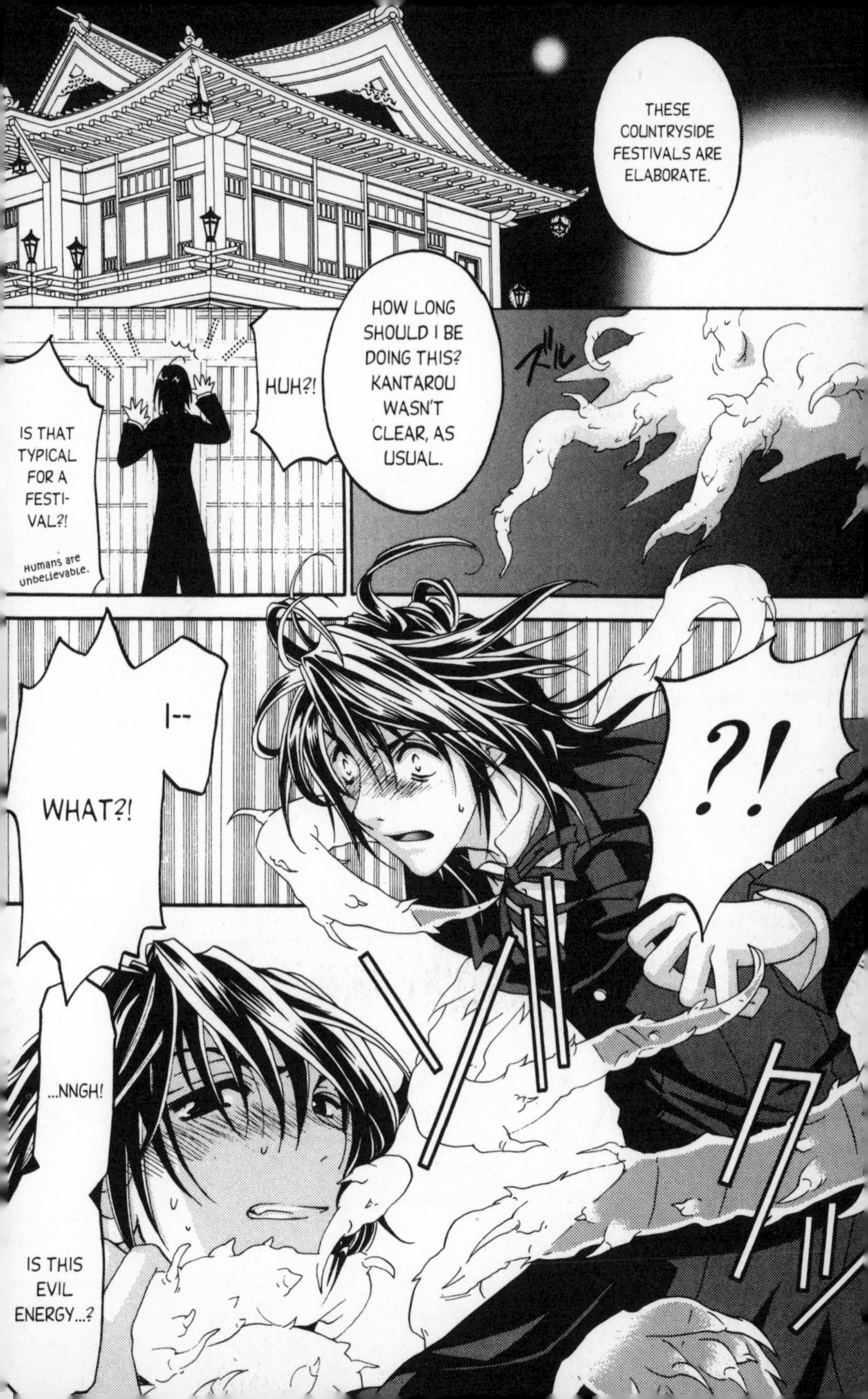
THESE COUNTRYSIDE FESTIVALS ARE ELABORATE.
ズル
HOW LONG SHOULD I BE DOING THIS? KANTAROU WASN'T CLEAR, AS USUAL.
HUH?!
IS THAT TYPICAL FOR A FESTI-VAL?!
Humans are unbelievable.
?!
I--
WHAT?!
...NNGH!
IS THIS EVIL ENERGY...?

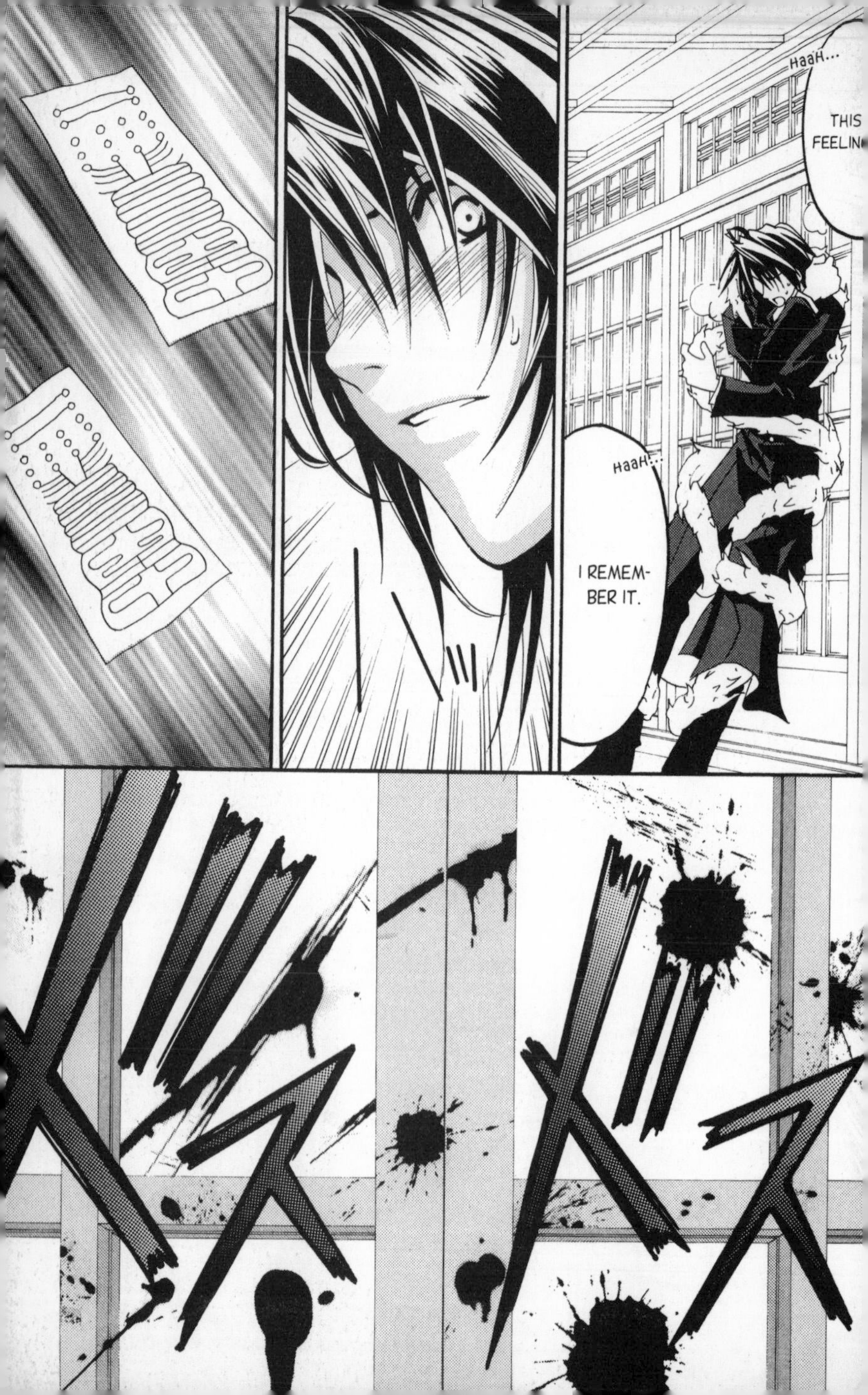
HaaH...
THIS FEELIN
HaaH...
I REMEMBER IT.

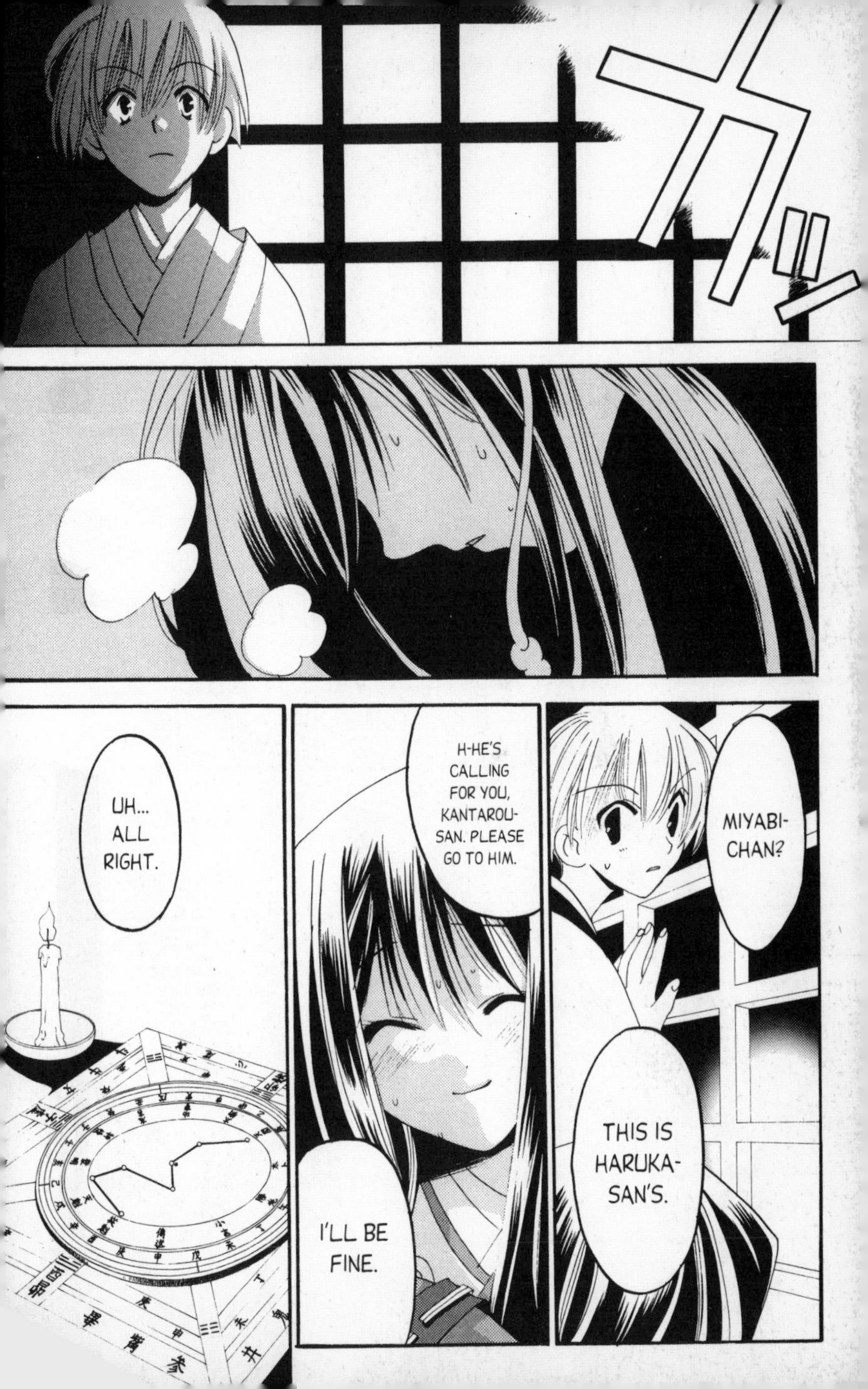
カッ
MIYABI-CHAN?
THIS IS HARUKA-SAN'S.
H-HE'S CALLING FOR YOU, KANTAROU-SAN. PLEASE GO TO HIM.
I'LL BE FINE.
UH... ALL RIGHT.

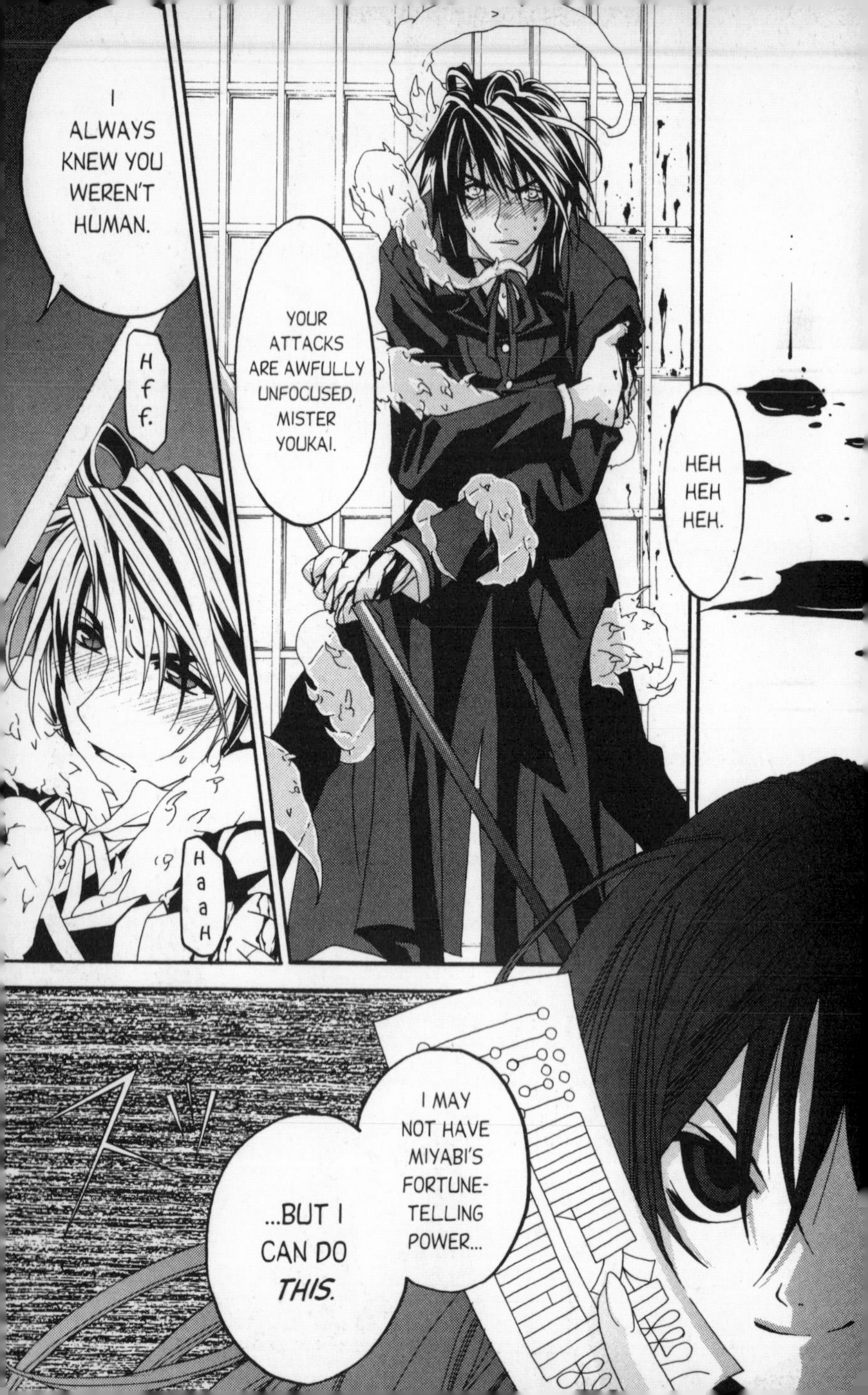
YOUR ATTACKS ARE AWFULLY UNFOCUSED, MISTER YOUKAI.
HEH HEH HEH.
I ALWAYS KNEW YOU WEREN'T HUMAN.
Hff.
Haah
I MAY NOT HAVE MIYABI'S FORTUNE-TELLING POWER...
...BUT I CAN DO *THIS.*

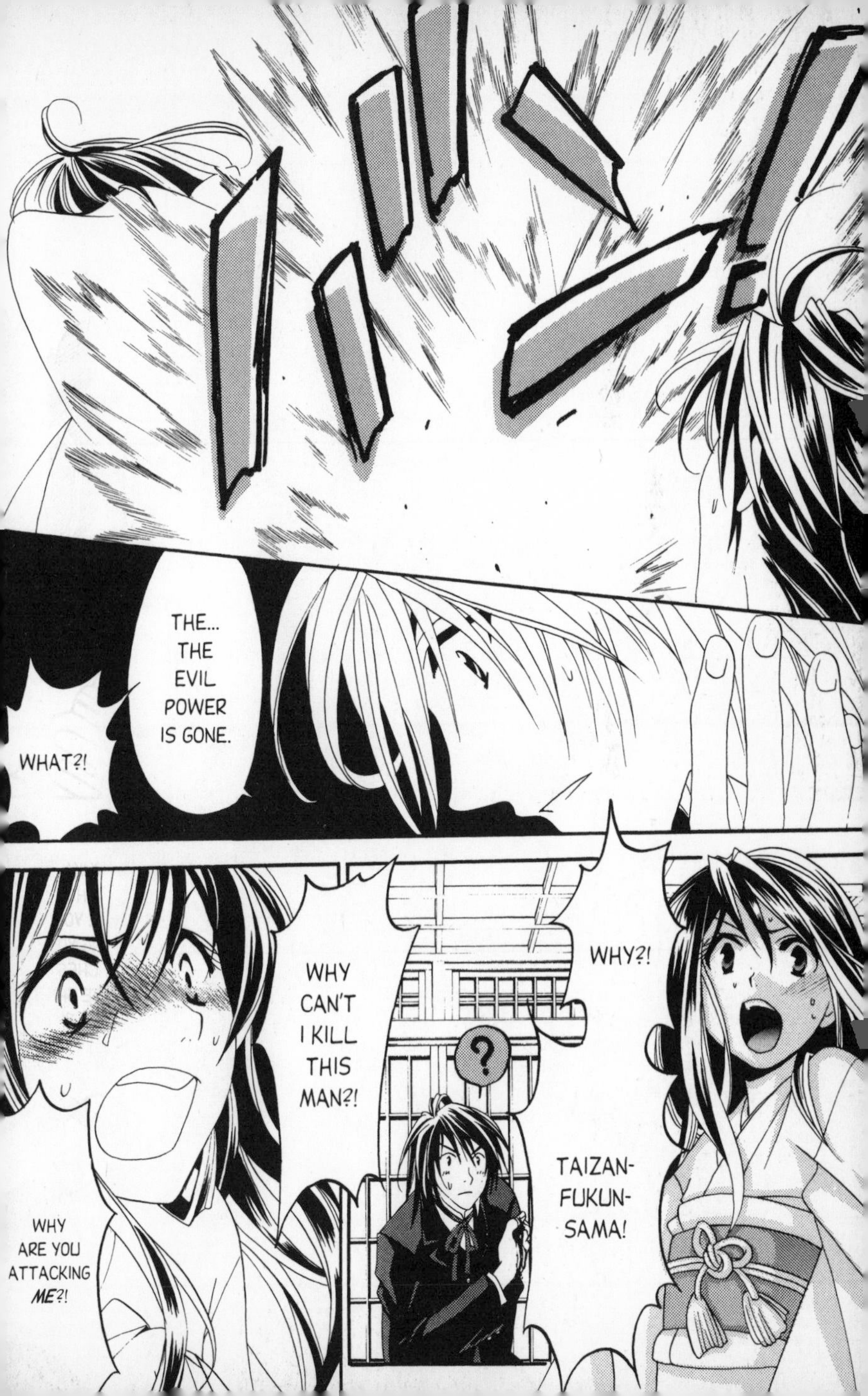
THE... THE EVIL POWER IS GONE.
WHAT?!
WHY?!
WHY CAN'T I KILL THIS MAN?!
?
TAIZAN-FUKUN-SAMA!
WHY ARE YOU ATTACKING *ME*?!

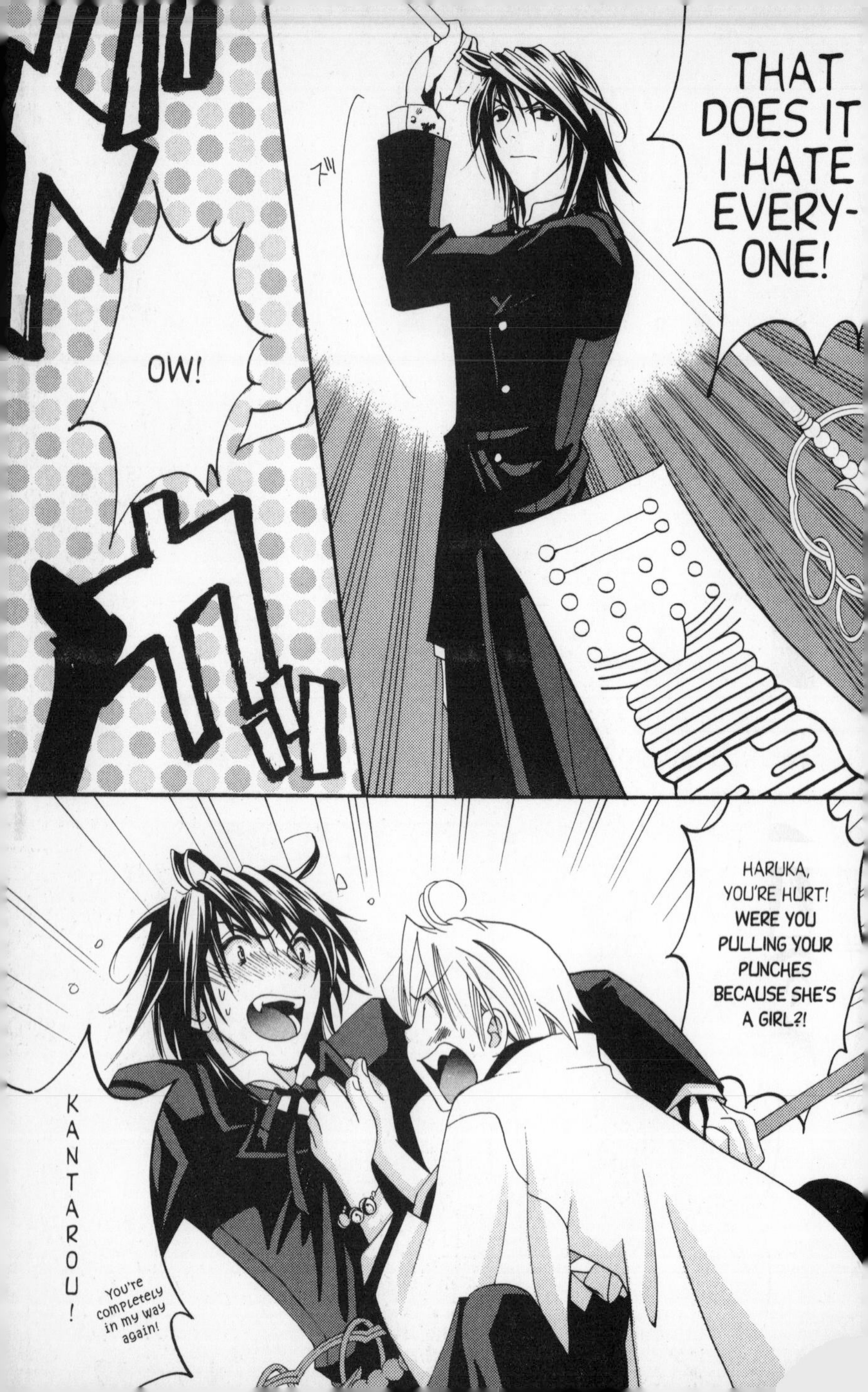
THAT DOES IT I HATE EVERY-ONE!
OW!
HARUKA, YOU'RE HURT! WERE YOU PULLING YOUR PUNCHES BECAUSE SHE'S A GIRL?!
KANTAROU!
You're completely in my way again!

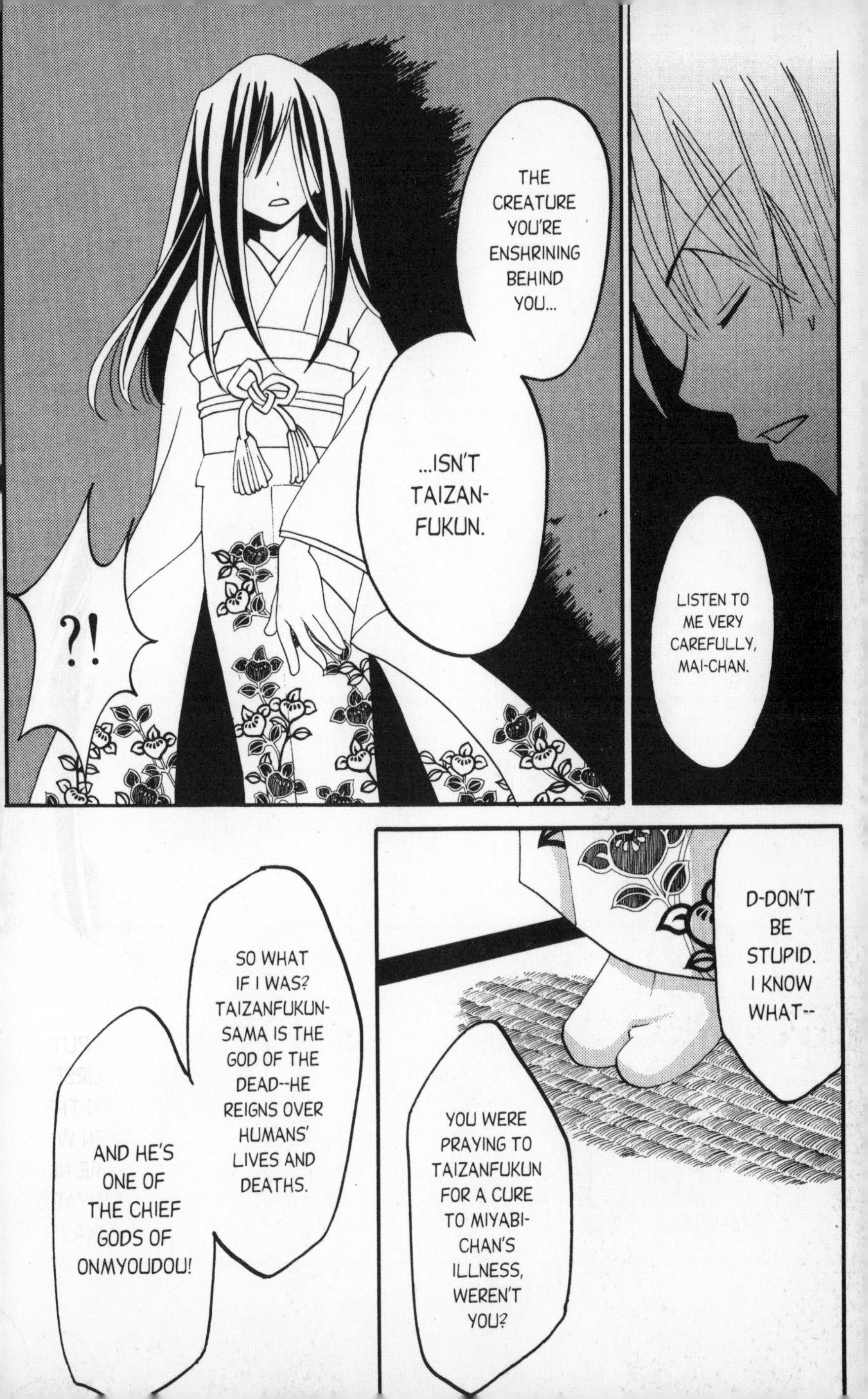
LISTEN TO ME VERY CAREFULLY, MAI-CHAN.
THE CREATURE YOU'RE ENSHRINING BEHIND YOU...
...ISN'T TAIZAN-FUKUN.
?!
D-DON'T BE STUPID. I KNOW WHAT--
YOU WERE PRAYING TO TAIZANFUKUN FOR A CURE TO MIYABI-CHAN'S ILLNESS, WEREN'T YOU?
SO WHAT IF I WAS? TAIZANFUKUN-SAMA IS THE GOD OF THE DEAD--HE REIGNS OVER HUMANS' LIVES AND DEATHS.
AND HE'S ONE OF THE CHIEF GODS OF ONMYOUDOU!

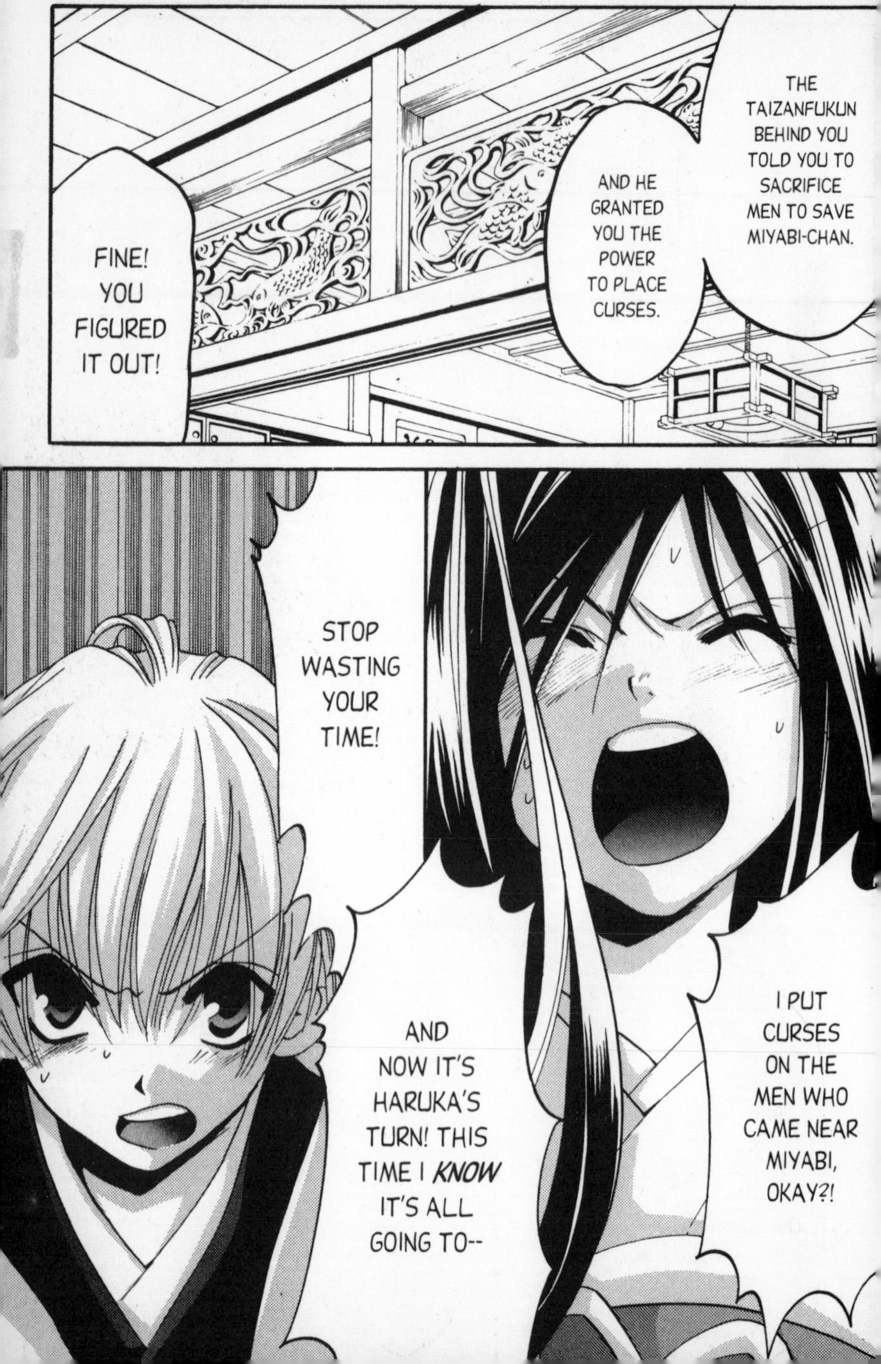
THE TAIZANFUKUN BEHIND YOU TOLD YOU TO SACRIFICE MEN TO SAVE MIYABI-CHAN.
AND HE GRANTED YOU THE POWER TO PLACE CURSES.
FINE! YOU FIGURED IT OUT!
STOP WASTING YOUR TIME!
I PUT CURSES ON THE MEN WHO CAME NEAR MIYABI, OKAY?!
AND NOW IT'S HARUKA'S TURN! THIS TIME I *KNOW* IT'S ALL GOING TO--

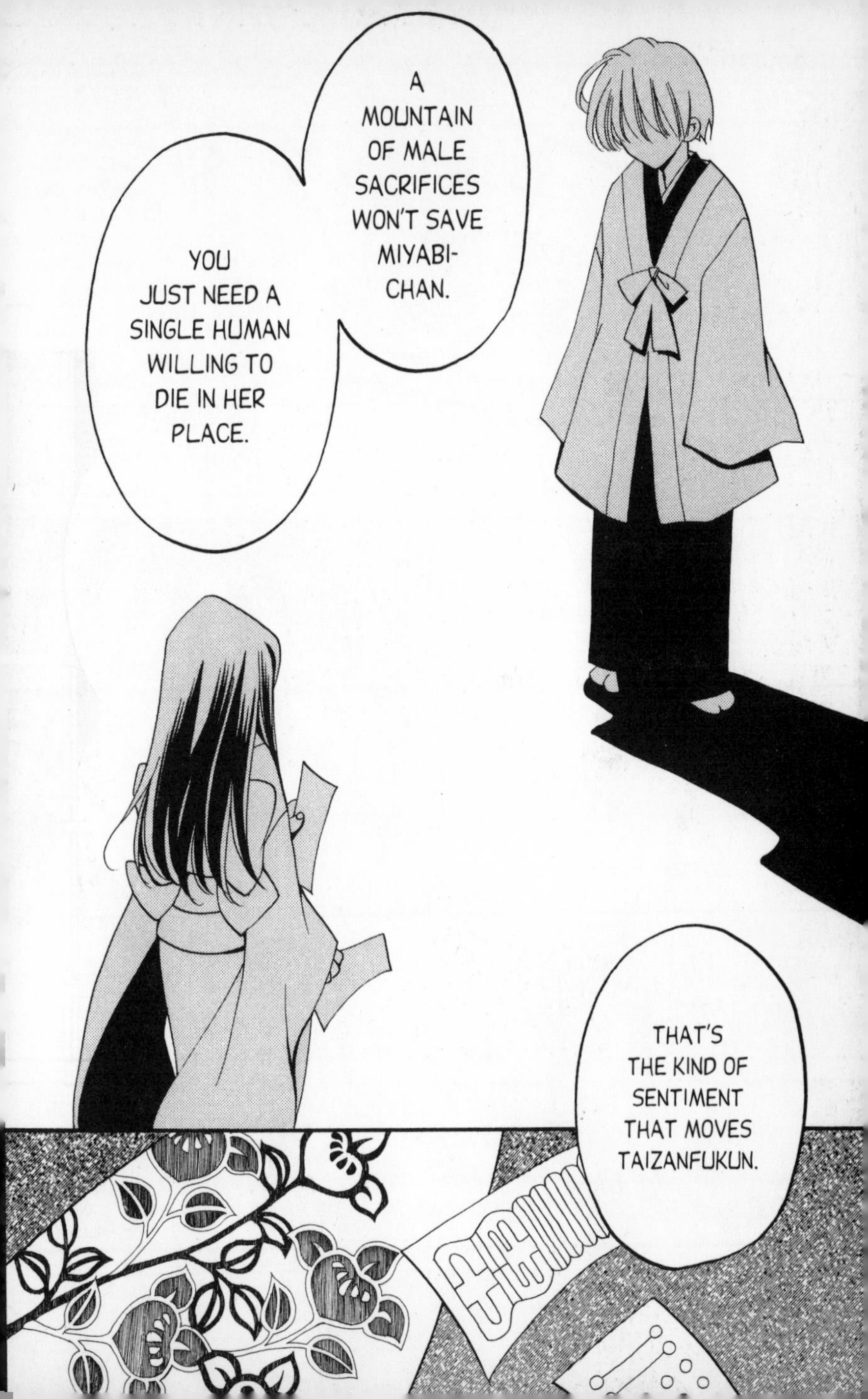
A MOUNTAIN OF MALE SACRIFICES WON'T SAVE MIYABI-CHAN.
YOU JUST NEED A SINGLE HUMAN WILLING TO DIE IN HER PLACE.
THAT'S THE KIND OF SENTIMENT THAT MOVES TAIZANFUKUN.

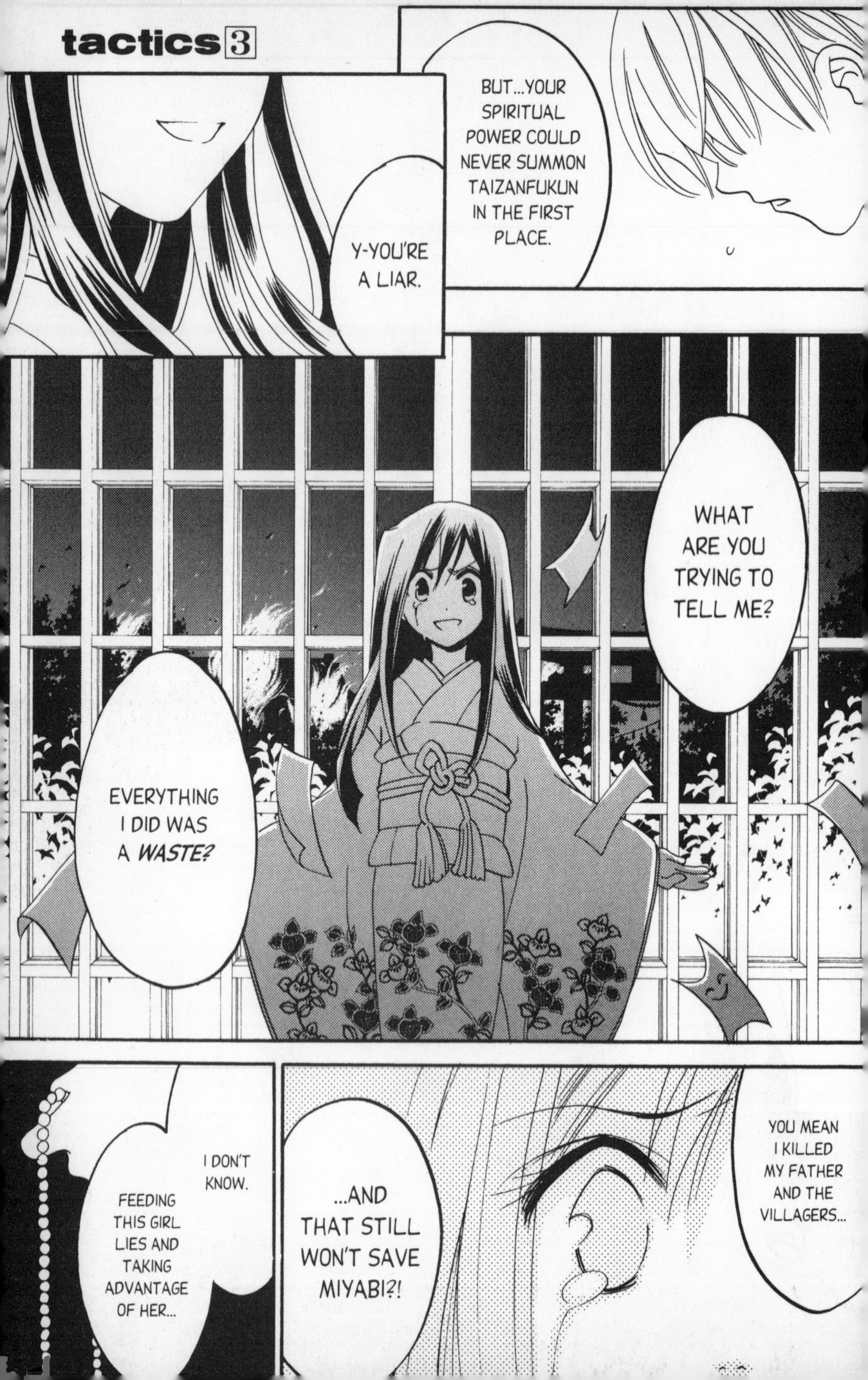
BUT...YOUR SPIRITUAL POWER COULD NEVER SUMMON TAIZANFUKUN IN THE FIRST PLACE.
Y-YOU'RE A LIAR.
WHAT ARE YOU TRYING TO TELL ME?
EVERYTHING I DID WAS A *WASTE?*
YOU MEAN I KILLED MY FATHER AND THE VILLAGERS...
...AND THAT STILL WON'T SAVE MIYABI?!
I DON'T KNOW.
FEEDING THIS GIRL LIES AND TAKING ADVANTAGE OF HER...

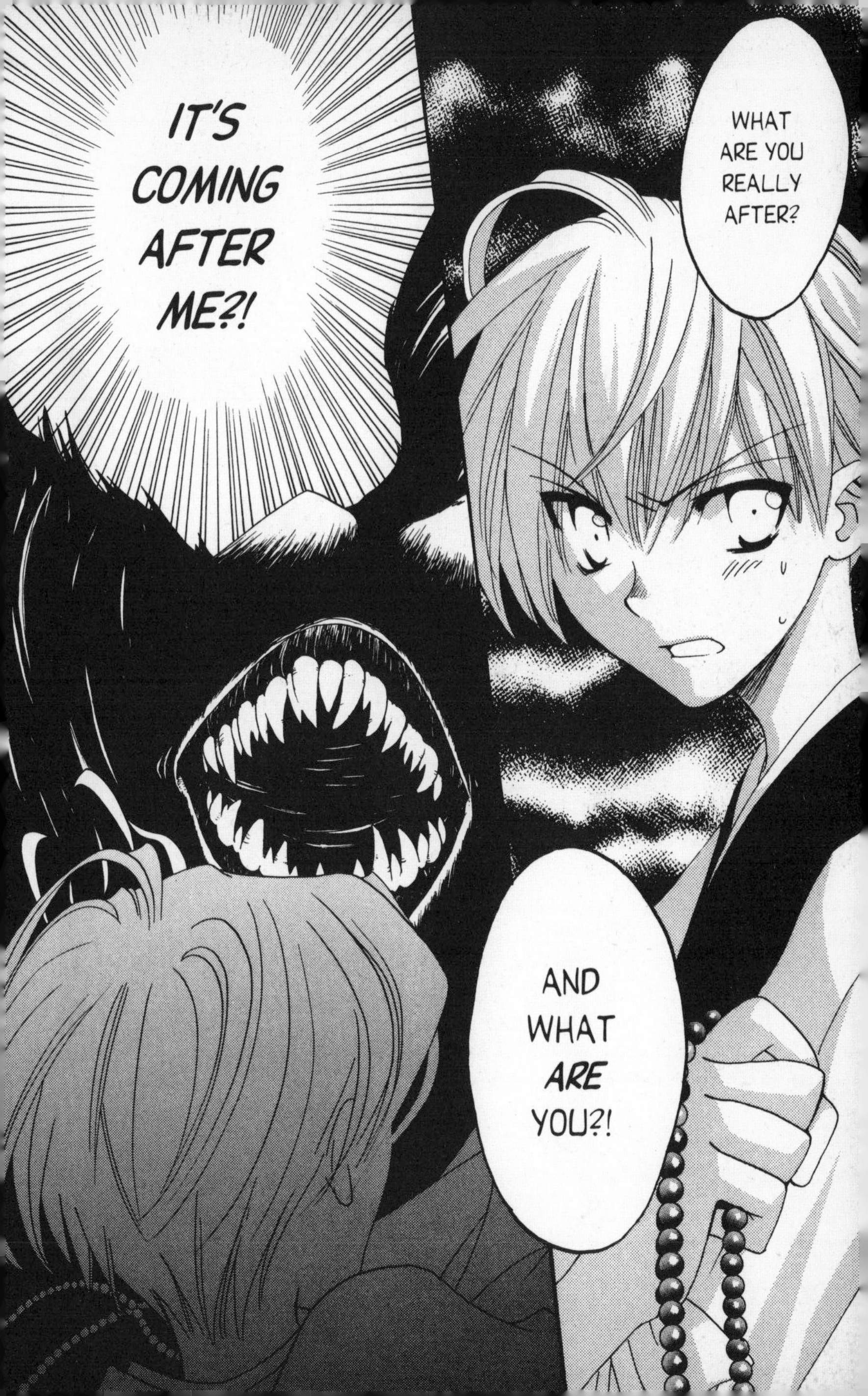
WHAT ARE YOU REALLY AFTER?
IT'S COMING AFTER ME?!
AND WHAT *ARE* YOU?!

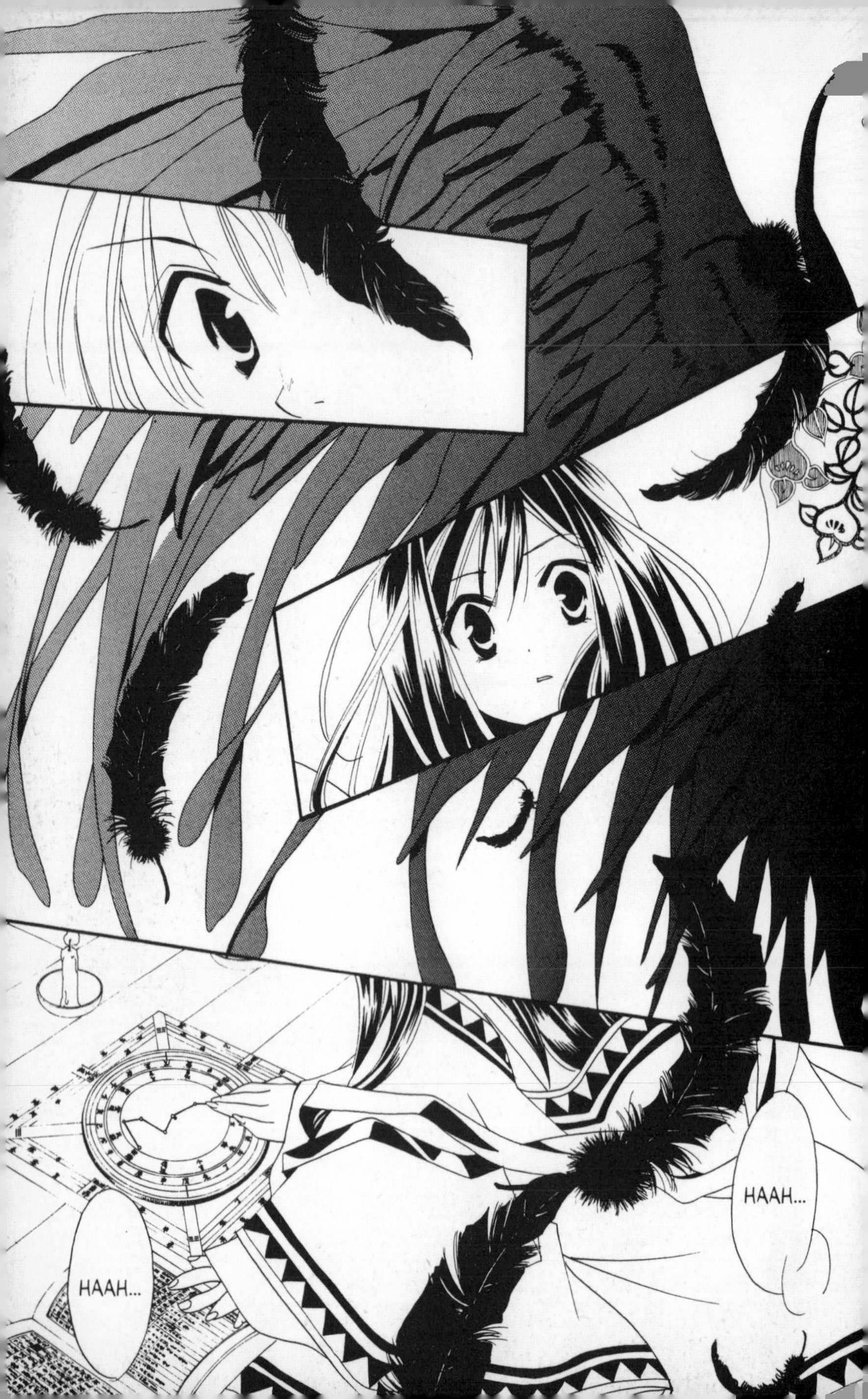
HAAH...
HAAH...

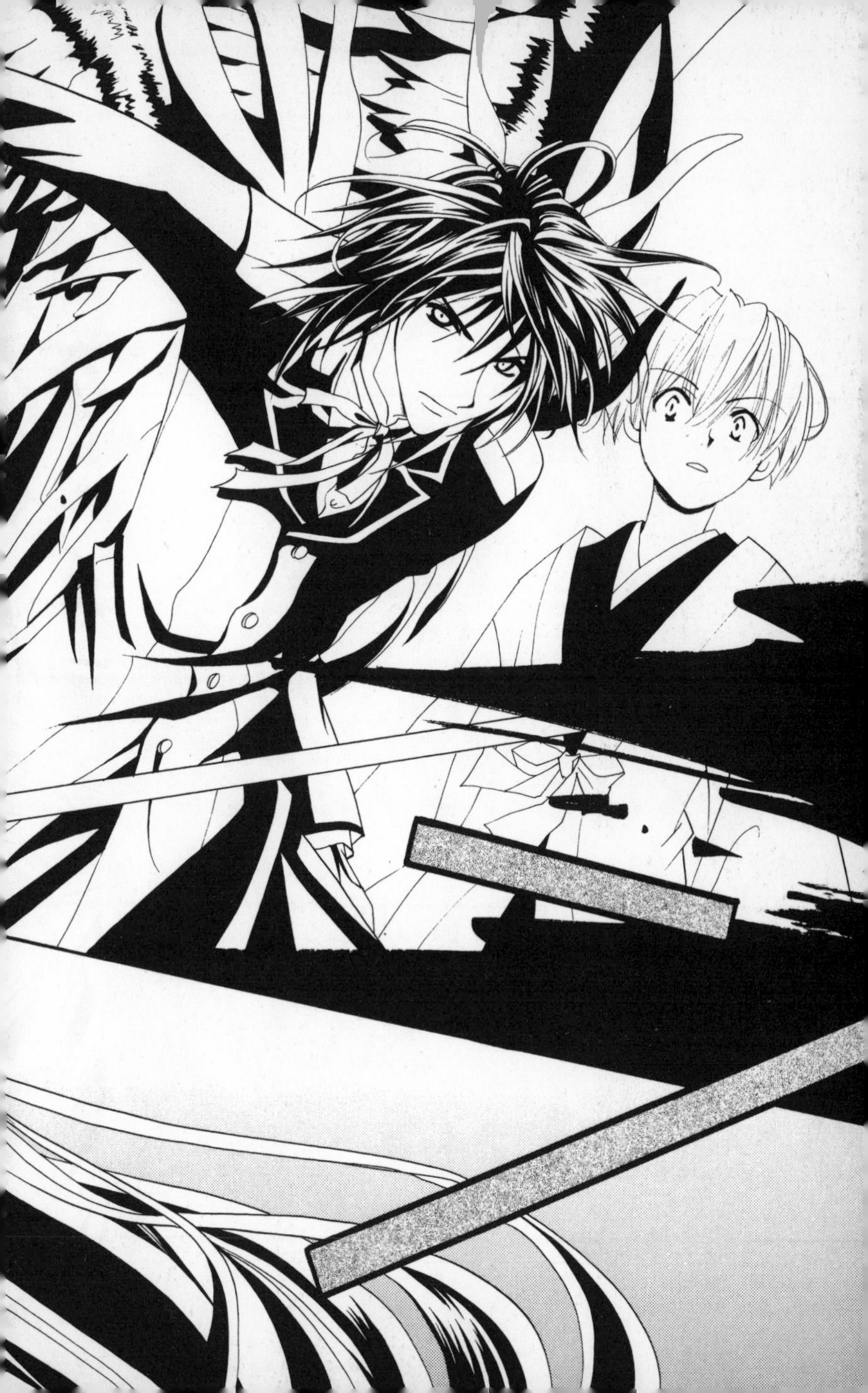

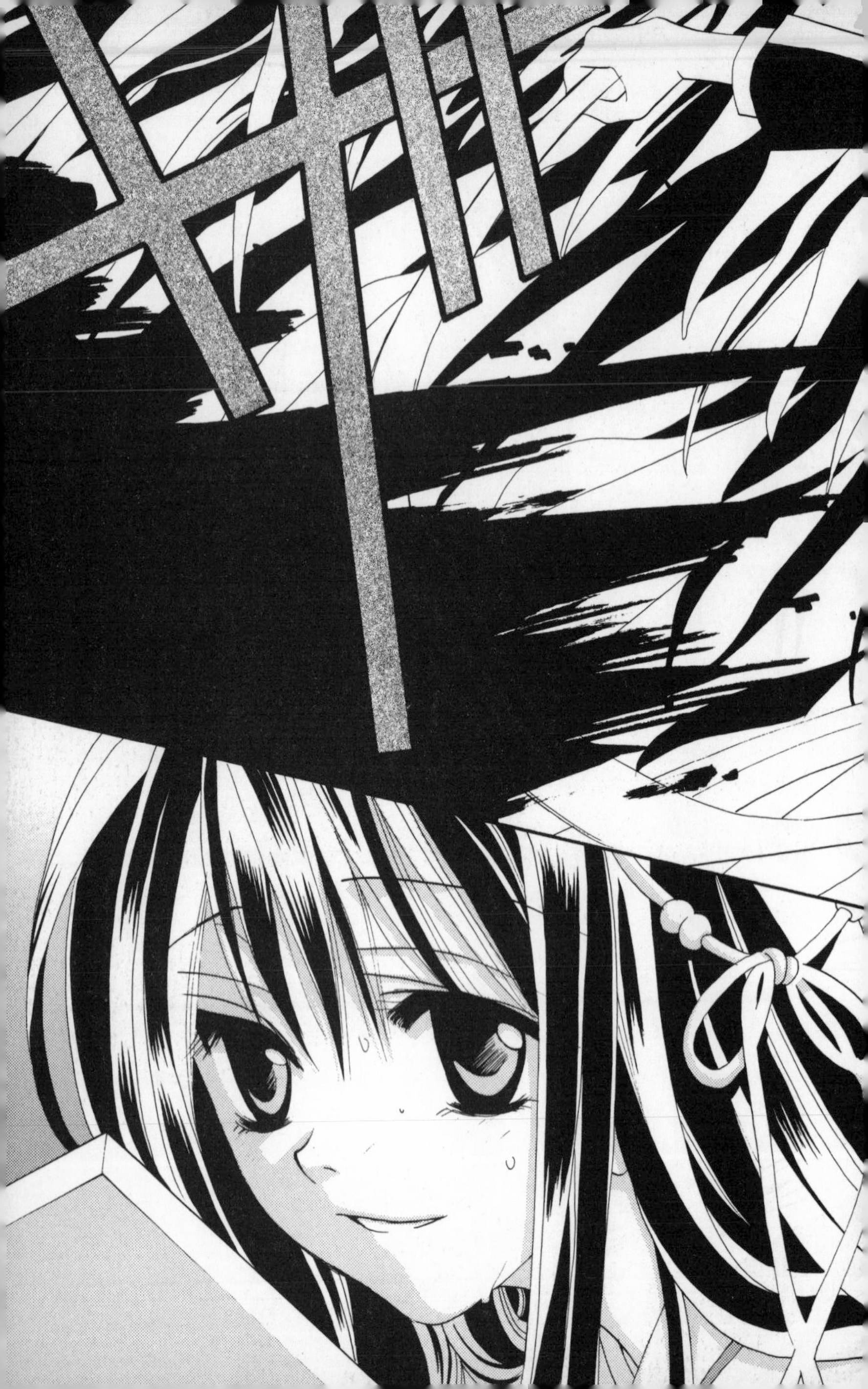

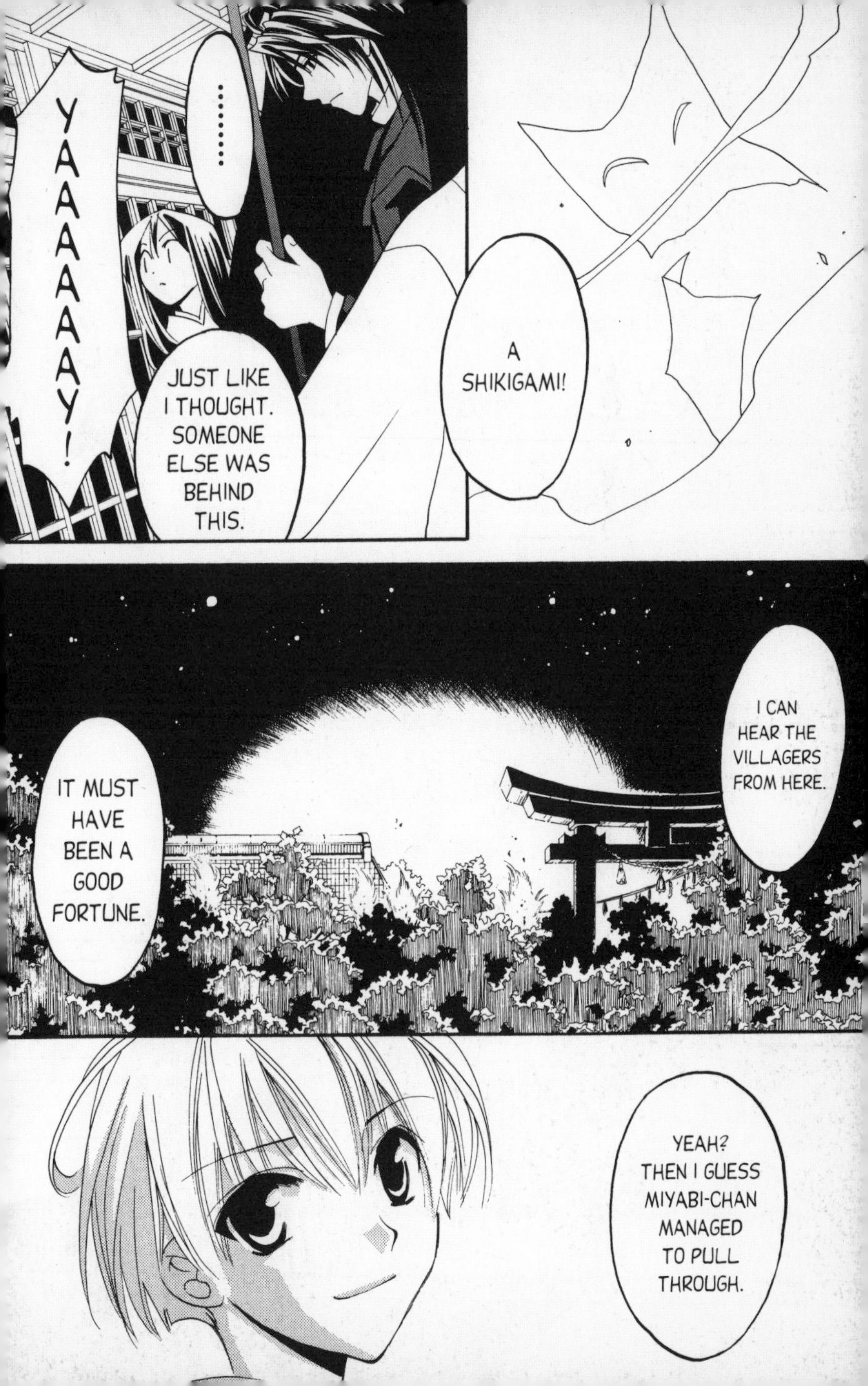
A SHIKIGAMI!
......
YAAAAAAY!
JUST LIKE I THOUGHT. SOMEONE ELSE WAS BEHIND THIS.
I CAN HEAR THE VILLAGERS FROM HERE.
IT MUST HAVE BEEN A GOOD FORTUNE.
YEAH? THEN I GUESS MIYABI-CHAN MANAGED TO PULL THROUGH.

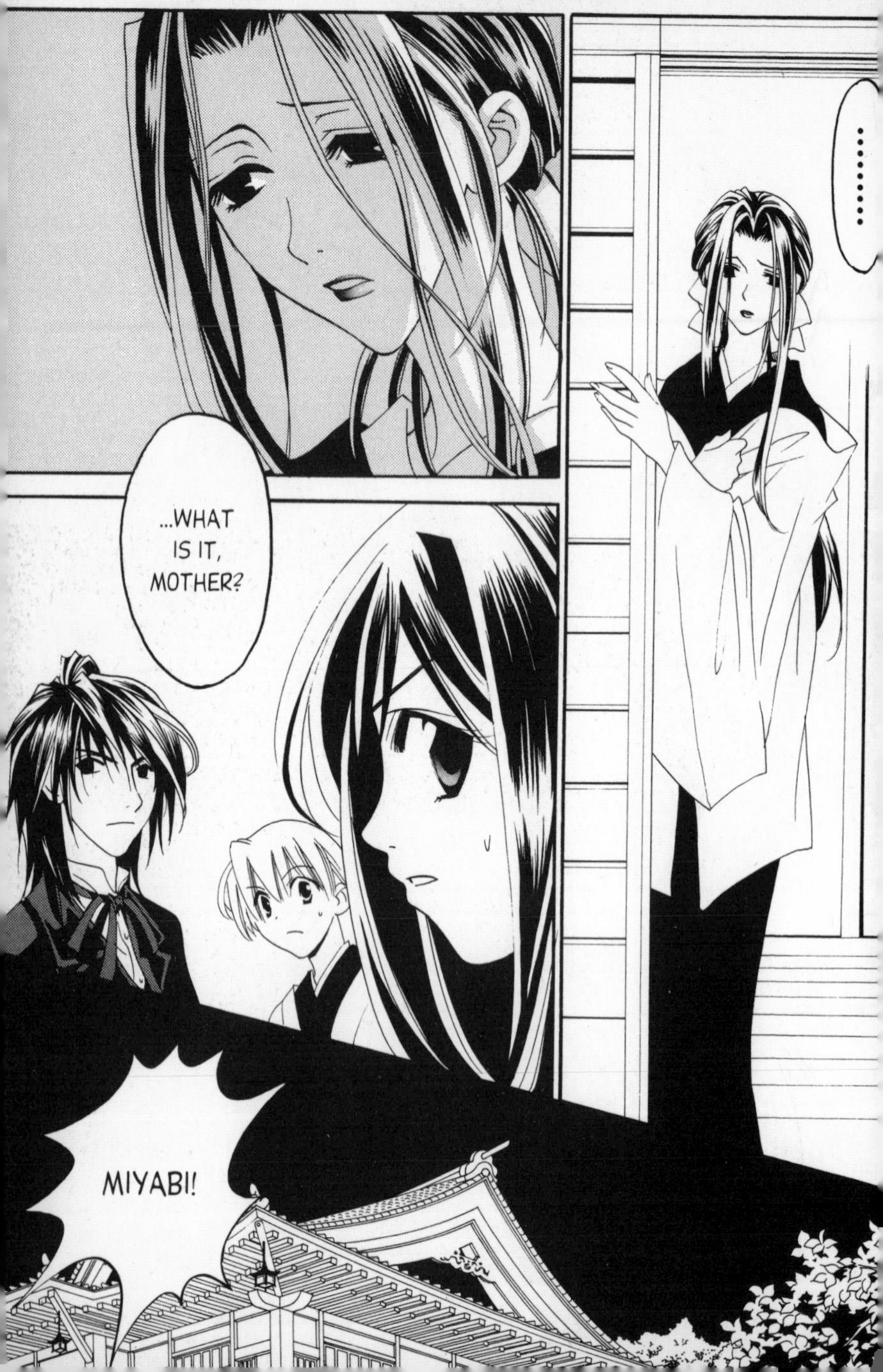
......
...WHAT IS IT, MOTHER?
MIYABI!

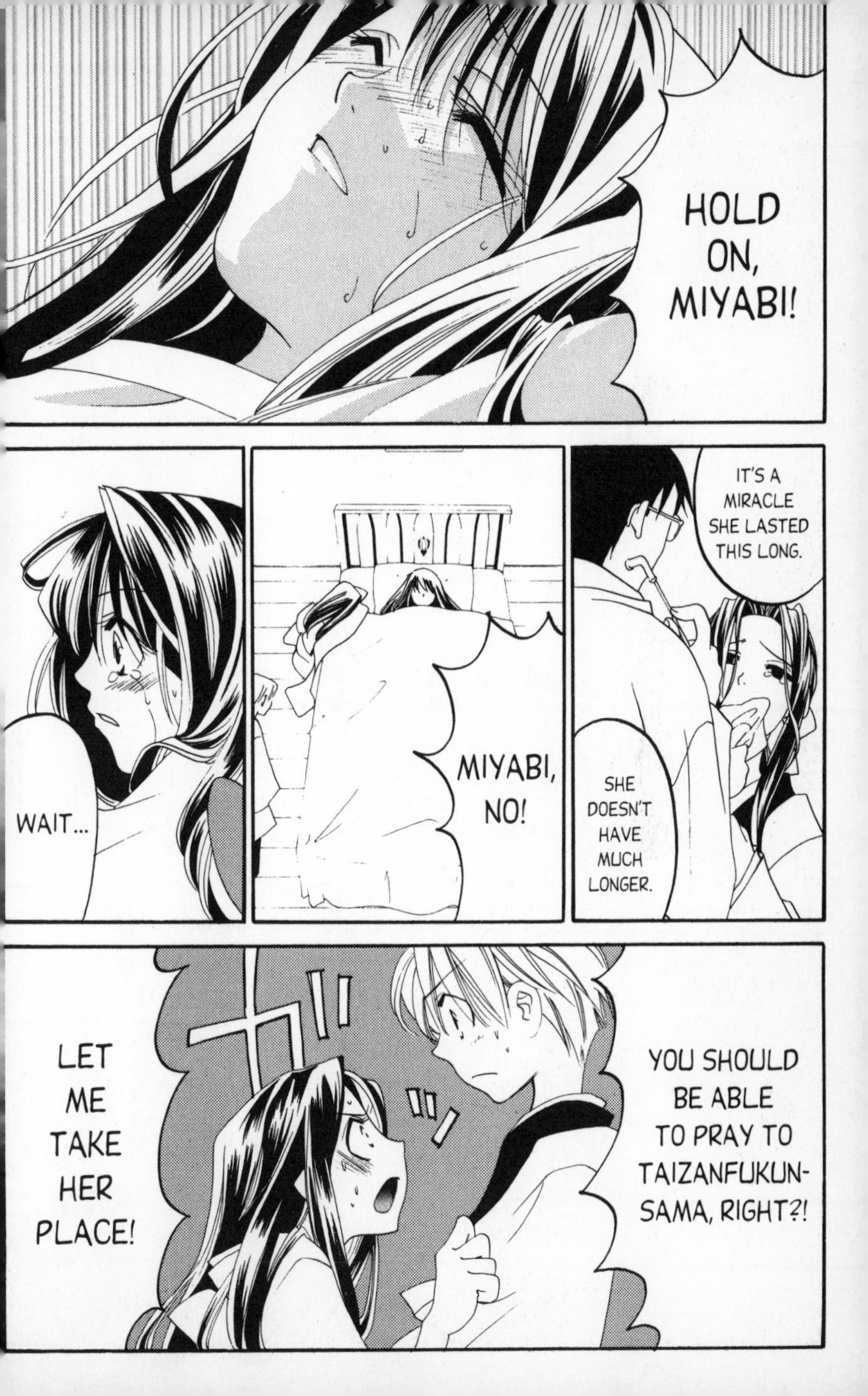
HOLD ON, MIYABI!
IT'S A MIRACLE SHE LASTED THIS LONG.
SHE DOESN'T HAVE MUCH LONGER.
MIYABI, NO!
WAIT...
YOU SHOULD BE ABLE TO PRAY TO TAIZANFUKUN-SAMA, RIGHT?!
LET ME TAKE HER PLACE!

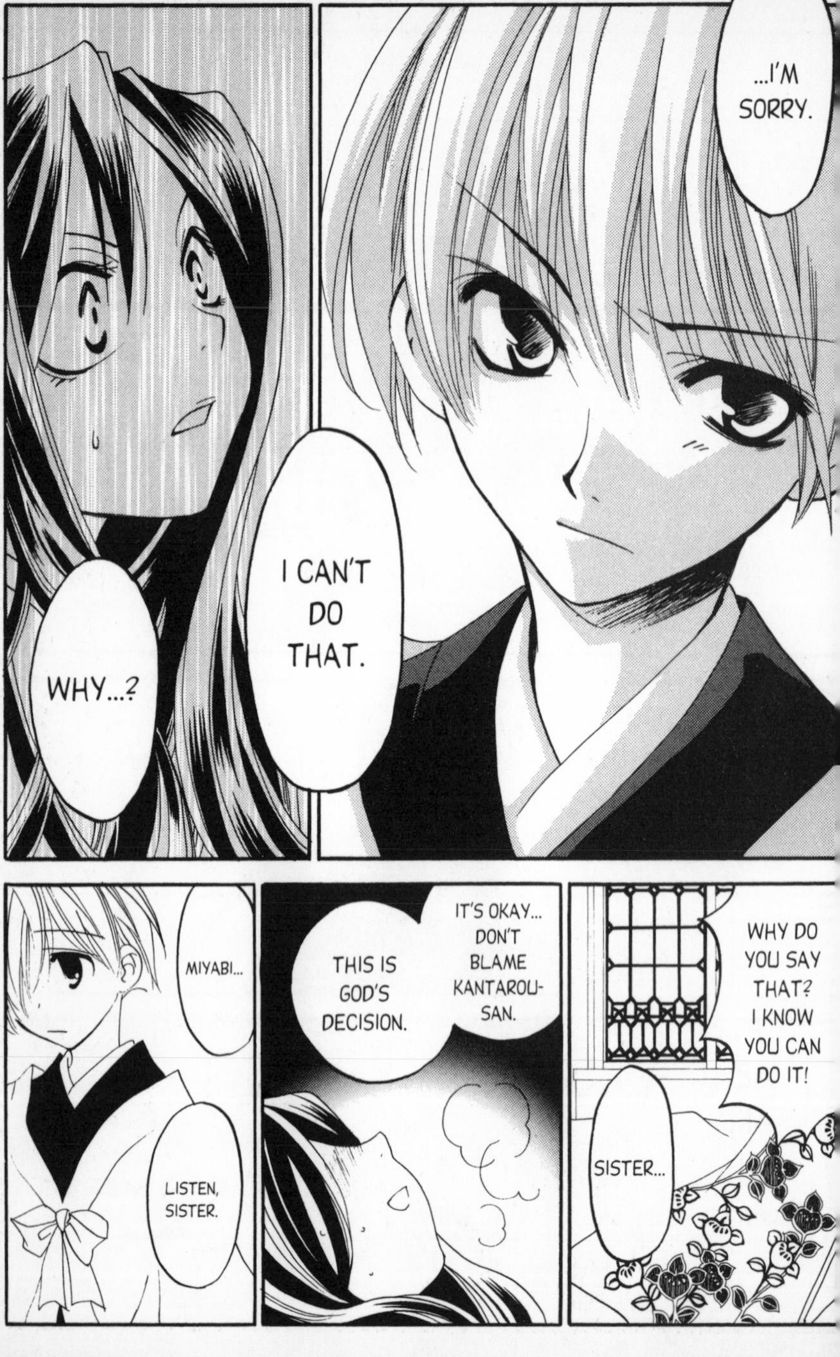
...I'M SORRY.
I CAN'T DO THAT.
WHY...?
WHY DO YOU SAY THAT? I KNOW YOU CAN DO IT!
SISTER...
IT'S OKAY... DON'T BLAME KANTAROU-SAN.
THIS IS GOD'S DECISION.
MIYABI...
LISTEN, SISTER.

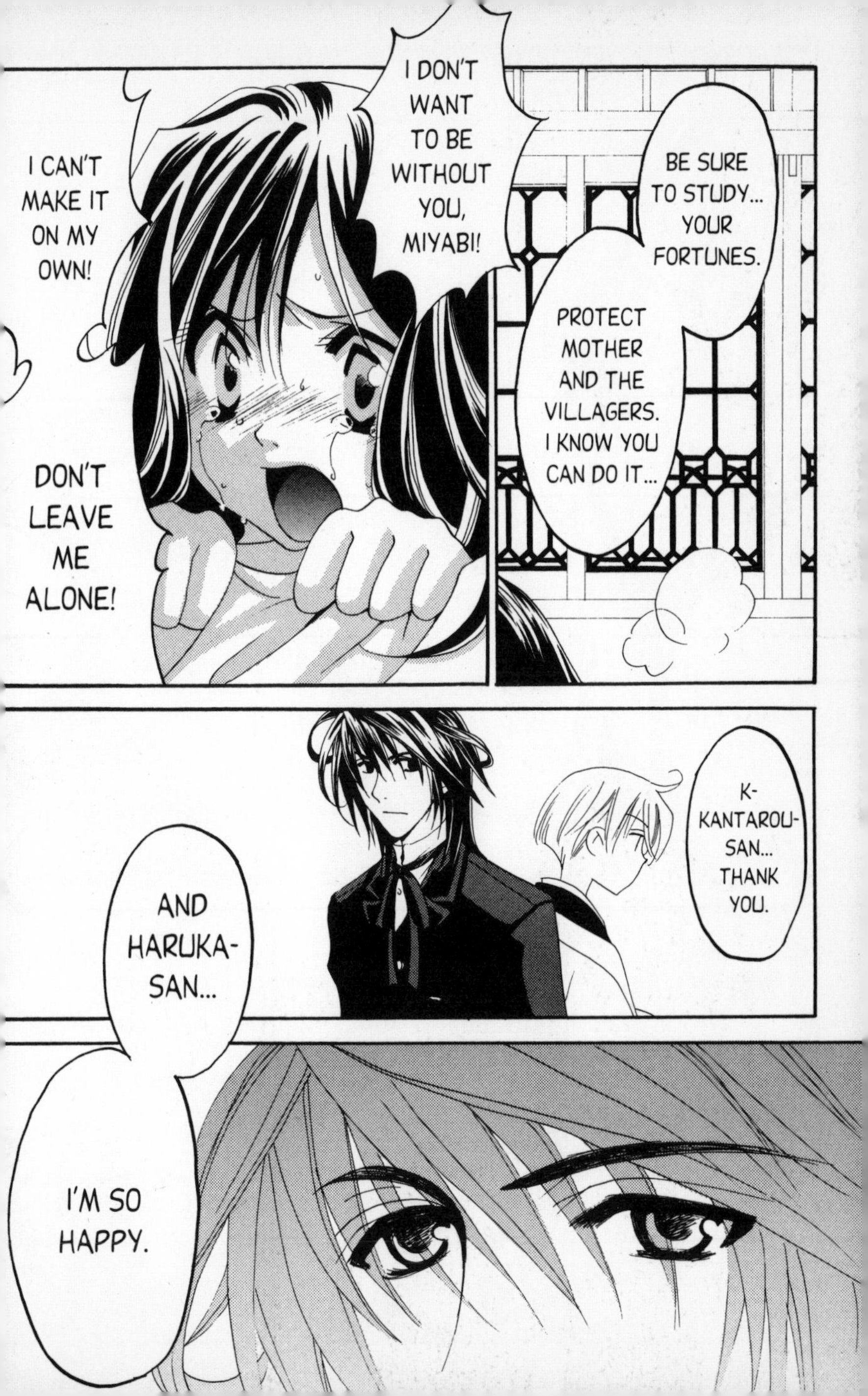
BE SURE TO STUDY... YOUR FORTUNES.
PROTECT MOTHER AND THE VILLAGERS. I KNOW YOU CAN DO IT...
I DON'T WANT TO BE WITHOUT YOU, MIYABI!
I CAN'T MAKE IT ON MY OWN!
DON'T LEAVE ME ALONE!
K-KANTAROU-SAN... THANK YOU.
AND HARUKA-SAN...
I'M SO HAPPY.

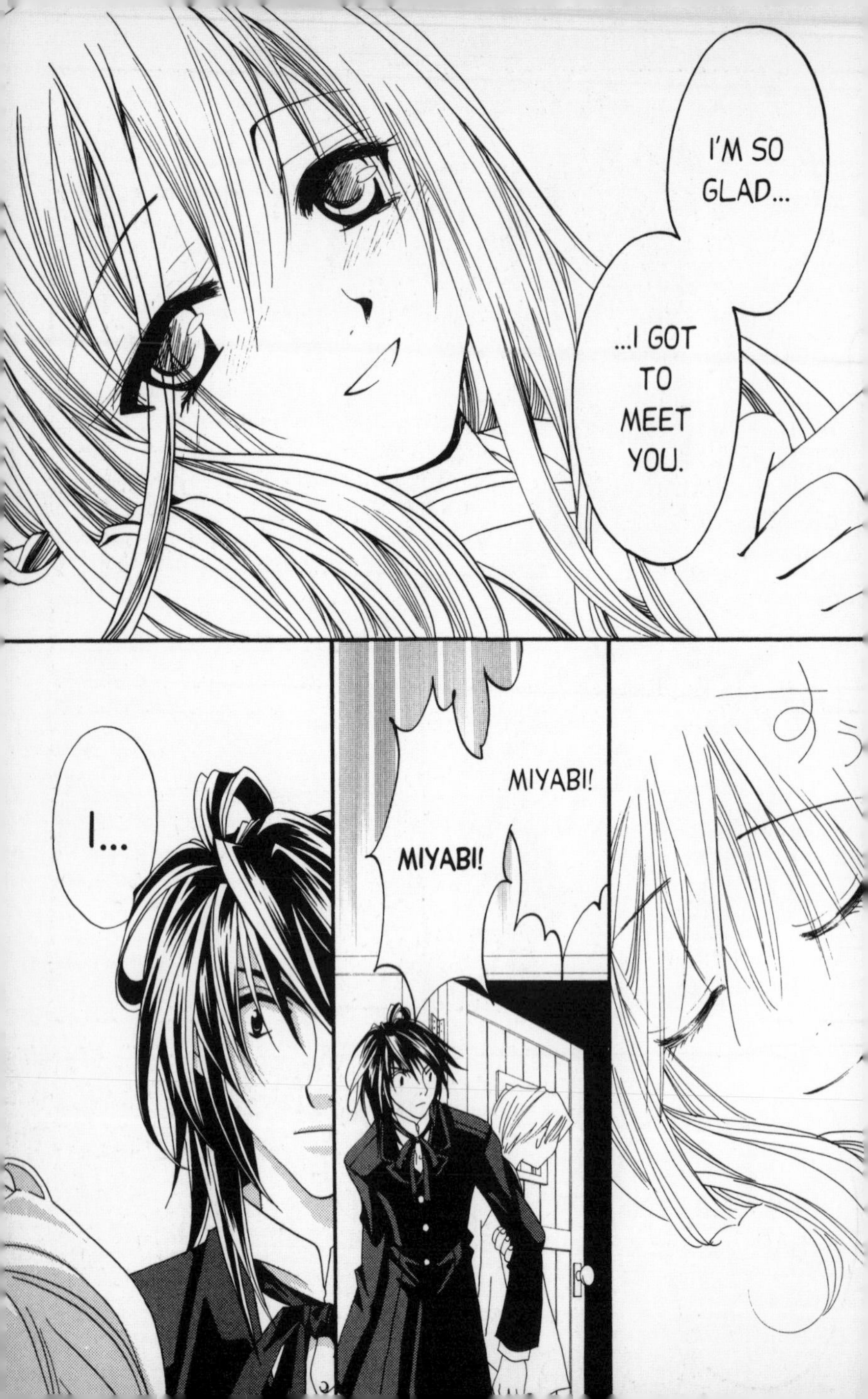
I'M SO GLAD...
...I GOT TO MEET YOU.
MIYABI!
MIYABI!
I...

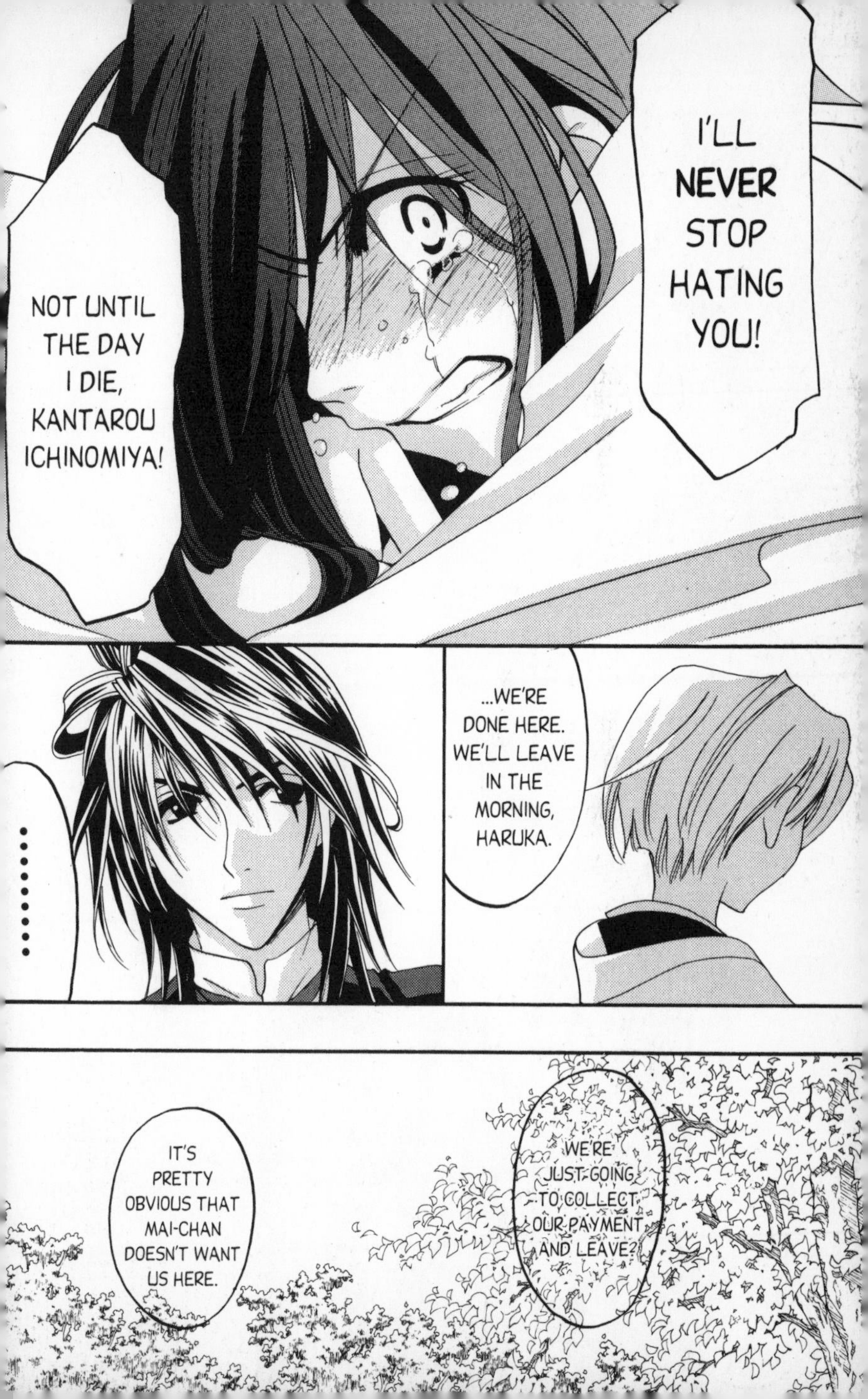
I'LL NEVER STOP HATING YOU!
NOT UNTIL THE DAY I DIE, KANTAROU ICHINOMIYA!
...WE'RE DONE HERE. WE'LL LEAVE IN THE MORNING, HARUKA.
....
WE'RE JUST GOING TO COLLECT OUR PAYMENT AND LEAVE?
IT'S PRETTY OBVIOUS THAT MAI-CHAN DOESN'T WANT US HERE.

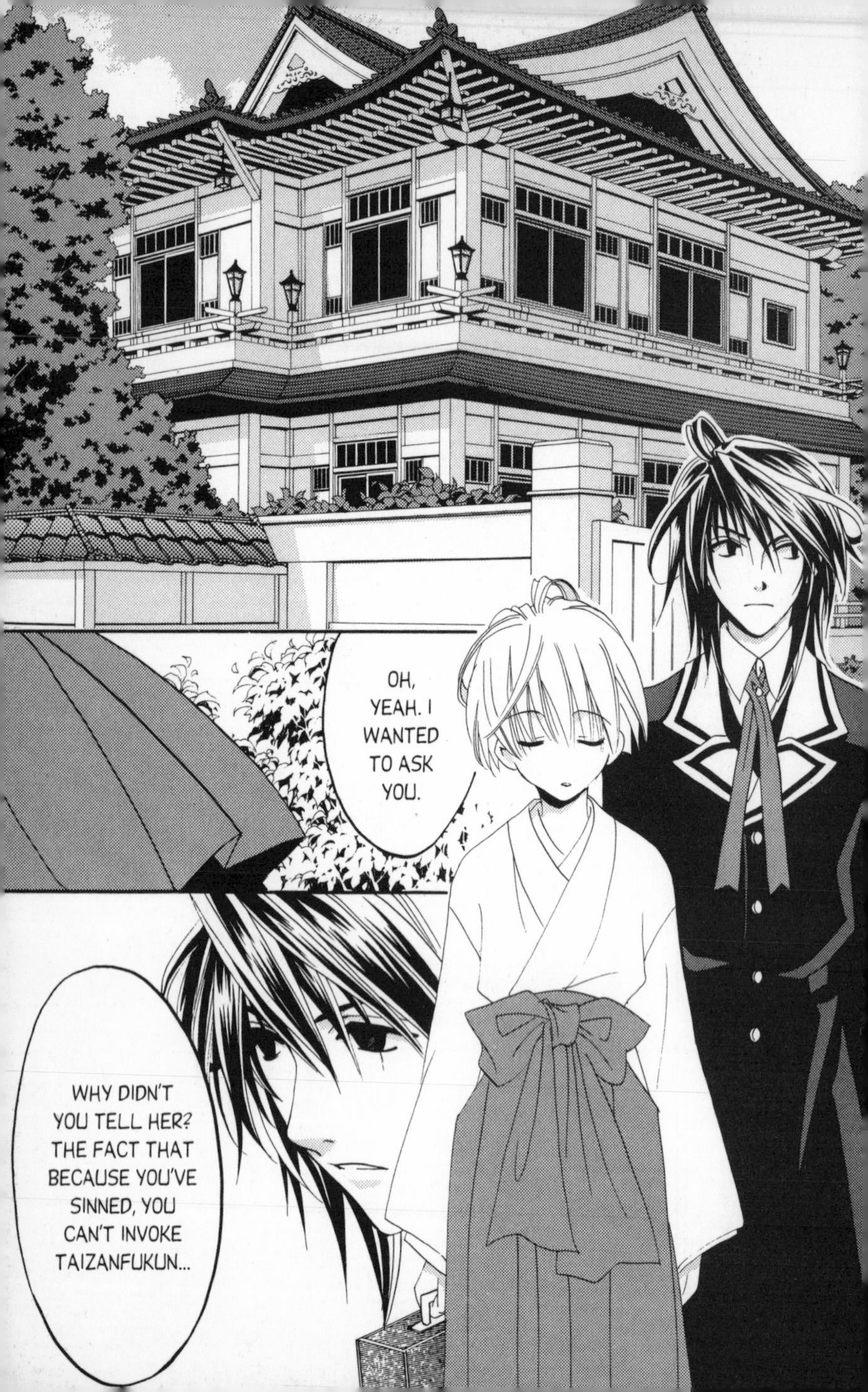
OH, YEAH. I WANTED TO ASK YOU.
WHY DIDN'T YOU TELL HER? THE FACT THAT BECAUSE YOU'VE SINNED, YOU CAN'T INVOKE TAIZANFUKUN...

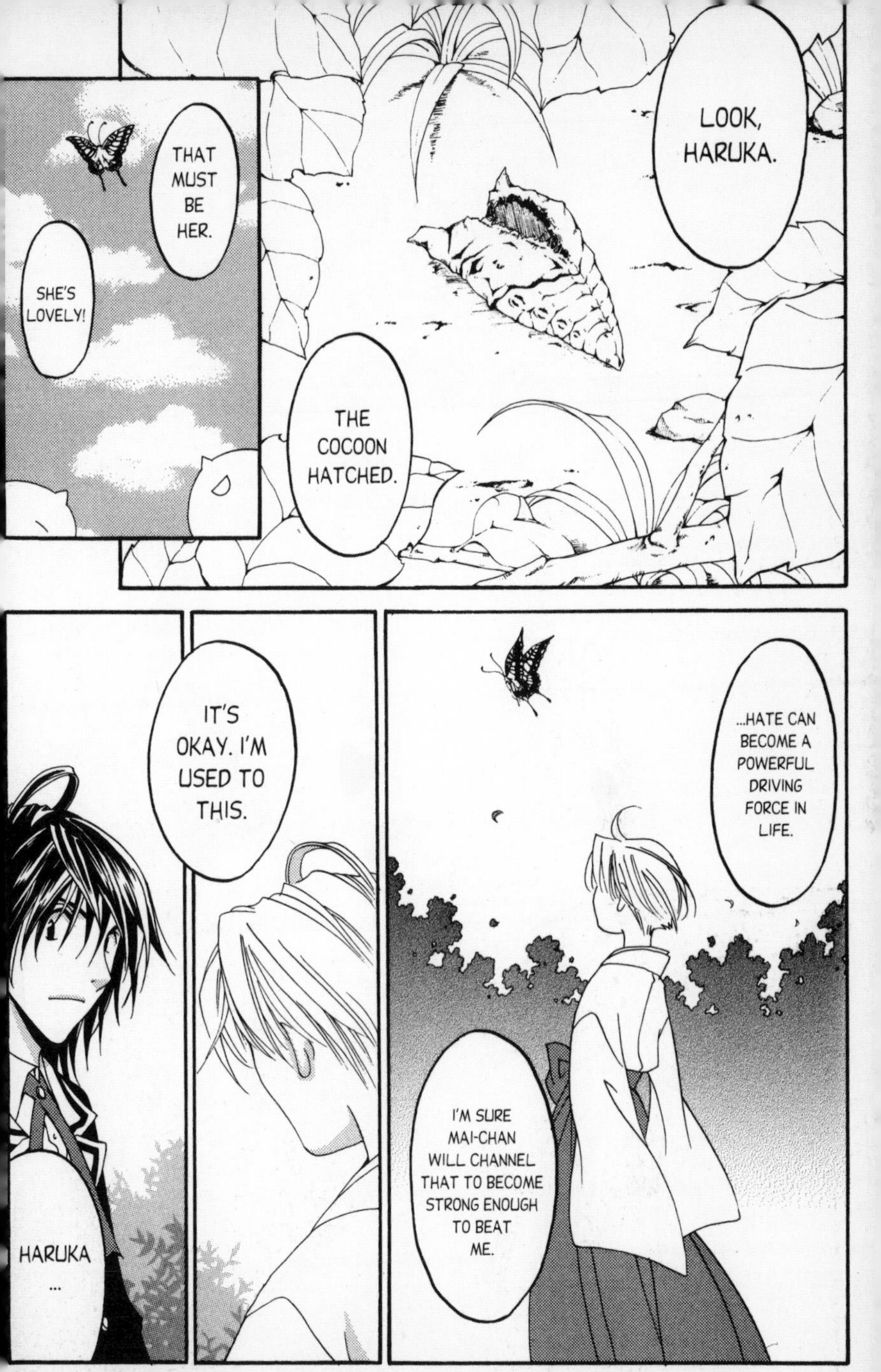
LOOK, HARUKA.
THE COCOON HATCHED.
THAT MUST BE HER.
SHE'S LOVELY!
...HATE CAN BECOME A POWERFUL DRIVING FORCE IN LIFE.
I'M SURE MAI-CHAN WILL CHANNEL THAT TO BECOME STRONG ENOUGH TO BEAT ME.
IT'S OKAY. I'M USED TO THIS.
HARUKA ...

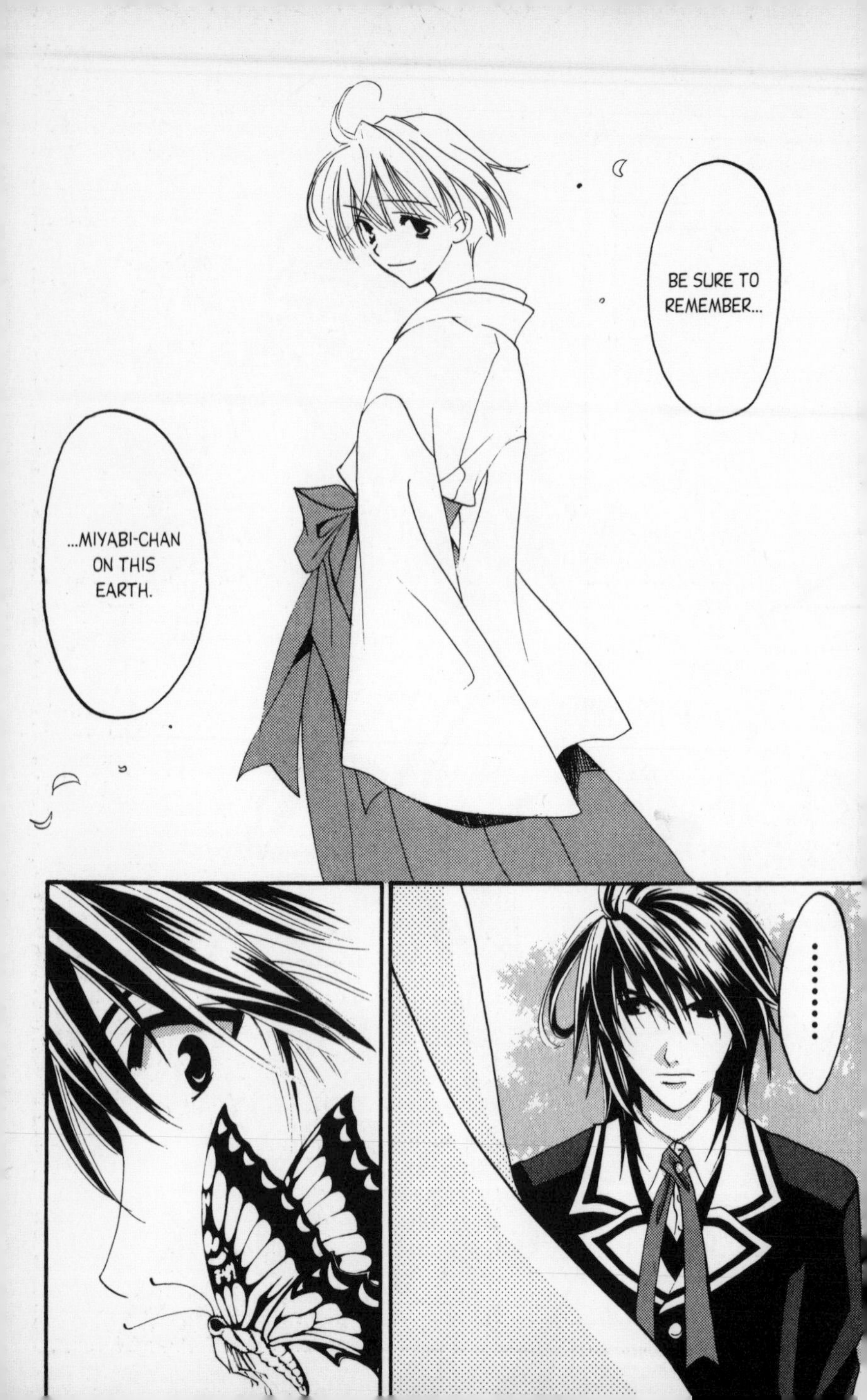
BE SURE TO REMEMBER...
...MIYABI-CHAN ON THIS EARTH.
......

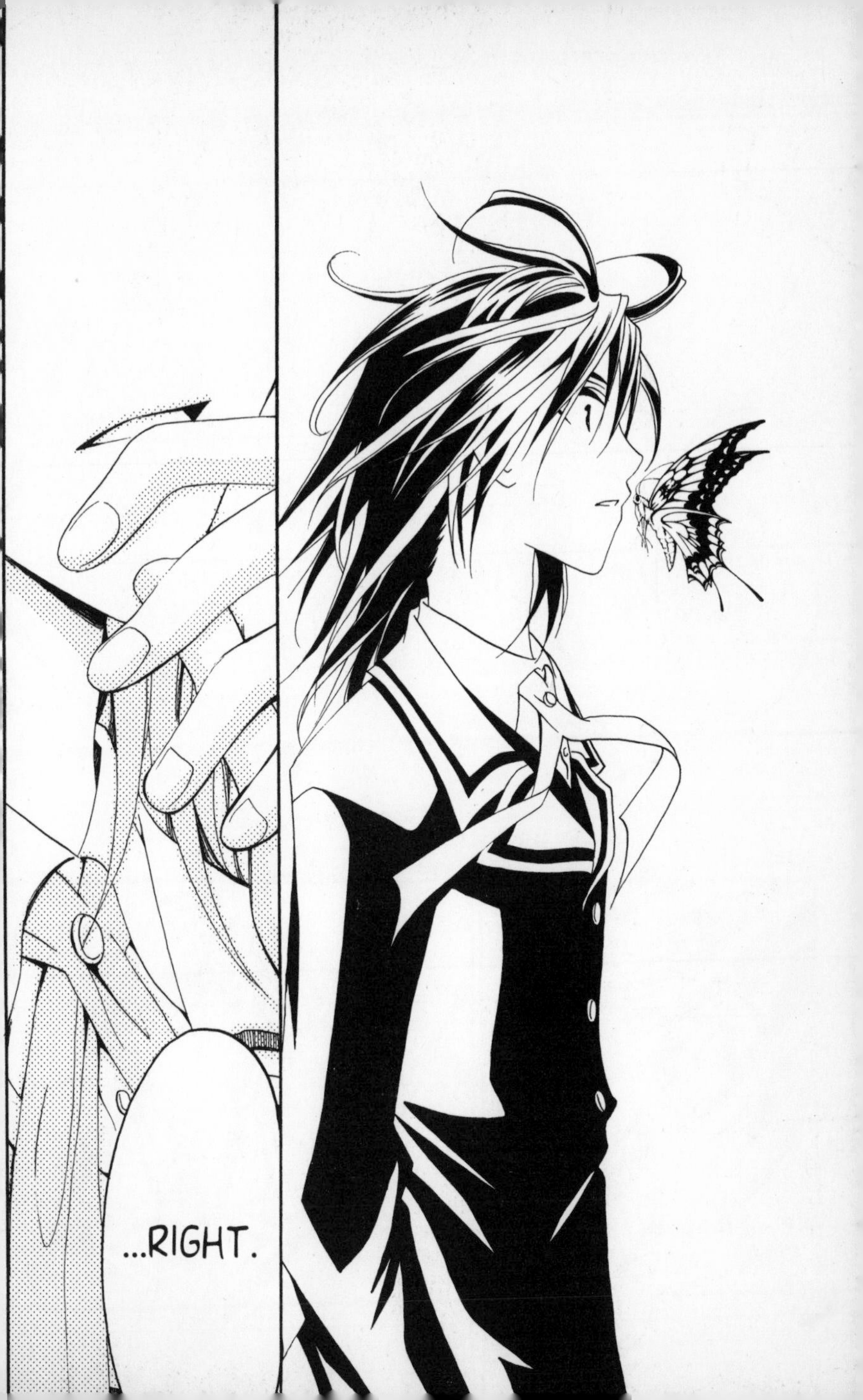
...RIGHT.

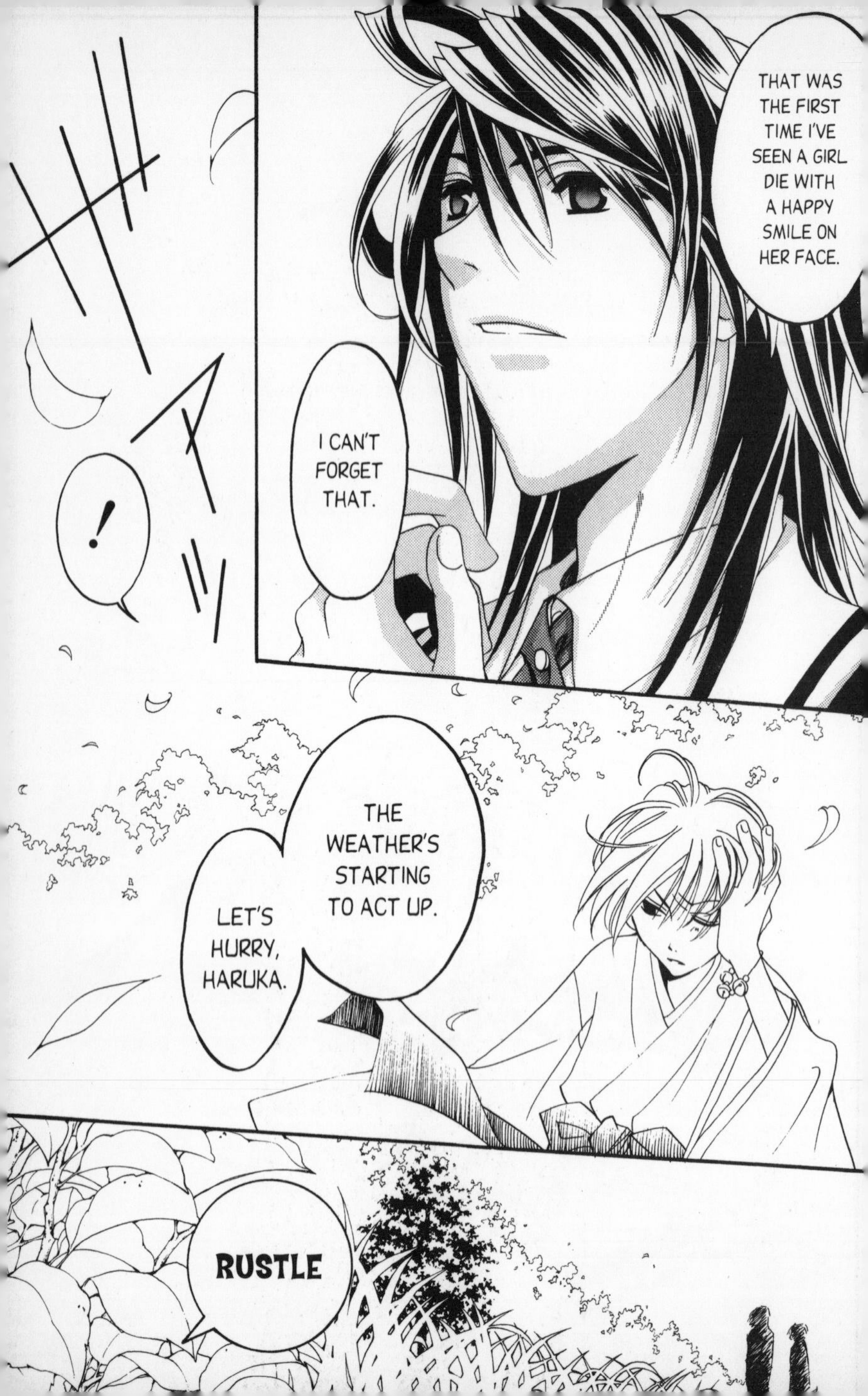
THAT WAS THE FIRST TIME I'VE SEEN A GIRL DIE WITH A HAPPY SMILE ON HER FACE.
I CAN'T FORGET THAT.
!
THE WEATHER'S STARTING TO ACT UP.
LET'S HURRY, HARUKA.
RUSTLE

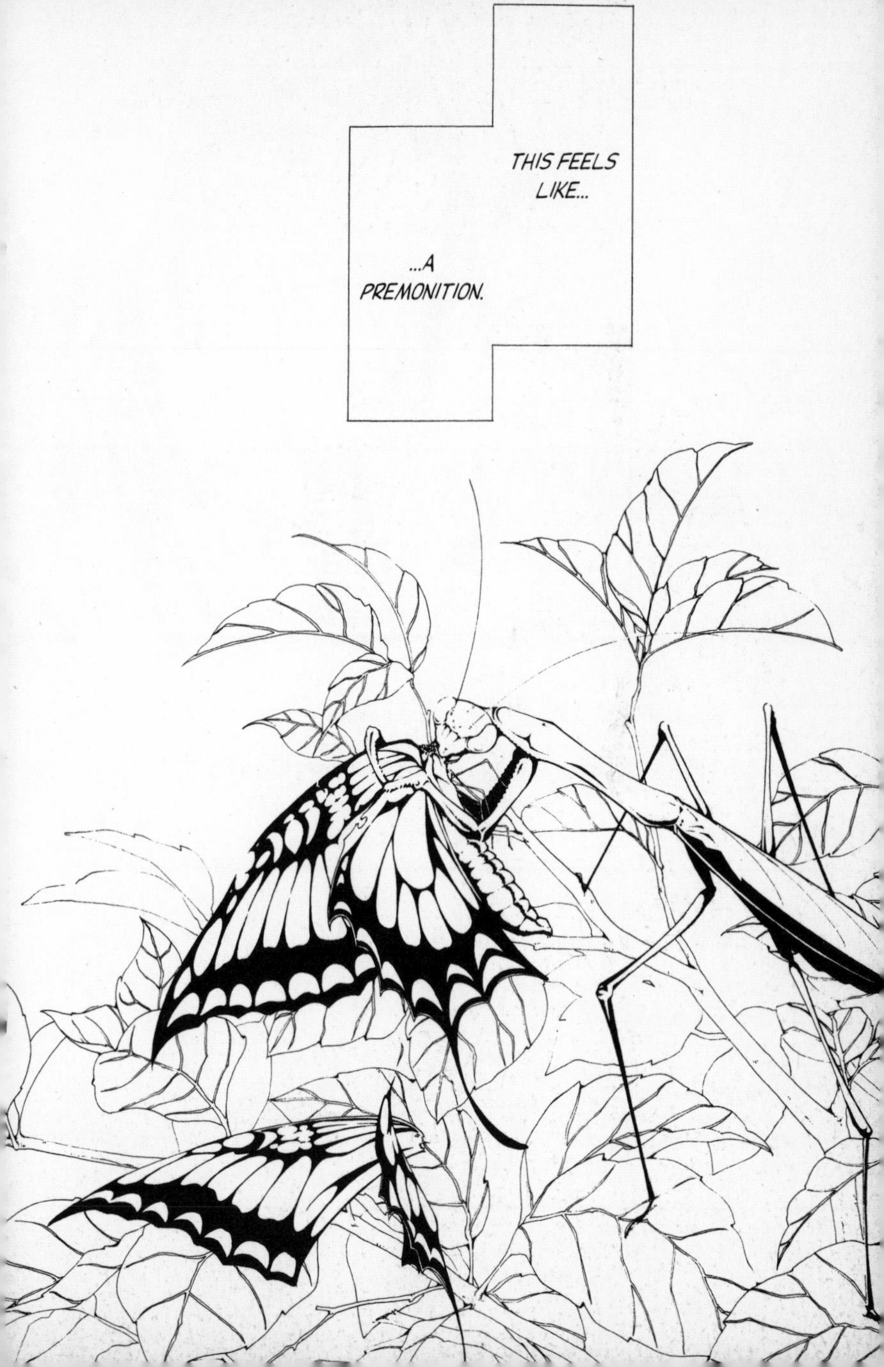
THIS FEELS LIKE...
...A PREMONITION.

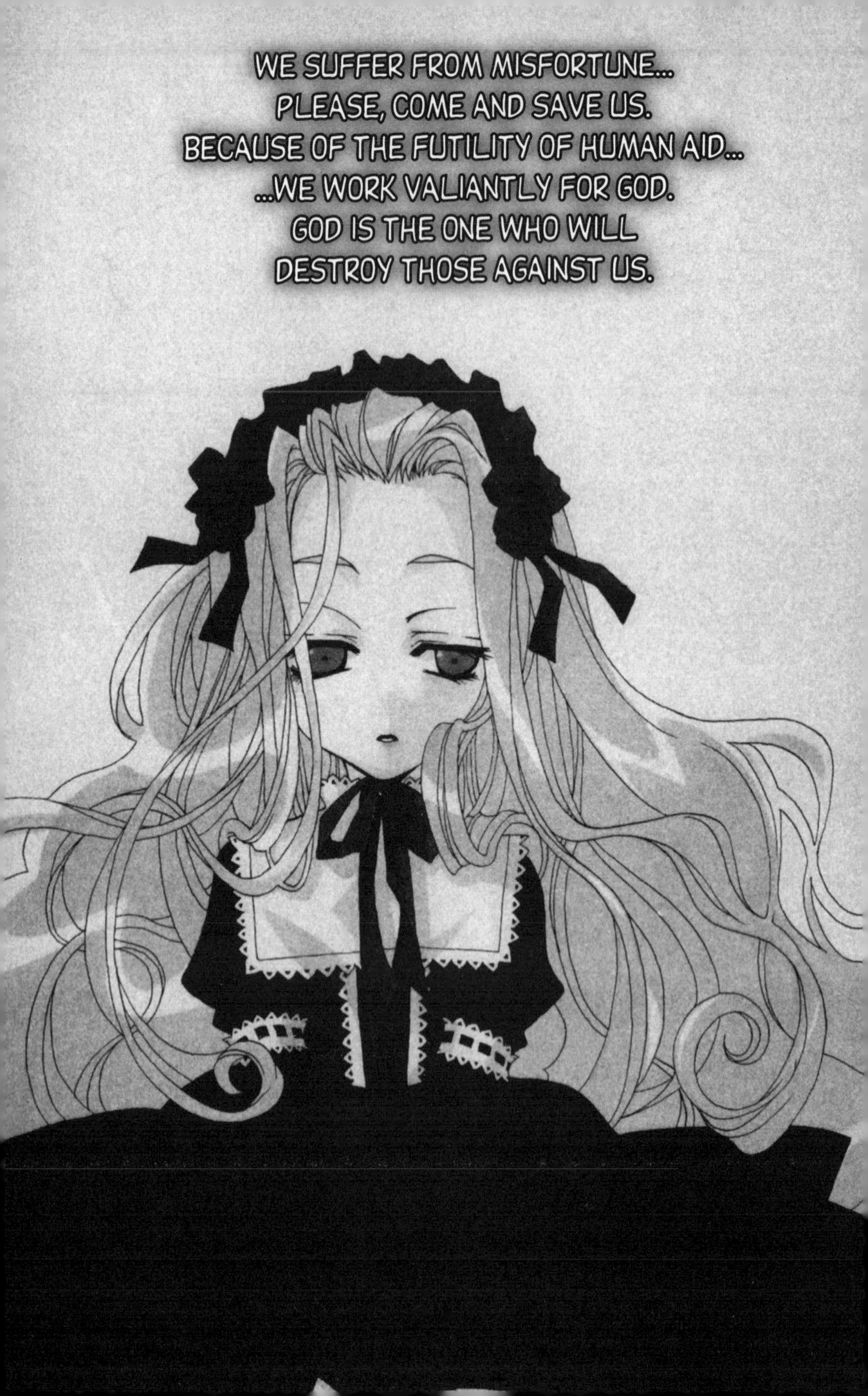
WE SUFFER FROM MISFORTUNE... PLEASE, COME AND SAVE US. BECAUSE OF THE FUTILITY OF HUMAN AID... ...WE WORK VALIANTLY FOR GOD. GOD IS THE ONE WHO WILL DESTROY THOSE AGAINST US.

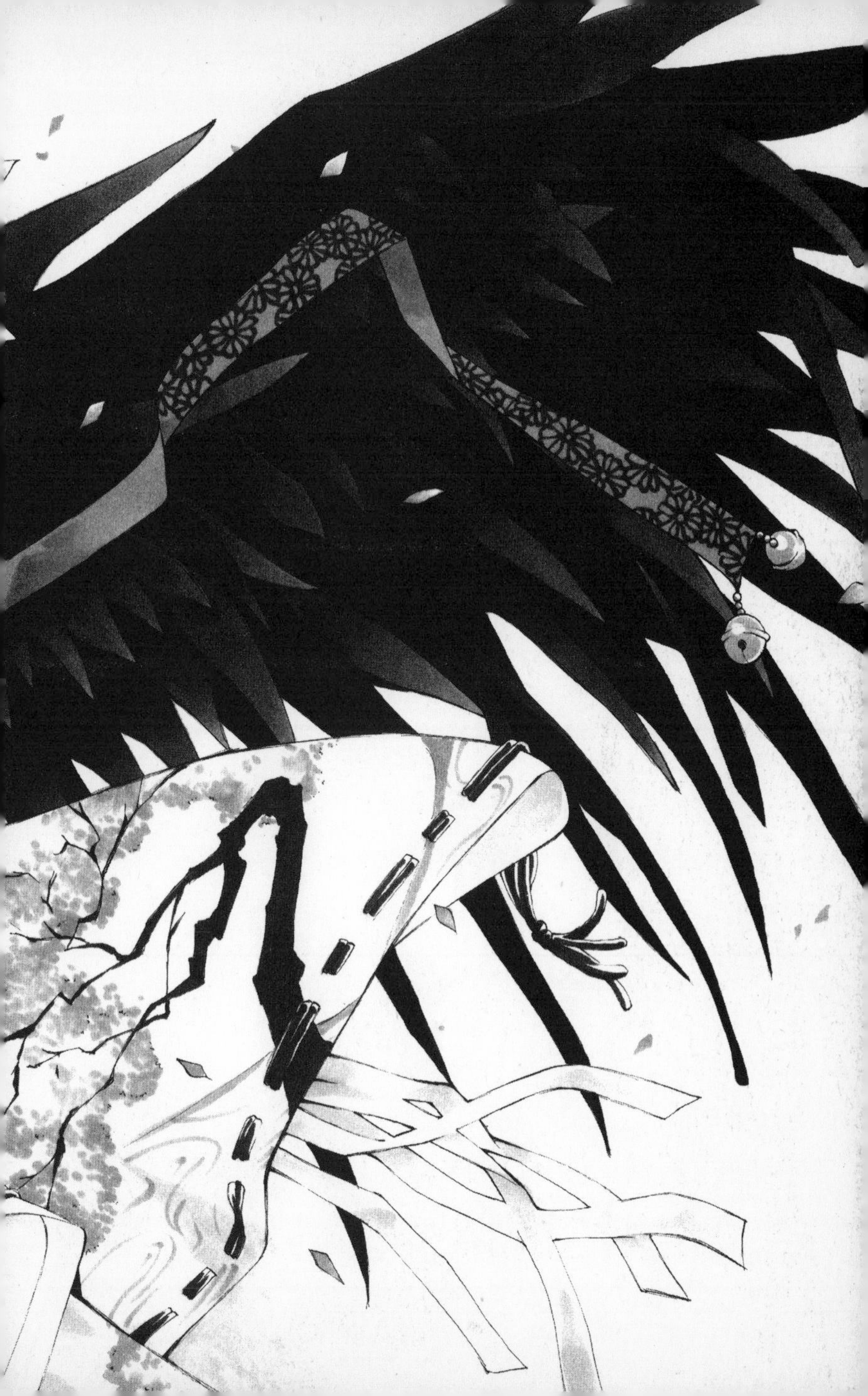

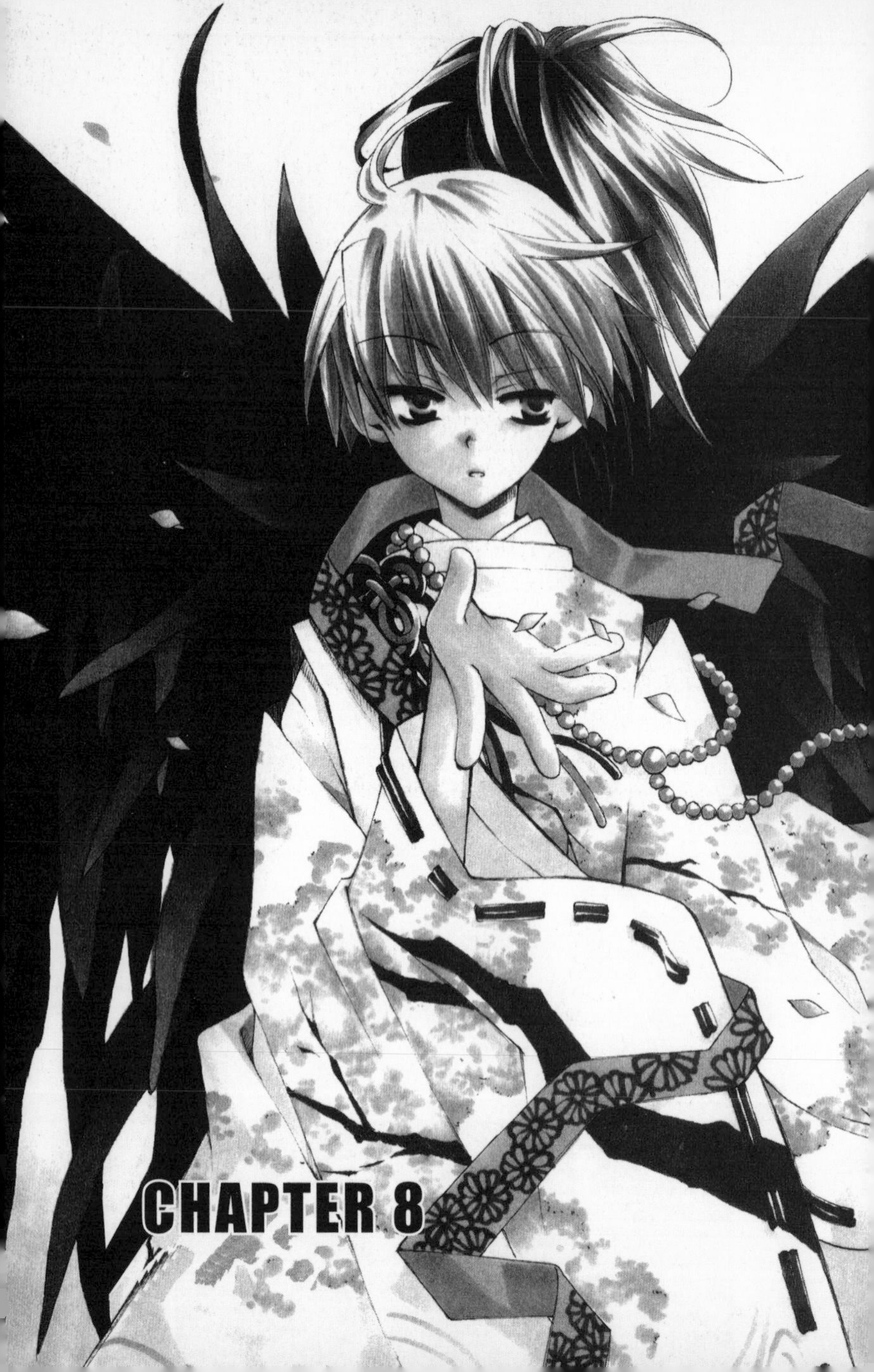
CHAPTER 8

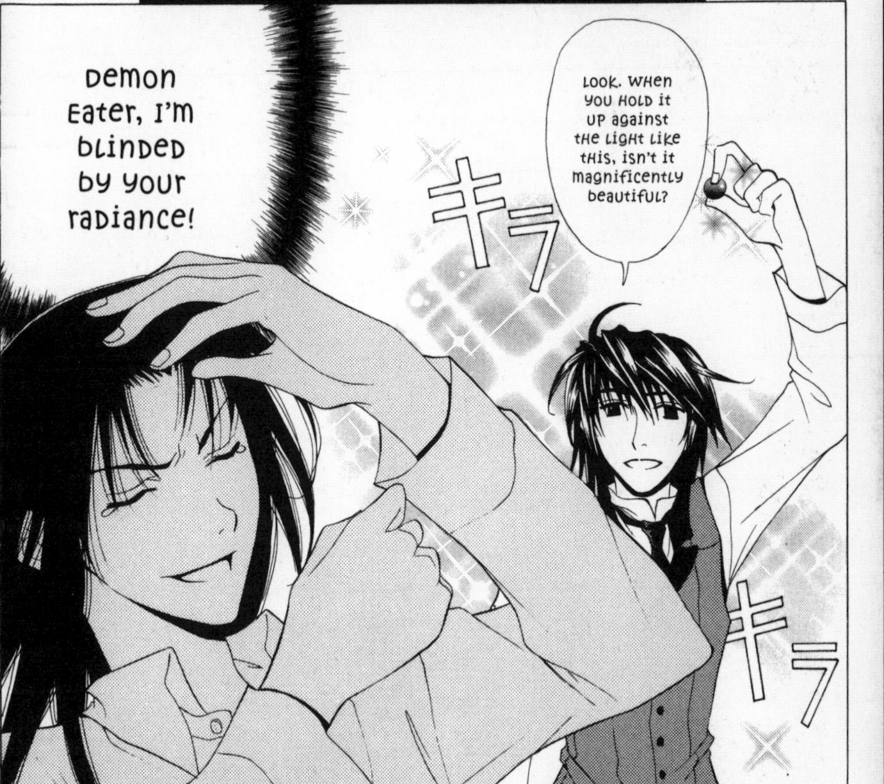
LOOK. WHEN YOU HOLD IT UP AGAINST THE LIGHT LIKE THIS, ISN'T IT MAGNIFICENTLY BEAUTIFUL?
キラ
キラ
Demon Eater, I'm blinded by your radiance!

tactics
3

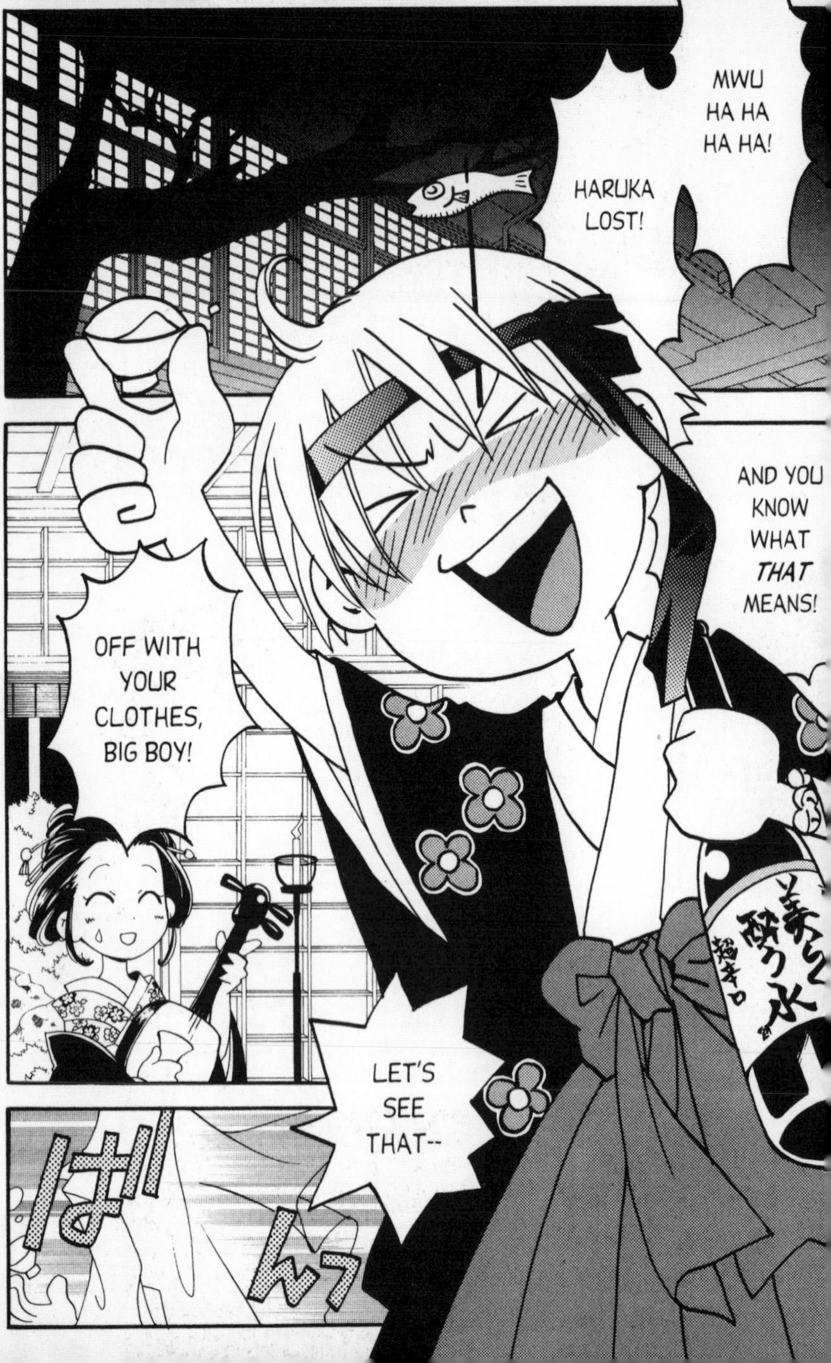
MWU HA HA HA HA!
HARUKA LOST!
AND YOU KNOW WHAT *THAT* MEANS!
OFF WITH YOUR CLOTHES, BIG BOY!
LET'S SEE THAT--
ぱんっ

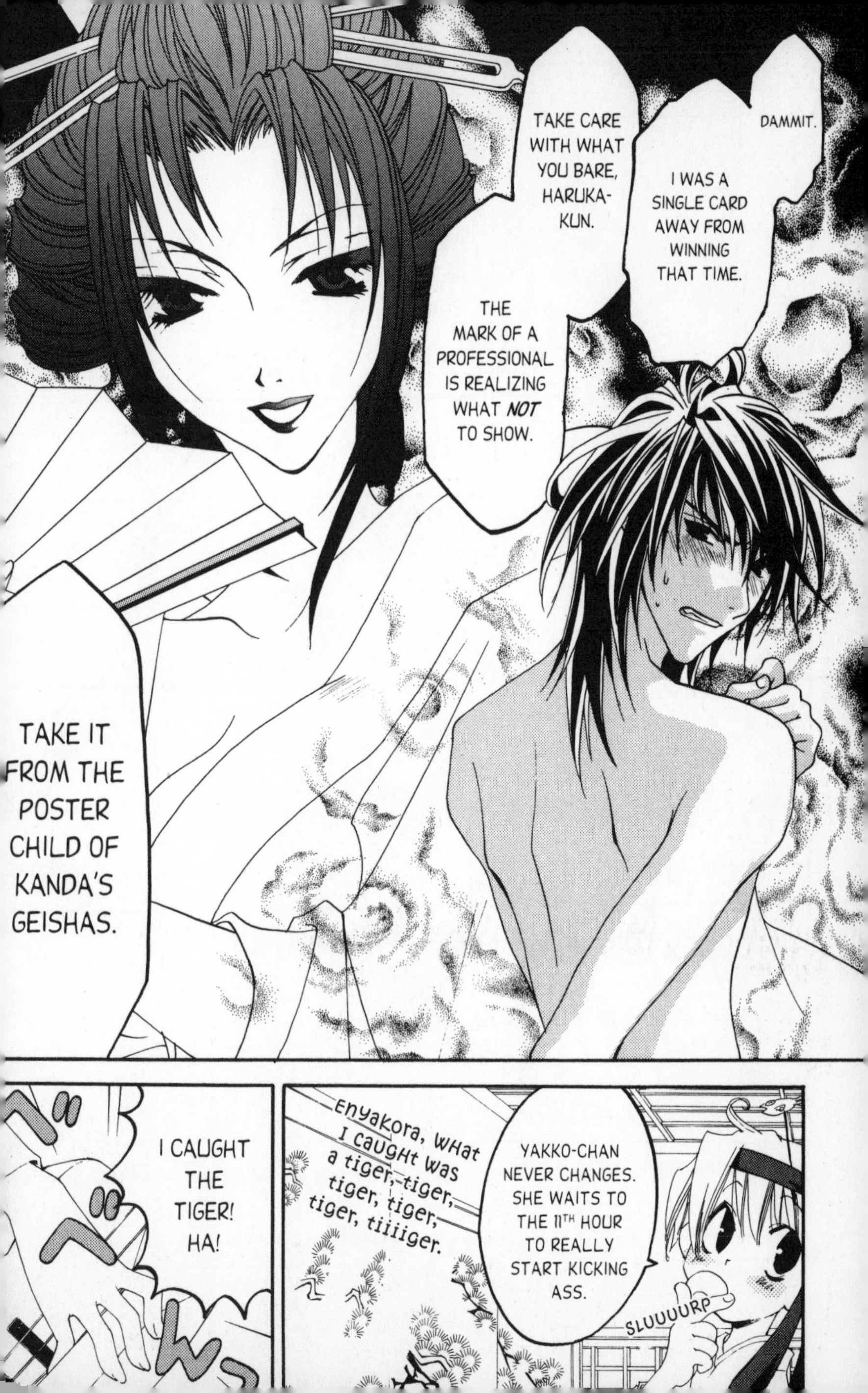
DAMMIT.
I WAS A SINGLE CARD AWAY FROM WINNING THAT TIME.
TAKE CARE WITH WHAT YOU BARE, HARUKA-KUN.
THE MARK OF A PROFESSIONAL IS REALIZING WHAT *NOT* TO SHOW.
TAKE IT FROM THE POSTER CHILD OF KANDA'S GEISHAS.
YAKKO-CHAN NEVER CHANGES. SHE WAITS TO THE 11TH HOUR TO REALLY START KICKING ASS.
SLUUUURP
Enyakora, what I caught was a tiger, tiger, tiger, tiger, tiger, tiiiiger.
I CAUGHT THE TIGER! HA!

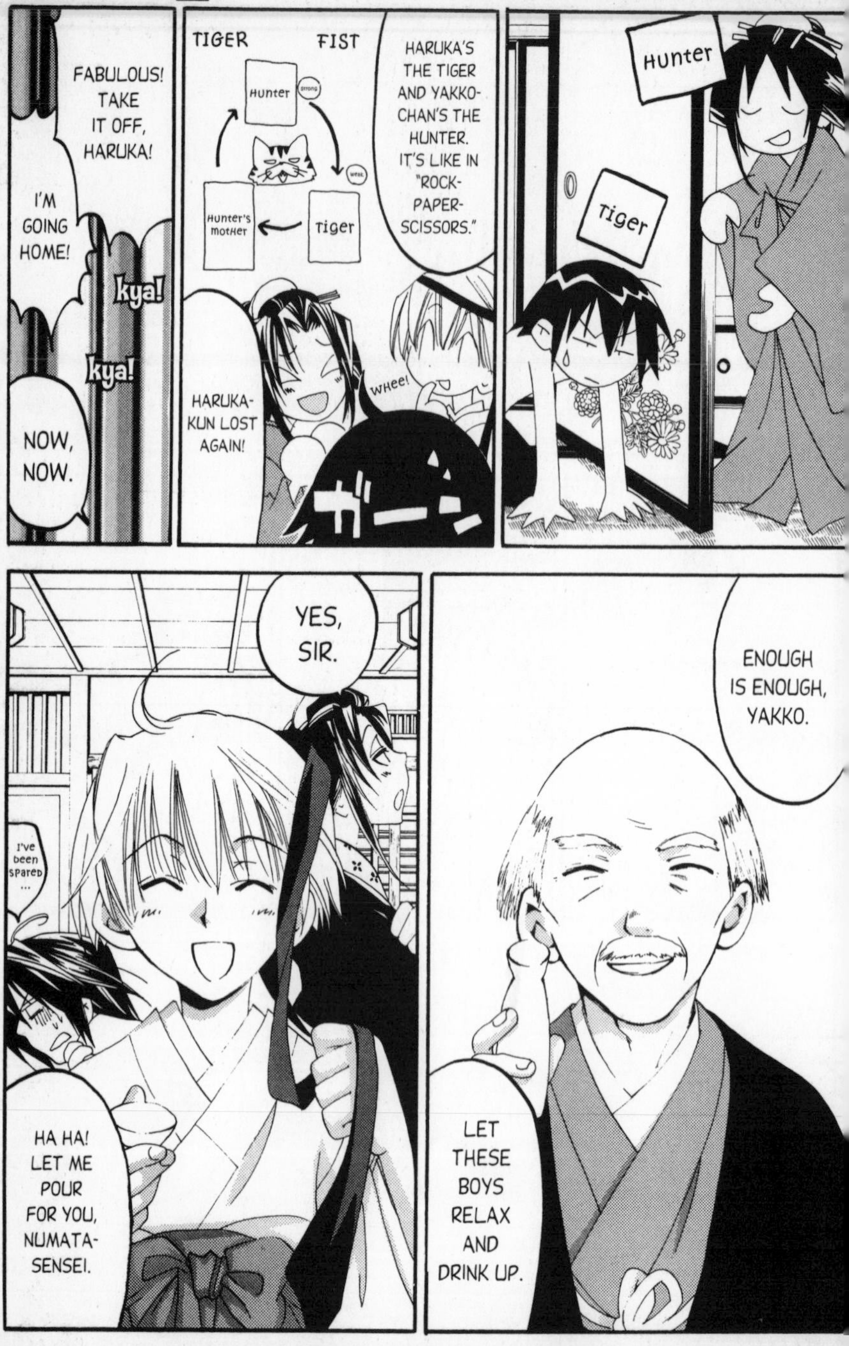
Hunter
Tiger
HARUKA'S THE TIGER AND YAKKO-CHAN'S THE HUNTER. IT'S LIKE IN "ROCK-PAPER-SCISSORS."
TIGER FIST
Hunter
strong
Hunter's mother
Tiger
weak
WHEE!
HARUKA-KUN LOST AGAIN!
FABULOUS! TAKE IT OFF, HARUKA!
I'M GOING HOME!
kya!
kya!
NOW, NOW.
ENOUGH IS ENOUGH, YAKKO.
LET THESE BOYS RELAX AND DRINK UP.
YES, SIR.
I've been spared...
HA HA! LET ME POUR FOR YOU, NUMATA-SENSEI.

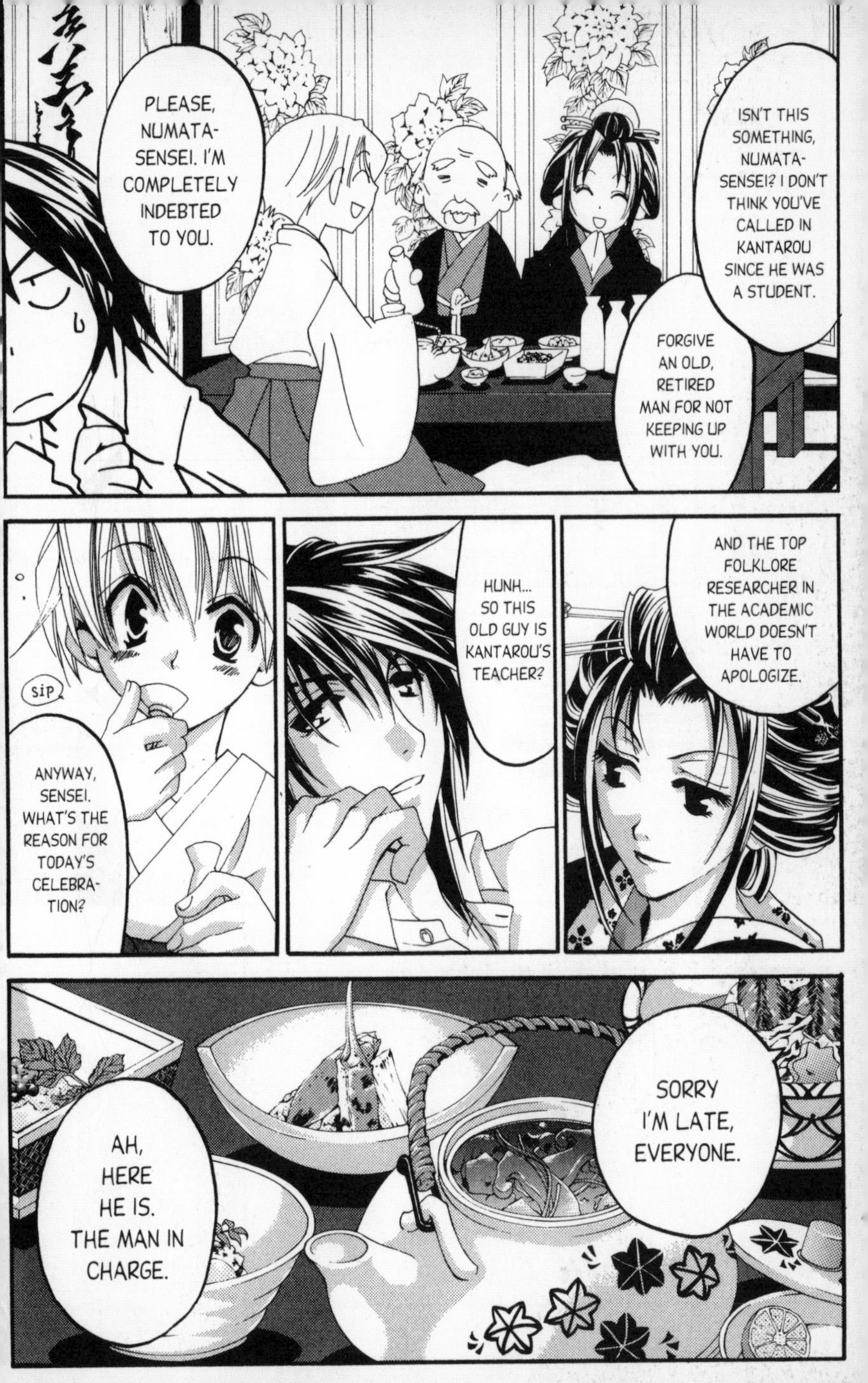
ISN'T THIS SOMETHING, NUMATA-SENSEI? I DON'T THINK YOU'VE CALLED IN KANTAROU SINCE HE WAS A STUDENT.
FORGIVE AN OLD, RETIRED MAN FOR NOT KEEPING UP WITH YOU.
PLEASE, NUMATA-SENSEI. I'M COMPLETELY INDEBTED TO YOU.
AND THE TOP FOLKLORE RESEARCHER IN THE ACADEMIC WORLD DOESN'T HAVE TO APOLOGIZE.
HUNH... SO THIS OLD GUY IS KANTAROU'S TEACHER?
sip
ANYWAY, SENSEI. WHAT'S THE REASON FOR TODAY'S CELEBRA-TION?
SORRY I'M LATE, EVERYONE.
AH, HERE HE IS. THE MAN IN CHARGE.

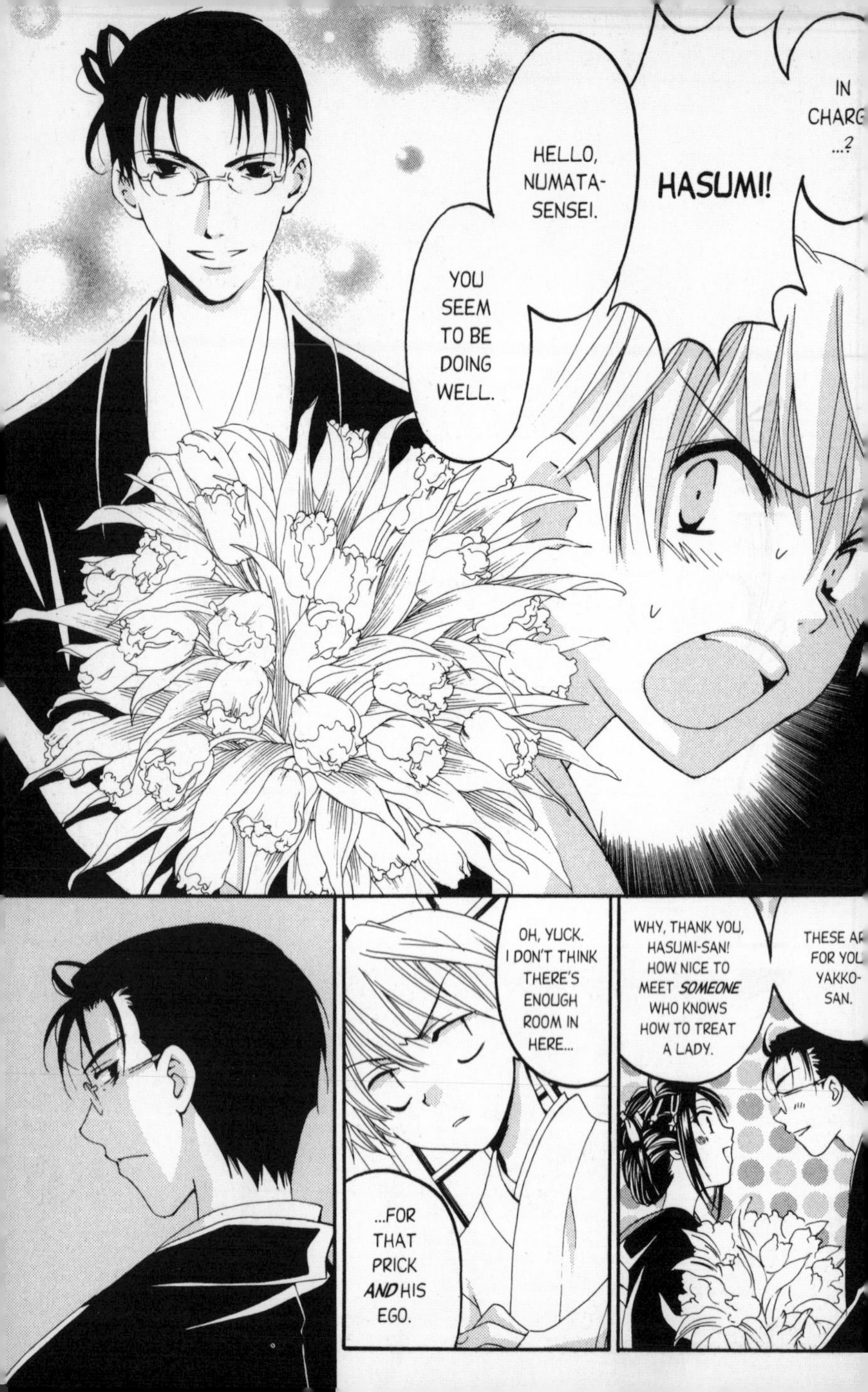
IN CHARG ...?
HASUMI!
HELLO, NUMATA-SENSEI.
YOU SEEM TO BE DOING WELL.
THESE AR FOR YOU YAKKO-SAN.
WHY, THANK YOU, HASUMI-SAN! HOW NICE TO MEET *SOMEONE* WHO KNOWS HOW TO TREAT A LADY.
OH, YUCK. I DON'T THINK THERE'S ENOUGH ROOM IN HERE...
...FOR THAT PRICK ***AND*** HIS EGO.

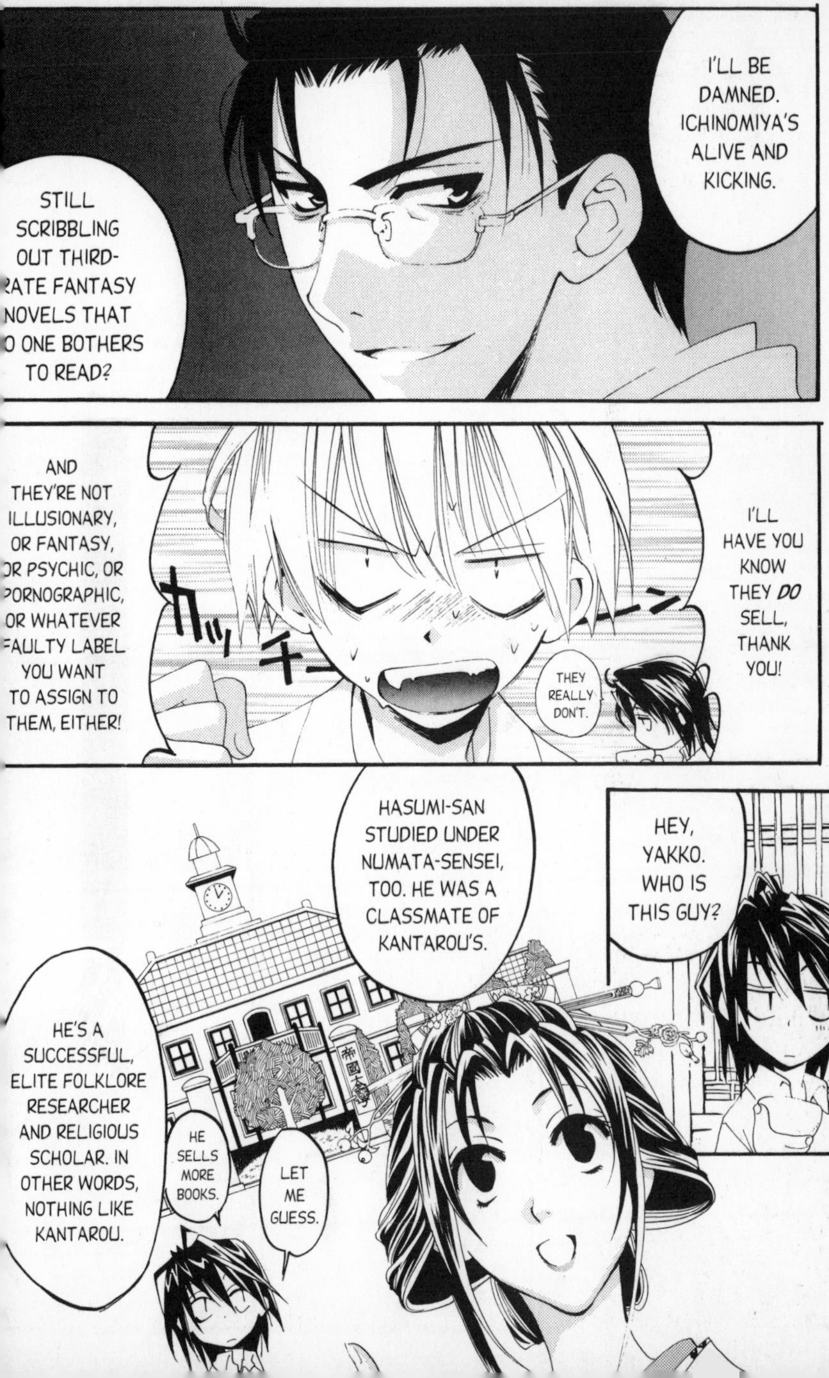
I'LL BE DAMNED. ICHINOMIYA'S ALIVE AND KICKING.
STILL SCRIBBLING OUT THIRD-RATE FANTASY NOVELS THAT NO ONE BOTHERS TO READ?
I'LL HAVE YOU KNOW THEY *DO* SELL, THANK YOU!
カッチーン
AND THEY'RE NOT ILLUSIONARY, OR FANTASY, OR PSYCHIC, OR PORNOGRAPHIC, OR WHATEVER FAULTY LABEL YOU WANT TO ASSIGN TO THEM, EITHER!
THEY REALLY DON'T.
HEY, YAKKO. WHO IS THIS GUY?
HASUMI-SAN STUDIED UNDER NUMATA-SENSEI, TOO. HE WAS A CLASSMATE OF KANTAROU'S.
HE'S A SUCCESSFUL, ELITE FOLKLORE RESEARCHER AND RELIGIOUS SCHOLAR. IN OTHER WORDS, NOTHING LIKE KANTAROU.
LET ME GUESS.
HE SELLS MORE BOOKS.

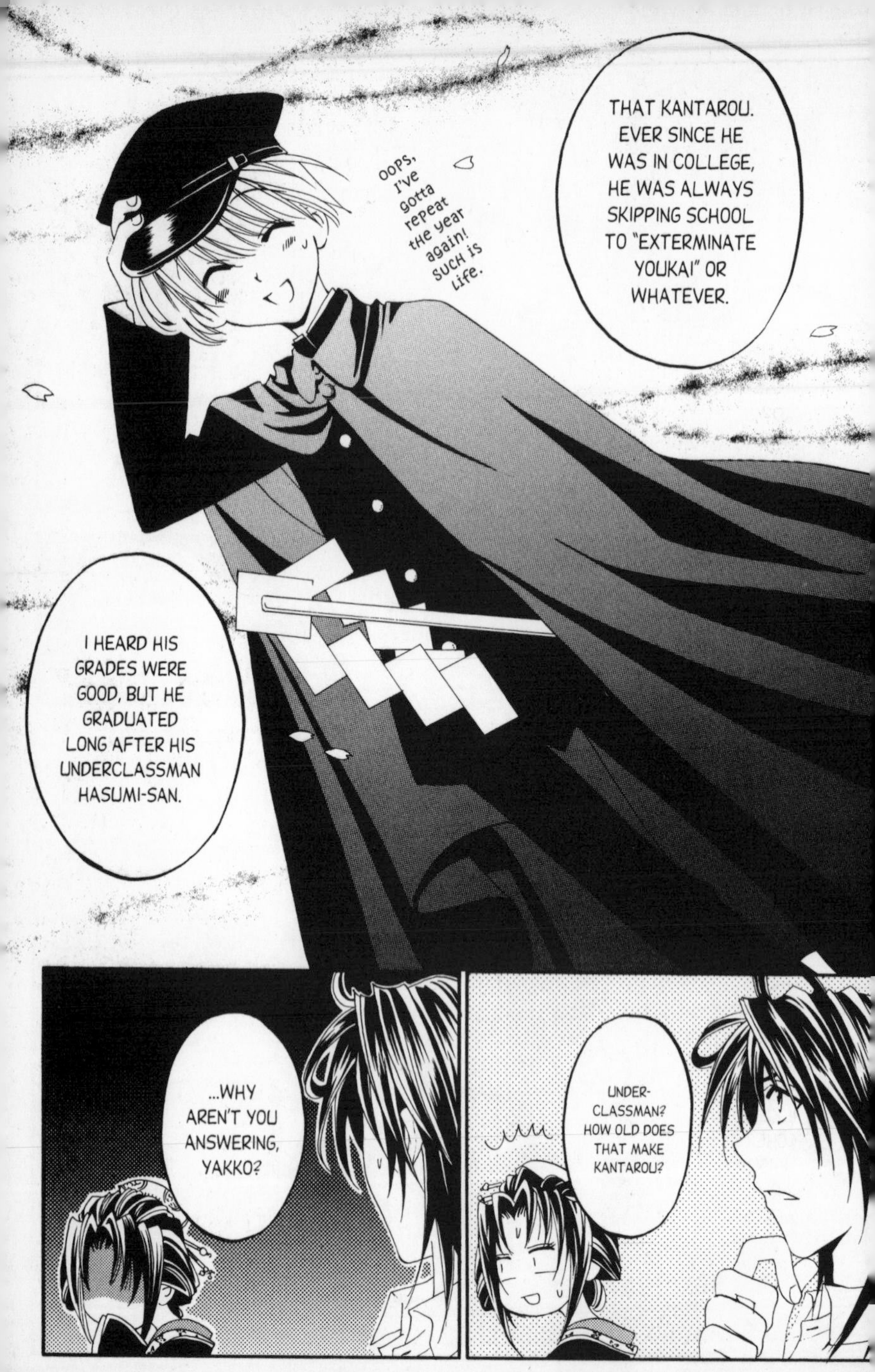
THAT KANTAROU. EVER SINCE HE WAS IN COLLEGE, HE WAS ALWAYS SKIPPING SCHOOL TO "EXTERMINATE YOUKAI" OR WHATEVER.
OOPS, I've gotta repeat the year again! SUCH is life.
I HEARD HIS GRADES WERE GOOD, BUT HE GRADUATED LONG AFTER HIS UNDERCLASSMAN HASUMI-SAN.
UNDER-CLASSMAN? HOW OLD DOES THAT MAKE KANTAROU?
...WHY AREN'T YOU ANSWERING, YAKKO?

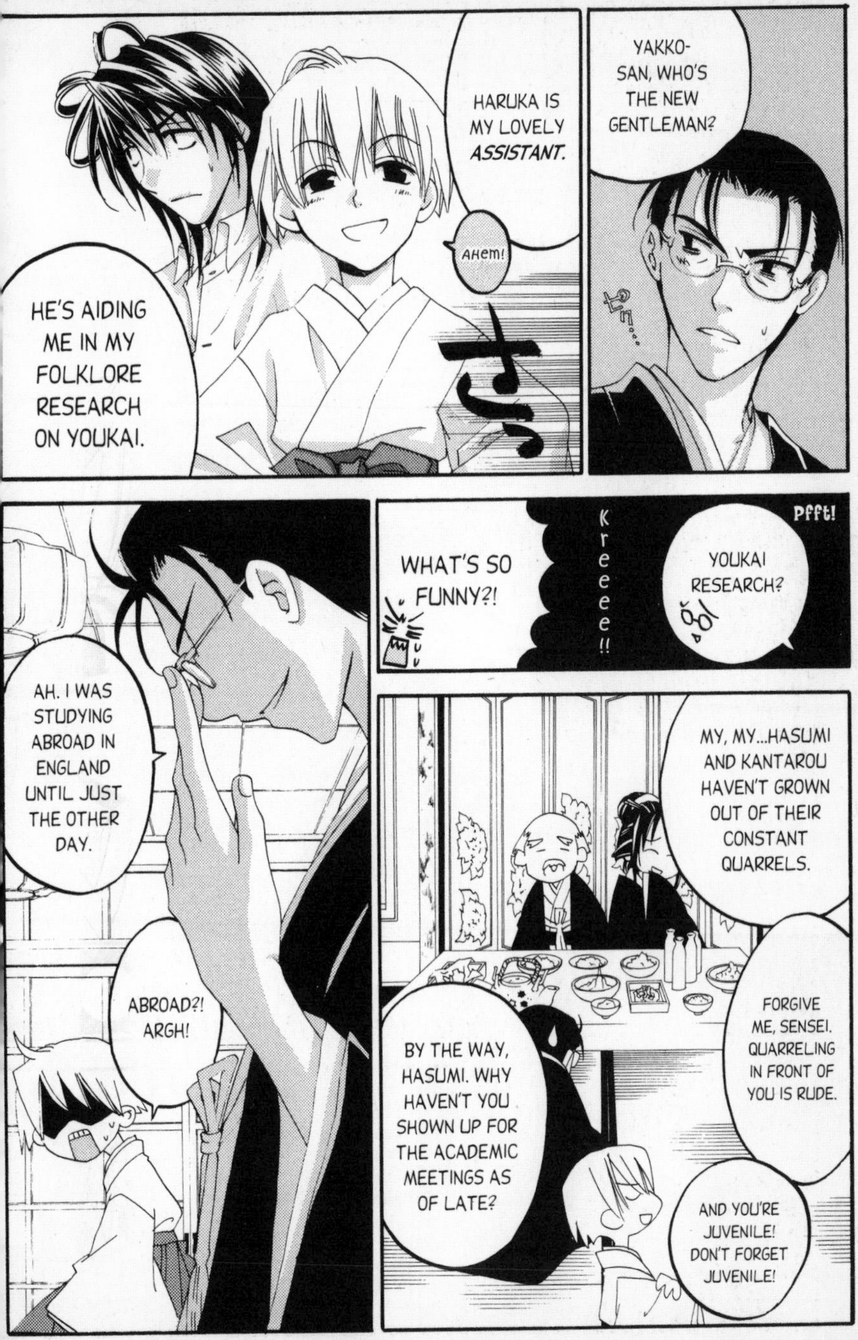
YAKKO-SAN, WHO'S THE NEW GENTLEMAN?
HARUKA IS MY LOVELY *ASSISTANT.*
AHEM!
HE'S AIDING ME IN MY FOLKLORE RESEARCH ON YOUKAI.
Pfft!
YOUKAI RESEARCH?
Kreeee!!
WHAT'S SO FUNNY?!
MY, MY...HASUMI AND KANTAROU HAVEN'T GROWN OUT OF THEIR CONSTANT QUARRELS.
FORGIVE ME, SENSEI. QUARRELING IN FRONT OF YOU IS RUDE.
AND YOU'RE JUVENILE! DON'T FORGET JUVENILE!
BY THE WAY, HASUMI. WHY HAVEN'T YOU SHOWN UP FOR THE ACADEMIC MEETINGS AS OF LATE?
AH. I WAS STUDYING ABROAD IN ENGLAND UNTIL JUST THE OTHER DAY.
ABROAD?! ARGH!

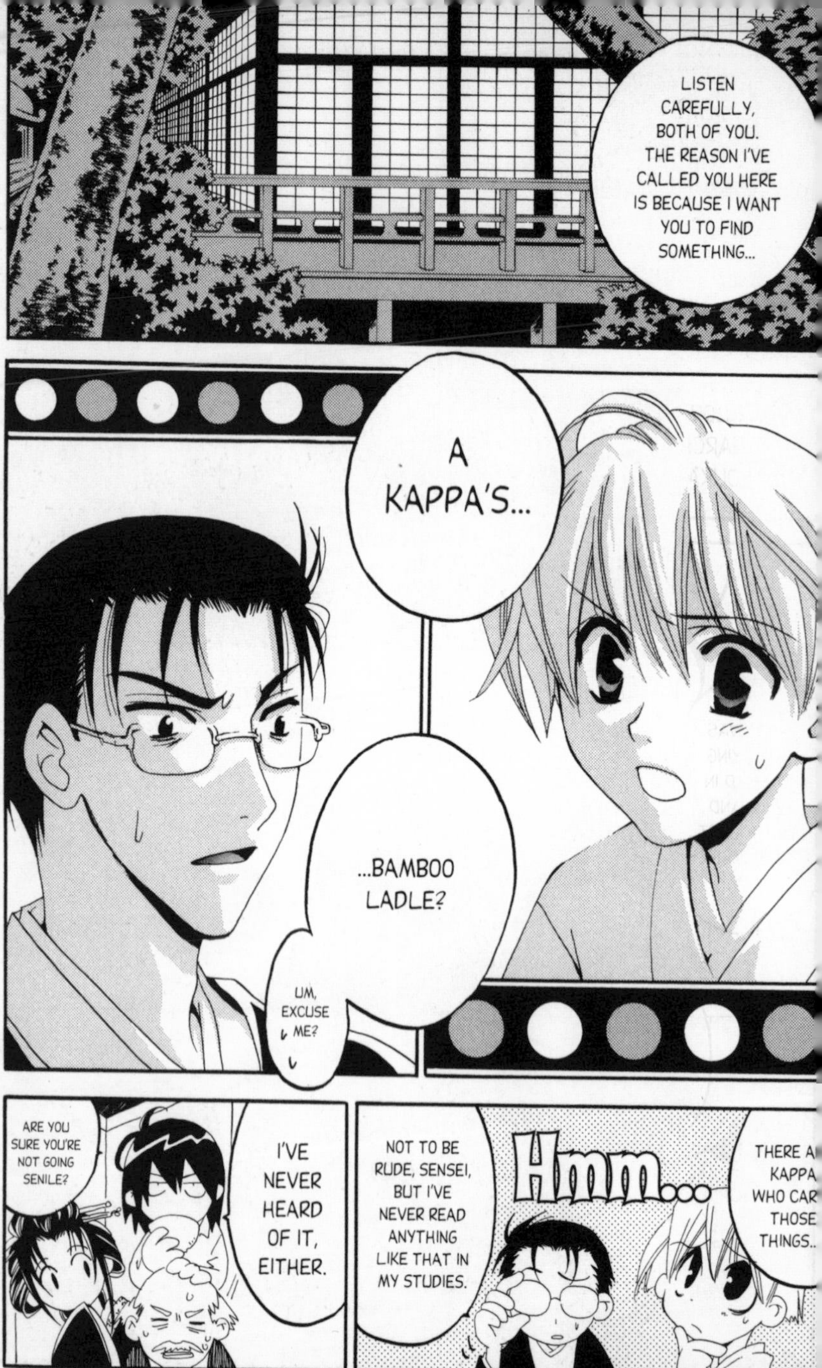
LISTEN CAREFULLY, BOTH OF YOU. THE REASON I'VE CALLED YOU HERE IS BECAUSE I WANT YOU TO FIND SOMETHING...
A KAPPA'S...
...BAMBOO LADLE?
UM, EXCUSE ME?
Hmm...
NOT TO BE RUDE, SENSEI, BUT I'VE NEVER READ ANYTHING LIKE THAT IN MY STUDIES.
I'VE NEVER HEARD OF IT, EITHER.
ARE YOU SURE YOU'RE NOT GOING SENILE?

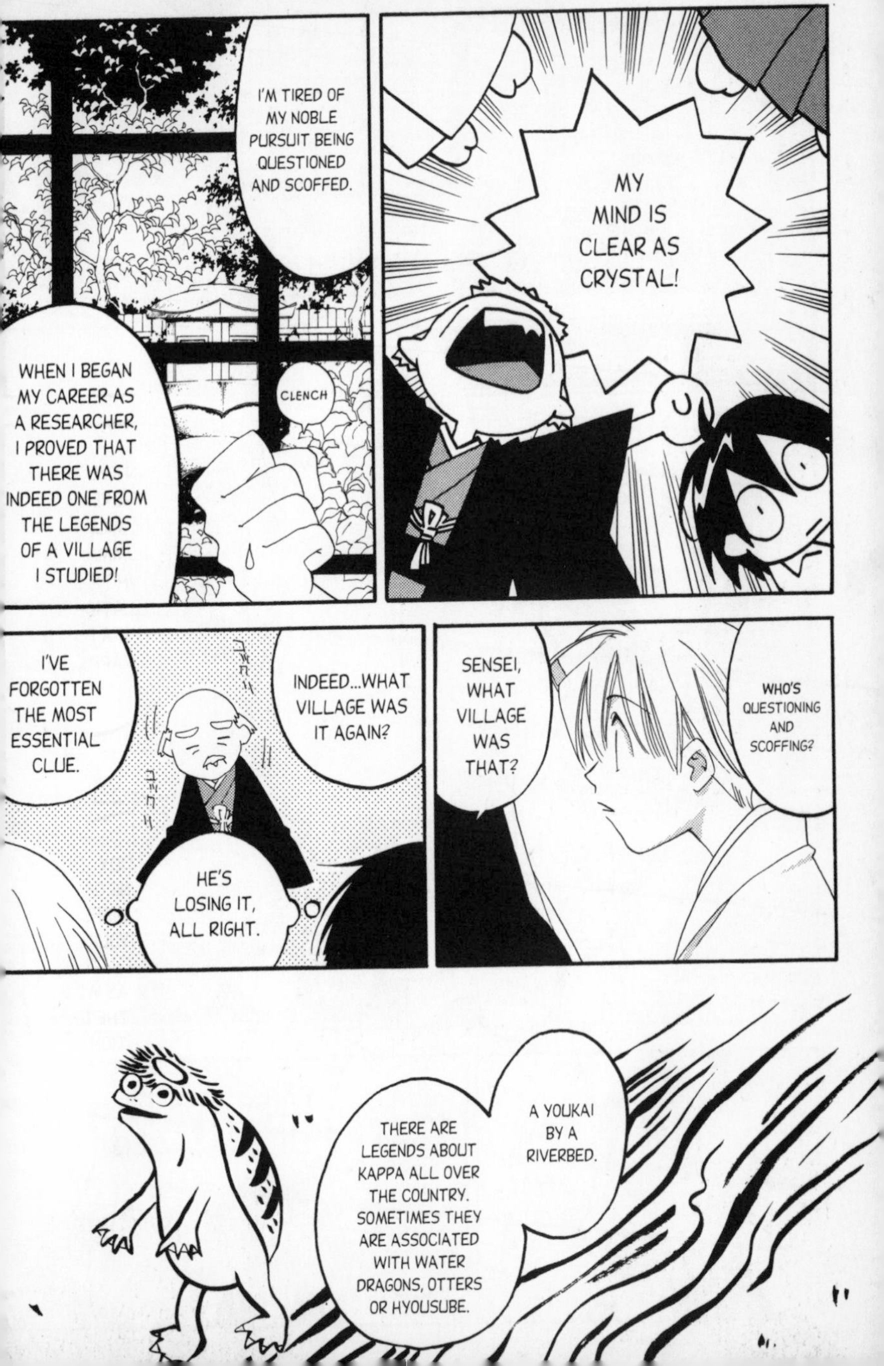
MY MIND IS CLEAR AS CRYSTAL!
I'M TIRED OF MY NOBLE PURSUIT BEING QUESTIONED AND SCOFFED.
CLENCH
WHEN I BEGAN MY CAREER AS A RESEARCHER, I PROVED THAT THERE WAS INDEED ONE FROM THE LEGENDS OF A VILLAGE I STUDIED!
WHO'S QUESTIONING AND SCOFFING?
SENSEI, WHAT VILLAGE WAS THAT?
INDEED...WHAT VILLAGE WAS IT AGAIN?
I'VE FORGOTTEN THE MOST ESSENTIAL CLUE.
HE'S LOSING IT, ALL RIGHT.
A YOUKAI BY A RIVERBED.
THERE ARE LEGENDS ABOUT KAPPA ALL OVER THE COUNTRY. SOMETIMES THEY ARE ASSOCIATED WITH WATER DRAGONS, OTTERS OR HYOUSUBE.

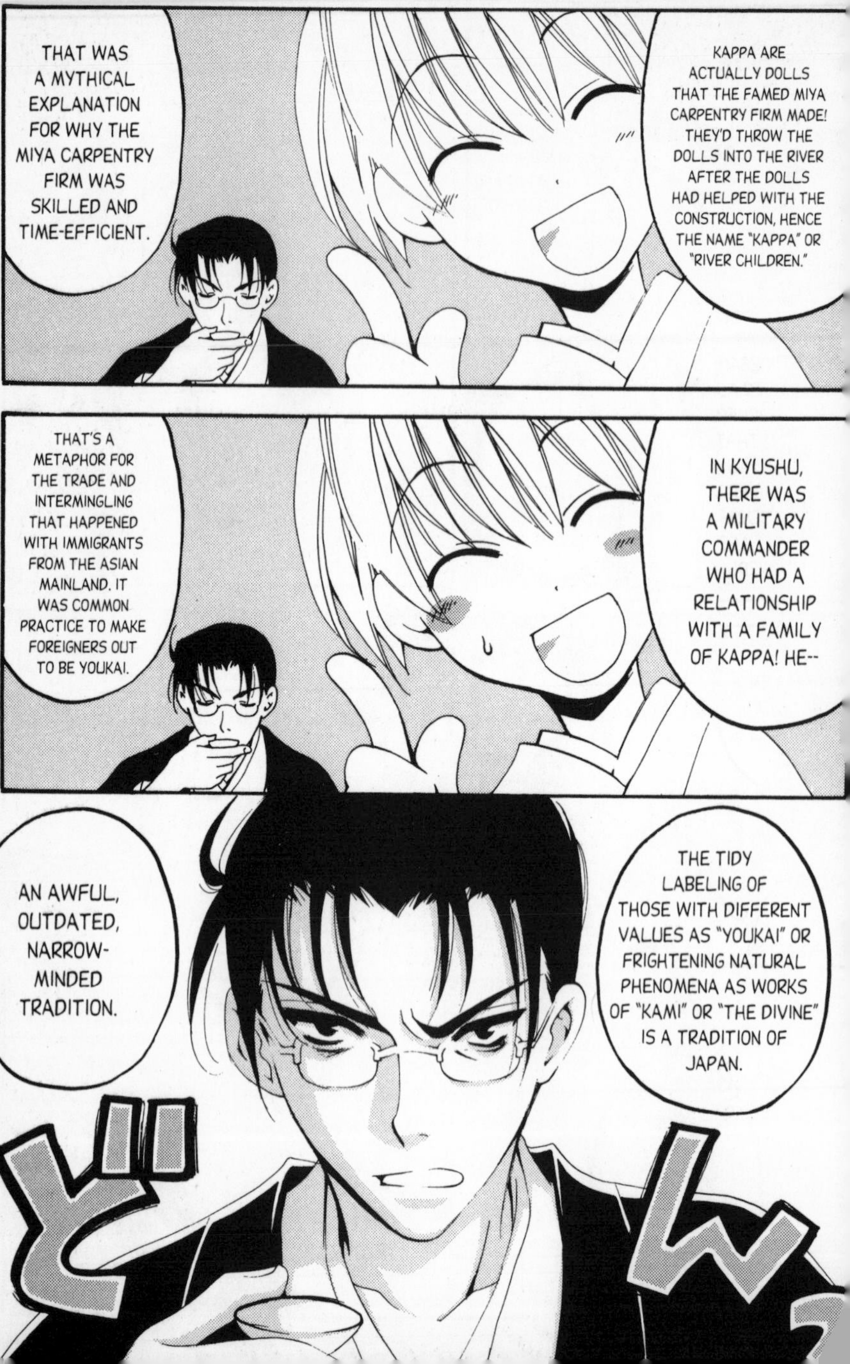
KAPPA ARE ACTUALLY DOLLS THAT THE FAMED MIYA CARPENTRY FIRM MADE! THEY'D THROW THE DOLLS INTO THE RIVER AFTER THE DOLLS HAD HELPED WITH THE CONSTRUCTION, HENCE THE NAME "KAPPA" OR "RIVER CHILDREN."
THAT WAS A MYTHICAL EXPLANATION FOR WHY THE MIYA CARPENTRY FIRM WAS SKILLED AND TIME-EFFICIENT.
IN KYUSHU, THERE WAS A MILITARY COMMANDER WHO HAD A RELATIONSHIP WITH A FAMILY OF KAPPA! HE--
THAT'S A METAPHOR FOR THE TRADE AND INTERMINGLING THAT HAPPENED WITH IMMIGRANTS FROM THE ASIAN MAINLAND. IT WAS COMMON PRACTICE TO MAKE FOREIGNERS OUT TO BE YOUKAI.
THE TIDY LABELING OF THOSE WITH DIFFERENT VALUES AS "YOUKAI" OR FRIGHTENING NATURAL PHENOMENA AS WORKS OF "KAMI" OR "THE DIVINE" IS A TRADITION OF JAPAN.
AN AWFUL, OUTDATED, NARROW-MINDED TRADITION.

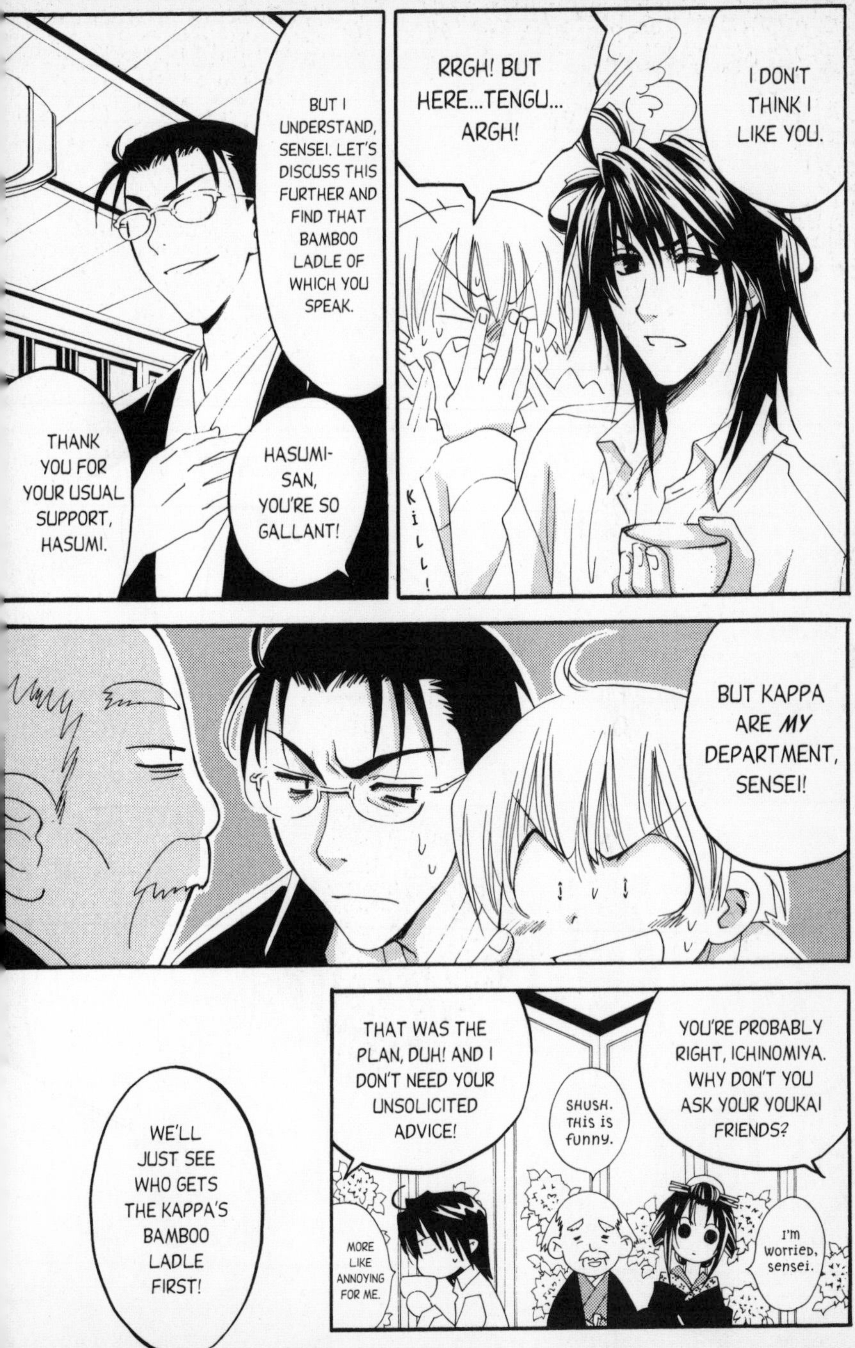
I DON'T THINK I LIKE YOU.
RRGH! BUT HERE...TENGU... ARGH!
KILL!
BUT I UNDERSTAND, SENSEI. LET'S DISCUSS THIS FURTHER AND FIND THAT BAMBOO LADLE OF WHICH YOU SPEAK.
HASUMI-SAN, YOU'RE SO GALLANT!
THANK YOU FOR YOUR USUAL SUPPORT, HASUMI.
BUT KAPPA ARE *MY* DEPARTMENT, SENSEI!
YOU'RE PROBABLY RIGHT, ICHINOMIYA. WHY DON'T YOU ASK YOUR YOUKAI FRIENDS?
SHUSH. This is funny.
THAT WAS THE PLAN, DUH! AND I DON'T NEED YOUR UNSOLICITED ADVICE!
I'm worried, sensei.
MORE LIKE ANNOYING FOR ME.
WE'LL JUST SEE WHO GETS THE KAPPA'S BAMBOO LADLE FIRST!

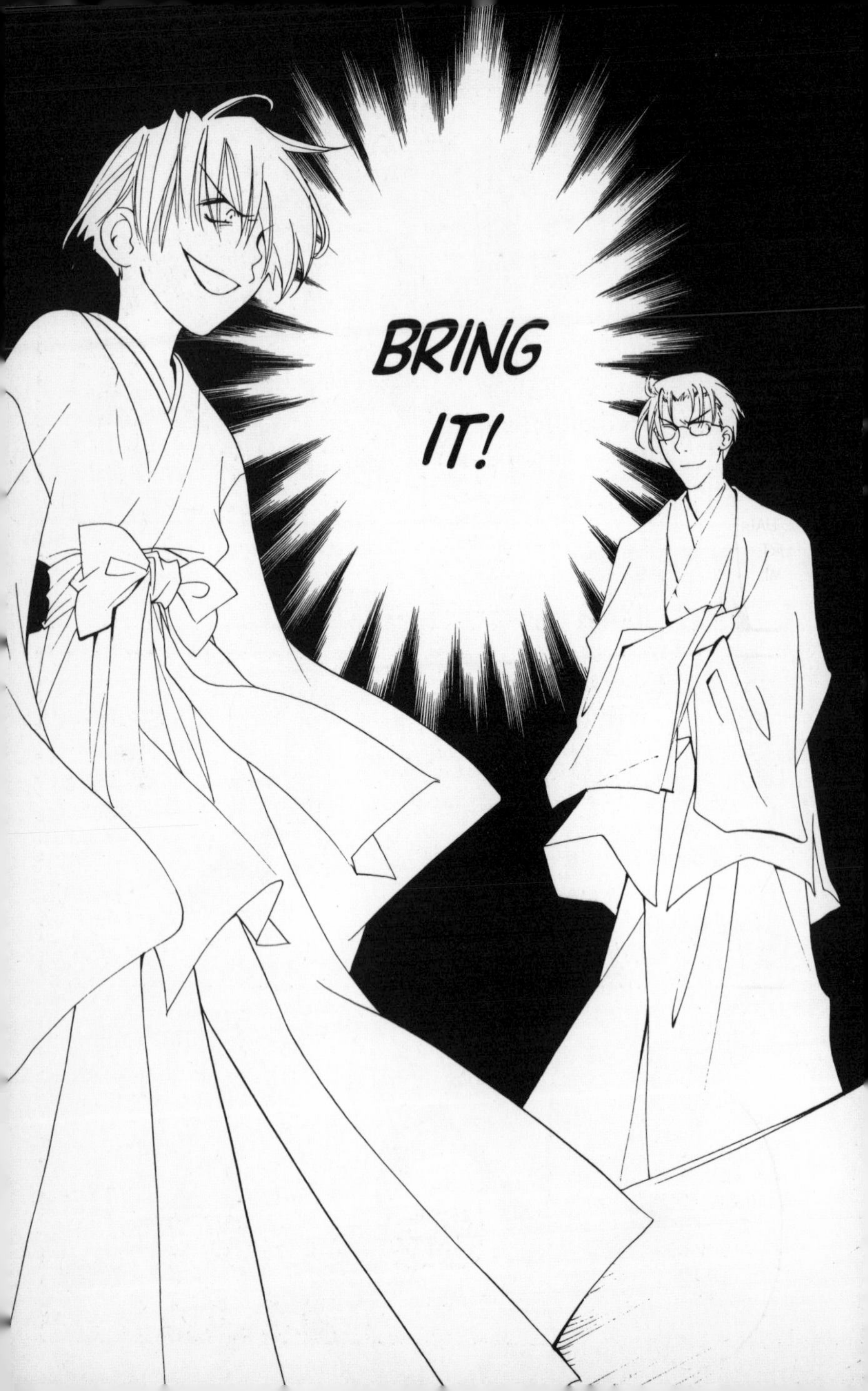
BRING IT!

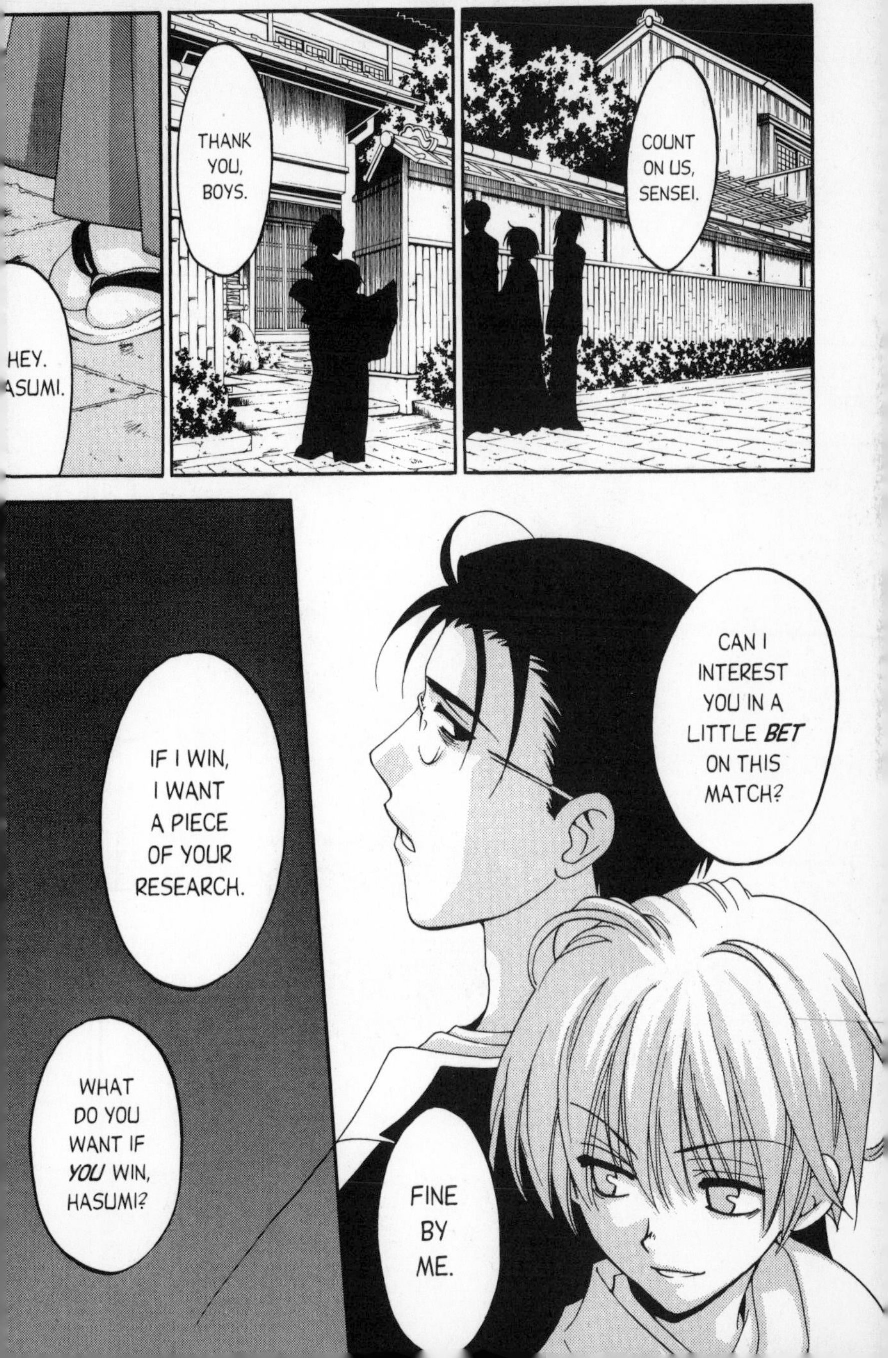
COUNT ON US, SENSEI.
THANK YOU, BOYS.
HEY. ASUMI.
CAN I INTEREST YOU IN A LITTLE *BET* ON THIS MATCH?
IF I WIN, I WANT A PIECE OF YOUR RESEARCH.
FINE BY ME.
WHAT DO YOU WANT IF *YOU* WIN, HASUMI?

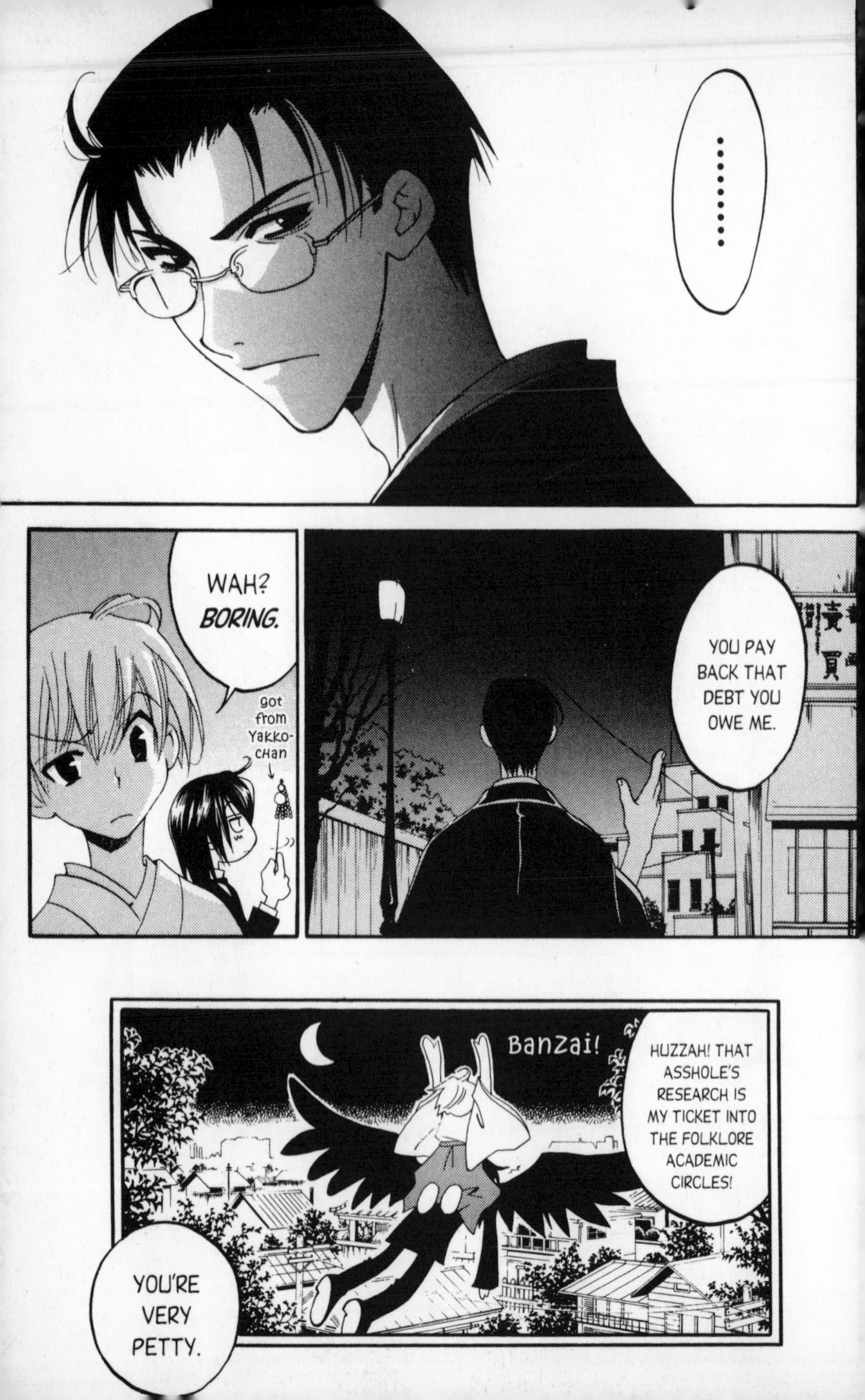
……
YOU PAY BACK THAT DEBT YOU OWE ME.
WAH? *BORING.*
got from Yakko-chan
HUZZAH! THAT ASSHOLE'S RESEARCH IS MY TICKET INTO THE FOLKLORE ACADEMIC CIRCLES!
Banzai!
YOU'RE VERY PETTY.

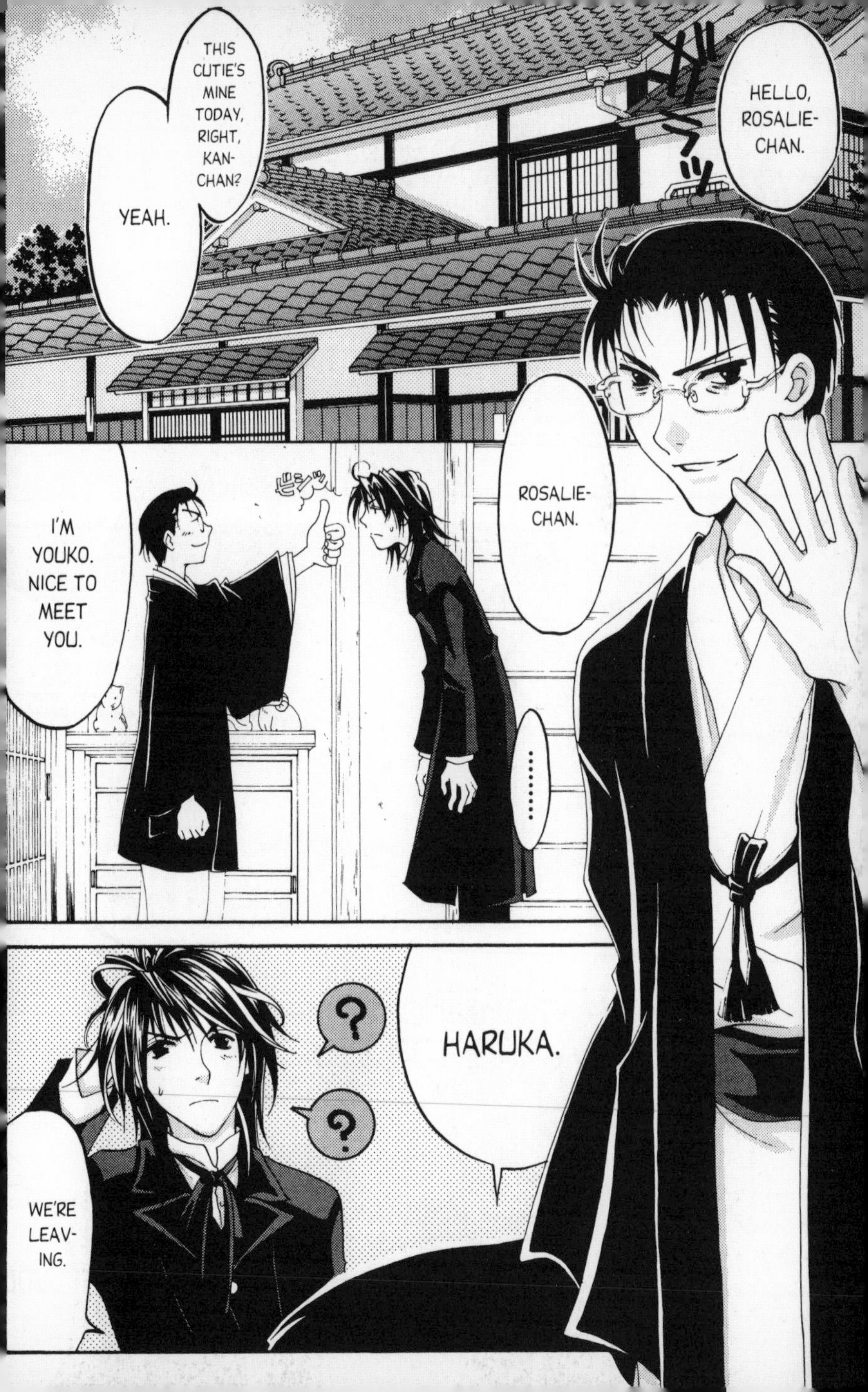
HELLO, ROSALIE-CHAN.
THIS CUTIE'S MINE TODAY, RIGHT, KAN-CHAN?
YEAH.
ROSALIE-CHAN.
....
ビシッ
I'M YOUKO. NICE TO MEET YOU.
HARUKA.
?
?
WE'RE LEAVING.

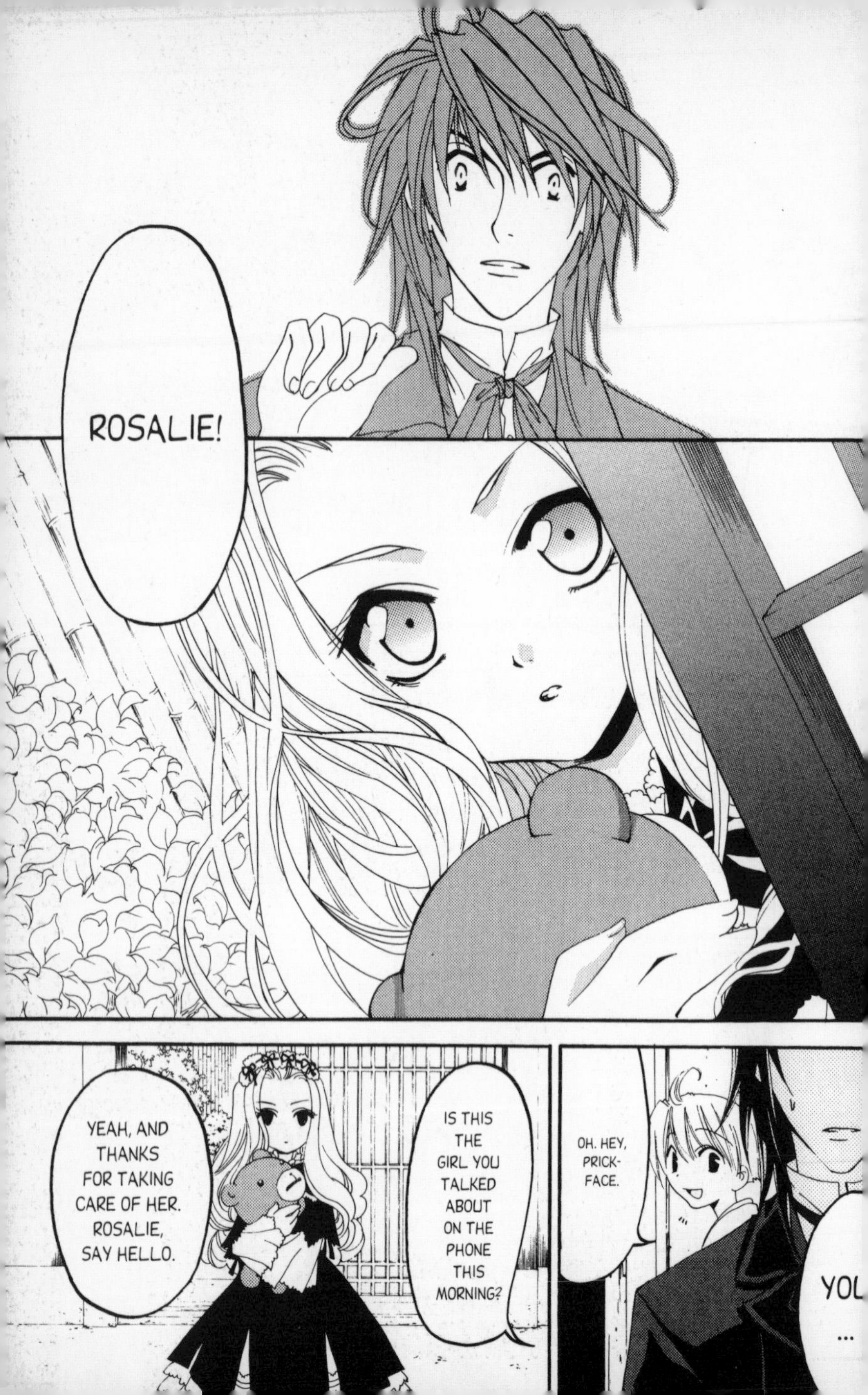
ROSALIE!
OH. HEY, PRICK-FACE.
YOU ...
IS THIS THE GIRL YOU TALKED ABOUT ON THE PHONE THIS MORNING?
YEAH, AND THANKS FOR TAKING CARE OF HER. ROSALIE, SAY HELLO.

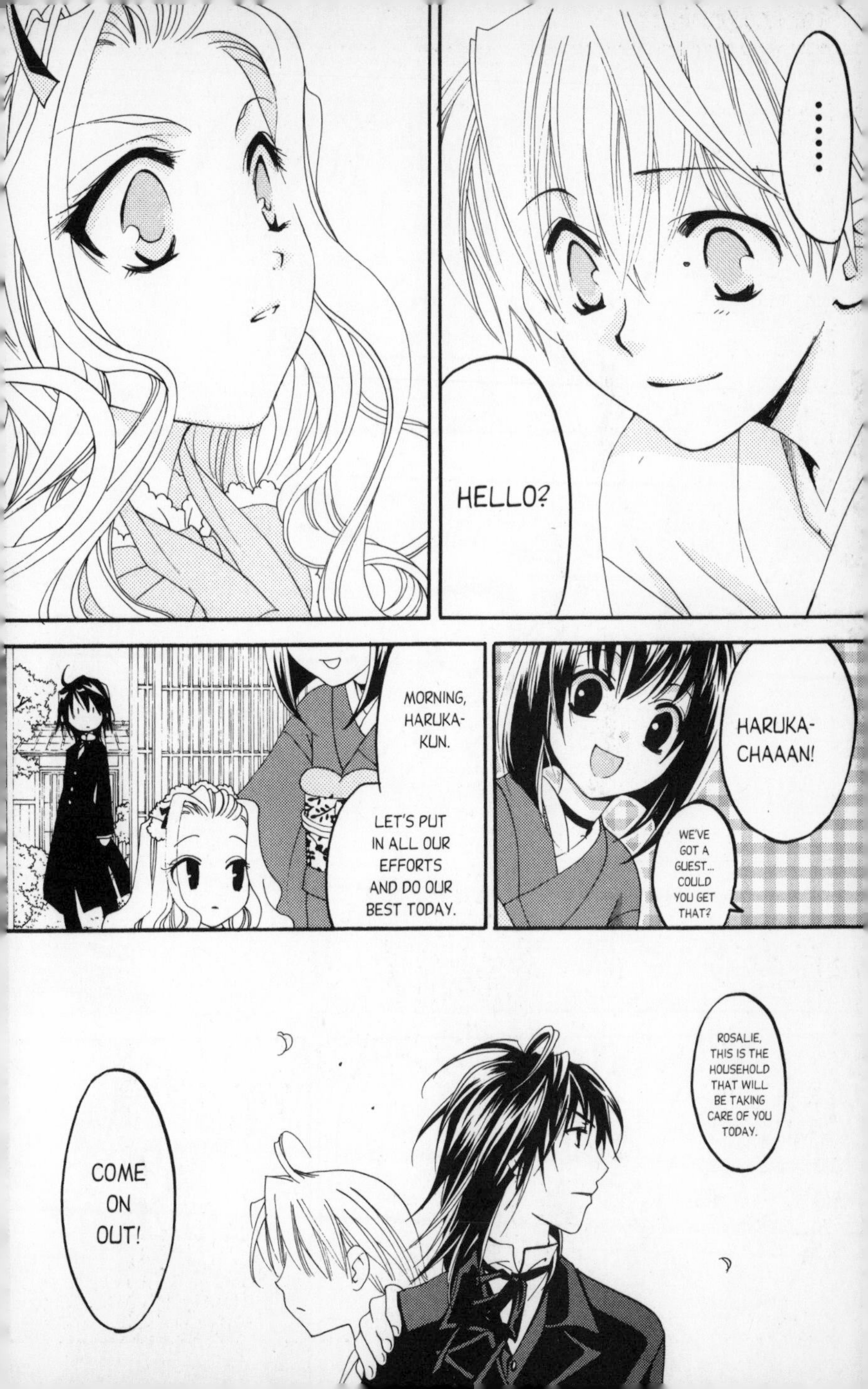
......
HELLO?
HARUKA-CHAAAN!
WE'VE GOT A GUEST... COULD YOU GET THAT?
MORNING, HARUKA-KUN.
LET'S PUT IN ALL OUR EFFORTS AND DO OUR BEST TODAY.
ROSALIE, THIS IS THE HOUSEHOLD THAT WILL BE TAKING CARE OF YOU TODAY.
COME ON OUT!

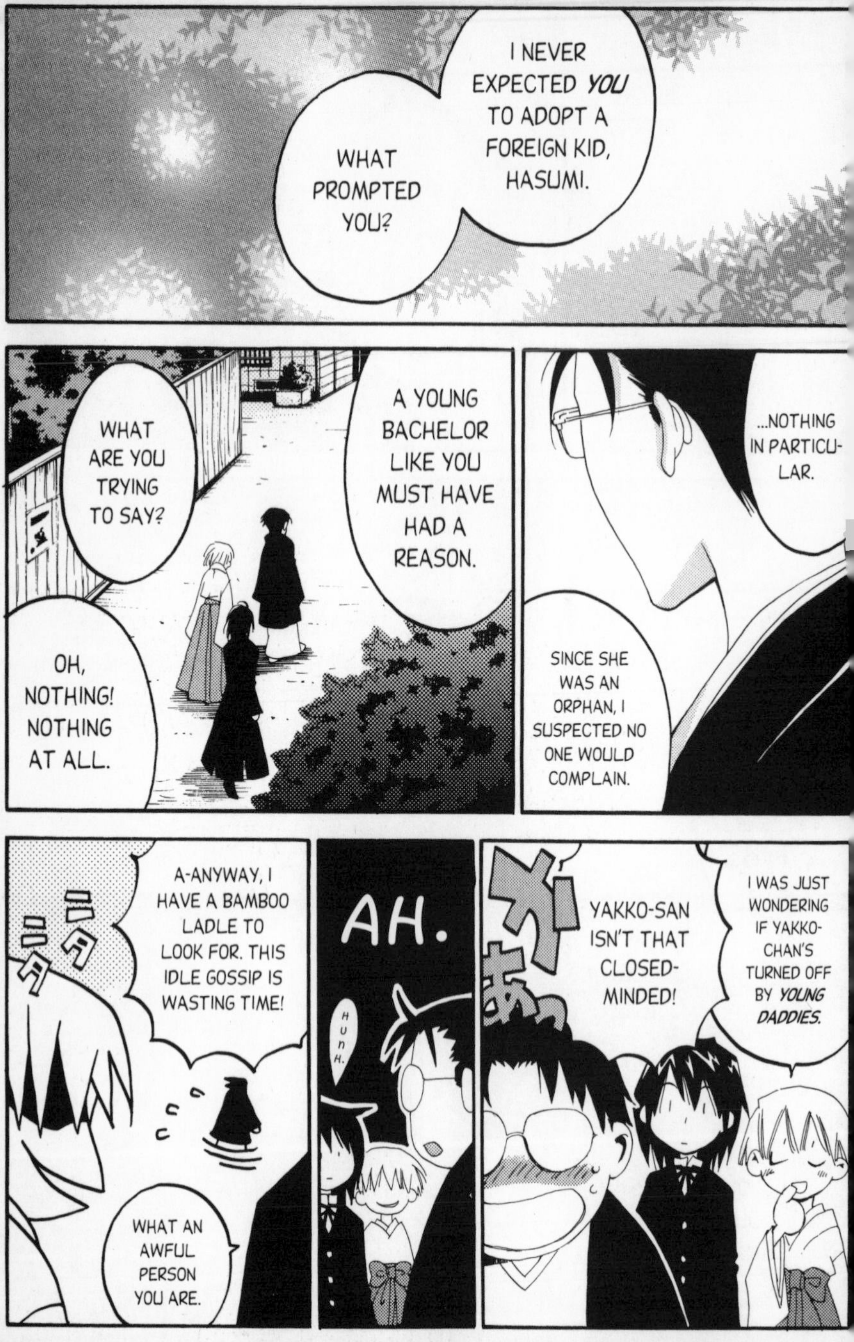
I NEVER EXPECTED *YOU* TO ADOPT A FOREIGN KID, HASUMI.
WHAT PROMPTED YOU?
...NOTHING IN PARTICULAR.
SINCE SHE WAS AN ORPHAN, I SUSPECTED NO ONE WOULD COMPLAIN.
A YOUNG BACHELOR LIKE YOU MUST HAVE HAD A REASON.
WHAT ARE YOU TRYING TO SAY?
OH, NOTHING! NOTHING AT ALL.
...
I WAS JUST WONDERING IF YAKKO-CHAN'S TURNED OFF BY *YOUNG DADDIES.*
YAKKO-SAN ISN'T THAT CLOSED-MINDED!
AH.
HUNH.
A-ANYWAY, I HAVE A BAMBOO LADLE TO LOOK FOR. THIS IDLE GOSSIP IS WASTING TIME!
WHAT AN AWFUL PERSON YOU ARE.

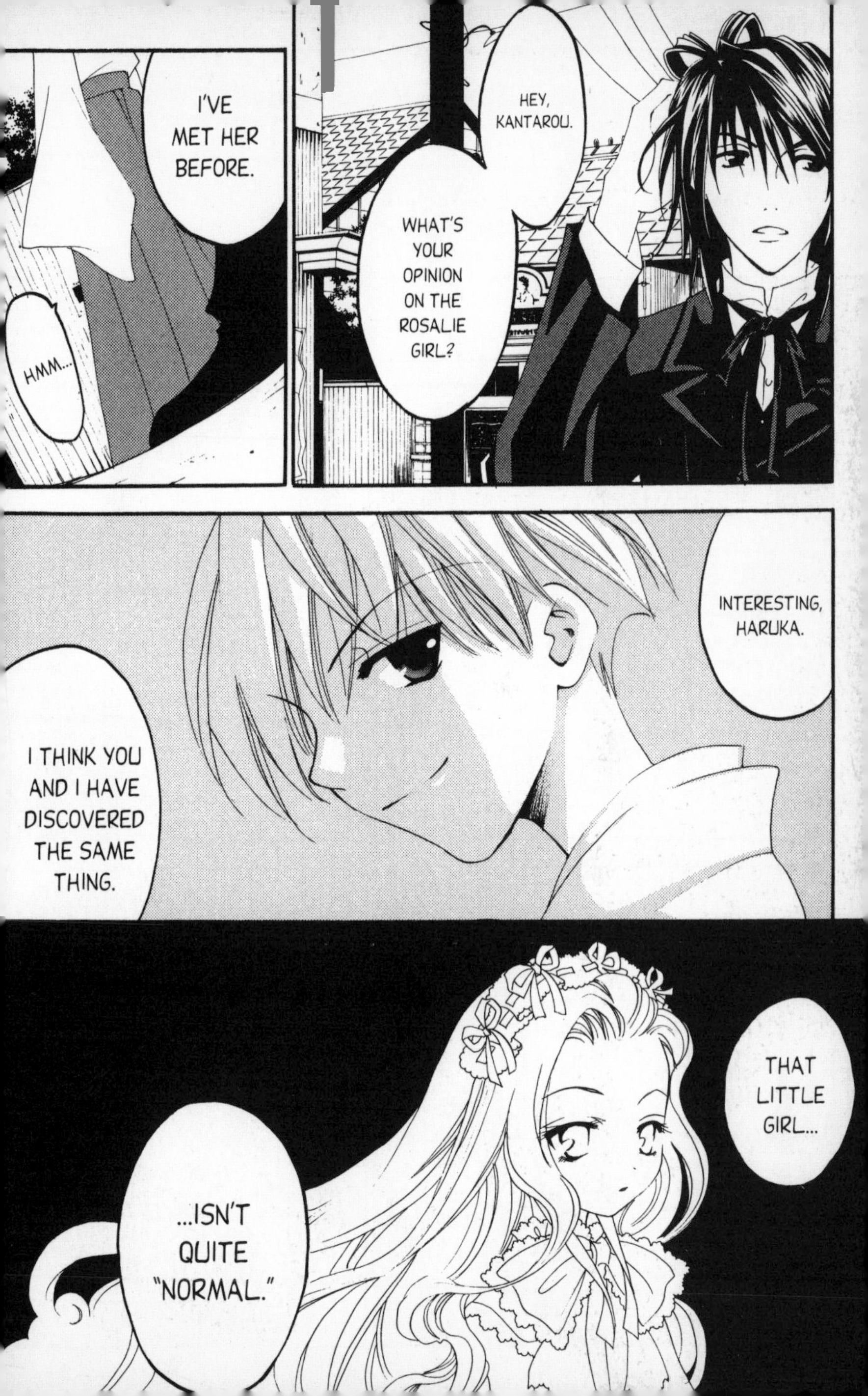
HEY, KANTAROU.
WHAT'S YOUR OPINION ON THE ROSALIE GIRL?
I'VE MET HER BEFORE.
HMM...
INTERESTING, HARUKA.
I THINK YOU AND I HAVE DISCOVERED THE SAME THING.
THAT LITTLE GIRL...
...ISN'T QUITE "NORMAL."

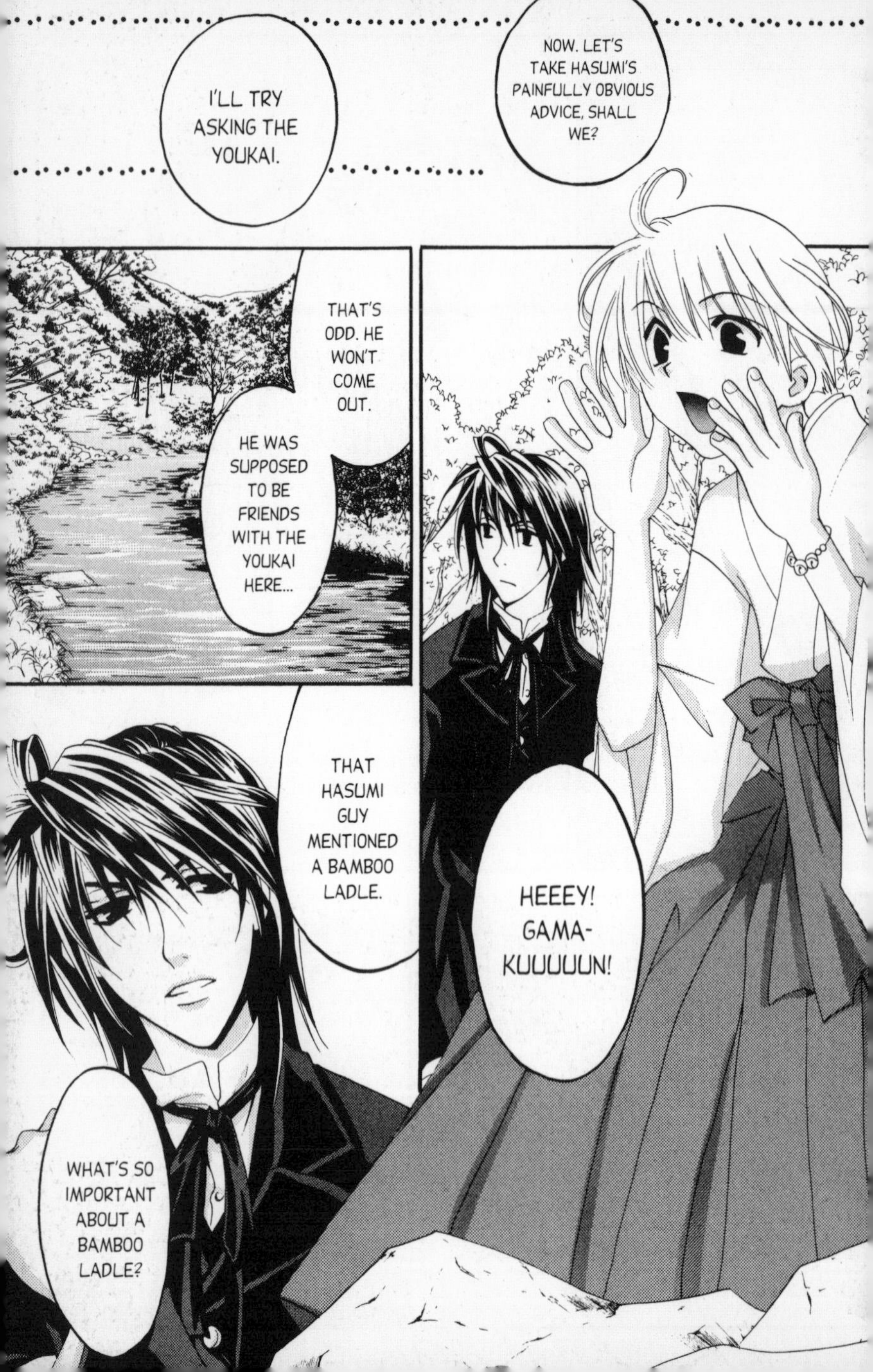
NOW. LET'S TAKE HASUMI'S PAINFULLY OBVIOUS ADVICE, SHALL WE?
I'LL TRY ASKING THE YOUKAI.
HEEEY! GAMA-KUUUUUN!
THAT'S ODD. HE WON'T COME OUT.
HE WAS SUPPOSED TO BE FRIENDS WITH THE YOUKAI HERE...
THAT HASUMI GUY MENTIONED A BAMBOO LADLE.
WHAT'S SO IMPORTANT ABOUT A BAMBOO LADLE?

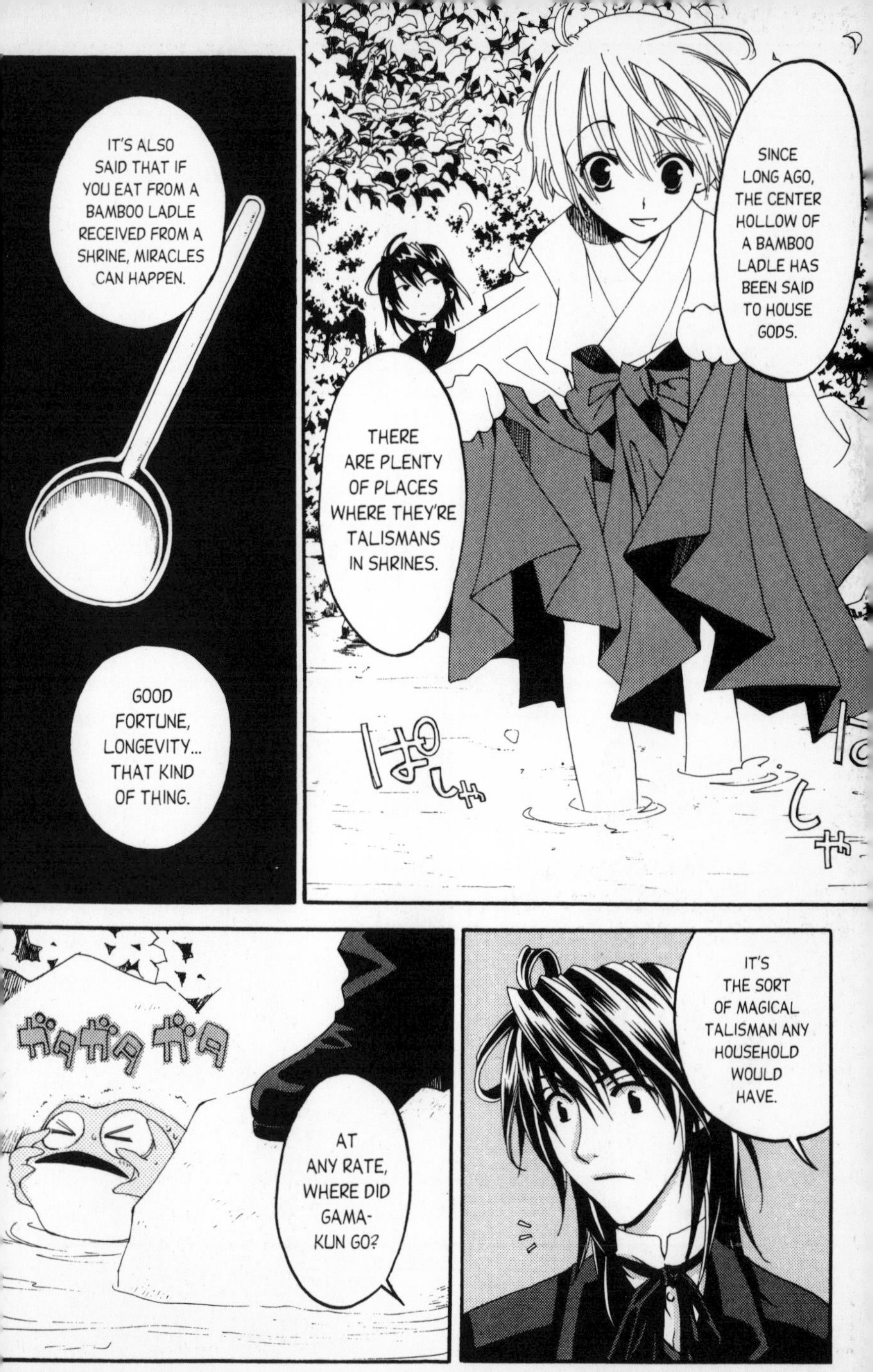
SINCE LONG AGO, THE CENTER HOLLOW OF A BAMBOO LADLE HAS BEEN SAID TO HOUSE GODS.
THERE ARE PLENTY OF PLACES WHERE THEY'RE TALISMANS IN SHRINES.
ぱしゃ
IT'S ALSO SAID THAT IF YOU EAT FROM A BAMBOO LADLE RECEIVED FROM A SHRINE, MIRACLES CAN HAPPEN.
GOOD FORTUNE, LONGEVITY... THAT KIND OF THING.
IT'S THE SORT OF MAGICAL TALISMAN ANY HOUSEHOLD WOULD HAVE.
ポタポタ ポタ
AT ANY RATE, WHERE DID GAMA-KUN GO?

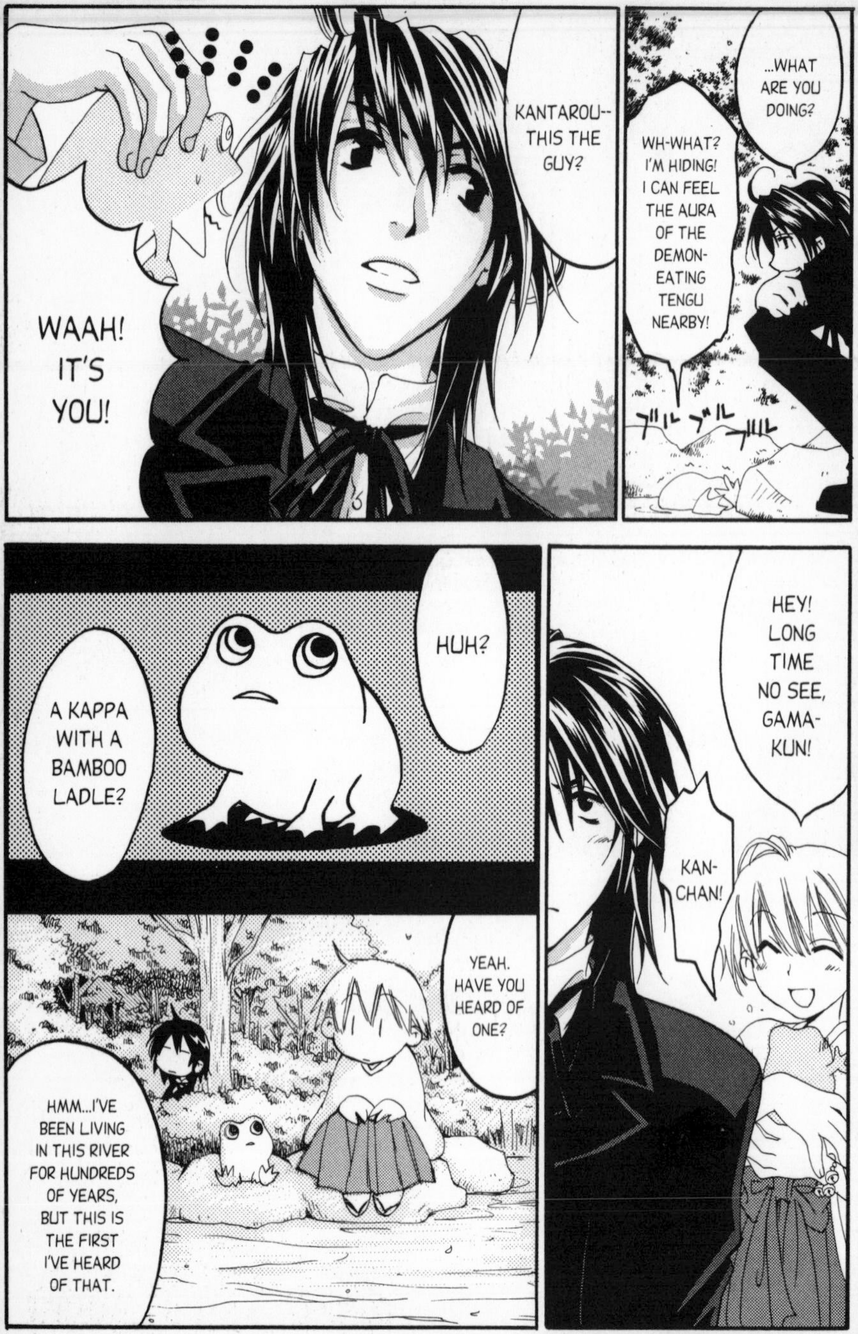
...WHAT ARE YOU DOING?
WH-WHAT? I'M HIDING! I CAN FEEL THE AURA OF THE DEMON-EATING TENGU NEARBY!
ブルブルブル
KANTAROU-- THIS THE GUY?
WAAH! IT'S YOU!
HEY! LONG TIME NO SEE, GAMA-KUN!
KAN-CHAN!
HUH?
A KAPPA WITH A BAMBOO LADLE?
YEAH. HAVE YOU HEARD OF ONE?
HMM...I'VE BEEN LIVING IN THIS RIVER FOR HUNDREDS OF YEARS, BUT THIS IS THE FIRST I'VE HEARD OF THAT.

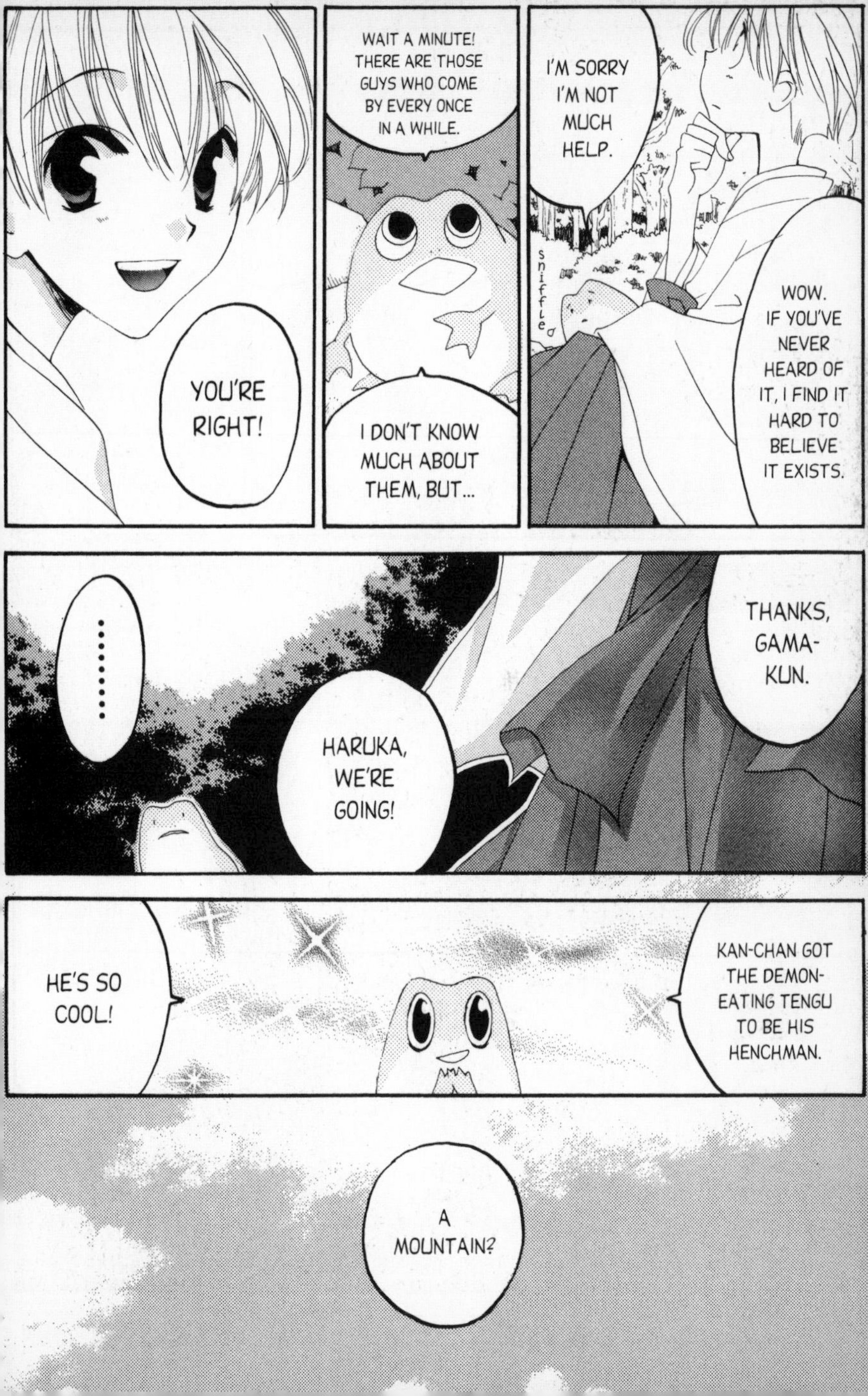
WOW. IF YOU'VE NEVER HEARD OF IT, I FIND IT HARD TO BELIEVE IT EXISTS.
I'M SORRY I'M NOT MUCH HELP.
sniffle
WAIT A MINUTE! THERE ARE THOSE GUYS WHO COME BY EVERY ONCE IN A WHILE.
I DON'T KNOW MUCH ABOUT THEM, BUT...
YOU'RE RIGHT!
THANKS, GAMA-KUN.
HARUKA, WE'RE GOING!
....
KAN-CHAN GOT THE DEMON-EATING TENGU TO BE HIS HENCHMAN.
HE'S SO COOL!
A MOUNTAIN?

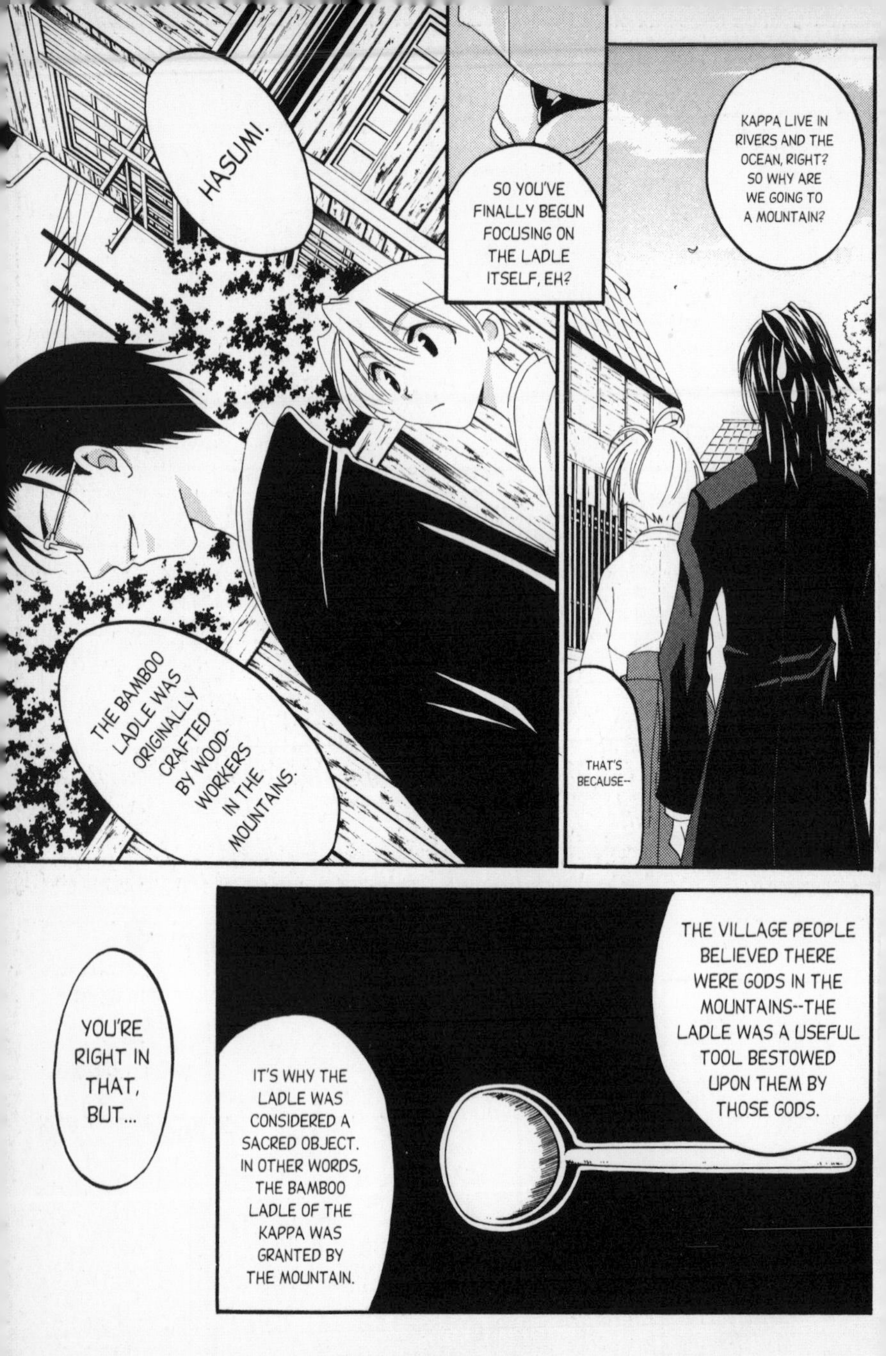
KAPPA LIVE IN RIVERS AND THE OCEAN, RIGHT? SO WHY ARE WE GOING TO A MOUNTAIN?
THAT'S BECAUSE--
SO YOU'VE FINALLY BEGUN FOCUSING ON THE LADLE ITSELF, EH?
HASUMI.
THE BAMBOO LADLE WAS ORIGINALLY CRAFTED BY WOOD-WORKERS IN THE MOUNTAINS.
THE VILLAGE PEOPLE BELIEVED THERE WERE GODS IN THE MOUNTAINS--THE LADLE WAS A USEFUL TOOL BESTOWED UPON THEM BY THOSE GODS.
IT'S WHY THE LADLE WAS CONSIDERED A SACRED OBJECT. IN OTHER WORDS, THE BAMBOO LADLE OF THE KAPPA WAS GRANTED BY THE MOUNTAIN.
YOU'RE RIGHT IN THAT, BUT...

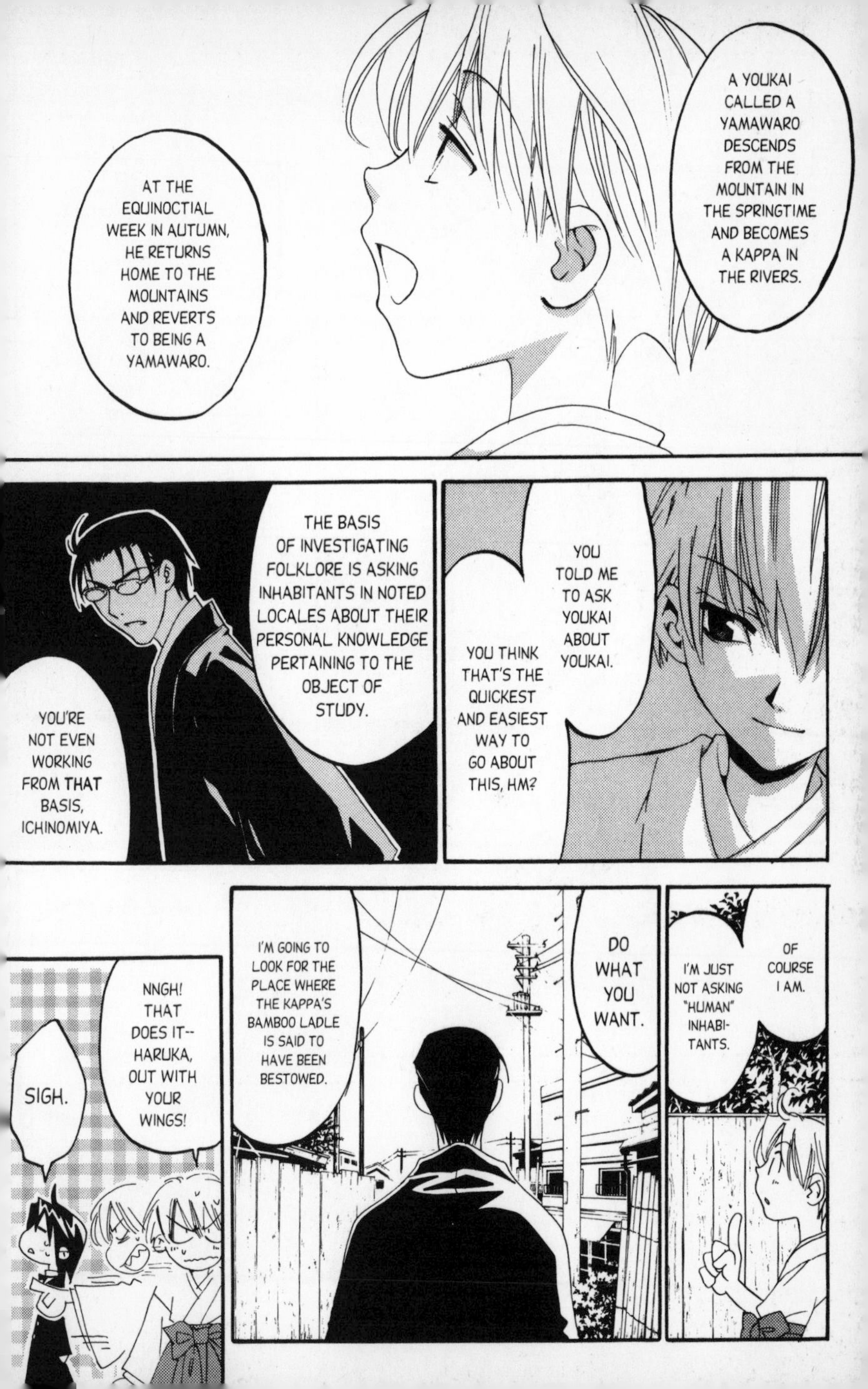
A YOUKAI CALLED A YAMAWARO DESCENDS FROM THE MOUNTAIN IN THE SPRINGTIME AND BECOMES A KAPPA IN THE RIVERS.
AT THE EQUINOCTIAL WEEK IN AUTUMN, HE RETURNS HOME TO THE MOUNTAINS AND REVERTS TO BEING A YAMAWARO.
YOU TOLD ME TO ASK YOUKAI ABOUT YOUKAI.
YOU THINK THAT'S THE QUICKEST AND EASIEST WAY TO GO ABOUT THIS, HM?
THE BASIS OF INVESTIGATING FOLKLORE IS ASKING INHABITANTS IN NOTED LOCALES ABOUT THEIR PERSONAL KNOWLEDGE PERTAINING TO THE OBJECT OF STUDY.
YOU'RE NOT EVEN WORKING FROM **THAT** BASIS, ICHINOMIYA.
OF COURSE I AM.
I'M JUST NOT ASKING "HUMAN" INHABI-TANTS.
DO WHAT YOU WANT.
I'M GOING TO LOOK FOR THE PLACE WHERE THE KAPPA'S BAMBOO LADLE IS SAID TO HAVE BEEN BESTOWED.
NNGH! THAT DOES IT-- HARUKA, OUT WITH YOUR WINGS!
SIGH.

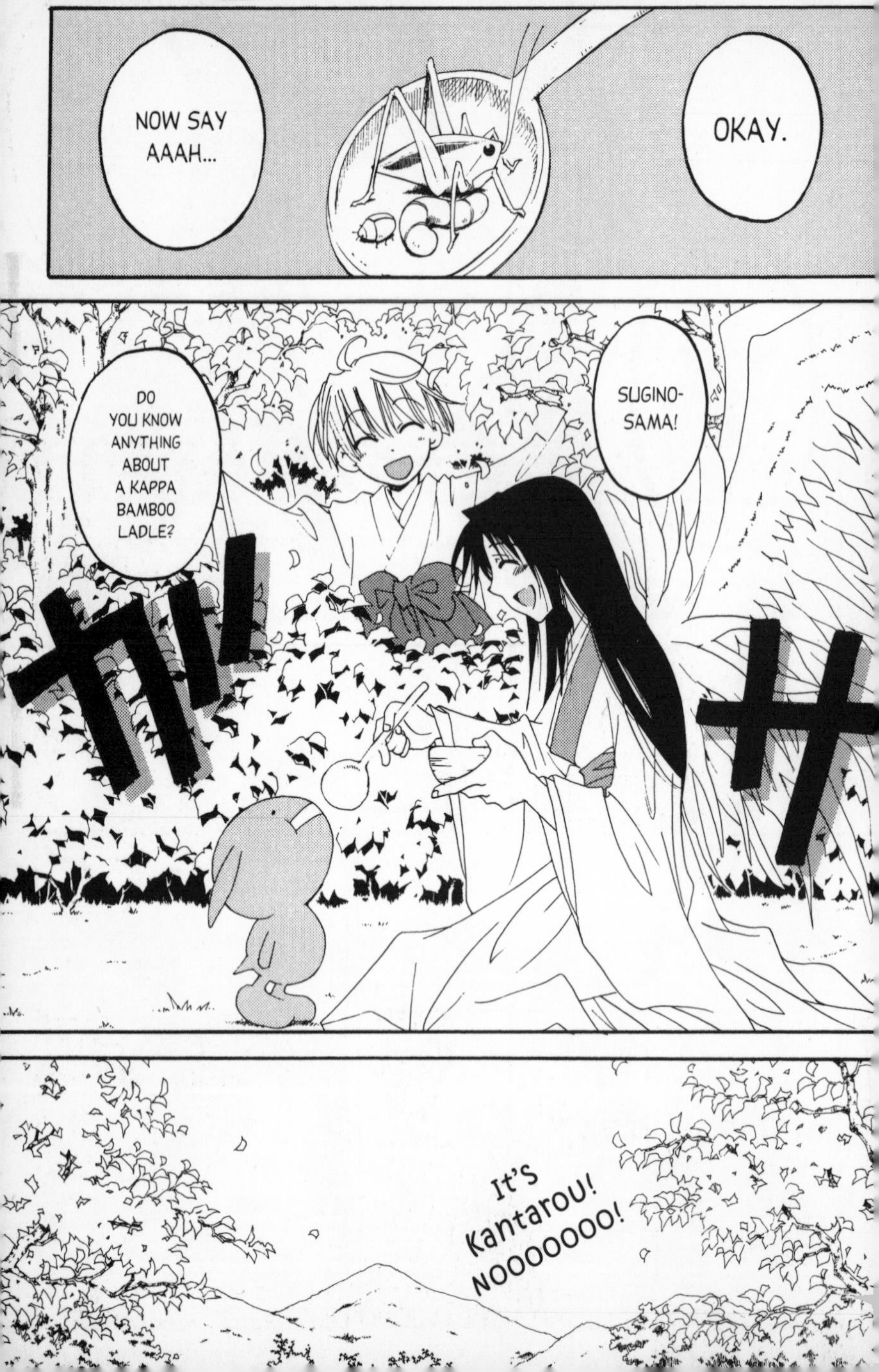
NOW SAY AAAH...
OKAY.
SUGINO-SAMA!
DO YOU KNOW ANYTHING ABOUT A KAPPA BAMBOO LADLE?
It'S Kantarou! NOOOOOOO!

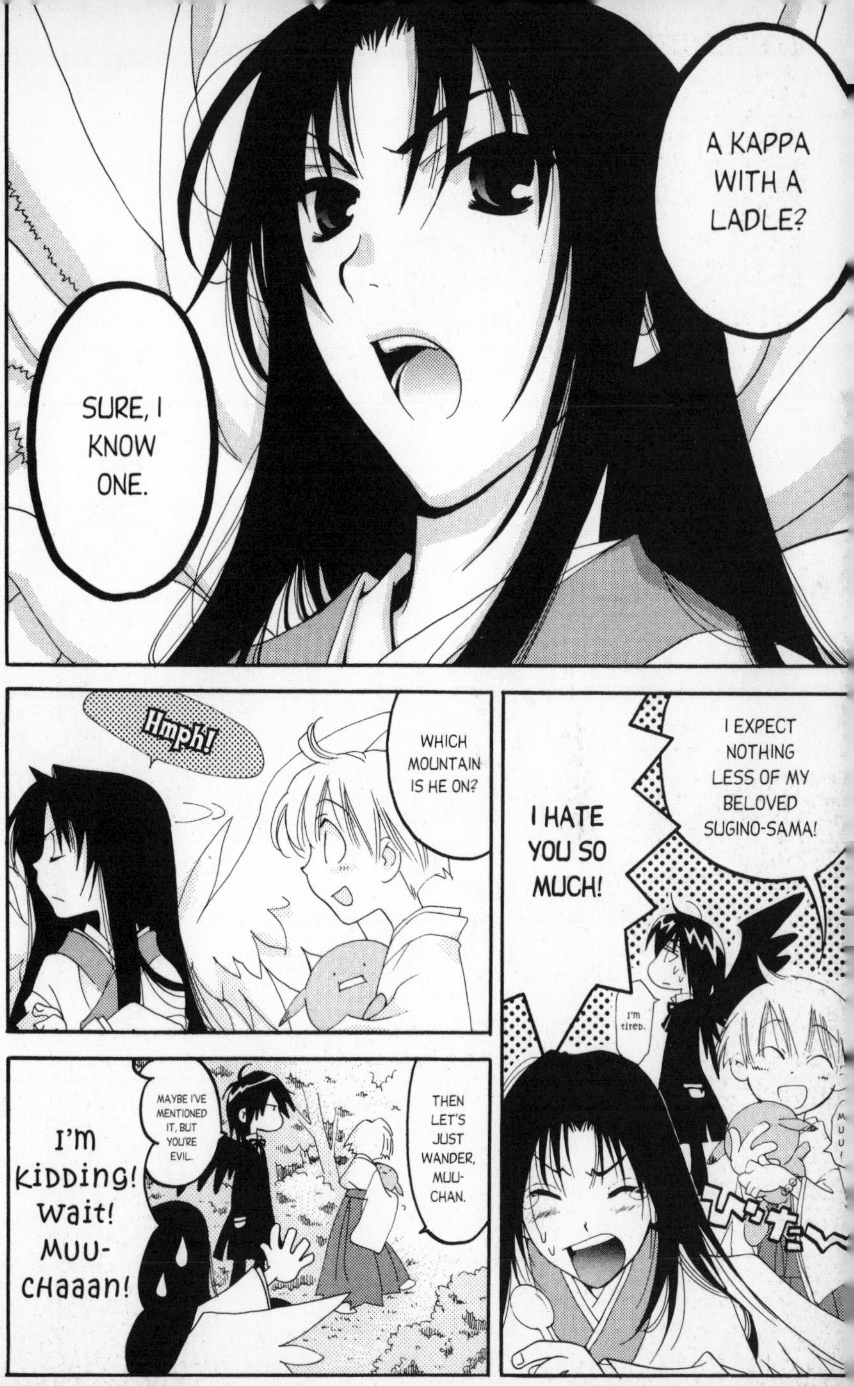
A KAPPA WITH A LADLE?
SURE, I KNOW ONE.
I EXPECT NOTHING LESS OF MY BELOVED SUGINO-SAMA!
I HATE YOU SO MUCH!
I'm tired.
MUU!
WHICH MOUNTAIN IS HE ON?
Hmph!
THEN LET'S JUST WANDER, MUU-CHAN.
MAYBE I'VE MENTIONED IT, BUT YOU'RE EVIL.
I'm KIDDING! Wait! MUU-CHaaan!

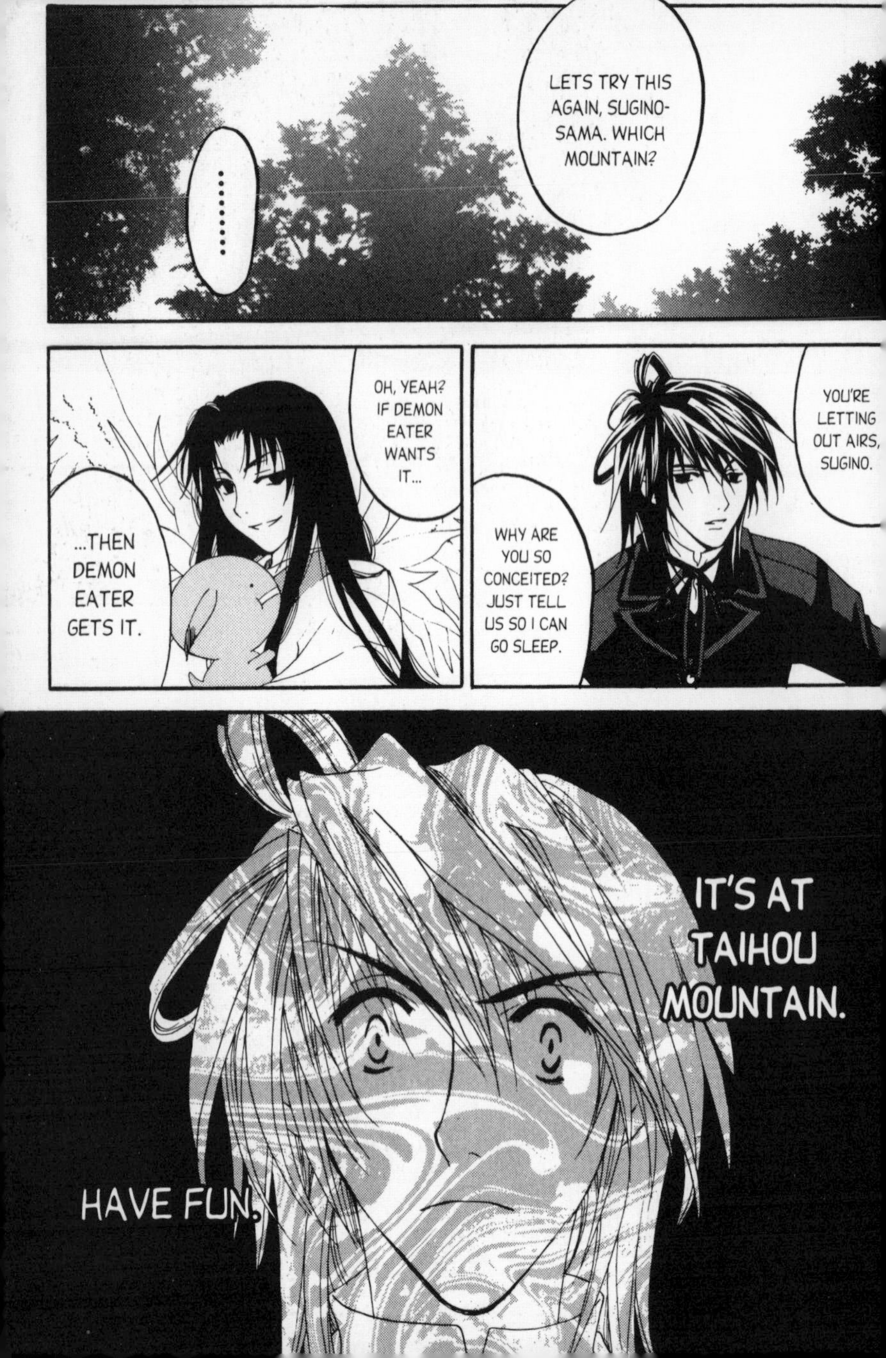
LETS TRY THIS AGAIN, SUGINO-SAMA. WHICH MOUNTAIN?
......
YOU'RE LETTING OUT AIRS, SUGINO.
WHY ARE YOU SO CONCEITED? JUST TELL US SO I CAN GO SLEEP.
OH, YEAH? IF DEMON EATER WANTS IT...
...THEN DEMON EATER GETS IT.
IT'S AT TAIHOU MOUNTAIN.
HAVE FUN.

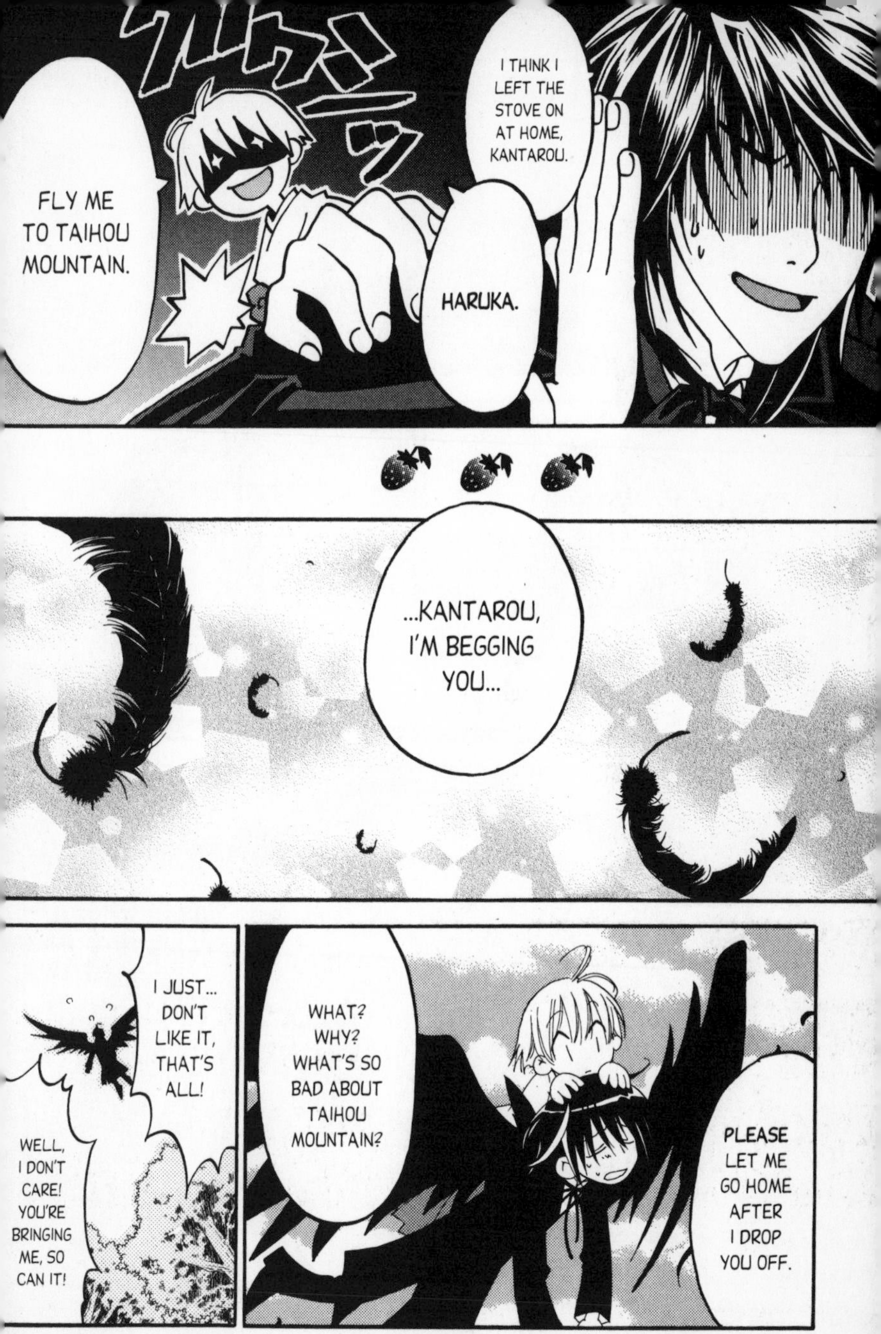
I THINK I LEFT THE STOVE ON AT HOME, KANTAROU.
HARUKA.
FLY ME TO TAIHOU MOUNTAIN.
...KANTAROU, I'M BEGGING YOU...
PLEASE LET ME GO HOME AFTER I DROP YOU OFF.
WHAT? WHY? WHAT'S SO BAD ABOUT TAIHOU MOUNTAIN?
I JUST... DON'T LIKE IT, THAT'S ALL!
WELL, I DON'T CARE! YOU'RE BRINGING ME, SO CAN IT!

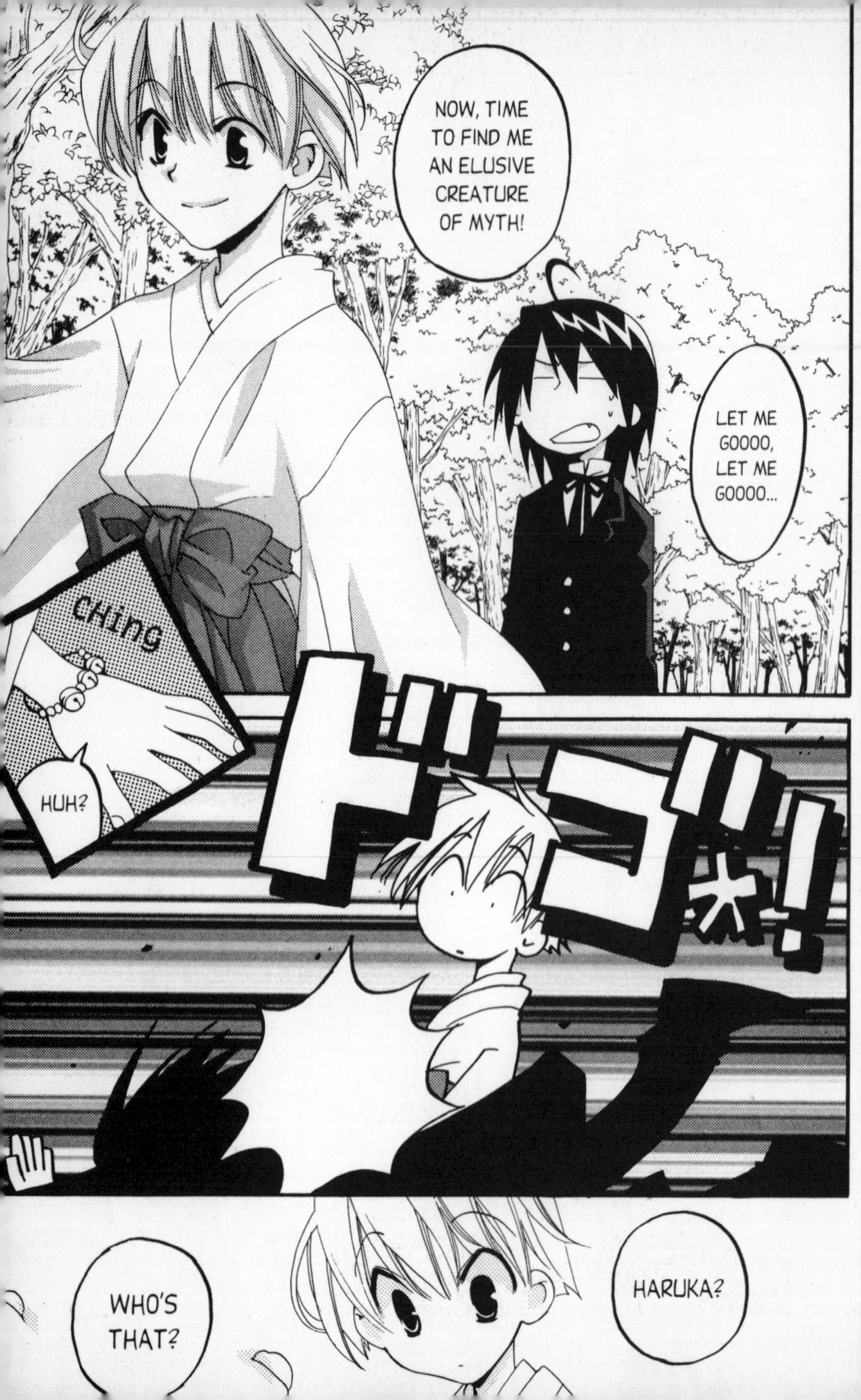
NOW, TIME TO FIND ME AN ELUSIVE CREATURE OF MYTH!
LET ME GOOOO, LET ME GOOOO...
CHing
HUH?
ドゴォ!
HARUKA?
WHO'S THAT?

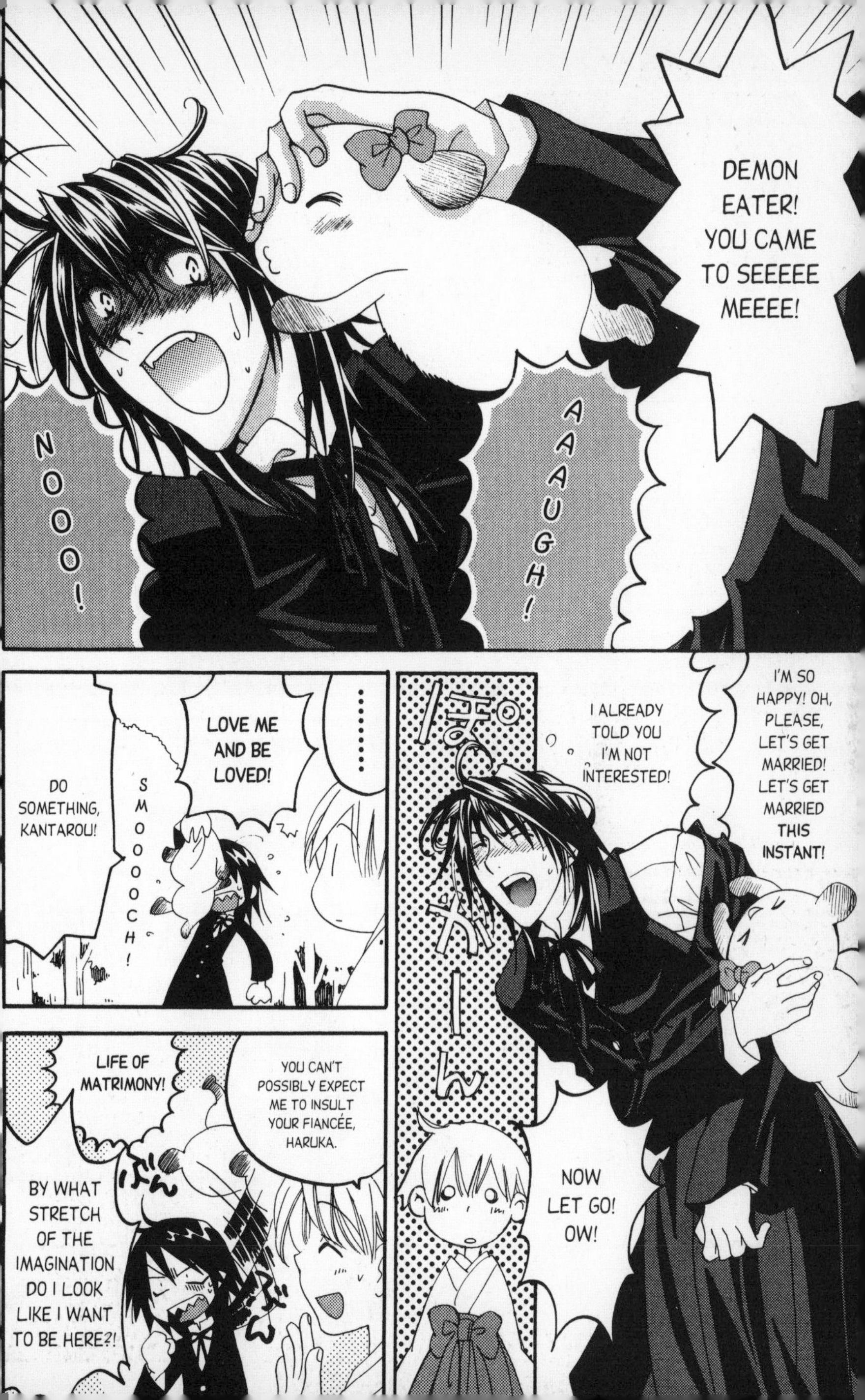
DEMON EATER! YOU CAME TO SEEEEE MEEEE!
AAAAUGH!
NOOOO!
I'M SO HAPPY! OH, PLEASE, LET'S GET MARRIED! LET'S GET MARRIED THIS INSTANT!
I ALREADY TOLD YOU I'M NOT INTERESTED!
NOW LET GO! OW!
......
LOVE ME AND BE LOVED!
SMOOOOOCH!
DO SOMETHING, KANTAROU!
YOU CAN'T POSSIBLY EXPECT ME TO INSULT YOUR FIANCÉE, HARUKA.
LIFE OF MATRIMONY!
BY WHAT STRETCH OF THE IMAGINATION DO I LOOK LIKE I WANT TO BE HERE?!

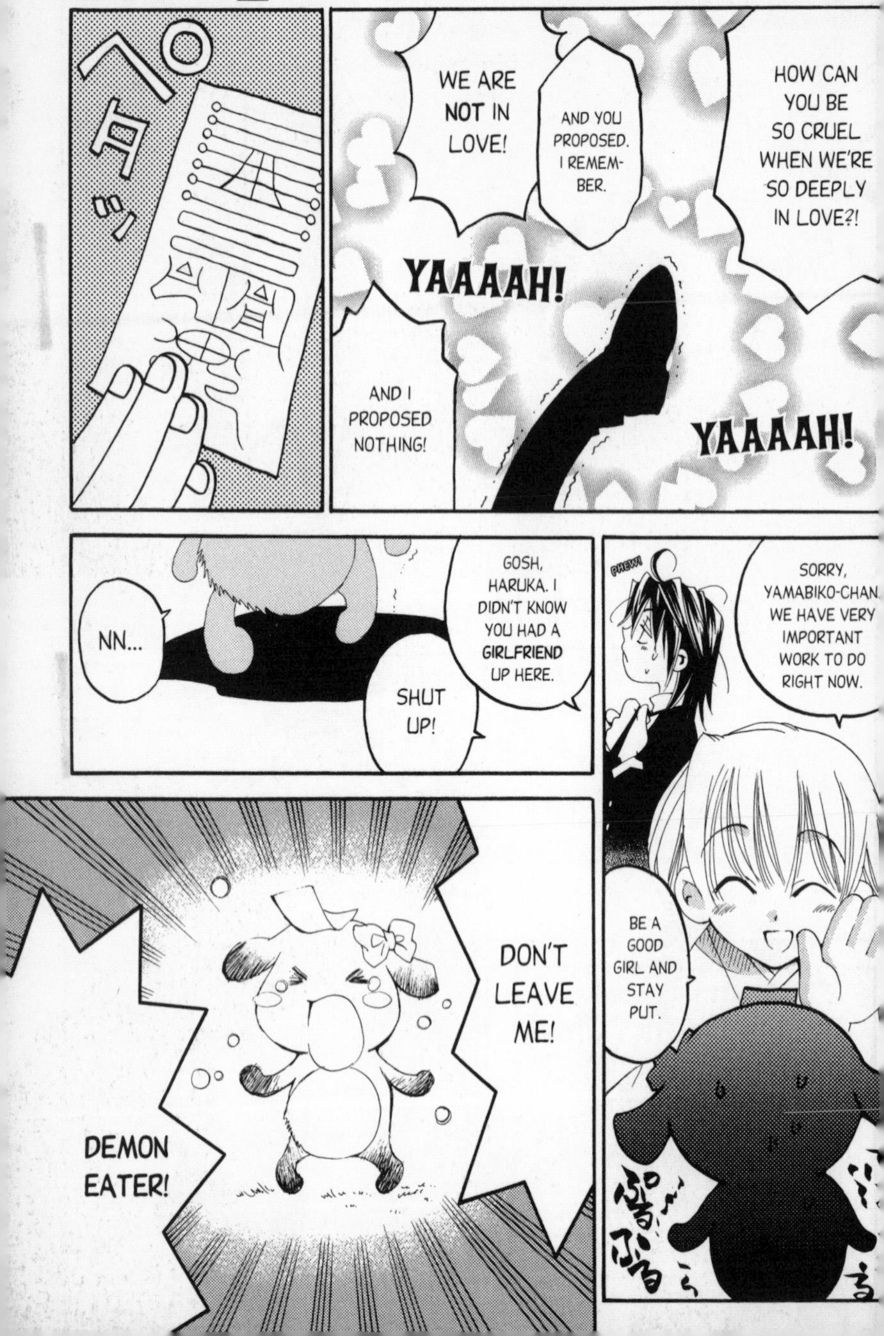
HOW CAN YOU BE SO CRUEL WHEN WE'RE SO DEEPLY IN LOVE?!
AND YOU PROPOSED. I REMEMBER.
WE ARE NOT IN LOVE!
YAAAAH!
YAAAAH!
AND I PROPOSED NOTHING!
SORRY, YAMABIKO-CHAN. WE HAVE VERY IMPORTANT WORK TO DO RIGHT NOW.
PHEW!
BE A GOOD GIRL AND STAY PUT.
GOSH, HARUKA. I DIDN'T KNOW YOU HAD A GIRLFRIEND UP HERE.
SHUT UP!
NN...
DON'T LEAVE ME!
DEMON EATER!

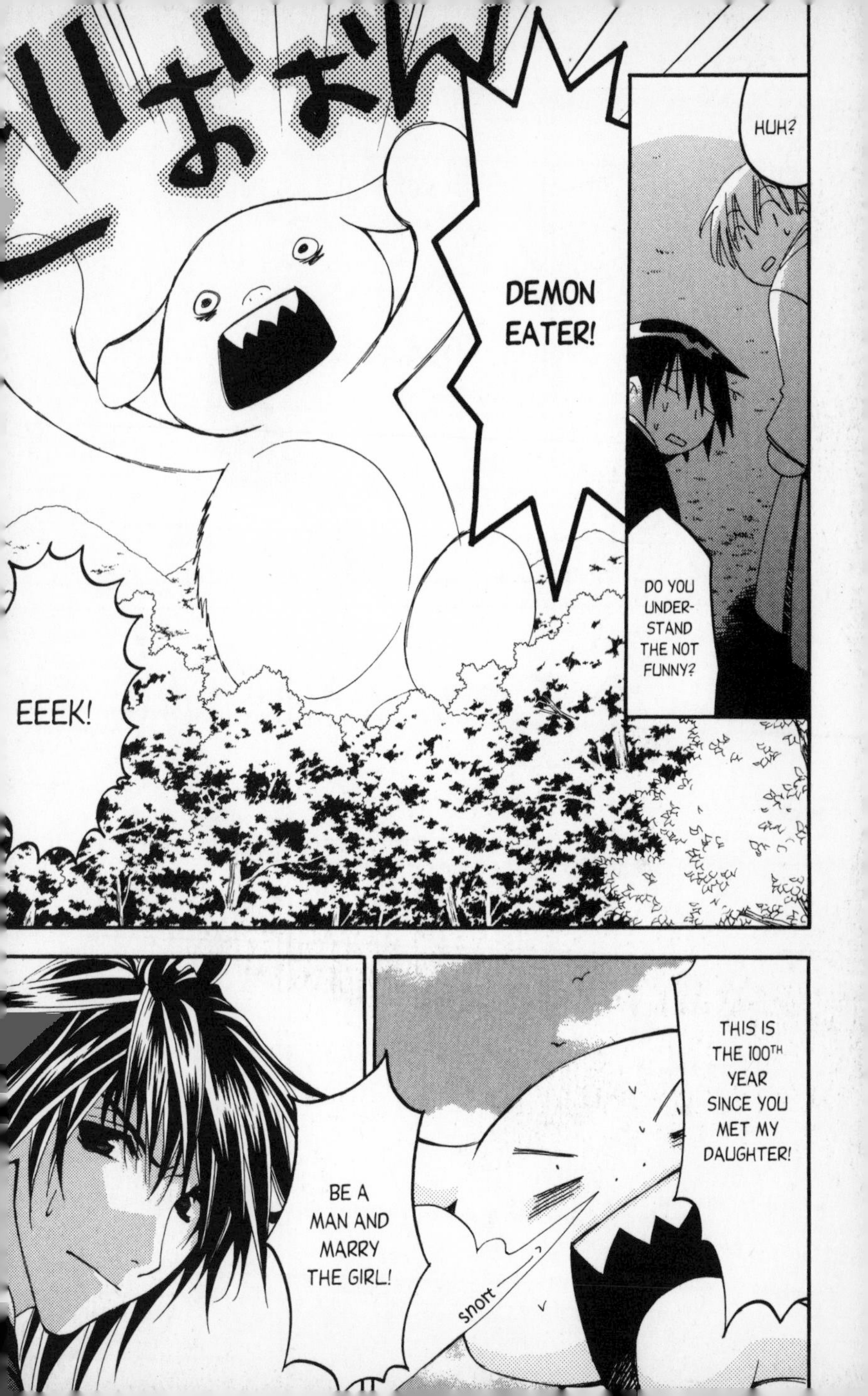
HUH?
DO YOU UNDERSTAND THE NOT FUNNY?
おおん
DEMON EATER!
EEEK!
THIS IS THE 100TH YEAR SINCE YOU MET MY DAUGHTER!
BE A MAN AND MARRY THE GIRL!
snort

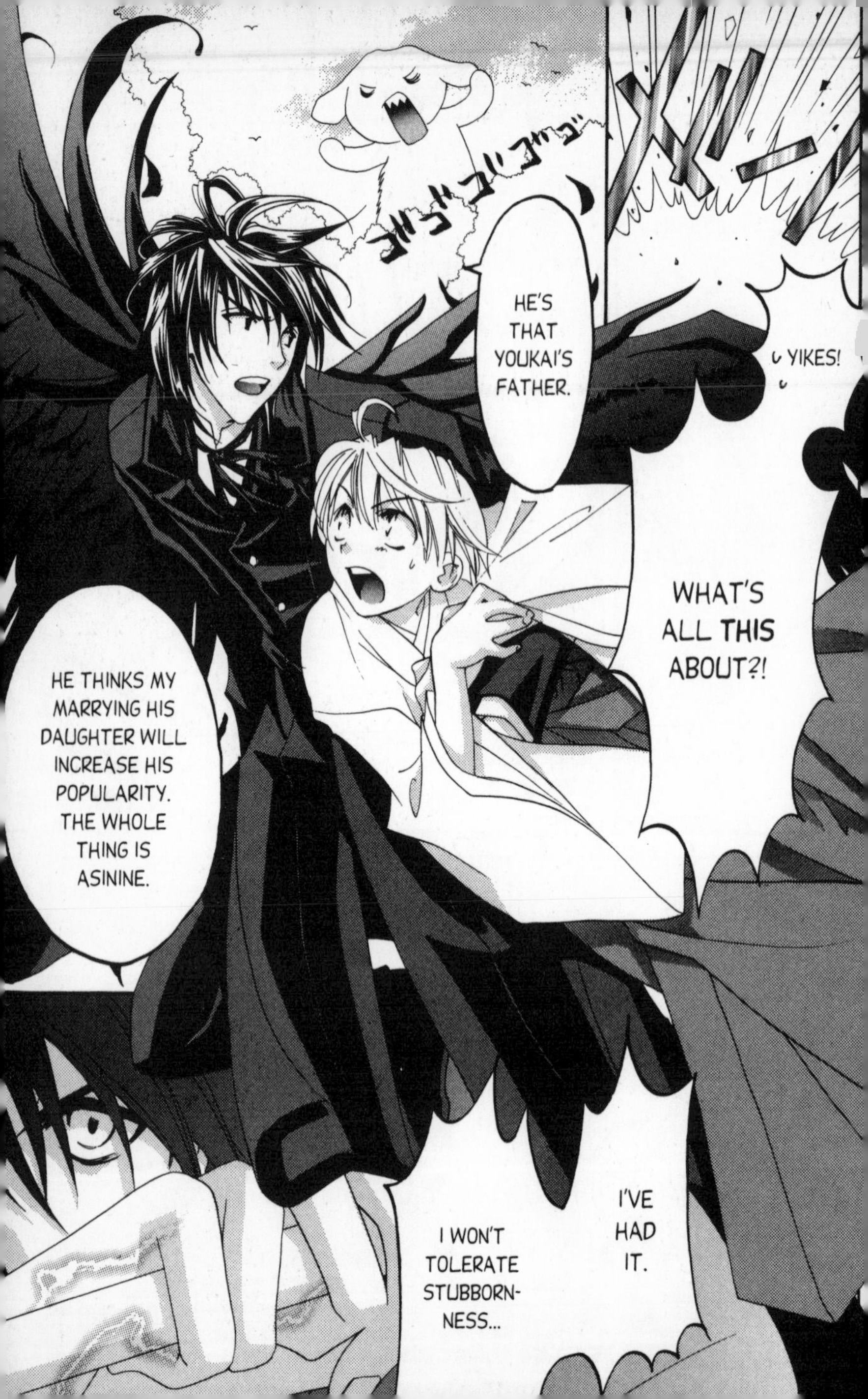
YIKES!
WHAT'S ALL THIS ABOUT?!
HE'S THAT YOUKAI'S FATHER.
HE THINKS MY MARRYING HIS DAUGHTER WILL INCREASE HIS POPULARITY. THE WHOLE THING IS ASININE.
I'VE HAD IT.
I WON'T TOLERATE STUBBORN-NESS...

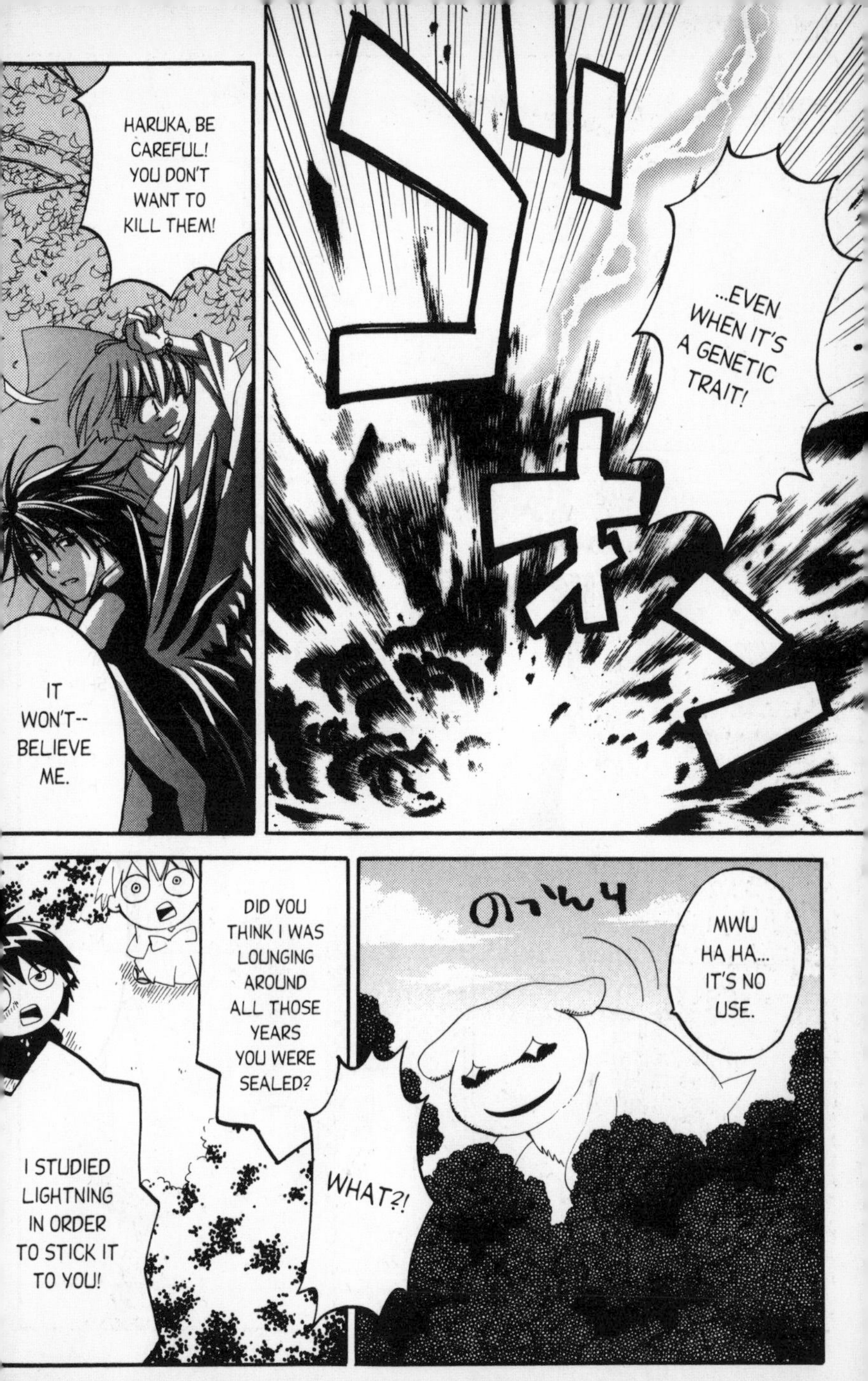
...EVEN WHEN IT'S A GENETIC TRAIT!
HARUKA, BE CAREFUL! YOU DON'T WANT TO KILL THEM!
IT WON'T-- BELIEVE ME.
MWU HA HA... IT'S NO USE.
DID YOU THINK I WAS LOUNGING AROUND ALL THOSE YEARS YOU WERE SEALED?
WHAT?!
I STUDIED LIGHTNING IN ORDER TO STICK IT TO YOU!

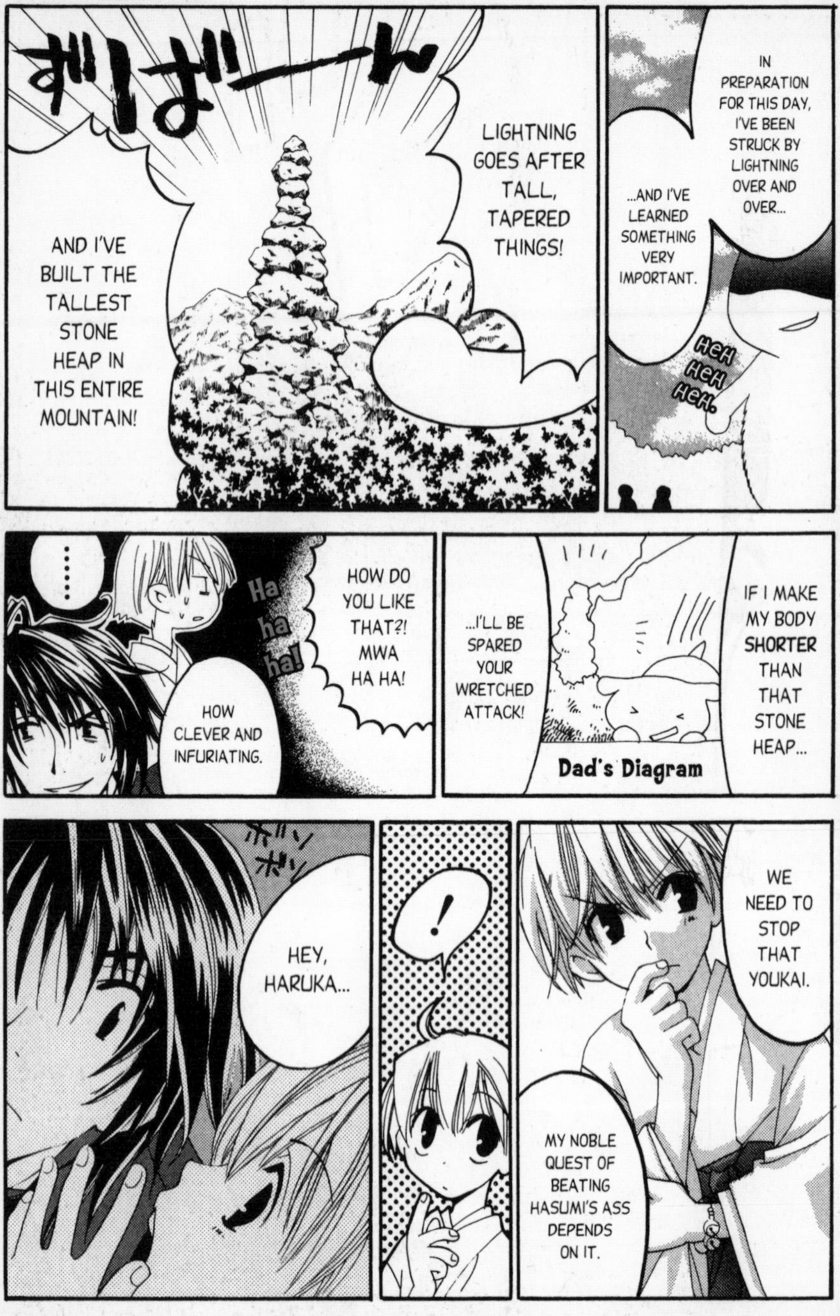
IN PREPARATION FOR THIS DAY, I'VE BEEN STRUCK BY LIGHTNING OVER AND OVER...
...AND I'VE LEARNED SOMETHING VERY IMPORTANT.
HEH HEH HEH.
ずばーーん
LIGHTNING GOES AFTER TALL, TAPERED THINGS!
AND I'VE BUILT THE TALLEST STONE HEAP IN THIS ENTIRE MOUNTAIN!
IF I MAKE MY BODY SHORTER THAN THAT STONE HEAP...
...I'LL BE SPARED YOUR WRETCHED ATTACK!
Dad's Diagram
HOW DO YOU LIKE THAT?! MWA HA HA!
Ha ha ha!
......
HOW CLEVER AND INFURIATING.
WE NEED TO STOP THAT YOUKAI.
MY NOBLE QUEST OF BEATING HASUMI'S ASS DEPENDS ON IT.
!
HEY, HARUKA...

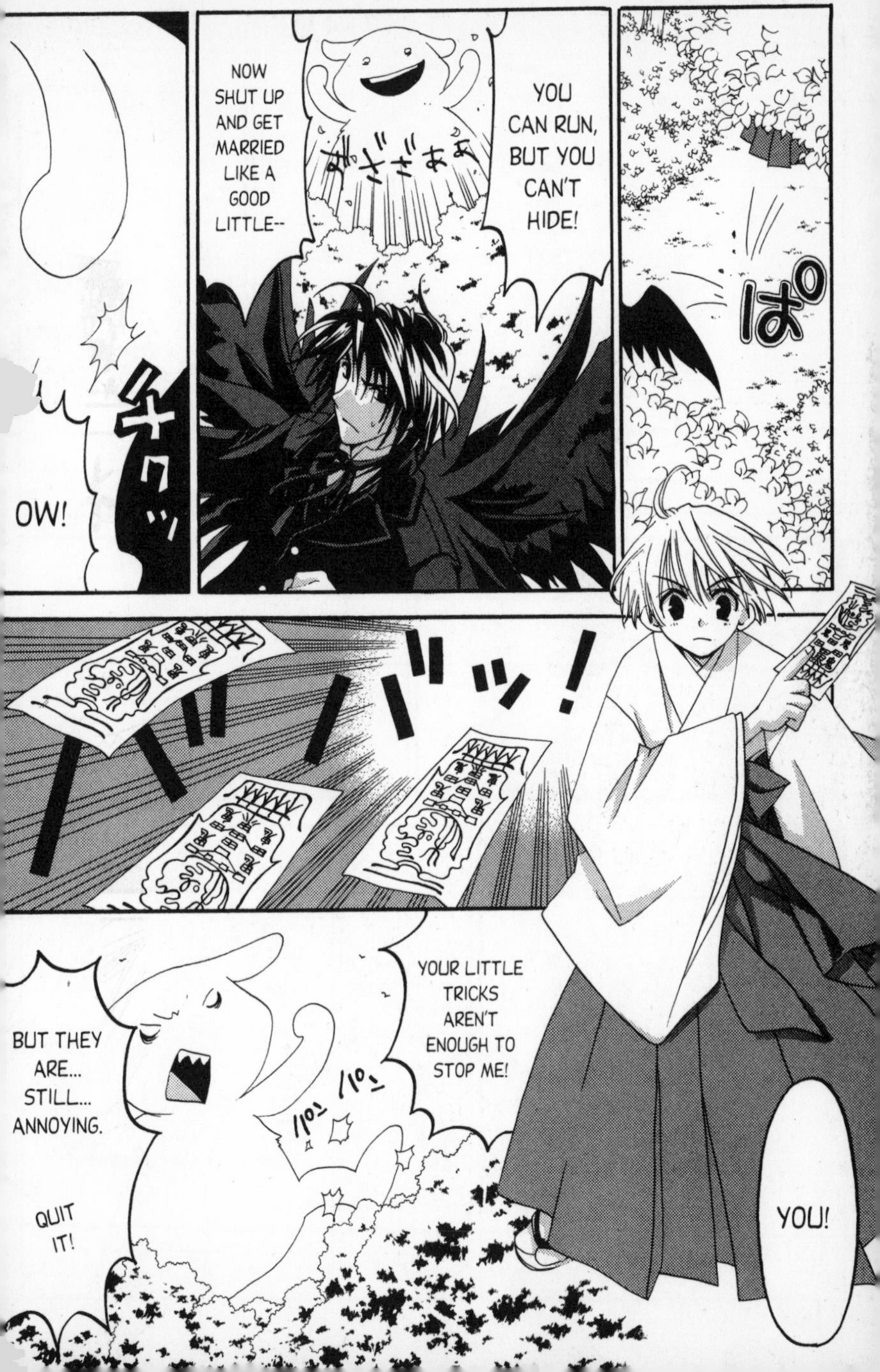
ぱ
YOU CAN RUN, BUT YOU CAN'T HIDE!
NOW SHUT UP AND GET MARRIED LIKE A GOOD LITTLE--
チクッ
OW!
バリッ!
YOU!
YOUR LITTLE TRICKS AREN'T ENOUGH TO STOP ME!
パン パン
BUT THEY ARE... STILL... ANNOYING.
QUIT IT!

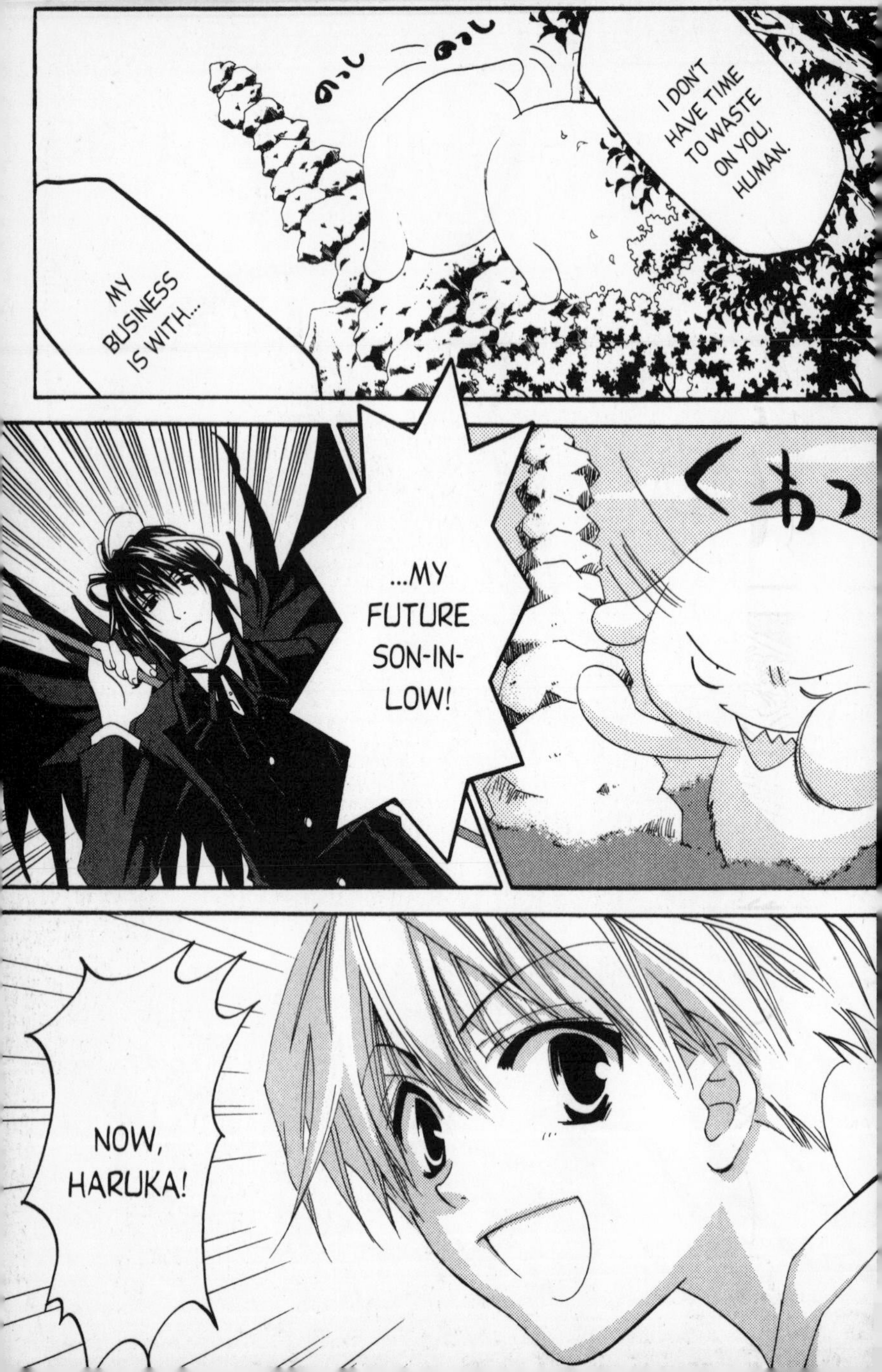
I DON'T HAVE TIME TO WASTE ON YOU, HUMAN.
のし のし
MY BUSINESS IS WITH...
くおっ
...MY FUTURE SON-IN-LOW!
NOW, HARUKA!

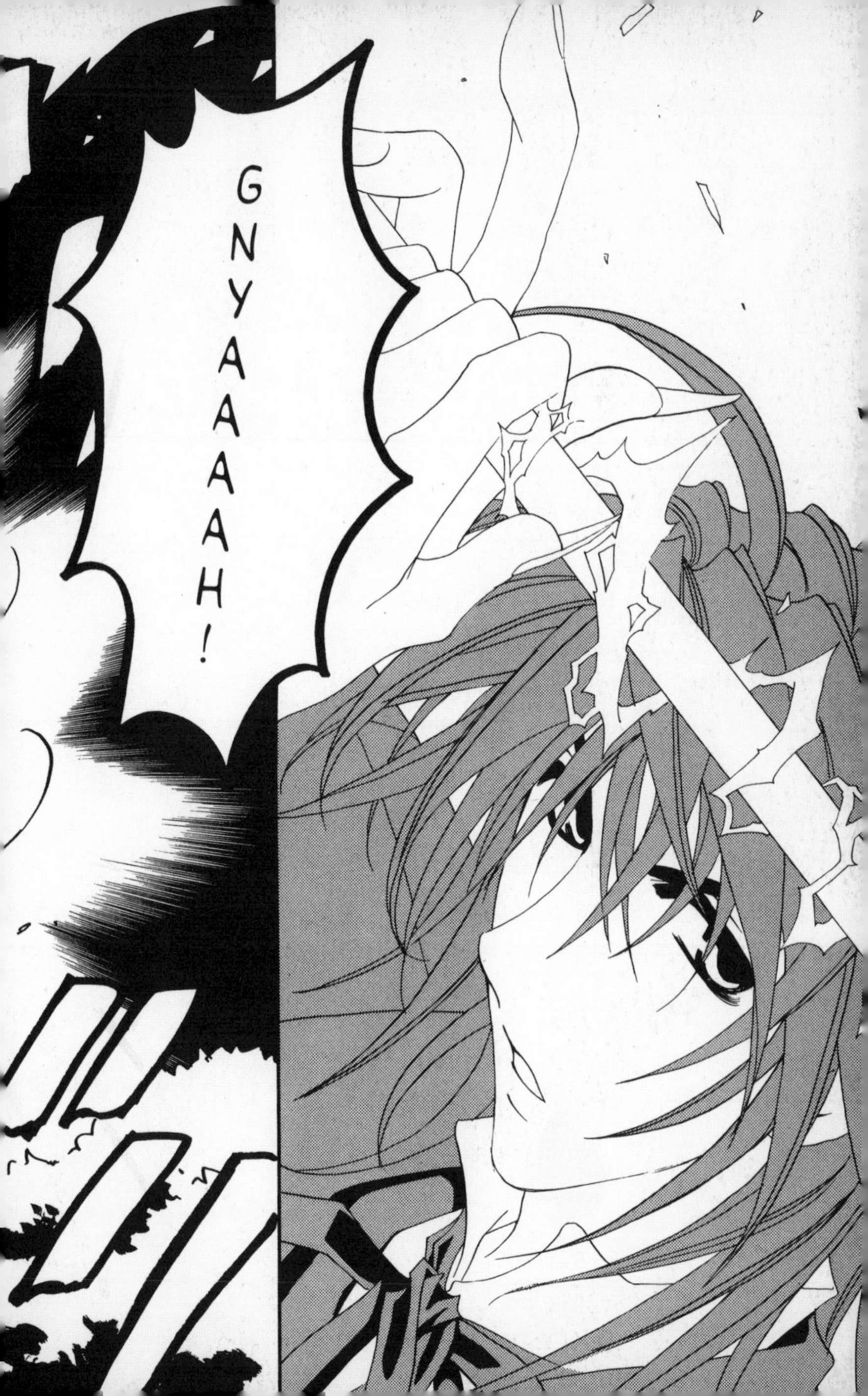
GNYAAAAH!

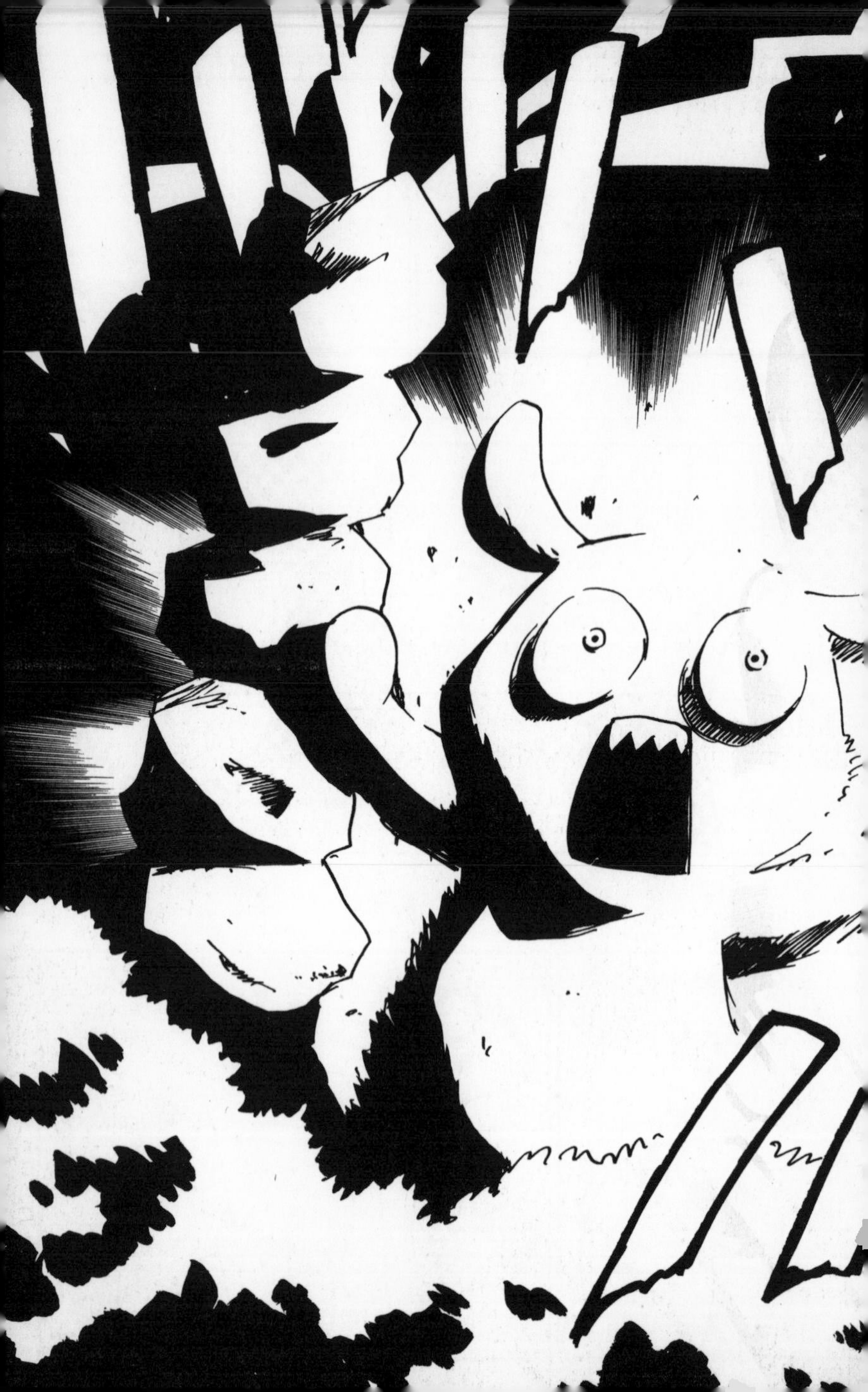

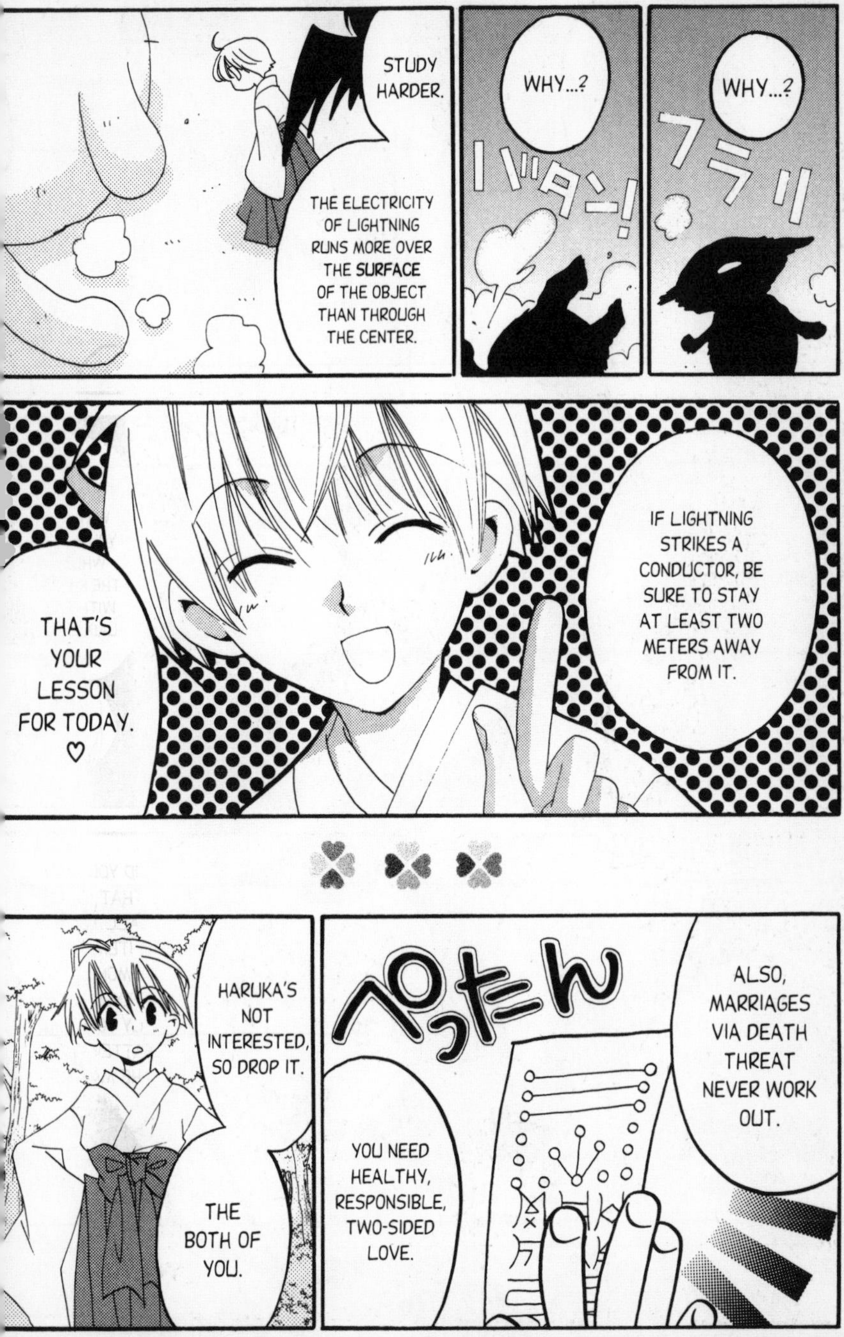
WHY...?
フラリ
WHY...?
バタン—!
STUDY HARDER.
THE ELECTRICITY OF LIGHTNING RUNS MORE OVER THE **SURFACE** OF THE OBJECT THAN THROUGH THE CENTER.
IF LIGHTNING STRIKES A CONDUCTOR, BE SURE TO STAY AT LEAST TWO METERS AWAY FROM IT.
THAT'S YOUR LESSON FOR TODAY. ♡
ALSO, MARRIAGES VIA DEATH THREAT NEVER WORK OUT.
ぺったん
YOU NEED HEALTHY, RESPONSIBLE, TWO-SIDED LOVE.
HARUKA'S NOT INTERESTED, SO DROP IT.
THE BOTH OF YOU.

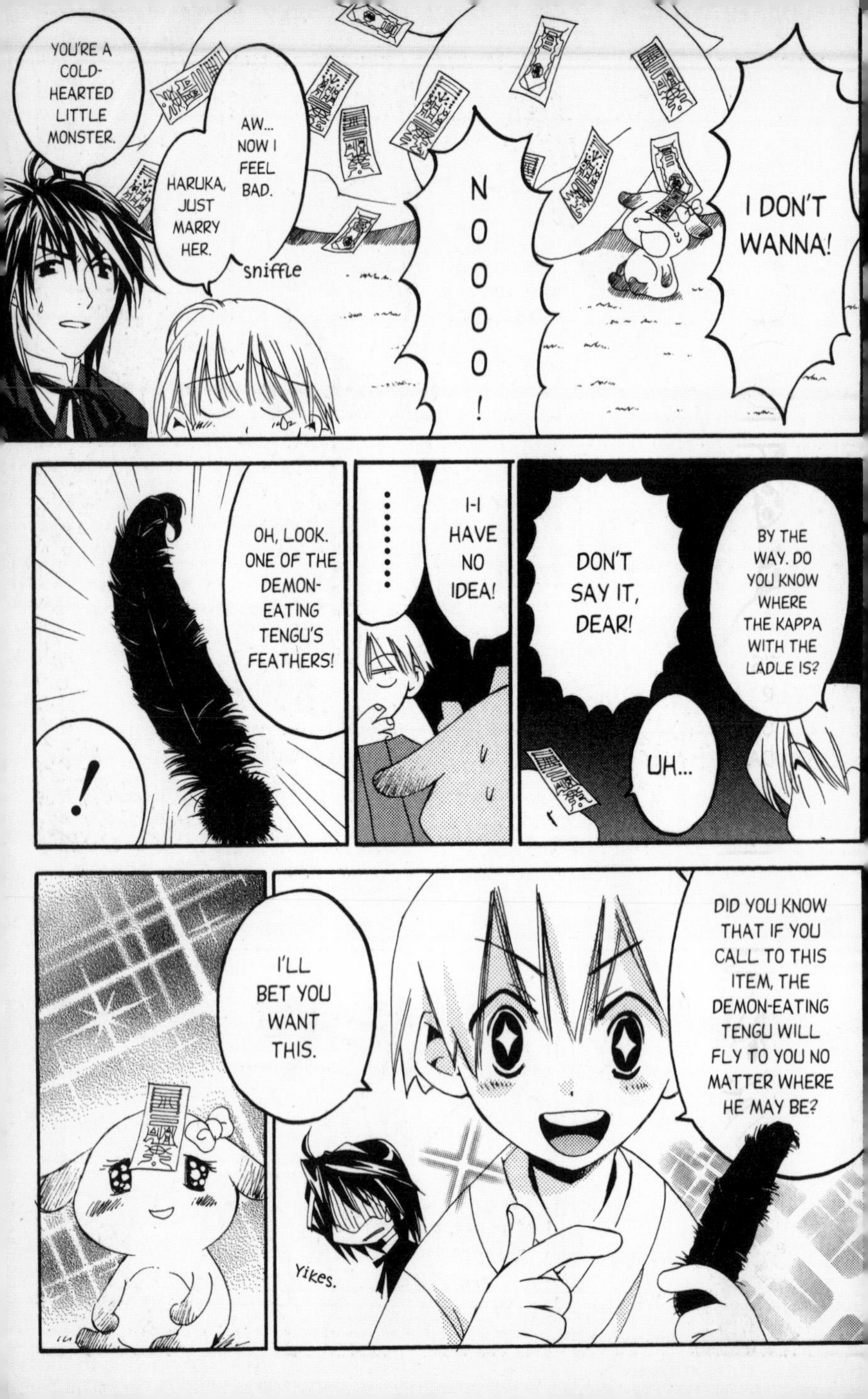
I DON'T WANNA!
NOOOO!
AW... NOW I FEEL BAD.
HARUKA, JUST MARRY HER.
sniffle
YOU'RE A COLD-HEARTED LITTLE MONSTER.
BY THE WAY. DO YOU KNOW WHERE THE KAPPA WITH THE LADLE IS?
DON'T SAY IT, DEAR!
UH...
I-I HAVE NO IDEA!
....
OH, LOOK. ONE OF THE DEMON-EATING TENGU'S FEATHERS!
!
DID YOU KNOW THAT IF YOU CALL TO THIS ITEM, THE DEMON-EATING TENGU WILL FLY TO YOU NO MATTER WHERE HE MAY BE?
Yikes.
I'LL BET YOU WANT THIS.

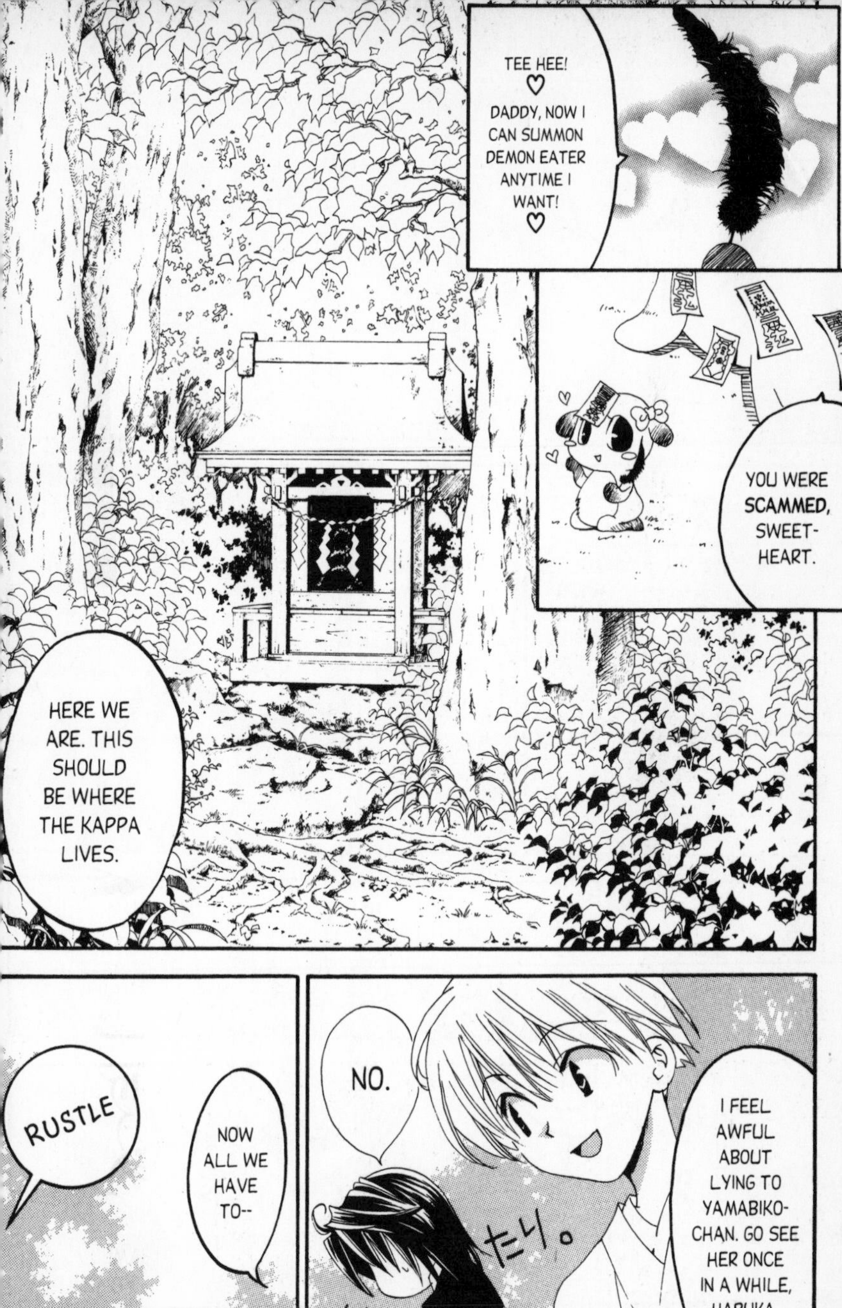
TEE HEE! ♡ DADDY, NOW I CAN SUMMON DEMON EATER ANYTIME I WANT! ♡
YOU WERE **SCAMMED**, SWEET-HEART.
HERE WE ARE. THIS SHOULD BE WHERE THE KAPPA LIVES.
I FEEL AWFUL ABOUT LYING TO YAMABIKO-CHAN. GO SEE HER ONCE IN A WHILE, HARUKA.
NO.
NOW ALL WE HAVE TO--
RUSTLE

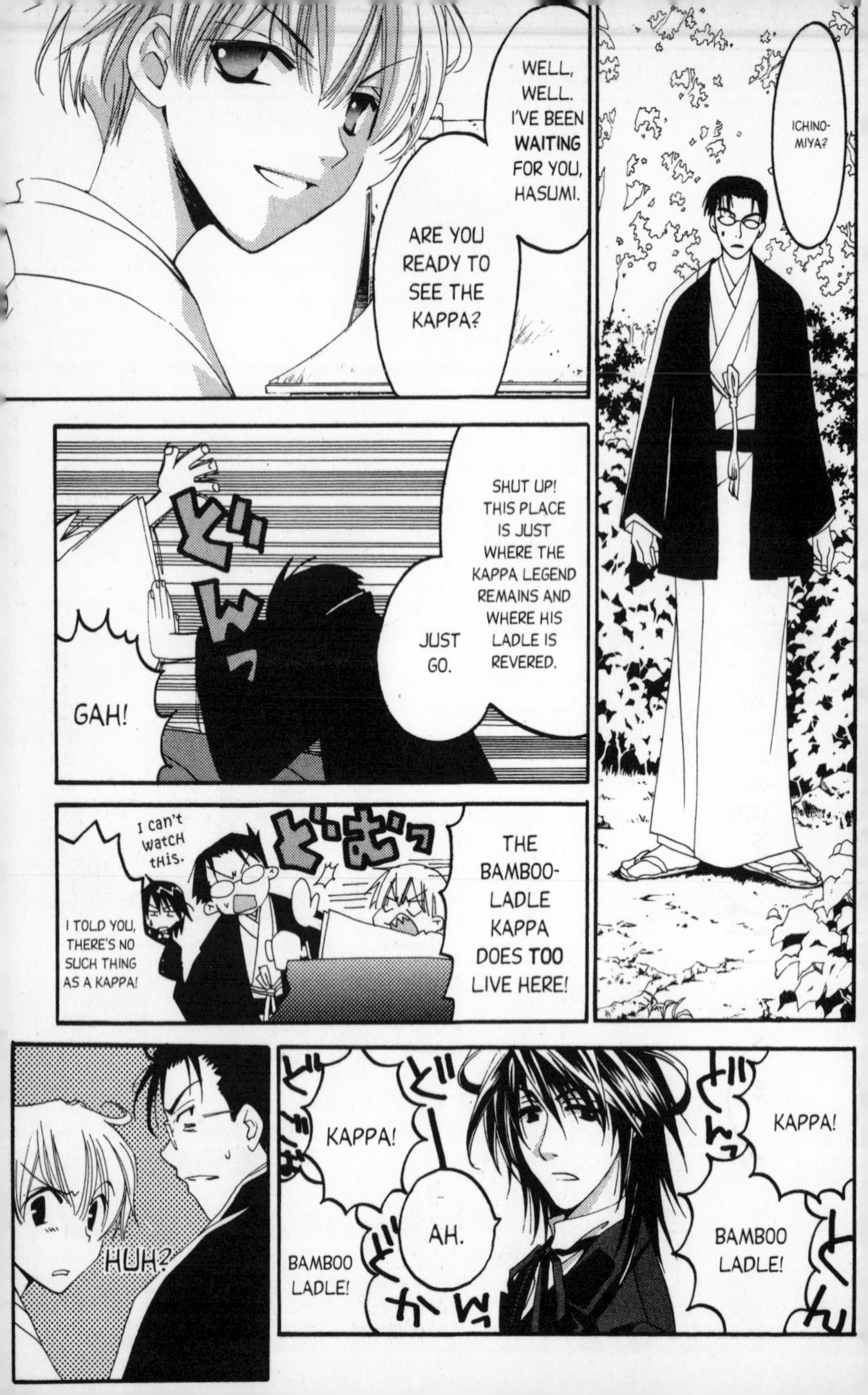
ICHINO-MIYA?
WELL, WELL. I'VE BEEN **WAITING** FOR YOU, HASUMI.
ARE YOU READY TO SEE THE KAPPA?
SHUT UP! THIS PLACE IS JUST WHERE THE KAPPA LEGEND REMAINS AND WHERE HIS LADLE IS REVERED.
JUST GO.
GAH!
THE BAMBOO-LADLE KAPPA DOES **TOO** LIVE HERE!
I TOLD YOU, THERE'S NO SUCH THING AS A KAPPA!
I can't watch this.
KAPPA!
BAMBOO LADLE!
KAPPA!
AH.
BAMBOO LADLE!
HUH?

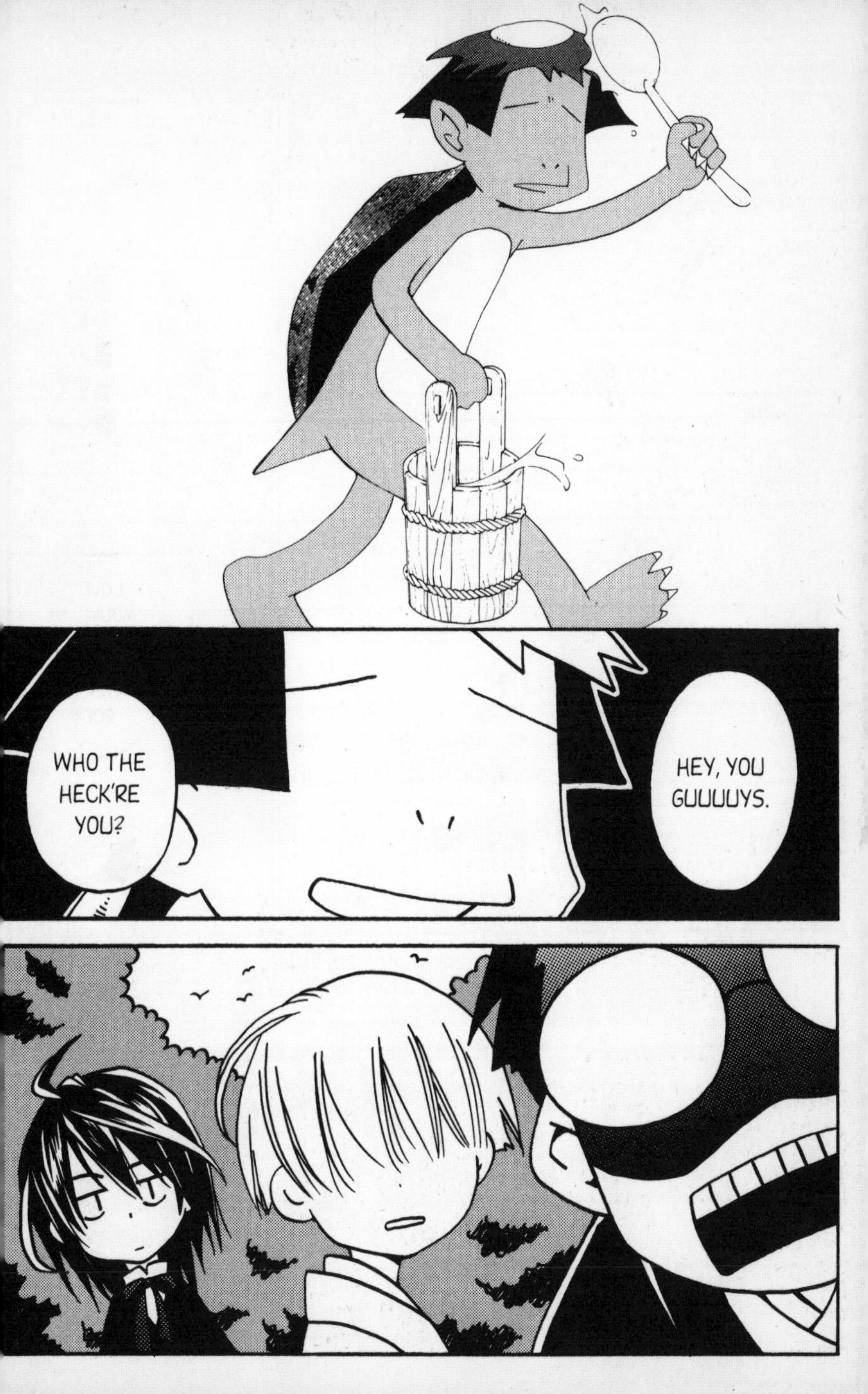
HEY, YOU GUUUUYS.
WHO THE HECK'RE YOU?

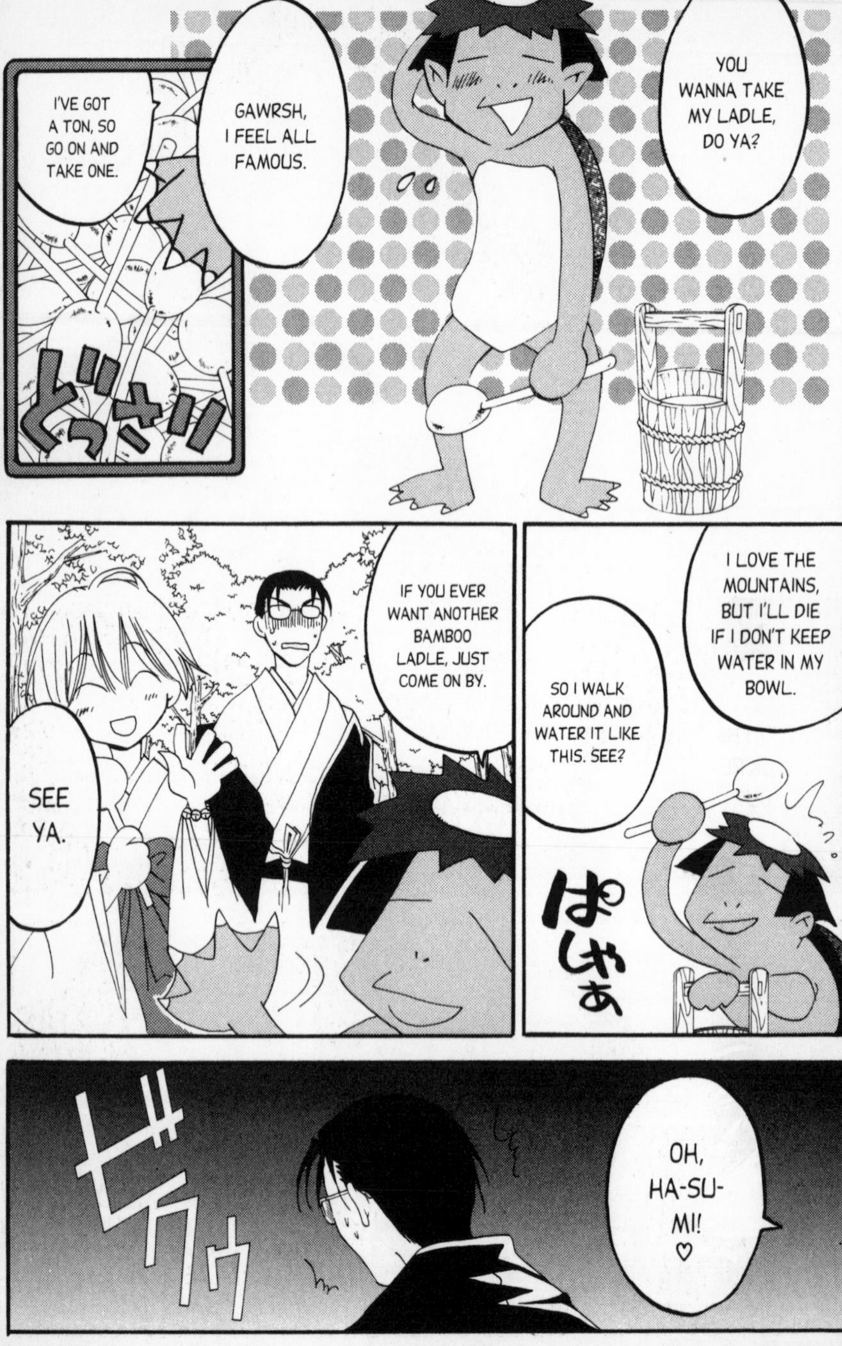
YOU WANNA TAKE MY LADLE, DO YA?
GAWRSH, I FEEL ALL FAMOUS.
I'VE GOT A TON, SO GO ON AND TAKE ONE.
どっさりッ
I LOVE THE MOUNTAINS, BUT I'LL DIE IF I DON'T KEEP WATER IN MY BOWL.
SO I WALK AROUND AND WATER IT LIKE THIS. SEE?
ぱしゃぁ
IF YOU EVER WANT ANOTHER BAMBOO LADLE, JUST COME ON BY.
SEE YA.
OH, HA-SU-MI! ♡
ビクゥ

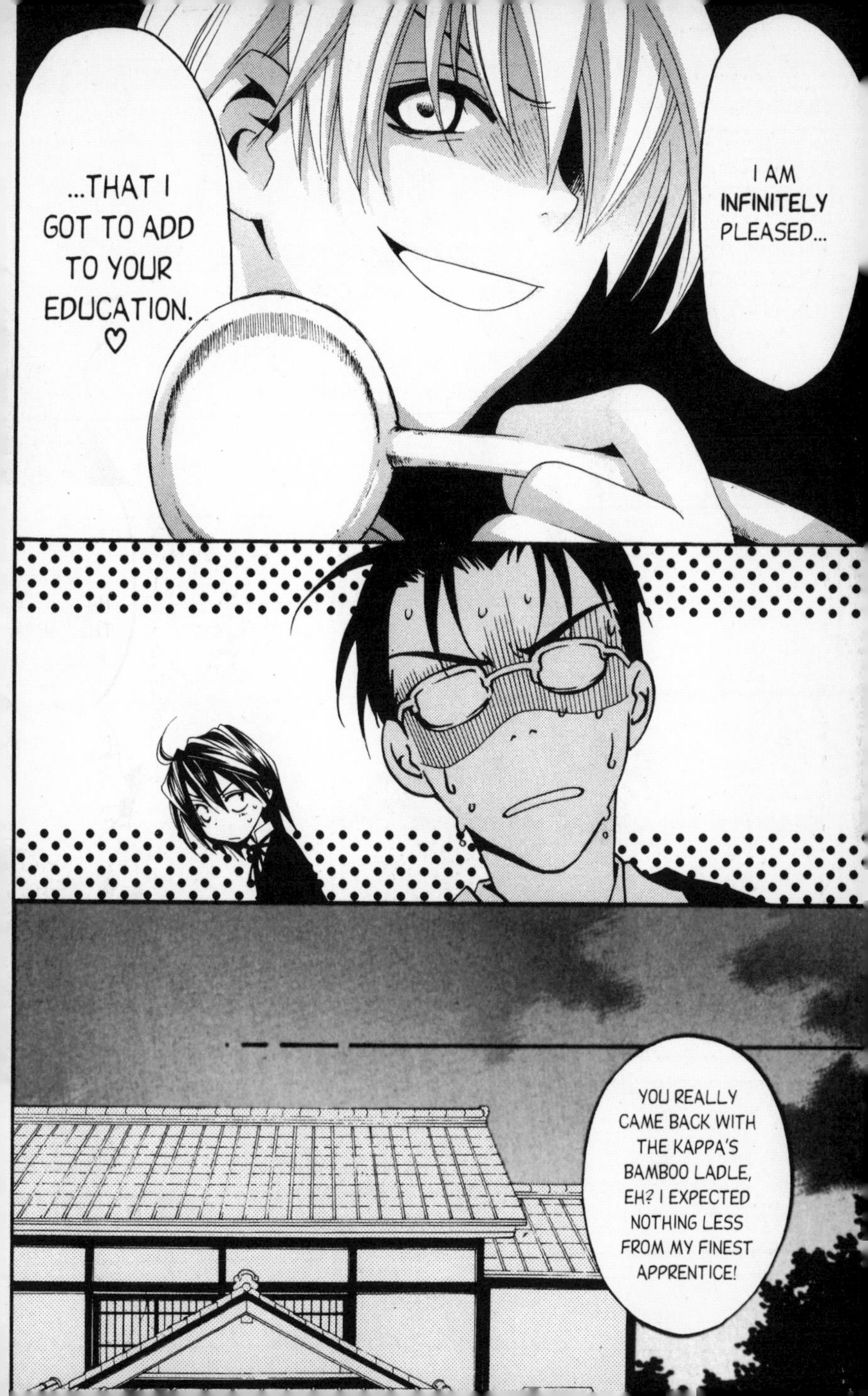
I AM **INFINITELY** PLEASED...
...THAT I GOT TO ADD TO YOUR EDUCATION. ♡
YOU REALLY CAME BACK WITH THE KAPPA'S BAMBOO LADLE, EH? I EXPECTED NOTHING LESS FROM MY FINEST APPRENTICE!

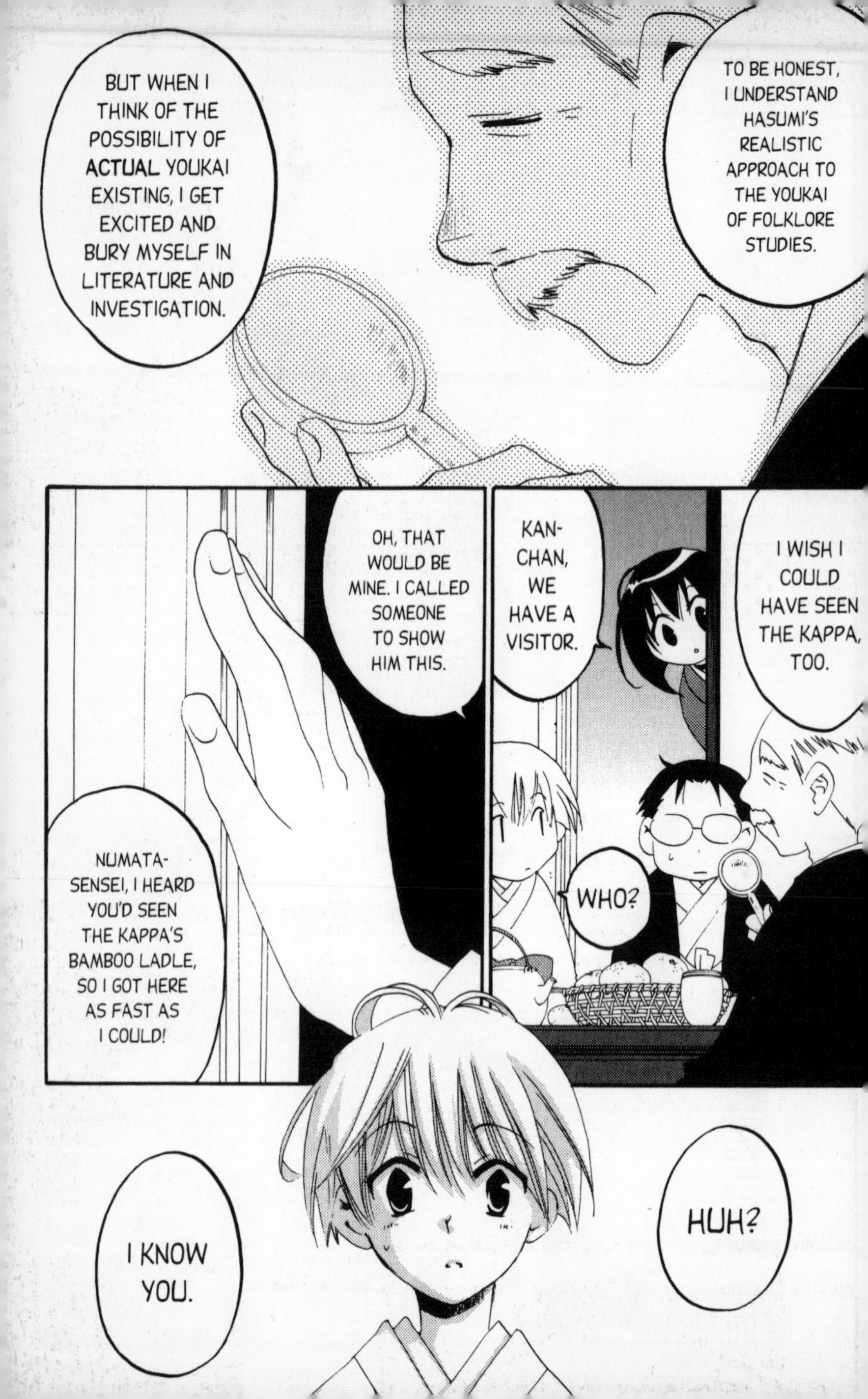
TO BE HONEST, I UNDERSTAND HASUMI'S REALISTIC APPROACH TO THE YOUKAI OF FOLKLORE STUDIES.
BUT WHEN I THINK OF THE POSSIBILITY OF **ACTUAL** YOUKAI EXISTING, I GET EXCITED AND BURY MYSELF IN LITERATURE AND INVESTIGATION.
I WISH I COULD HAVE SEEN THE KAPPA, TOO.
KAN-CHAN, WE HAVE A VISITOR.
WHO?
OH, THAT WOULD BE MINE. I CALLED SOMEONE TO SHOW HIM THIS.
NUMATA-SENSEI, I HEARD YOU'D SEEN THE KAPPA'S BAMBOO LADLE, SO I GOT HERE AS FAST AS I COULD!
HUH?
I KNOW YOU.

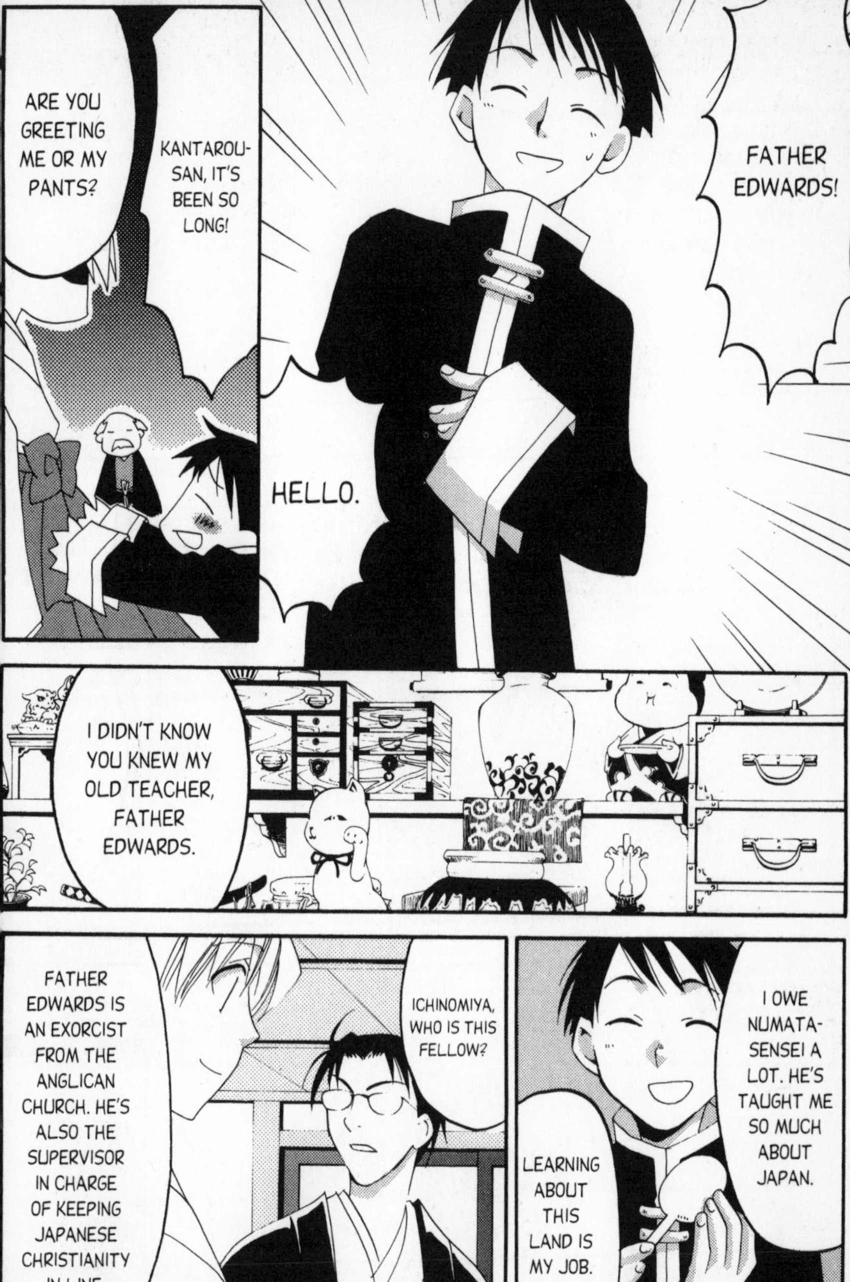
FATHER EDWARDS!
HELLO.
KANTAROU-SAN, IT'S BEEN SO LONG!
ARE YOU GREETING ME OR MY PANTS?
I DIDN'T KNOW YOU KNEW MY OLD TEACHER, FATHER EDWARDS.
I OWE NUMATA-SENSEI A LOT. HE'S TAUGHT ME SO MUCH ABOUT JAPAN.
LEARNING ABOUT THIS LAND IS MY JOB.
ICHINOMIYA, WHO IS THIS FELLOW?
FATHER EDWARDS IS AN EXORCIST FROM THE ANGLICAN CHURCH. HE'S ALSO THE SUPERVISOR IN CHARGE OF KEEPING JAPANESE CHRISTIANITY IN LINE.

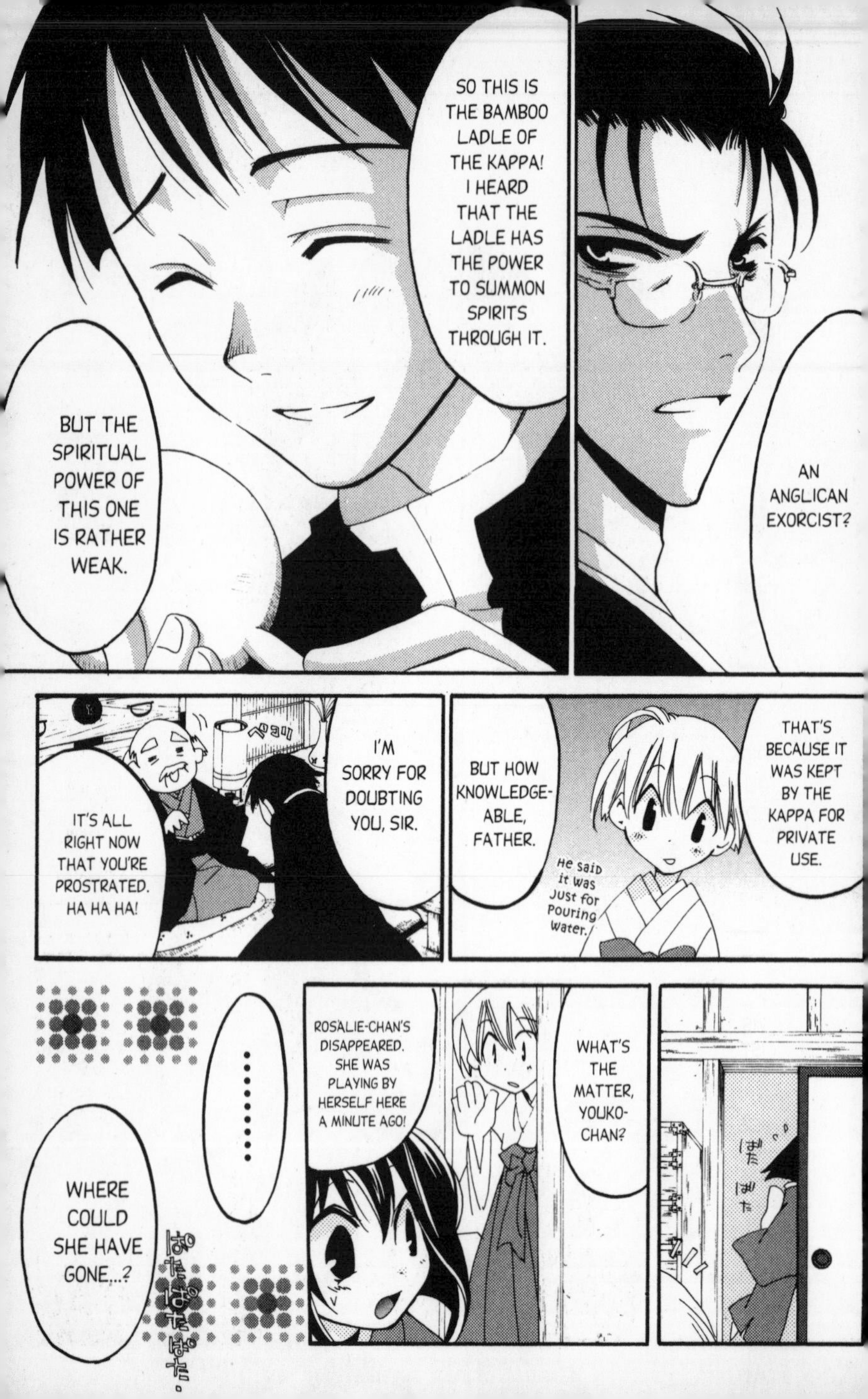

AN ANGLICAN EXORCIST?
SO THIS IS THE BAMBOO LADLE OF THE KAPPA! I HEARD THAT THE LADLE HAS THE POWER TO SUMMON SPIRITS THROUGH IT.
BUT THE SPIRITUAL POWER OF THIS ONE IS RATHER WEAK.
THAT'S BECAUSE IT WAS KEPT BY THE KAPPA FOR PRIVATE USE.
BUT HOW KNOWLEDGE-ABLE, FATHER.
He said it was just for pouring water.
I'M SORRY FOR DOUBTING YOU, SIR.
IT'S ALL RIGHT NOW THAT YOU'RE PROSTRATED. HA HA HA!
ばた ばた
WHAT'S THE MATTER, YOUKO-CHAN?
ROSALIE-CHAN'S DISAPPEARED. SHE WAS PLAYING BY HERSELF HERE A MINUTE AGO!
....
WHERE COULD SHE HAVE GONE...?

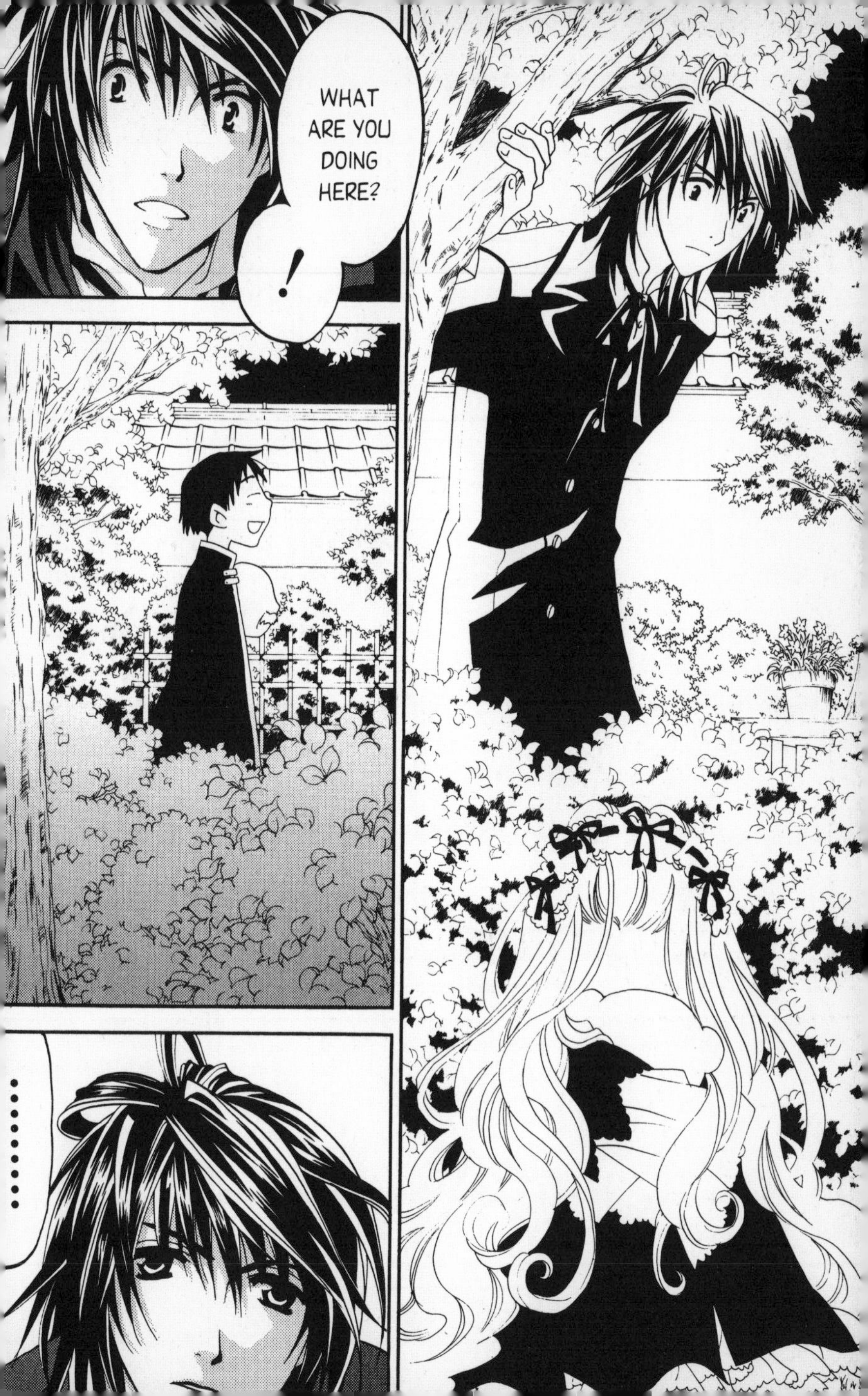
WHAT ARE YOU DOING HERE?
!
......

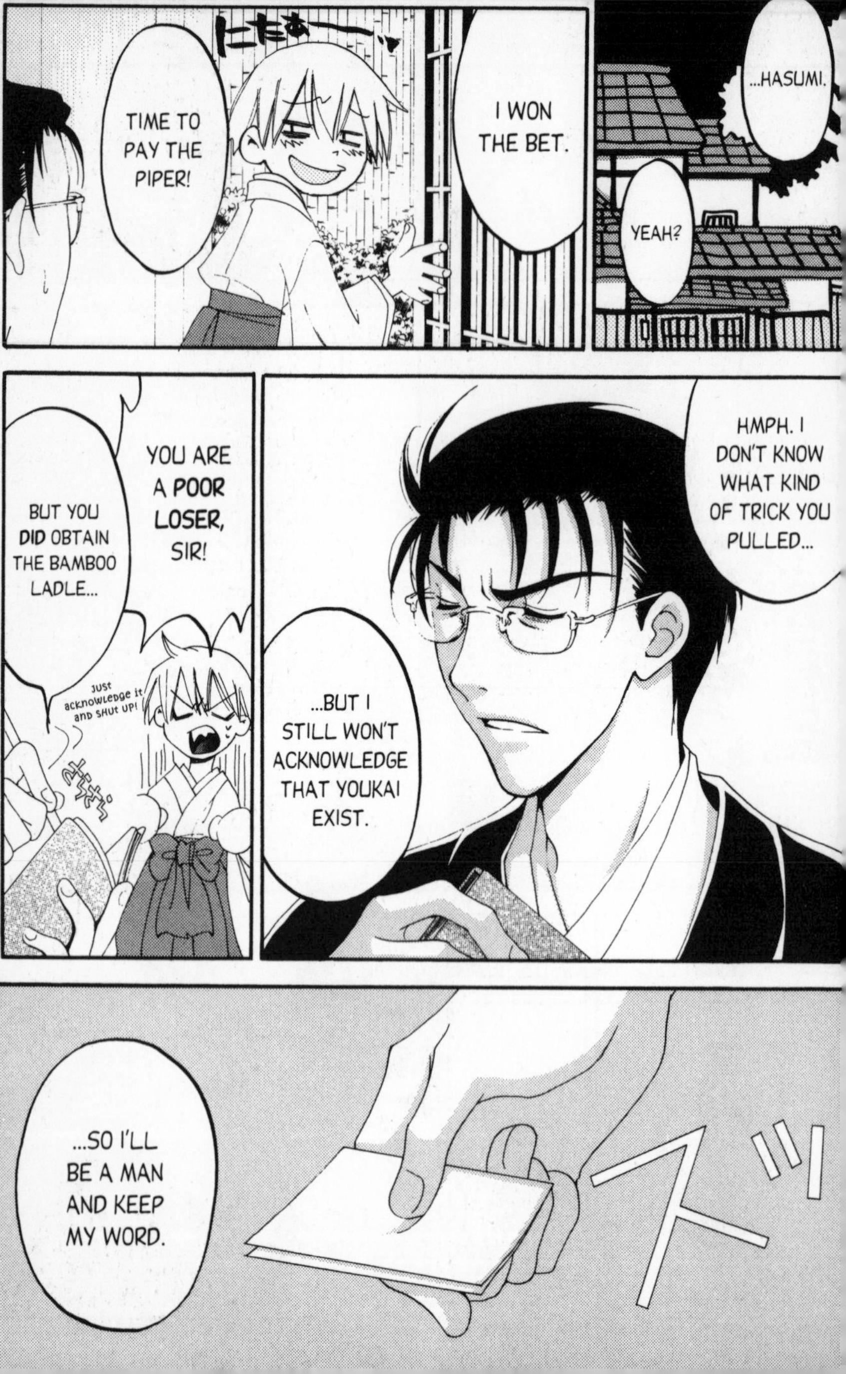
...HASUMI.
YEAH?
I WON THE BET.
にたぁーー
TIME TO PAY THE PIPER!
HMPH. I DON'T KNOW WHAT KIND OF TRICK YOU PULLED...
...BUT I STILL WON'T ACKNOWLEDGE THAT YOUKAI EXIST.
YOU ARE A POOR LOSER, SIR!
BUT YOU DID OBTAIN THE BAMBOO LADLE...
Just acknowledge it and SHut UP!
...SO I'LL BE A MAN AND KEEP MY WORD.
スッ

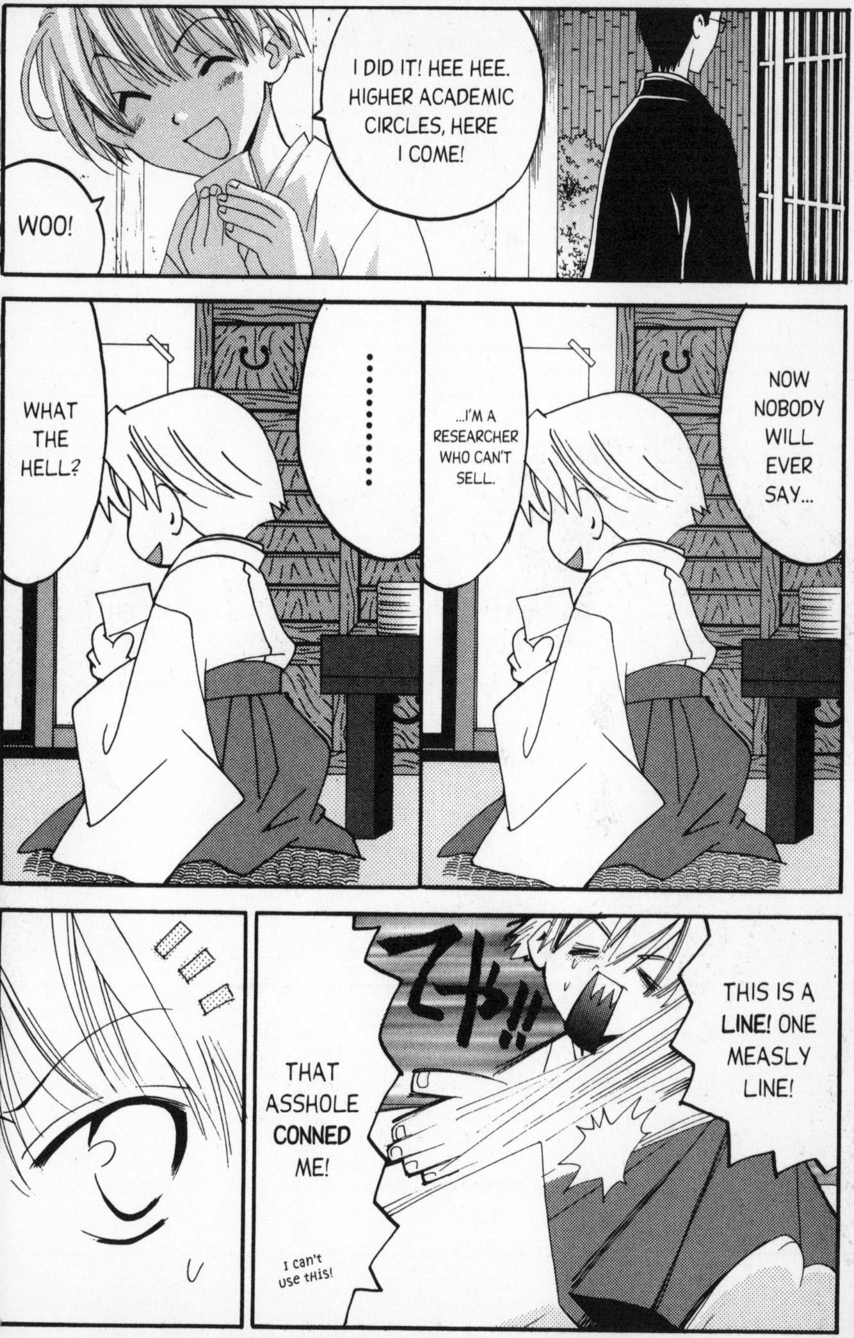
I DID IT! HEE HEE. HIGHER ACADEMIC CIRCLES, HERE I COME!
WOO!
NOW NOBODY WILL EVER SAY...
...I'M A RESEARCHER WHO CAN'T SELL.
......
WHAT THE HELL?
THIS IS A LINE! ONE MEASLY LINE!
THAT ASSHOLE CONNED ME!
I can't use this!

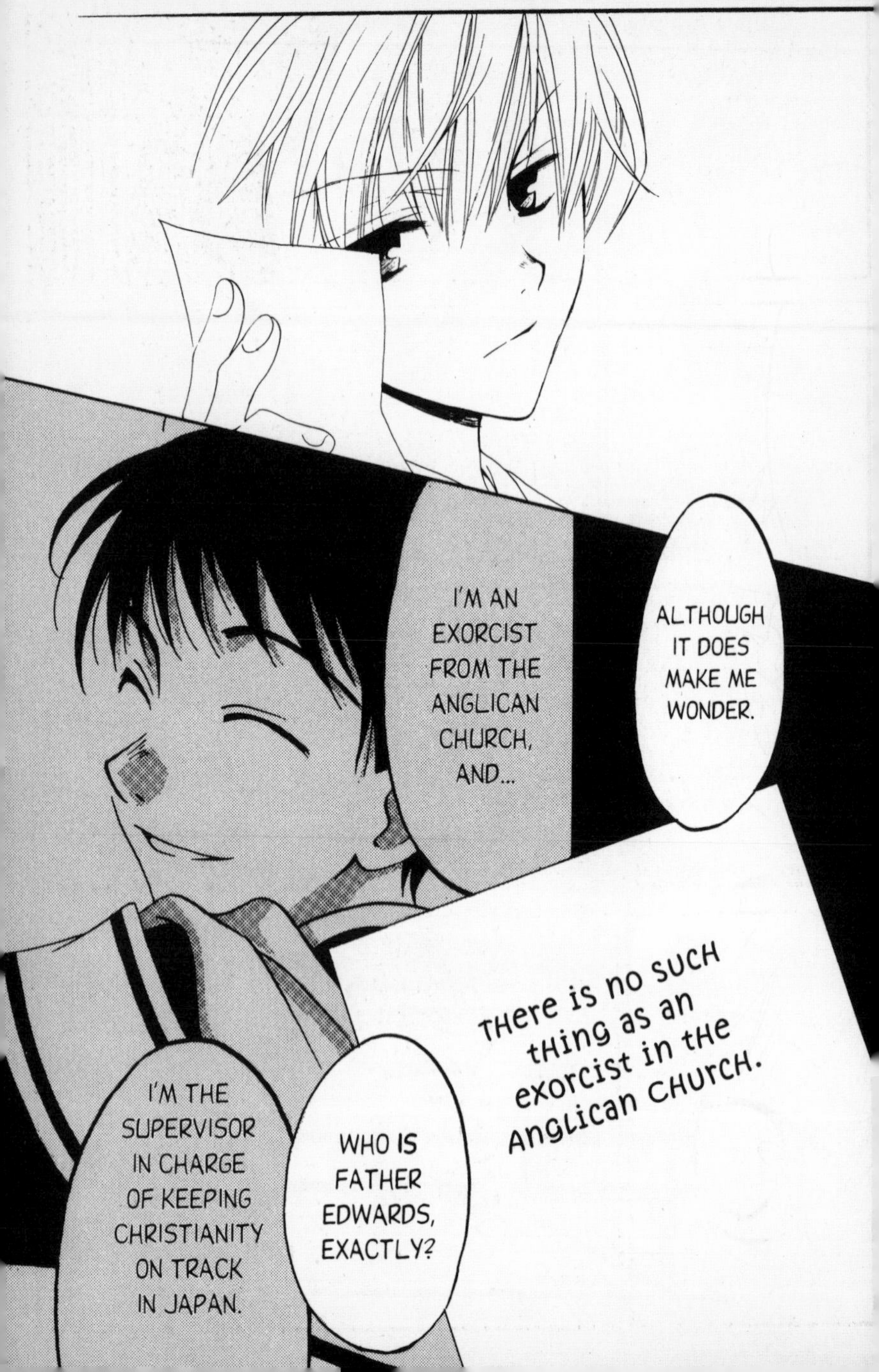
ALTHOUGH IT DOES MAKE ME WONDER.
I'M AN EXORCIST FROM THE ANGLICAN CHURCH, AND...
There is no SUCH tHing as an exorcist in tHe AngLican CHUrcH.
WHO IS FATHER EDWARDS, EXACTLY?
I'M THE SUPERVISOR IN CHARGE OF KEEPING CHRISTIANITY ON TRACK IN JAPAN.

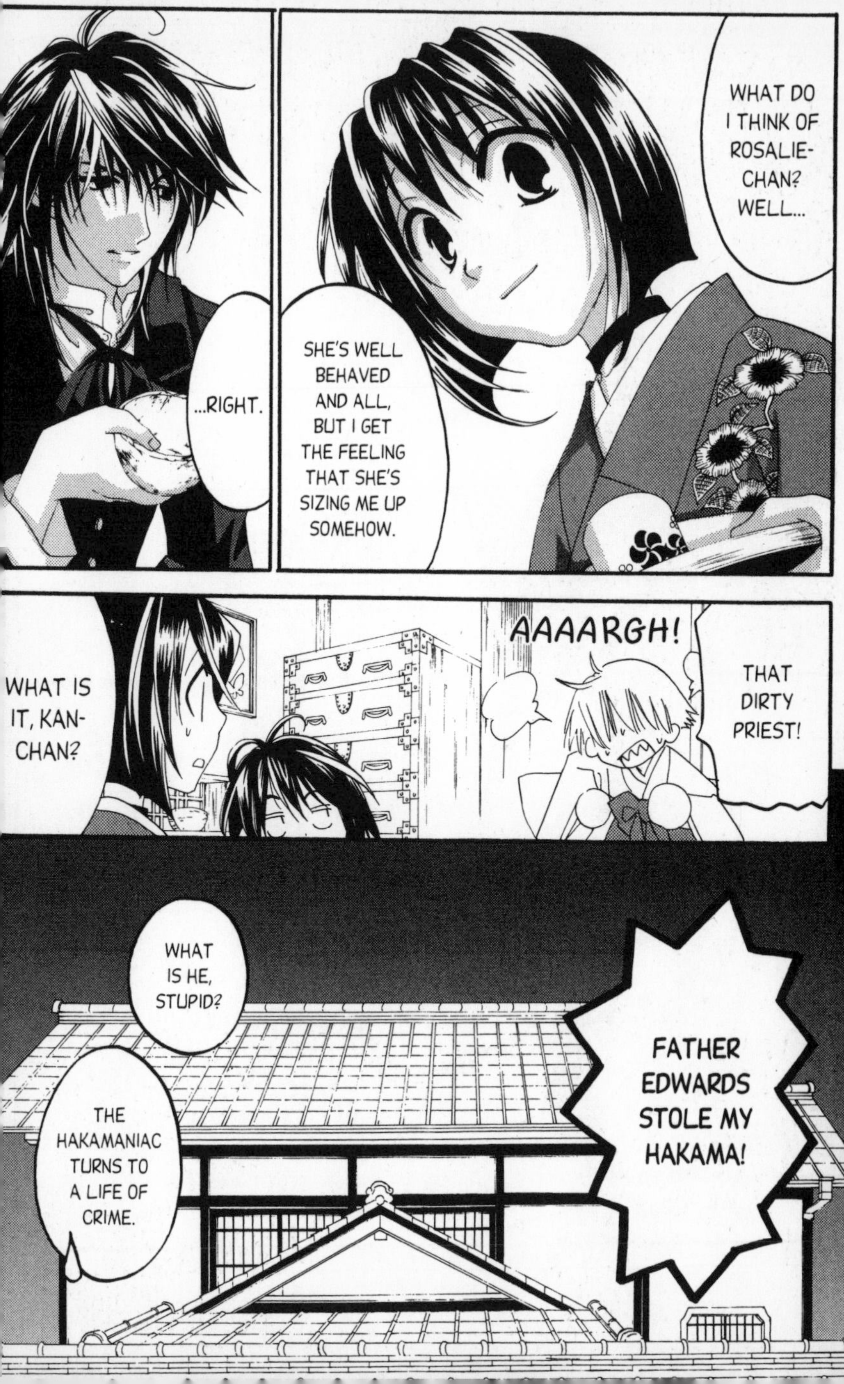
WHAT DO I THINK OF ROSALIE-CHAN? WELL...
SHE'S WELL BEHAVED AND ALL, BUT I GET THE FEELING THAT SHE'S SIZING ME UP SOMEHOW.
...RIGHT.
THAT DIRTY PRIEST!
AAAARGH!
WHAT IS IT, KAN-CHAN?
FATHER EDWARDS STOLE MY HAKAMA!
WHAT IS HE, STUPID?
THE HAKAMANIAC TURNS TO A LIFE OF CRIME.

tactics Special 滑稽画報 Preview Comic

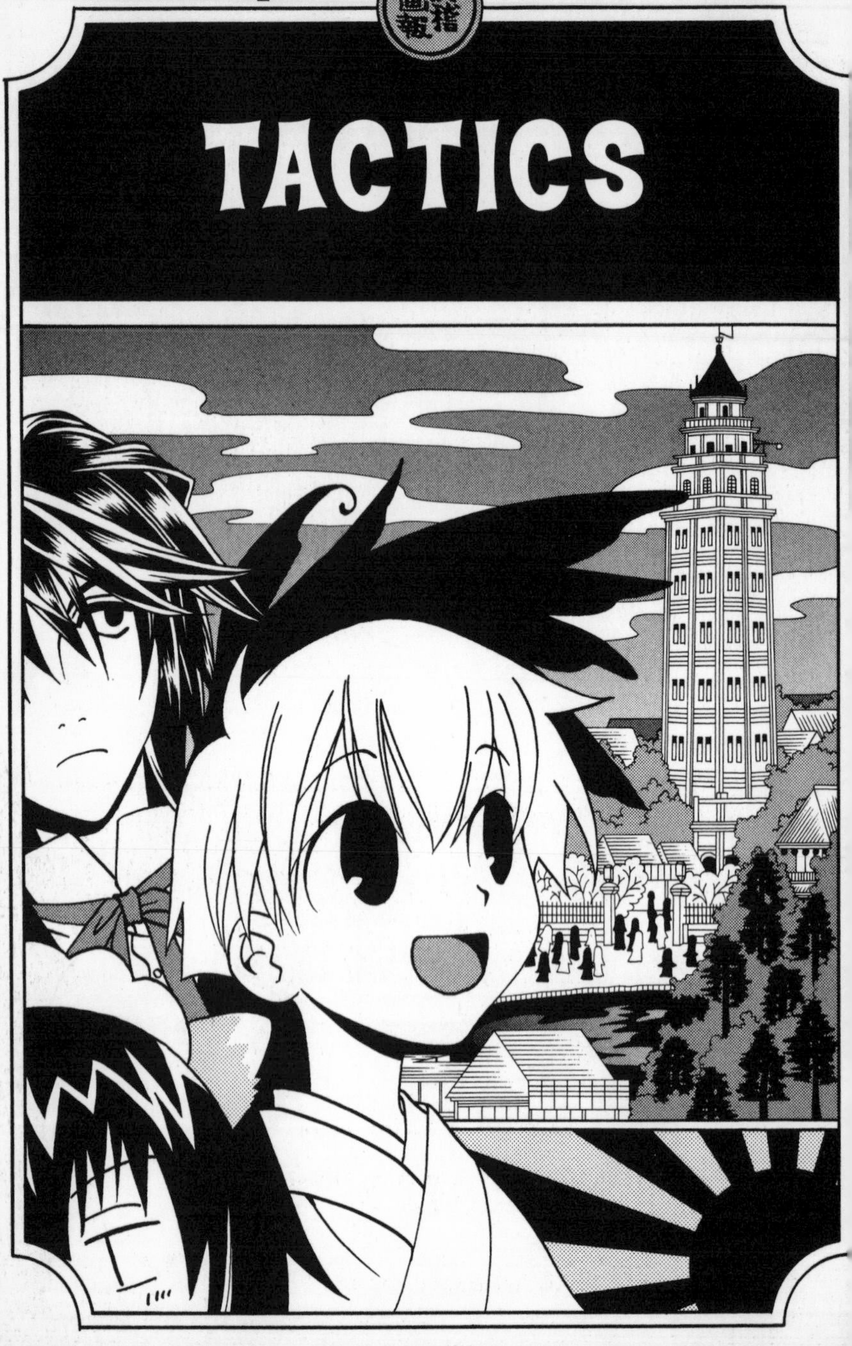
TACTICS

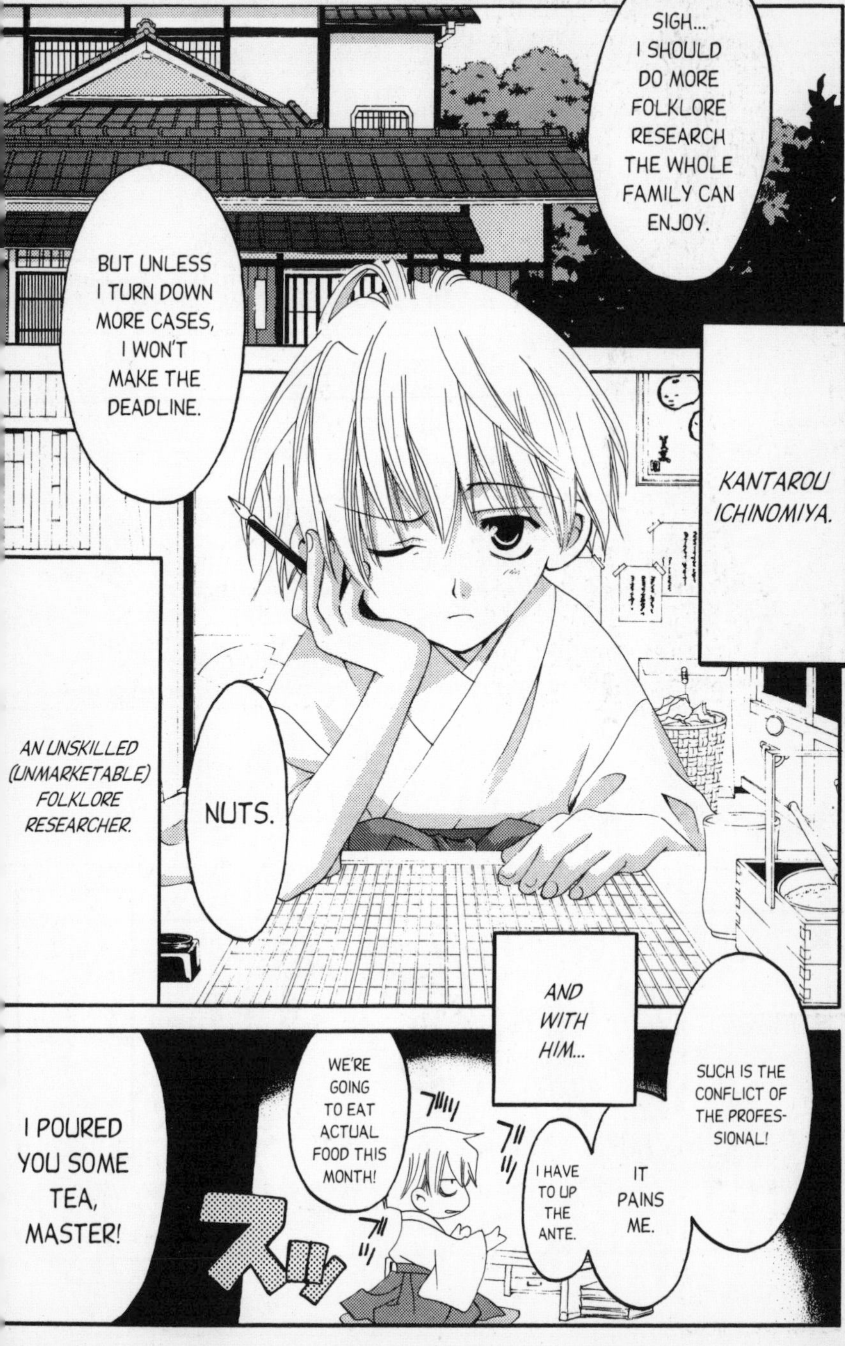
SIGH... I SHOULD DO MORE FOLKLORE RESEARCH THE WHOLE FAMILY CAN ENJOY.
BUT UNLESS I TURN DOWN MORE CASES, I WON'T MAKE THE DEADLINE.
KANTAROU ICHINOMIYA.
NUTS.
AN UNSKILLED (UNMARKETABLE) FOLKLORE RESEARCHER.
AND WITH HIM...
SUCH IS THE CONFLICT OF THE PROFES-SIONAL!
IT PAINS ME.
I HAVE TO UP THE ANTE.
WE'RE GOING TO EAT ACTUAL FOOD THIS MONTH!
I POURED YOU SOME TEA, MASTER!

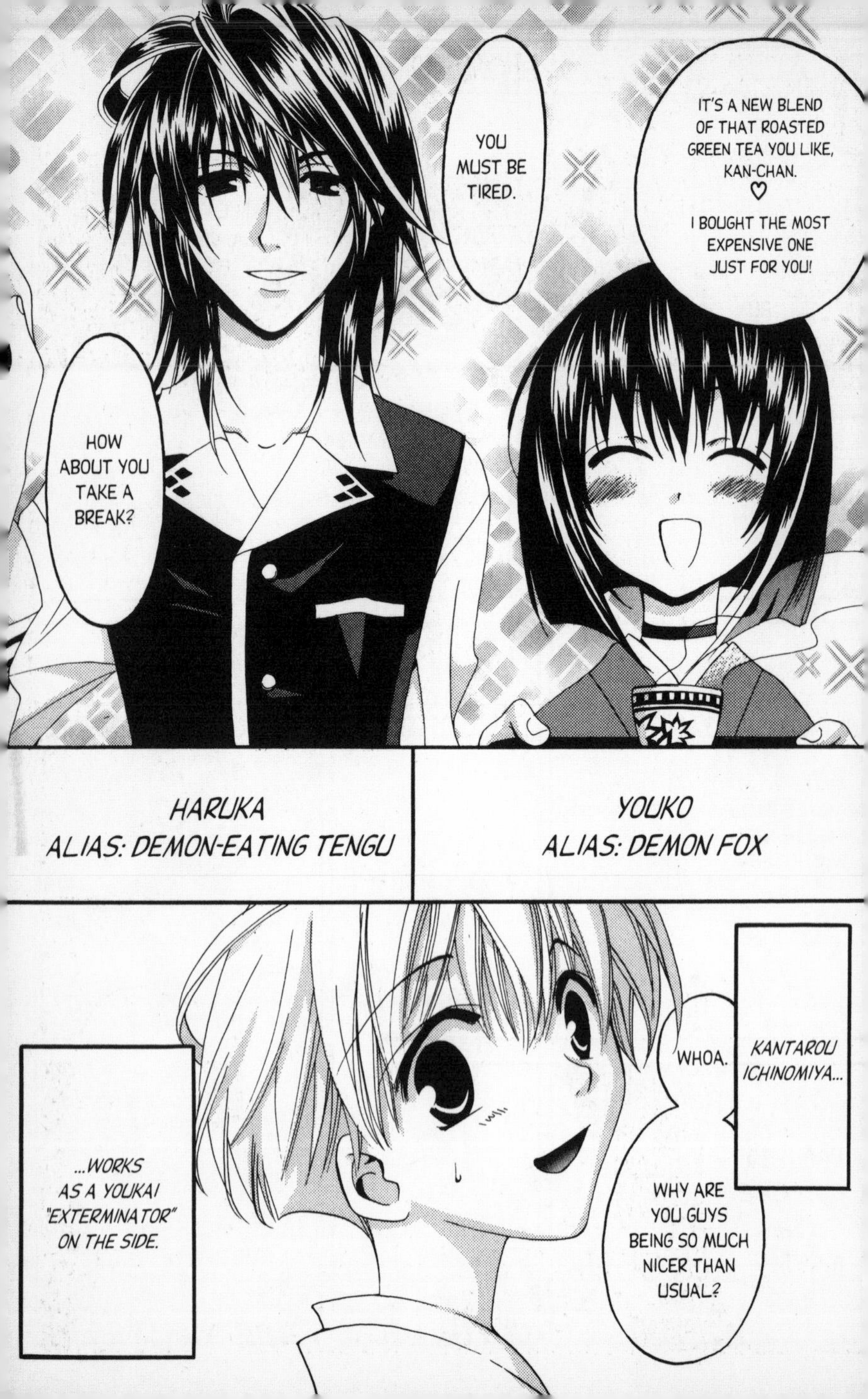
IT'S A NEW BLEND OF THAT ROASTED GREEN TEA YOU LIKE, KAN-CHAN. ♡
I BOUGHT THE MOST EXPENSIVE ONE JUST FOR YOU!
YOU MUST BE TIRED.
HOW ABOUT YOU TAKE A BREAK?
YOUKO
ALIAS: DEMON FOX
HARUKA
ALIAS: DEMON-EATING TENGU
KANTAROU ICHINOMIYA...
WHOA.
WHY ARE YOU GUYS BEING SO MUCH NICER THAN USUAL?
...WORKS AS A YOUKAI "EXTERMINATOR" ON THE SIDE.

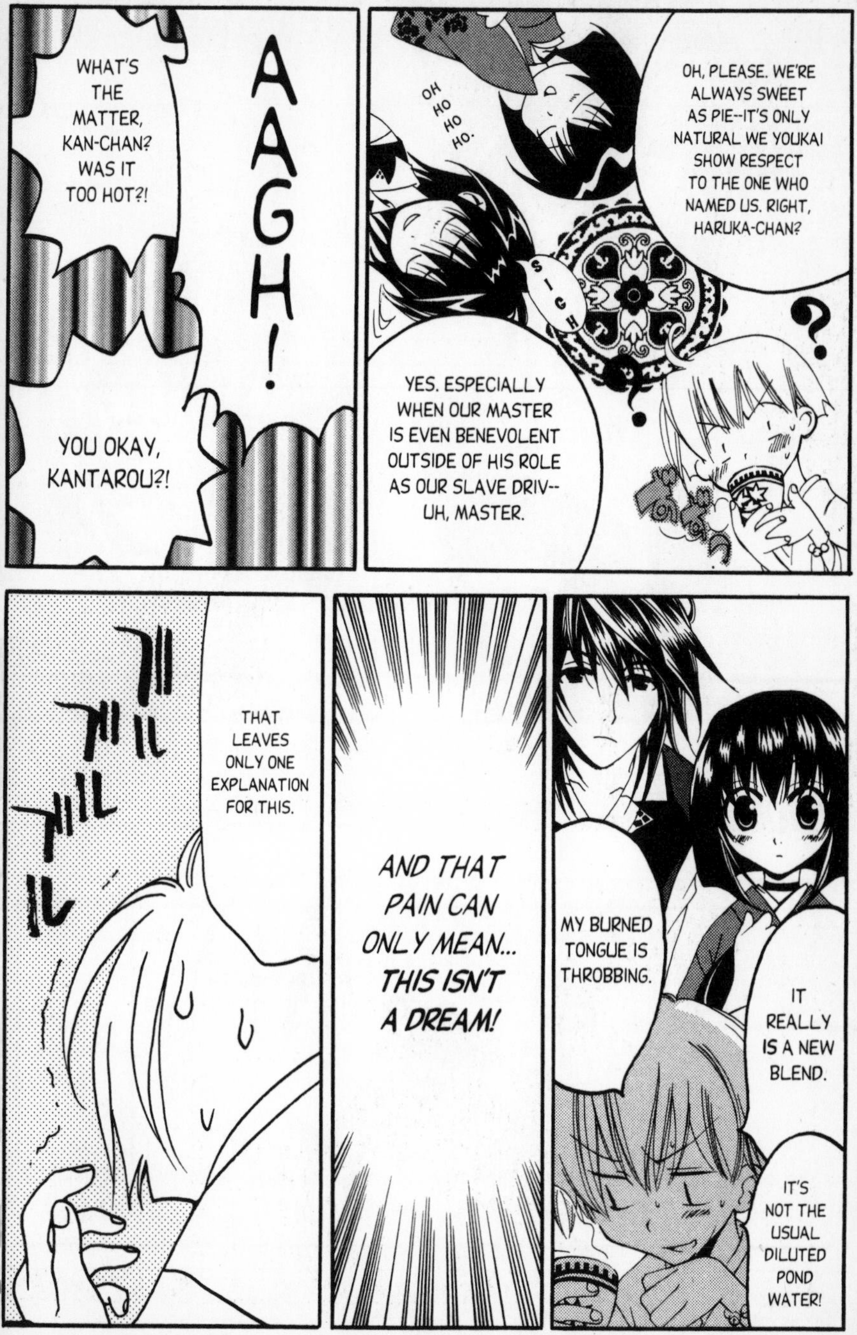
OH, PLEASE. WE'RE ALWAYS SWEET AS PIE--IT'S ONLY NATURAL WE YOUKAI SHOW RESPECT TO THE ONE WHO NAMED US. RIGHT, HARUKA-CHAN?
OH HO HO HO.
SIGH
YES. ESPECIALLY WHEN OUR MASTER IS EVEN BENEVOLENT OUTSIDE OF HIS ROLE AS OUR SLAVE DRIV-- UH, MASTER.
?
?
AAGH!
WHAT'S THE MATTER, KAN-CHAN? WAS IT TOO HOT?!
YOU OKAY, KANTAROU?!
MY BURNED TONGUE IS THROBBING.
IT REALLY IS A NEW BLEND.
IT'S NOT THE USUAL DILUTED POND WATER!
AND THAT PAIN CAN ONLY MEAN... THIS ISN'T A DREAM!
THAT LEAVES ONLY ONE EXPLANATION FOR THIS.

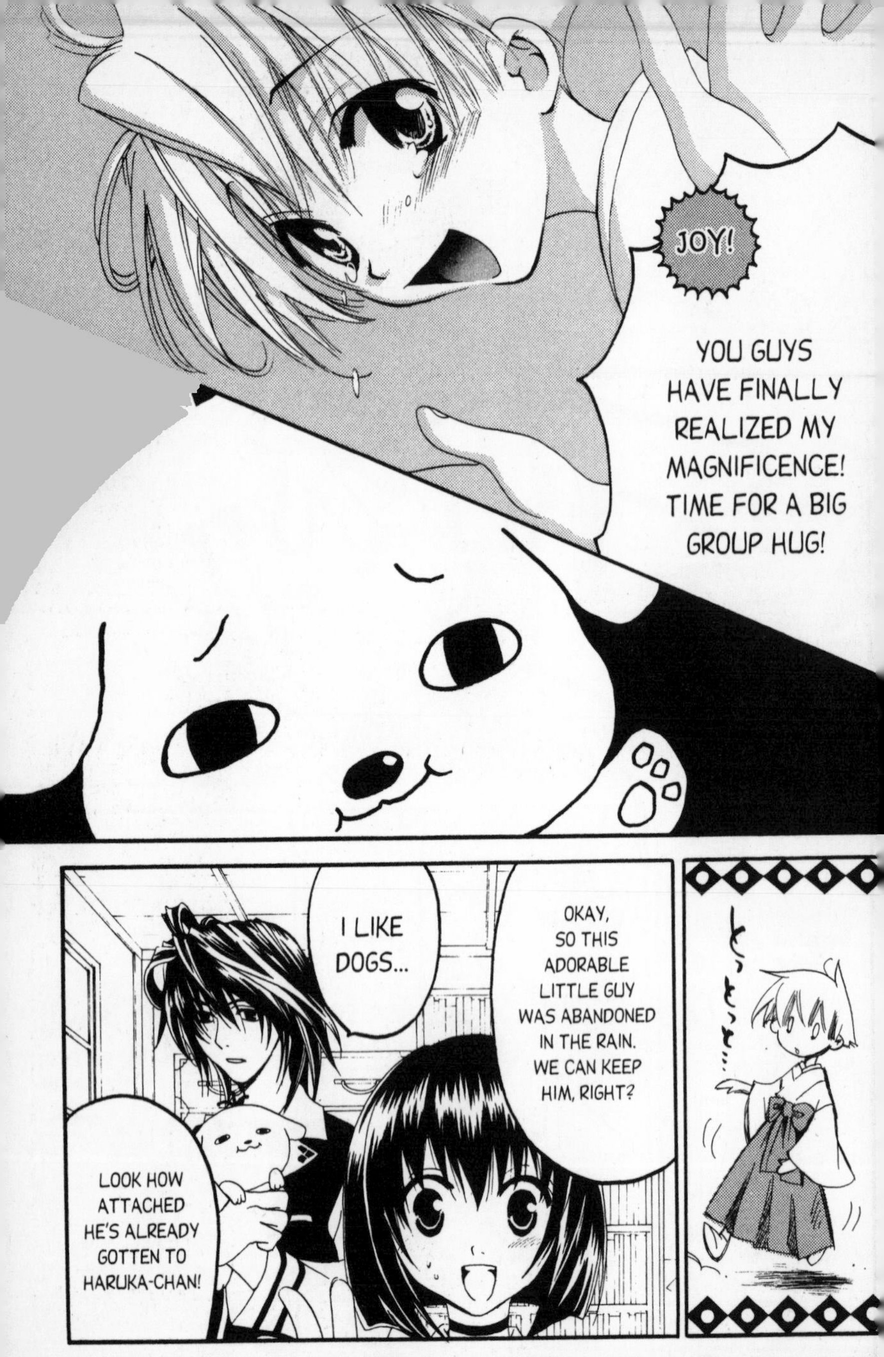
JOY!
YOU GUYS HAVE FINALLY REALIZED MY MAGNIFICENCE! TIME FOR A BIG GROUP HUG!
とっとっと…
OKAY, SO THIS ADORABLE LITTLE GUY WAS ABANDONED IN THE RAIN. WE CAN KEEP HIM, RIGHT?
I LIKE DOGS...
LOOK HOW ATTACHED HE'S ALREADY GOTTEN TO HARUKA-CHAN!

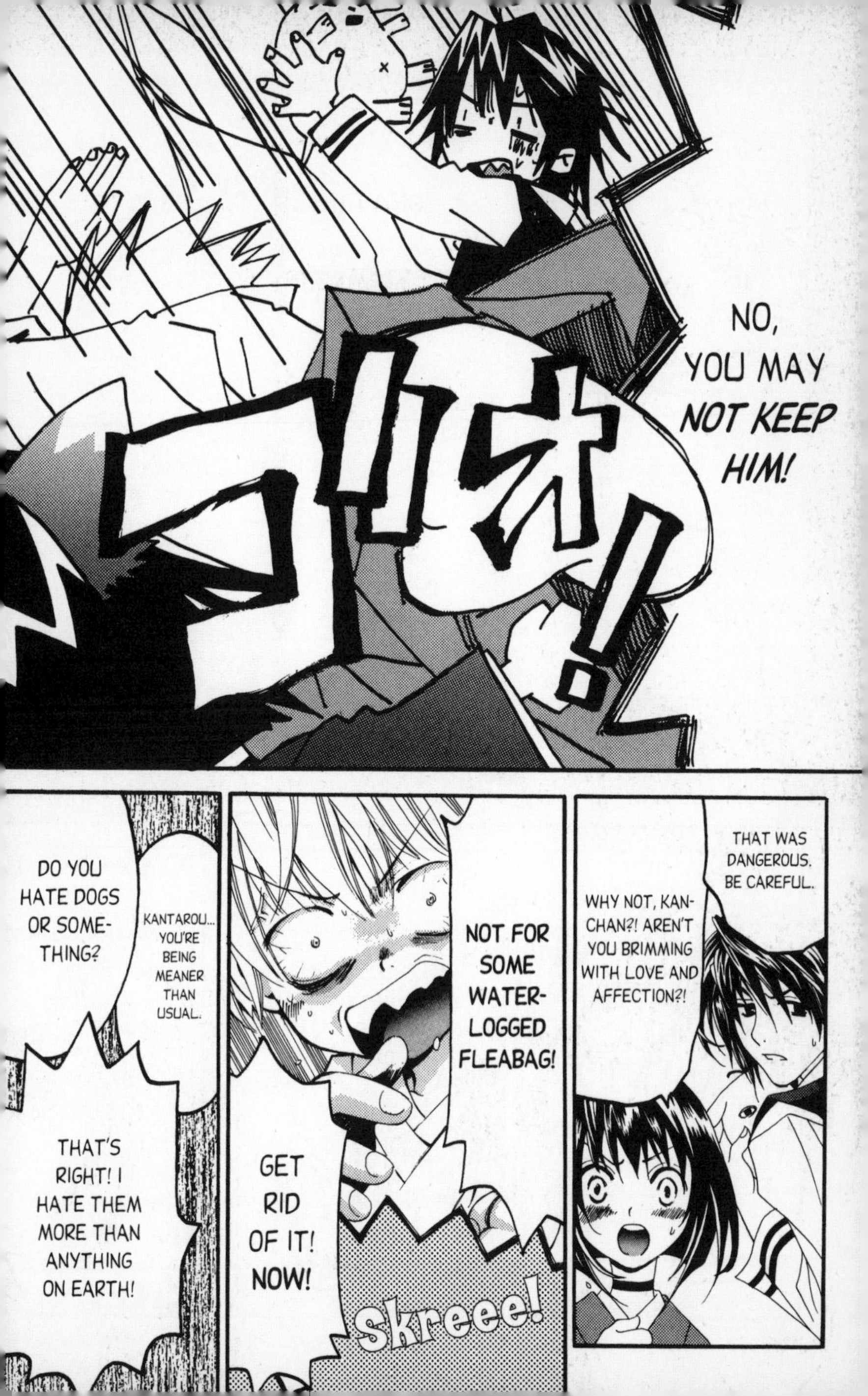
NO, YOU MAY NOT KEEP HIM!
THAT WAS DANGEROUS. BE CAREFUL.
WHY NOT, KAN-CHAN?! AREN'T YOU BRIMMING WITH LOVE AND AFFECTION?!
NOT FOR SOME WATER-LOGGED FLEABAG!
GET RID OF IT! NOW!
Skreee!
KANTAROU... YOU'RE BEING MEANER THAN USUAL.
DO YOU HATE DOGS OR SOME-THING?
THAT'S RIGHT! I HATE THEM MORE THAN ANYTHING ON EARTH!

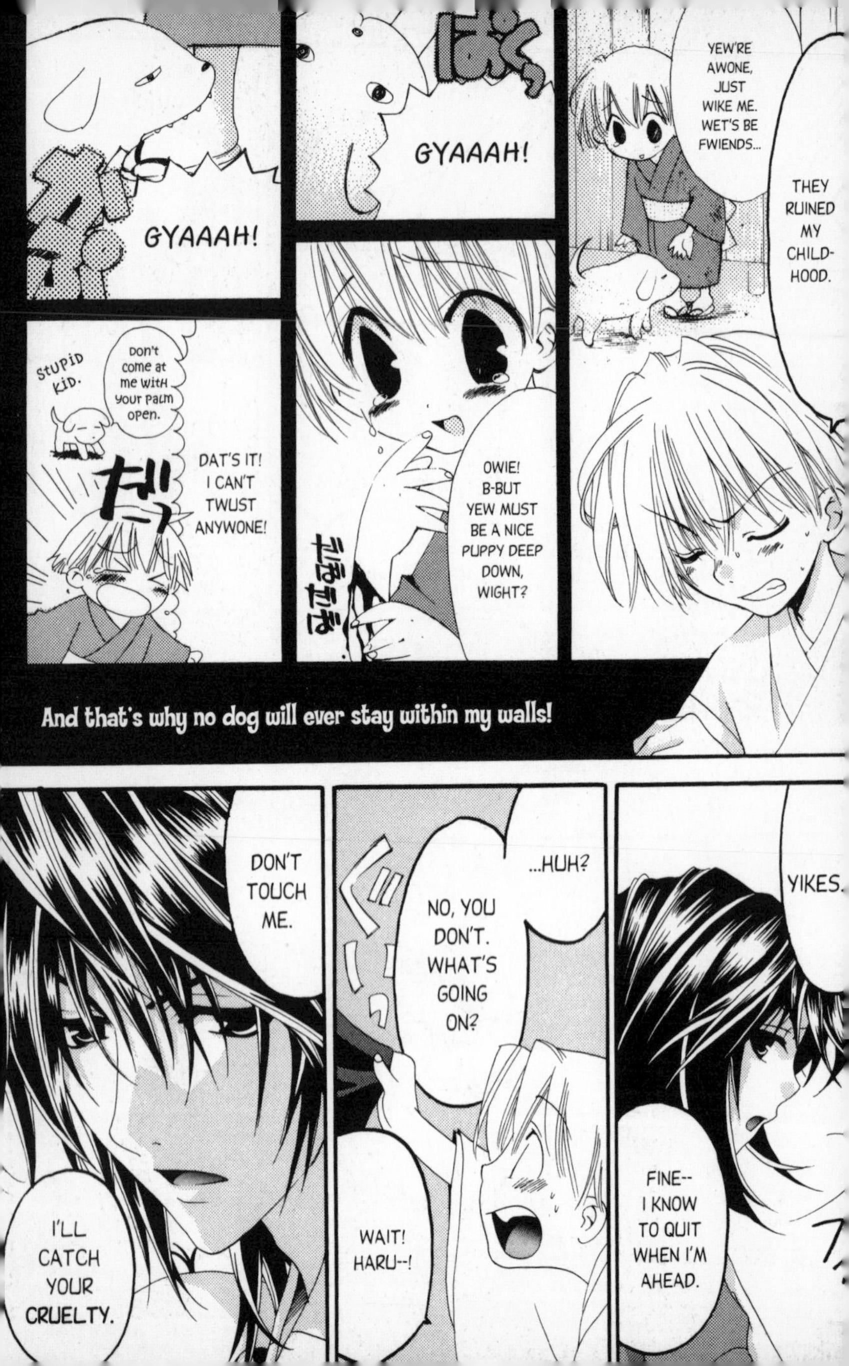
YEW'RE AWONE, JUST WIKE ME. WET'S BE FWIENDS...
THEY RUINED MY CHILDHOOD.
ぱくっ
GYAAAH!
GYAAAH!
OWIE! B-BUT YEW MUST BE A NICE PUPPY DEEP DOWN, WIGHT?
だばだば
STUPID KID.
Don't come at me with your palm open.
DAT'S IT! I CAN'T TWUST ANYWONE!
だっ
And that's why no dog will ever stay within my walls!
YIKES.
FINE-- I KNOW TO QUIT WHEN I'M AHEAD.
...HUH?
NO, YOU DON'T. WHAT'S GOING ON?
WAIT! HARU--!
DON'T TOUCH ME.
I'LL CATCH YOUR CRUELTY.

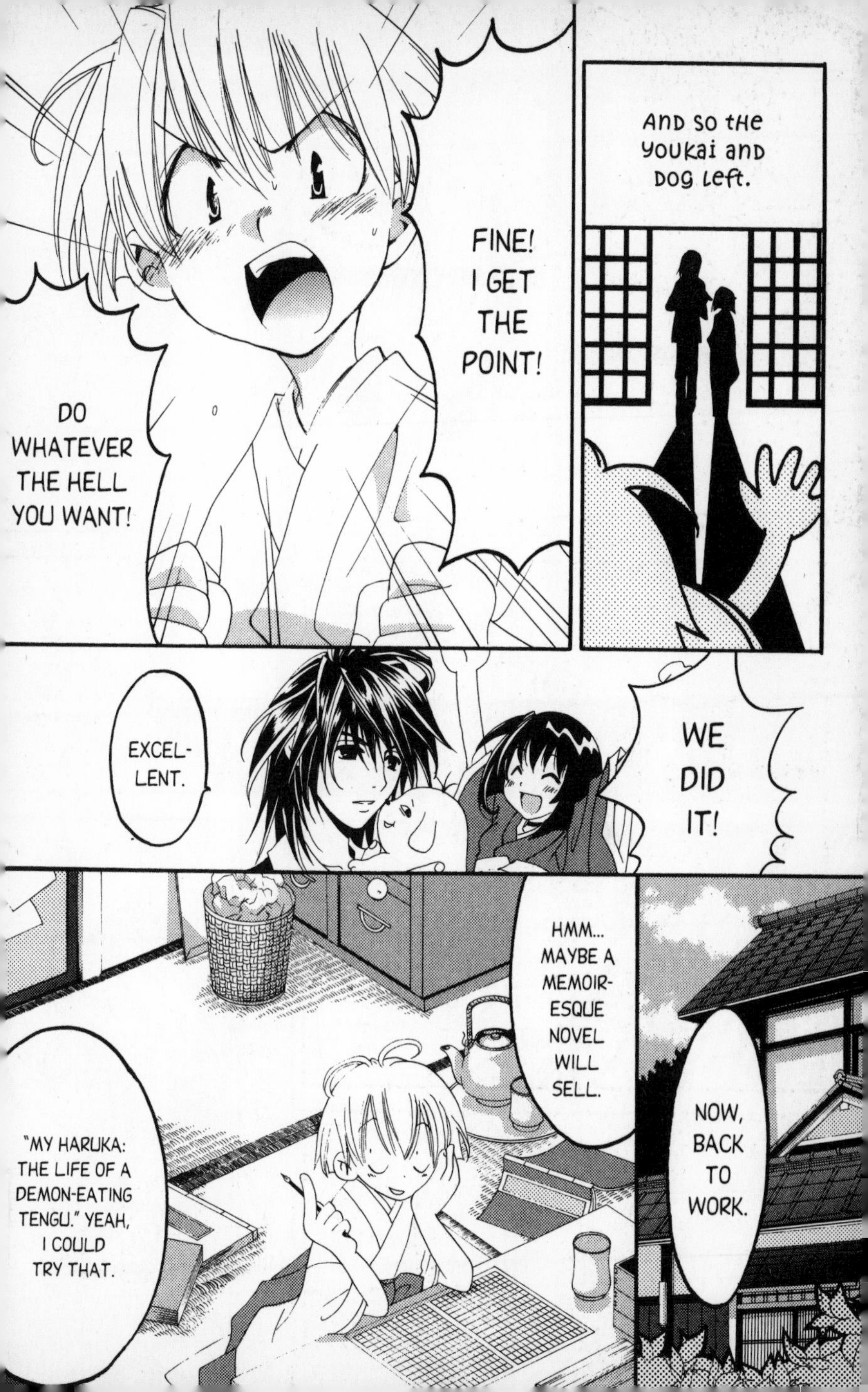
And so the youkai and dog left.
FINE! I GET THE POINT!
DO WHATEVER THE HELL YOU WANT!
WE DID IT!
EXCEL-LENT.
NOW, BACK TO WORK.
HMM... MAYBE A MEMOIR-ESQUE NOVEL WILL SELL.
"MY HARUKA: THE LIFE OF A DEMON-EATING TENGU." YEAH, I COULD TRY THAT.

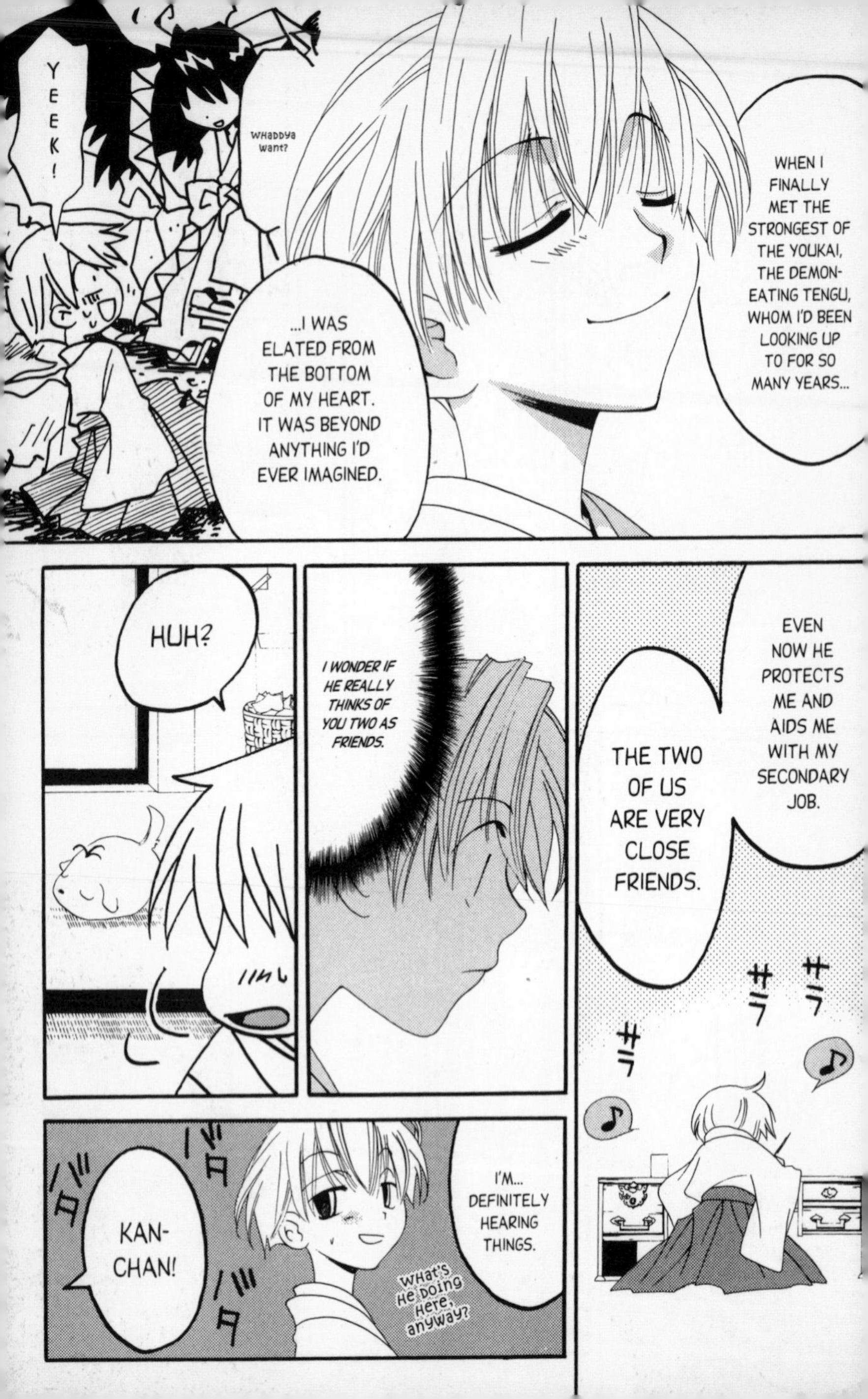
WHEN I FINALLY MET THE STRONGEST OF THE YOUKAI, THE DEMON-EATING TENGU, WHOM I'D BEEN LOOKING UP TO FOR SO MANY YEARS...
...I WAS ELATED FROM THE BOTTOM OF MY HEART. IT WAS BEYOND ANYTHING I'D EVER IMAGINED.
Whaddya want?
YEEK!
EVEN NOW HE PROTECTS ME AND AIDS ME WITH MY SECONDARY JOB.
THE TWO OF US ARE VERY CLOSE FRIENDS.
サラ
サラ
サラ
I WONDER IF HE REALLY THINKS OF YOU TWO AS FRIENDS.
HUH?
I'M... DEFINITELY HEARING THINGS.
What's he doing here, anyway?
KAN-CHAN!

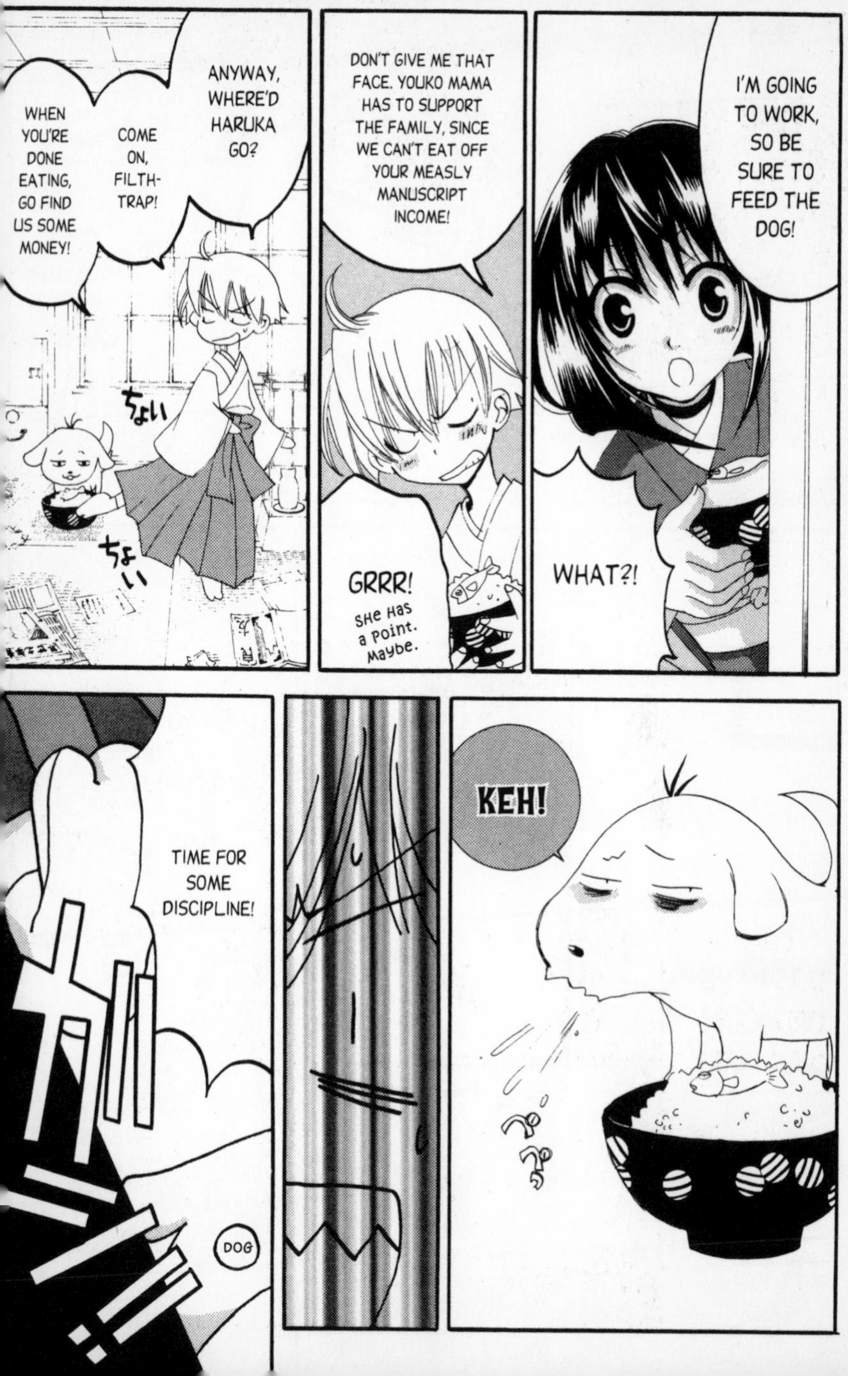
I'M GOING TO WORK, SO BE SURE TO FEED THE DOG!
WHAT?!
DON'T GIVE ME THAT FACE. YOUKO MAMA HAS TO SUPPORT THE FAMILY, SINCE WE CAN'T EAT OFF YOUR MEASLY MANUSCRIPT INCOME!
GRRR!
SHE HAS A POINT. MAYBE.
ANYWAY, WHERE'D HARUKA GO?
COME ON, FILTH-TRAP!
WHEN YOU'RE DONE EATING, GO FIND US SOME MONEY!
ちょい
ちょい
KEH!
TIME FOR SOME DISCIPLINE!
DOG

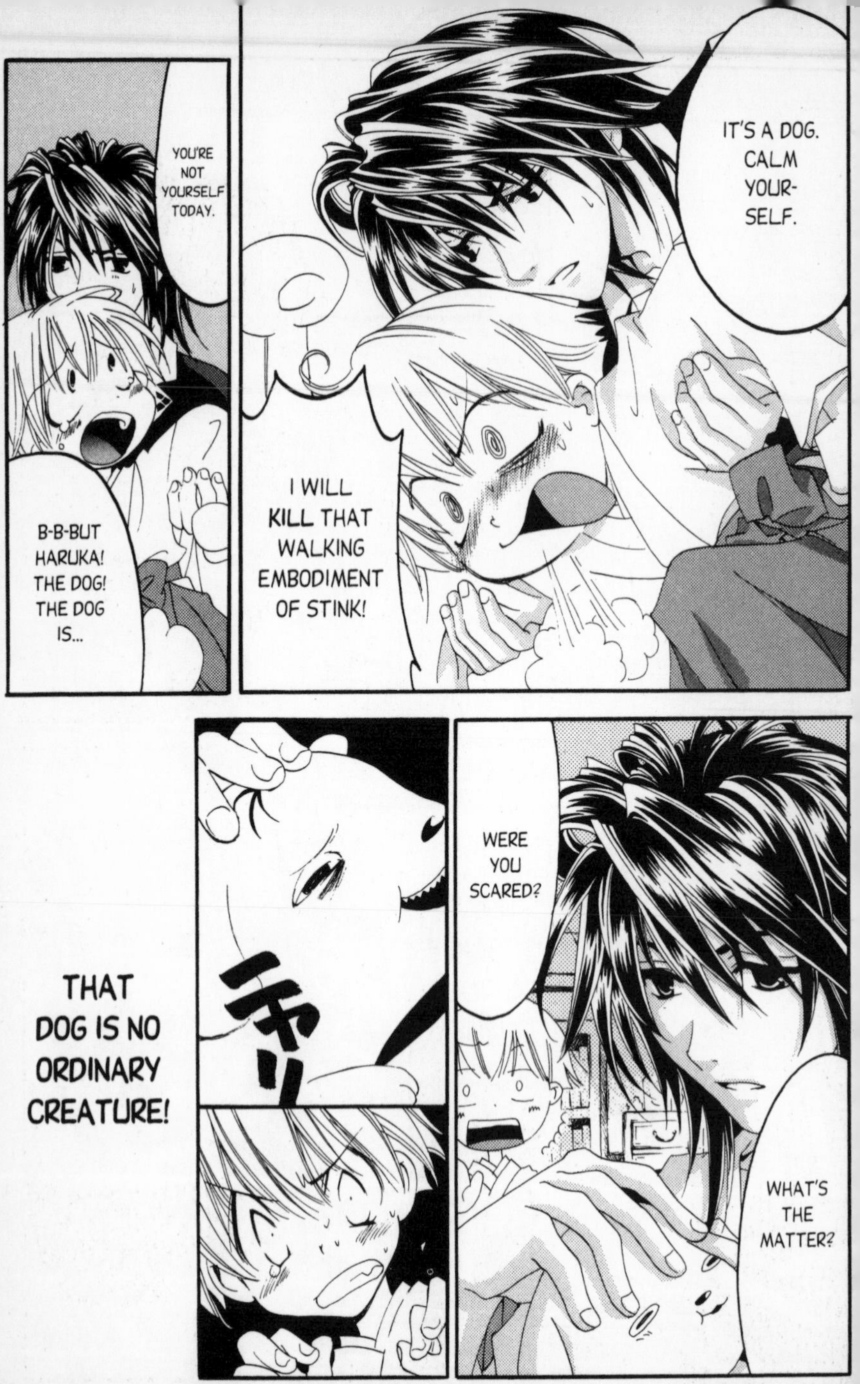
IT'S A DOG. CALM YOURSELF.
I WILL KILL THAT WALKING EMBODIMENT OF STINK!
YOU'RE NOT YOURSELF TODAY.
B-B-BUT HARUKA! THE DOG! THE DOG IS...
WERE YOU SCARED?
WHAT'S THE MATTER?
ニヤリ
THAT DOG IS NO ORDINARY CREATURE!

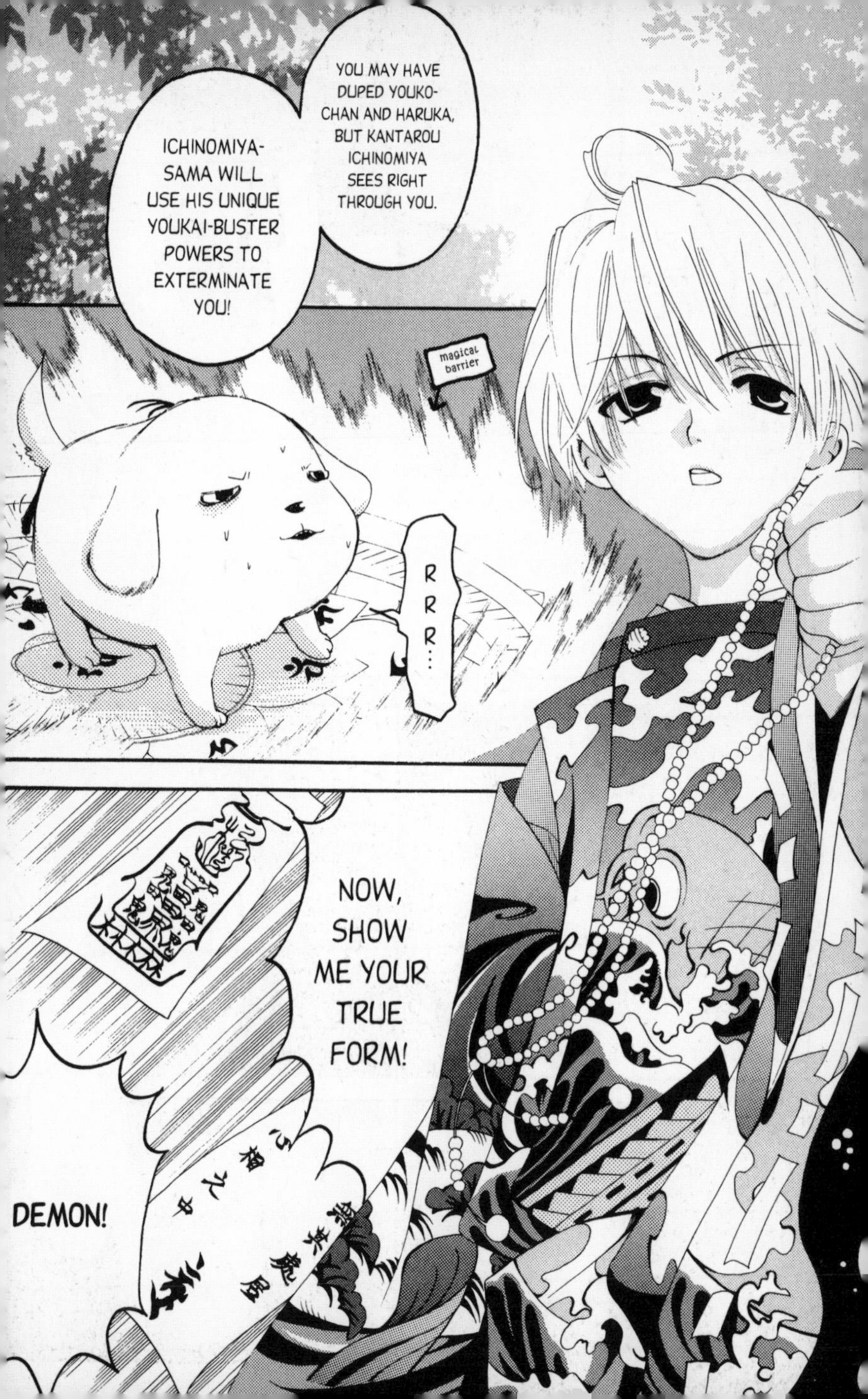
YOU MAY HAVE DUPED YOUKO-CHAN AND HARUKA, BUT KANTAROU ICHINOMIYA SEES RIGHT THROUGH YOU.
ICHINOMIYA-SAMA WILL USE HIS UNIQUE YOUKAI-BUSTER POWERS TO EXTERMINATE YOU!
magical barrier
RRR...
NOW, SHOW ME YOUR TRUE FORM!
DEMON!

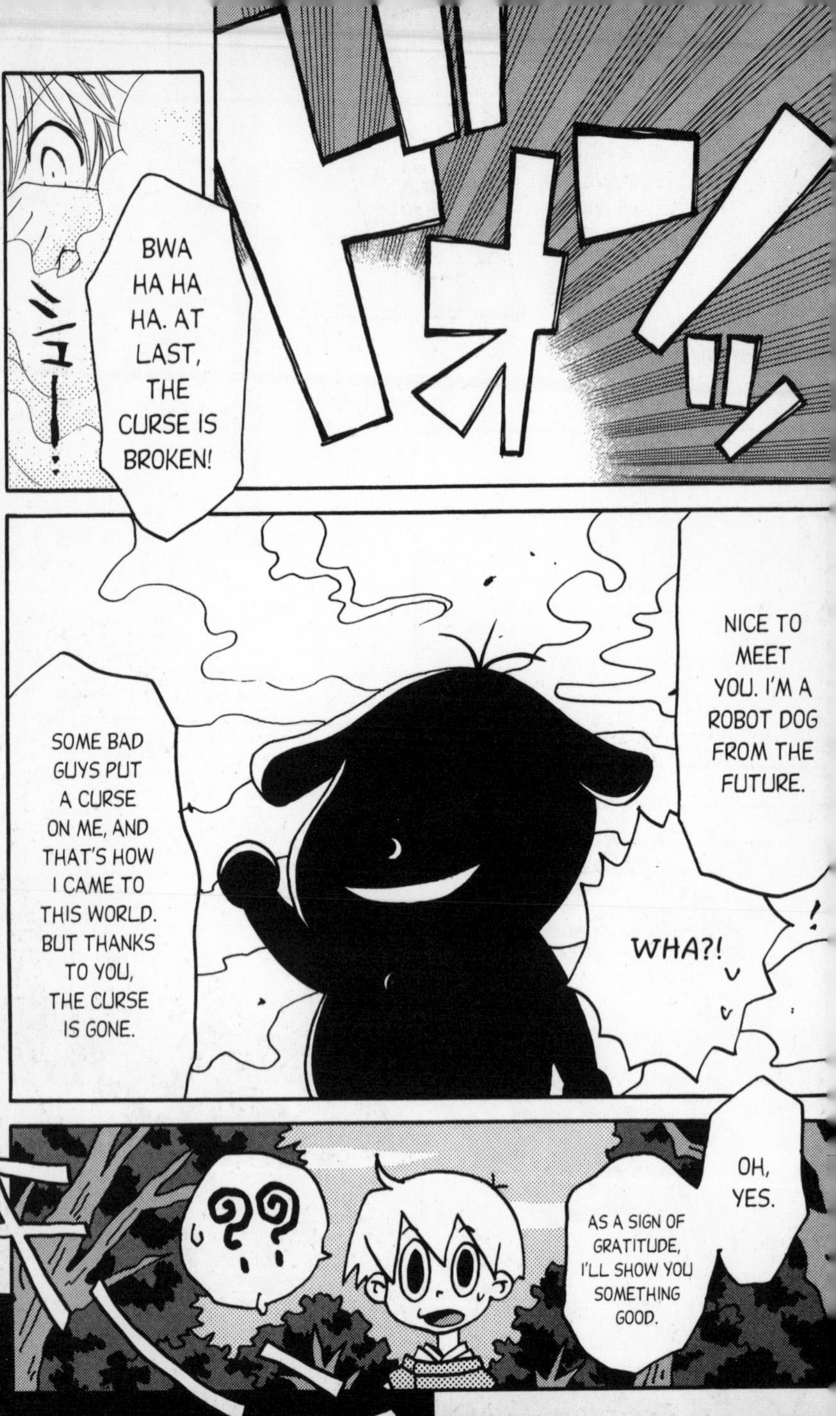
BWA HA HA HA. AT LAST, THE CURSE IS BROKEN!
NICE TO MEET YOU. I'M A ROBOT DOG FROM THE FUTURE.
WHA?!
SOME BAD GUYS PUT A CURSE ON ME, AND THAT'S HOW I CAME TO THIS WORLD. BUT THANKS TO YOU, THE CURSE IS GONE.
OH, YES.
AS A SIGN OF GRATITUDE, I'LL SHOW YOU SOMETHING GOOD.
??

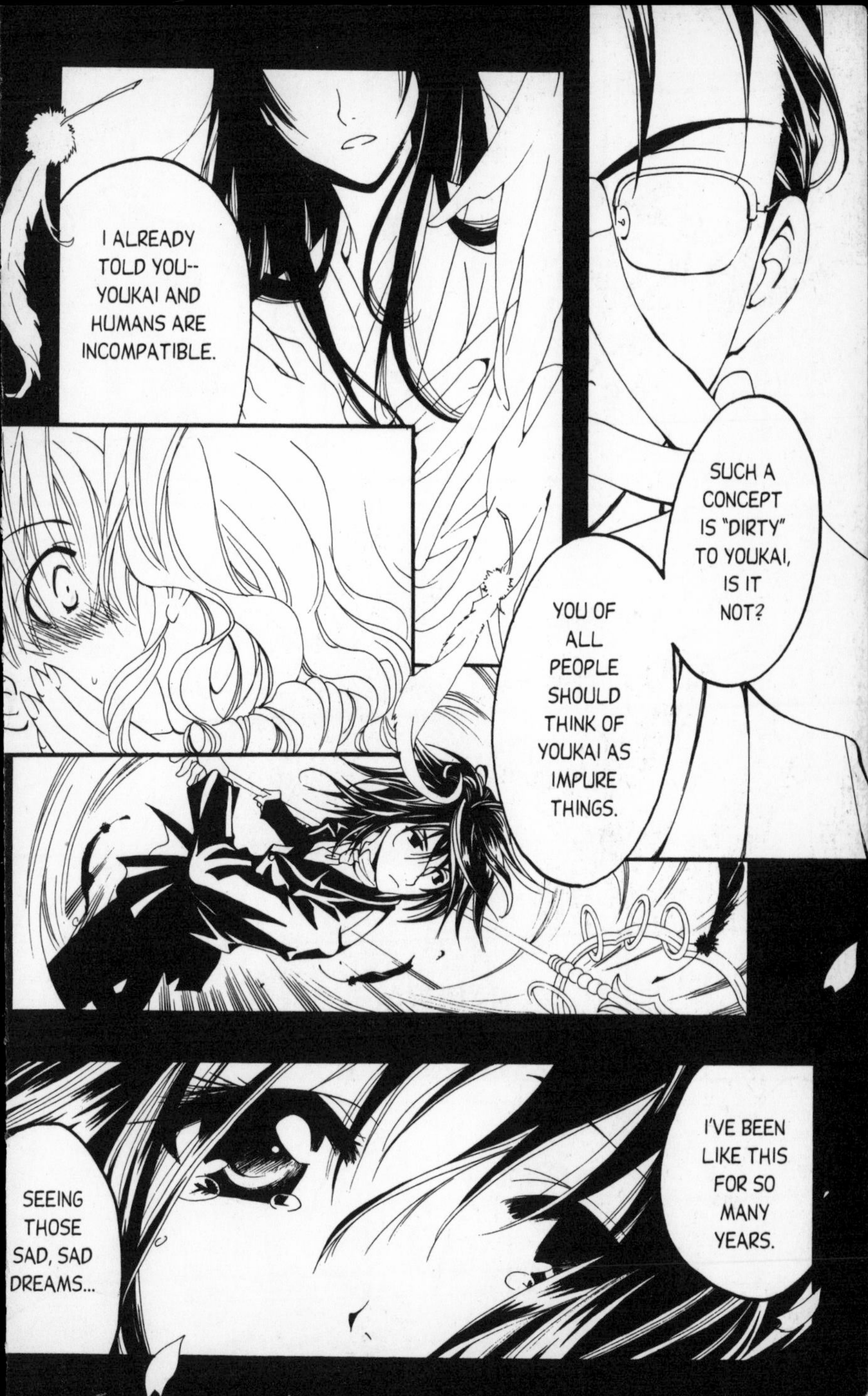
SUCH A CONCEPT IS "DIRTY" TO YOUKAI, IS IT NOT?
YOU OF ALL PEOPLE SHOULD THINK OF YOUKAI AS IMPURE THINGS.
I ALREADY TOLD YOU-- YOUKAI AND HUMANS ARE INCOMPATIBLE.
I'VE BEEN LIKE THIS FOR SO MANY YEARS.
SEEING THOSE SAD, SAD DREAMS...

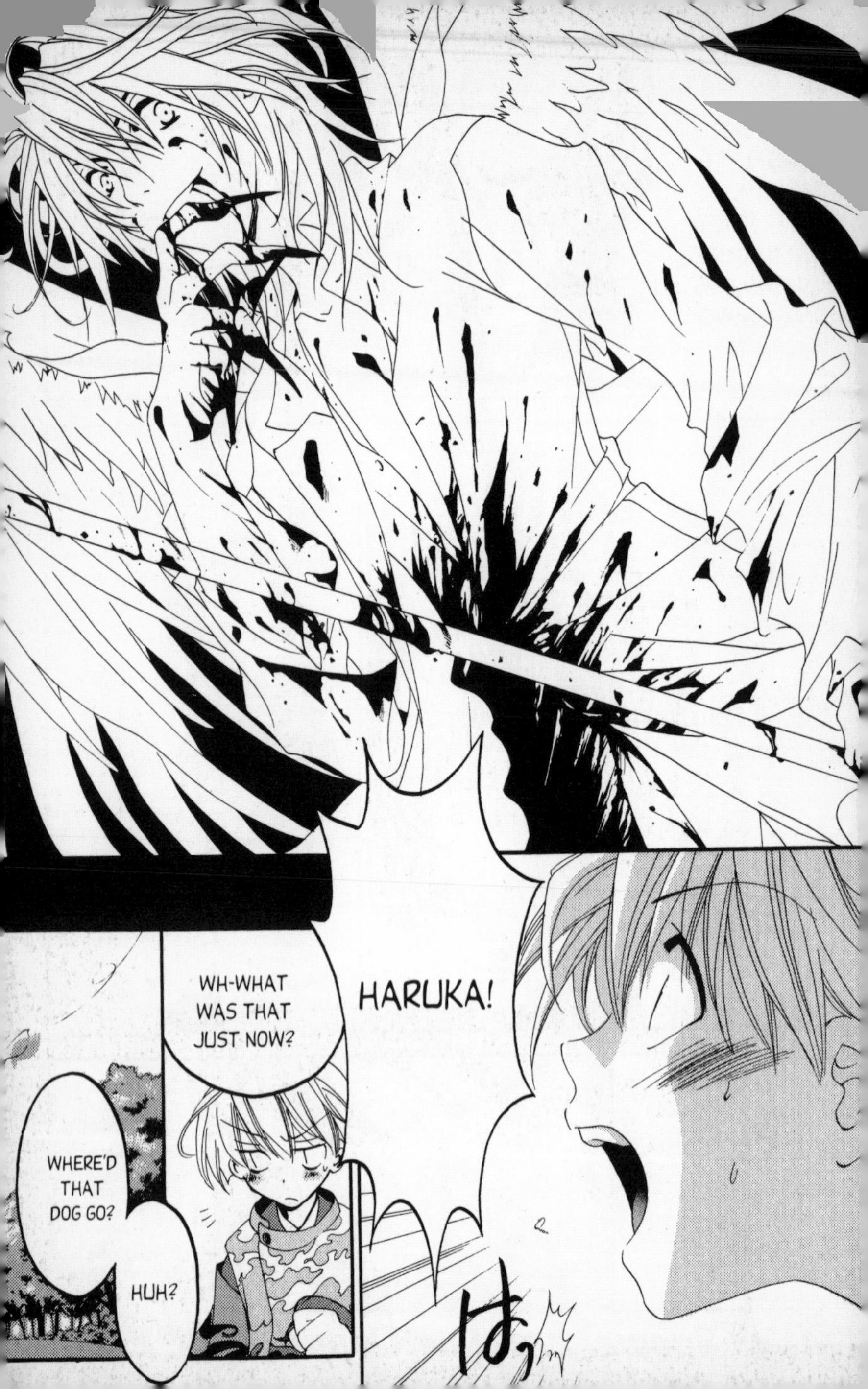
HARUKA!
はっ
WH-WHAT WAS THAT JUST NOW?
WHERE'D THAT DOG GO?
HUH?

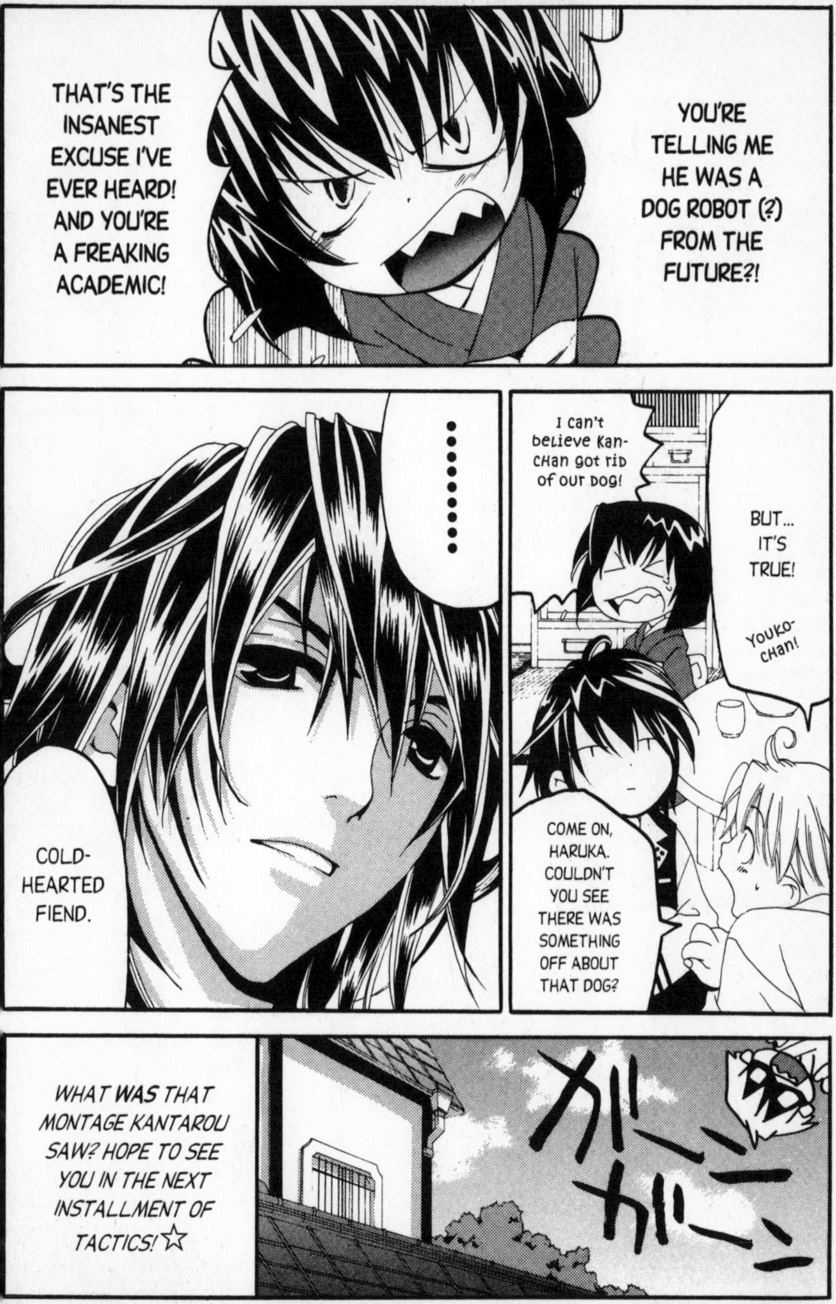
YOU'RE TELLING ME HE WAS A DOG ROBOT (?) FROM THE FUTURE?!
THAT'S THE INSANEST EXCUSE I'VE EVER HEARD! AND YOU'RE A FREAKING ACADEMIC!
I can't believe Kan-chan got rid of our dog!
BUT... IT'S TRUE!
YOUKO-CHAN!
COME ON, HARUKA. COULDN'T YOU SEE THERE WAS SOMETHING OFF ABOUT THAT DOG?
....
COLD-HEARTED FIEND.
カー
カー
WHAT WAS THAT MONTAGE KANTAROU SAW? HOPE TO SEE YOU IN THE NEXT INSTALLMENT OF TACTICS! ☆

tactics Special Preview Comic···THE END!

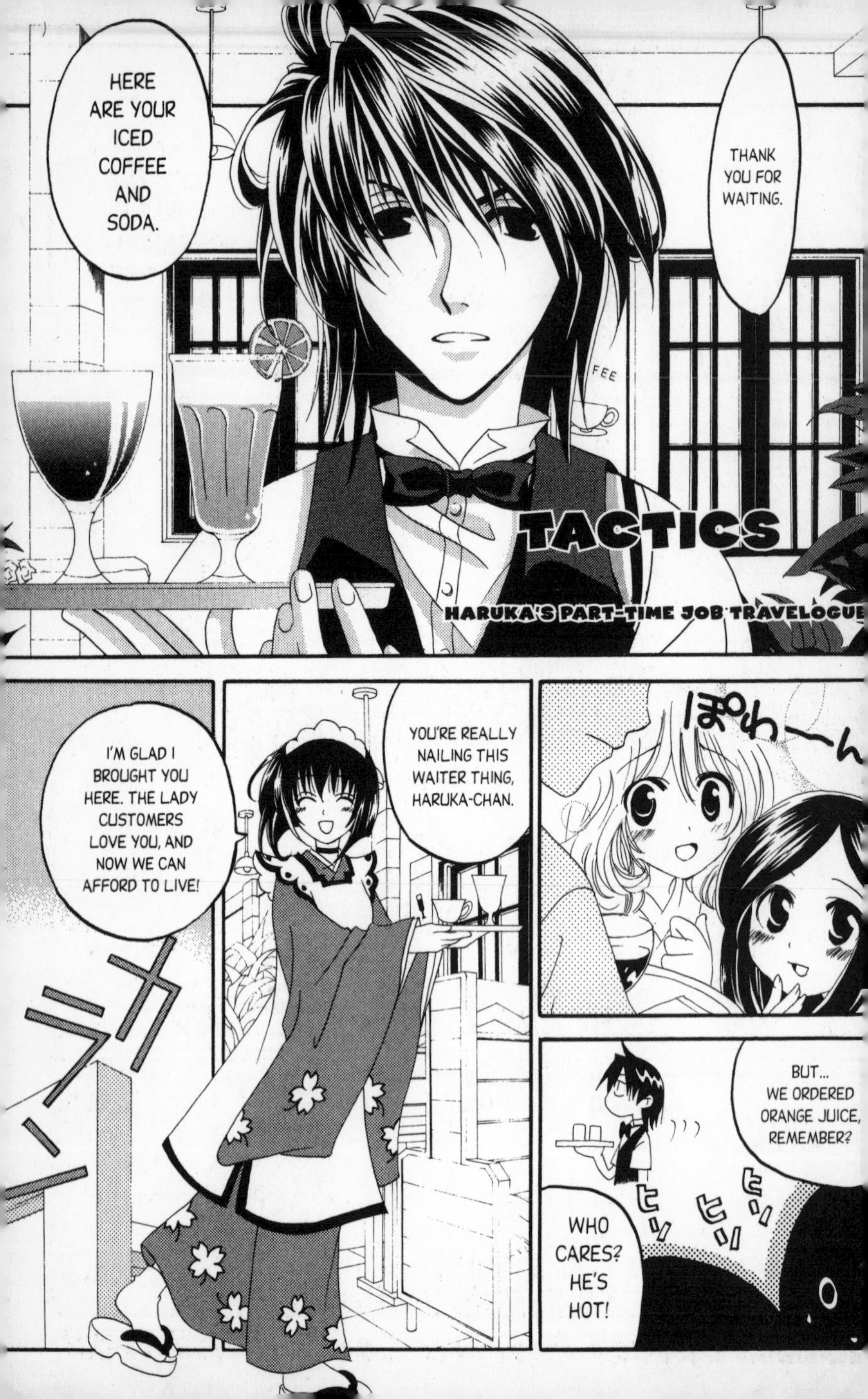
THANK YOU FOR WAITING.
HERE ARE YOUR ICED COFFEE AND SODA.
TACTICS
HARUKA'S PART-TIME JOB TRAVELOGUE
ぽわ～ん
YOU'RE REALLY NAILING THIS WAITER THING, HARUKA-CHAN.
BUT... WE ORDERED ORANGE JUICE, REMEMBER?
ヒソ ヒソ
WHO CARES? HE'S HOT!
I'M GLAD I BROUGHT YOU HERE. THE LADY CUSTOMERS LOVE YOU, AND NOW WE CAN AFFORD TO LIVE!

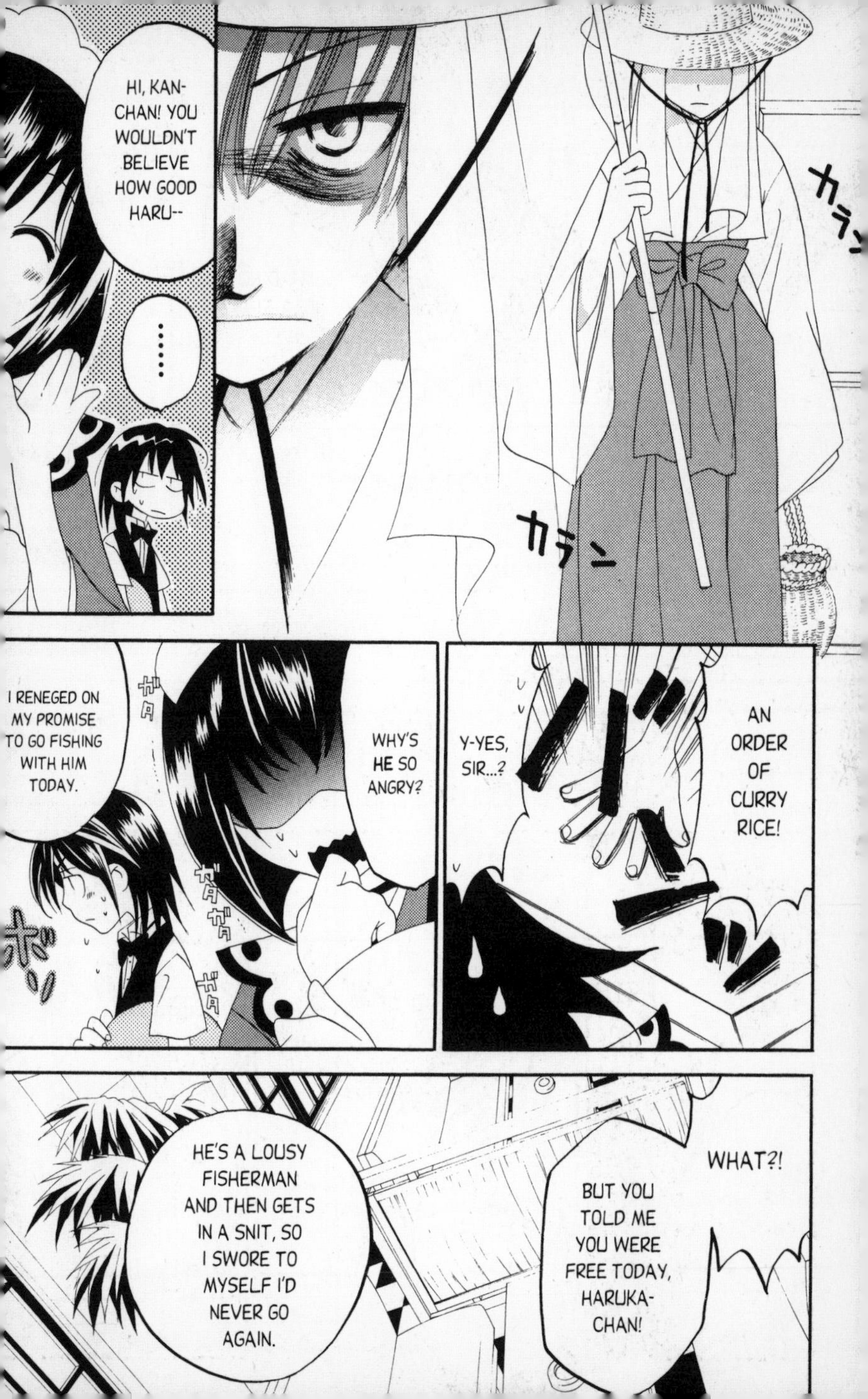

カラン
カラン
HI, KAN-CHAN! YOU WOULDN'T BELIEVE HOW GOOD HARU--
......
AN ORDER OF CURRY RICE!
Y-YES, SIR...?
WHY'S HE SO ANGRY?
ガタ
ガタ
ガタ
ガタ
I RENEGED ON MY PROMISE TO GO FISHING WITH HIM TODAY.
WHAT?!
BUT YOU TOLD ME YOU WERE FREE TODAY, HARUKA-CHAN!
HE'S A LOUSY FISHERMAN AND THEN GETS IN A SNIT, SO I SWORE TO MYSELF I'D NEVER GO AGAIN.

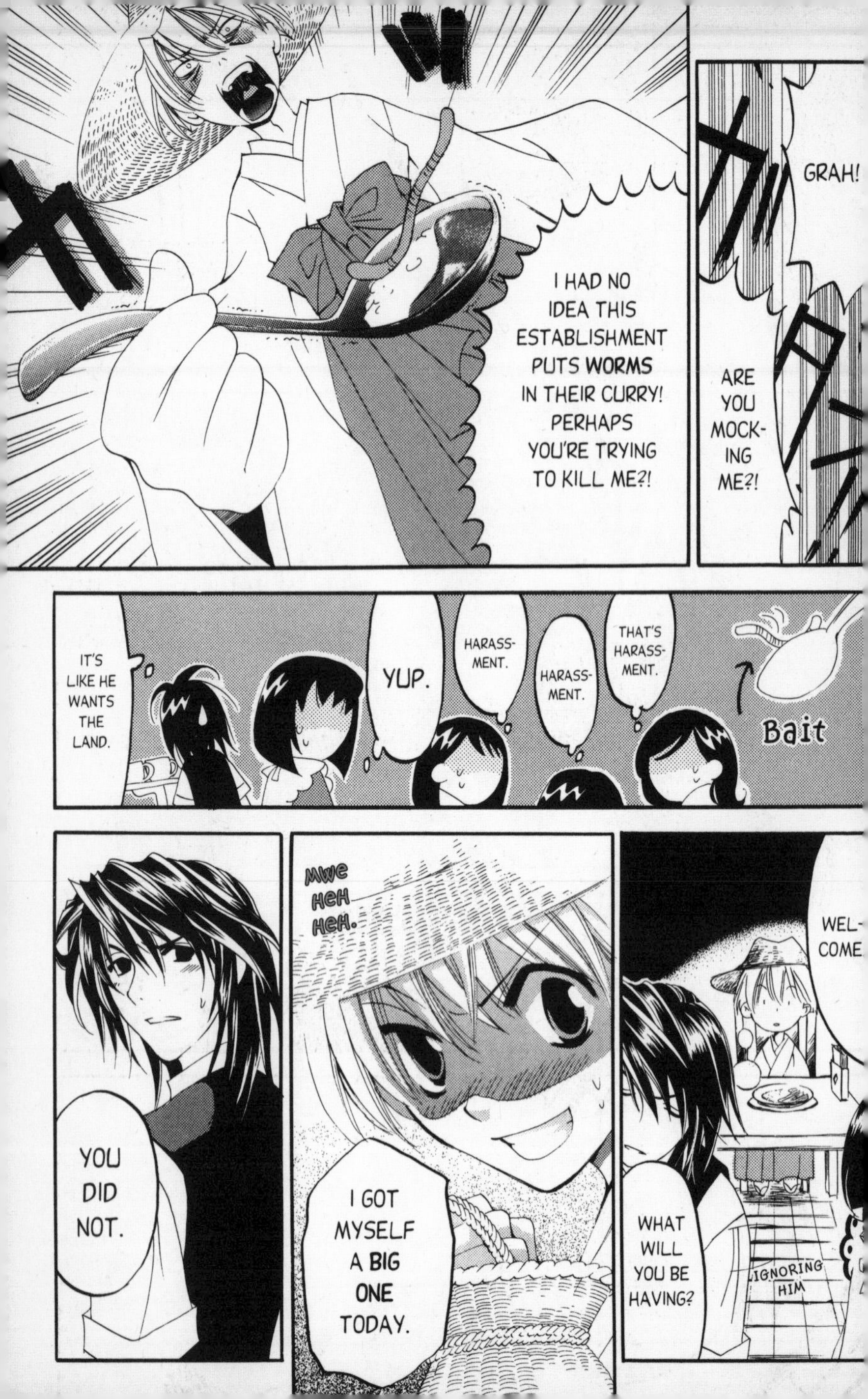
GRAH!
ARE YOU MOCKING ME?!
I HAD NO IDEA THIS ESTABLISHMENT PUTS **WORMS** IN THEIR CURRY! PERHAPS YOU'RE TRYING TO KILL ME?!
Bait
THAT'S HARASSMENT.
HARASSMENT.
HARASSMENT.
YUP.
IT'S LIKE HE WANTS THE LAND.
WELCOME.
WHAT WILL YOU BE HAVING?
IGNORING HIM
MWE HEH HEH.
I GOT MYSELF A **BIG ONE** TODAY.
YOU DID NOT.

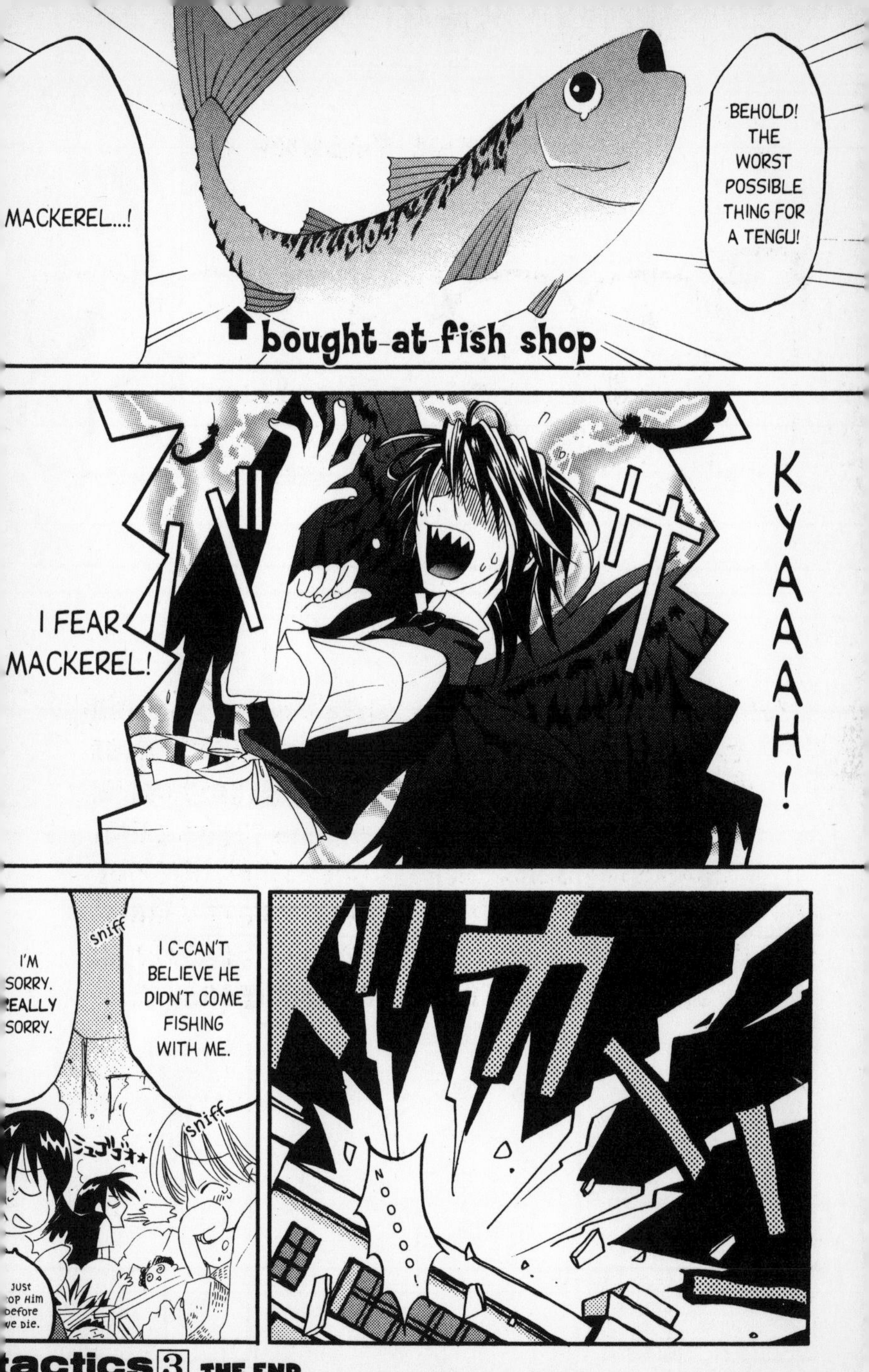
BEHOLD! THE WORST POSSIBLE THING FOR A TENGU!
MACKEREL...!
bought at fish shop
KYAAAH!
I FEAR MACKEREL!
NOOOOOO!
I C-CAN'T BELIEVE HE DIDN'T COME FISHING WITH ME.
sniff
I'M SORRY. EALLY SORRY.
sniff
シュゴゴォ
JUST OP HIM BEFORE E DIE.

tactics 3 THE END

IN THE NEXT VOLUME OF

tactics

Kantarou and company sign up to handle a seemingly
endless stream of youkai infesting the mansion
of a wealthy and powerful young businesswoman.
But Haruka's sudden sneezing fits suggest that
there's something mysterious and malevolent
going on with rich Ms. Sakurazawa, and they
may all be in grave danger. Kantarou and Haruka
apparently have a new and deadly enemy...

Language and Culture Notes on *Tactics* vol. 3!

Chapter 7:

~Tatsu no Hi: literally means "day of the Dragon." From the Chinese Zodiac/Calendar system, which uses animals to represent months, days and hours, this an auspicious day found once a month.

~Abe no Seimei: a famous onmyouji who would advise the emperors and the Heian government on the spiritually correct way to deal with issues thanks to all his astrological/spiritual knowledge.

~Onmyoudou (yin-yang magic): a fortune-telling system that uses calendars, astronomy, etc.

~Five elements: In Taoist practice, and much of Asian culture, the five base elements are Water, Fire, Earth, Metal and Wood, as opposed to the Western, Aristotelian elements, Water, Fire, Air, Earth and Aether.

~On amiriti un hatta: a mantra that protects the speaker from outside evils.

~Naumaku sanmanda bazaradan kan: a mantra that supposedly gives you the power of Acala The Immovable to curse your opponent.

~Taizanfukun: the ancient Chinese name for the King of Hell who judges the dead and decides their fate.

~Shikigami: a spiritual entity that can perform many mysterious acts under an onmyoji's command.

Chapter 8:

~Yakko's song: Basically a kind of "nyah nyah, I won!" song.

~Hyousube: monkey-like creatures that are kin to the kappa.

Special Preview Comic One:

The splash page for this section totally threw me for a loop the first time I saw it. The translator had "SUKUTEIKUTA" written as the heading in the big black box, and even with my moderate Japanese language capabilities, I was like, "WTF?!" In the original book, the word is written in katakana, the Japanese writing system most often used for writing words borrowed from other languages, including English, so usually you can sound out what it's supposed to be if you think about it long enough. So I sat there, thinking, "Sukuteikuta, sukuteikuta...what could that mean?!" for a good fifteen minutes before I realized that it was actually another historical reference! Japanese is usually read from right-to-left, but the exception is when words are horizontal, like on signs or titles, in which case it's left-to-right. However! This was not always the case. If you look at old woodblock prints from the Meiji and early Taisho period, a lot of the time the title above the image is written right-to-left. (The giveaway for me is usually when the two characters for Japan are "backwards.") And that's what the joke here is. What's SUKUTEIKUTA backwards in Japanese? TAKUTEIKUSU. "Tactics." :-) But we reversed it in translation, because SCITCAT just looks silly.

STOP!

This is the back of the book.
You wouldn't want to spoil a great ending!

This book is printed "manga-style," in the authentic Japanese right-to-left format. Since none of the artwork has been flipped or altered, readers get to experience the story just as the creator intended. You've been asking for it, so TOKYOPOP® delivered: authentic, hot-off-the-press, and far more fun!

DIRECTIONS

If this is your first time reading manga-style, here's a quick guide to help you understand how it works.

It's easy... just start in the top right panel and follow the numbers. Have fun, and look for more 100% authentic manga from TOKYOPOP®!

tactics

3

Sakura Kinoshita × Kazuko Higashiyama

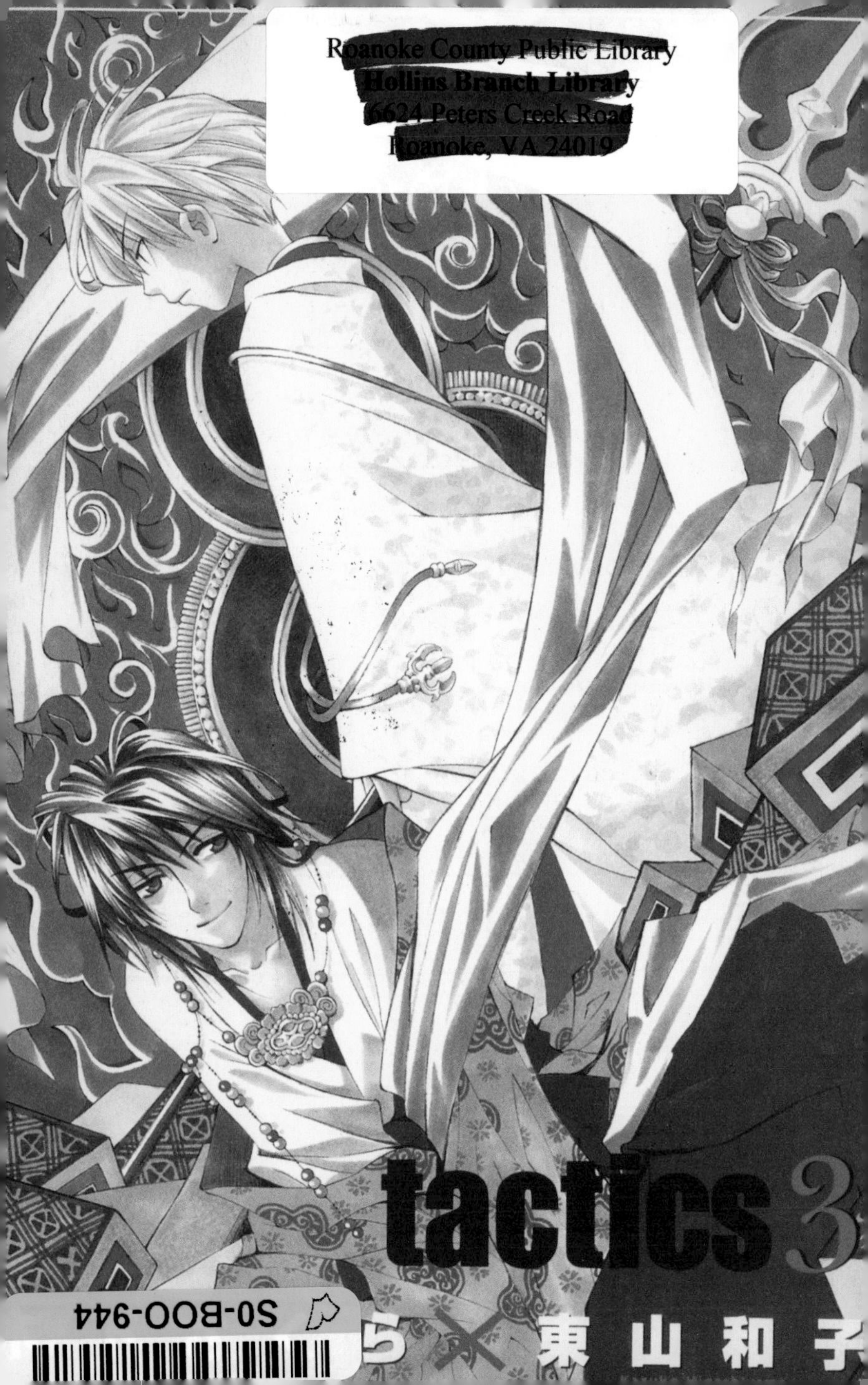

tactics 3

ら × 東山和子